Escape from Predicament

Studies of the East Asian Institute

Columbia University

THOMAS A. METZGER

Escape from
Predicament

NEO-CONFUCIANISM AND
CHINA'S EVOLVING POLITICAL CULTURE

Columbia University Press New York

Thomas A. Metzger is Associate Professor of History
University of California, San Diego

Library of Congress Cataloging in Publication Data
Metzger, Thomas A.
    Escape from predicament.
    Bibliography: p.
    Includes index.
    1. Political science—History—China. 2. China—
Civilization. 3. China—Politics and government.
I. Title.
JA84.06M43   320'.0951   76–25445
ISBN 0–231–03979–4
ISBN 0–231–03980–8 (pa.)

Columbia University Press
New York   Guildford, Surrey
Copyright © 1977 by Columbia University Press
All Rights Reserved
Printed in the United States of America

FOR
SUZANNE,
JULIA,
AND
JESSICA

The East Asian Institute of Columbia University

THE East Asian Institute of Columbia University was established in 1949 to prepare graduate students for careers dealing with East Asia, and to aid research and publication on East Asia during the modern period. The faculty of the Institute are grateful to the Ford Foundation and the Rockefeller Foundation for their financial assistance.

The Studies of the East Asian Institute were inaugurated in 1962 to bring to a wider public the results of significant new research on modern and contemporary East Asia.

Acknowledgments

THIS study began with the kind encouragement of H. D. Harootunian as an attempt to write a review article exploring some of the current Chinese perspectives on Chinese culture. It still has the form of a critique of these perspectives, and it does not cover all relevant primary and secondary sources. Whatever its deficiencies, it has been concretely strengthened by revisions made to try to meet the criticisms of a number of scholars, to whom I am, therefore, truly grateful. These are especially Guy S. Alito, Robert N. Bellah, Hao Chang, Wm. Theodore de Bary, Charlotte Furth, David K. Jordan, Kwang-Ching Liu, Yen-lung Liu, David S. Luft, Ramon H. Myers, Andrew J. Nathan, Don C. Price, Lawrence A. Schneider, Wei-ming Tu, and Frederic Wakeman, Jr. I also owe a special debt to Professor Myers for the moral support he gave me at an early stage in the writing of this manuscript; to Professor Liu for arranging a memorable seminar at my home on June 15, 1974, in the course of which important issues were raised forcing me to reconsider aspects of my thesis; and to Professor Chang for once more acting as my mentor. Some of the ideas in this essay stem from a course on "Tradition and Modernity in Europe and China" which Professor Gabriel Jackson and I gave together at the University of California, San Diego, in 1973–1974. This is not to say that all these distinguished scholars necessarily subscribe to all the views in this book. Some of these views are at odds with those in the two most distinguished contributions to the problem of China's ideological turn to the West, Hao Chang's study of Liang Ch'i-ch'ao and Benjamin I. Schwartz's study of Yen Fu, but the debt I owe these two works will be obvious. Finally, the reader may note in my study a curious variety of reactions to the writings of T'ang Chün-i, whom I alternately criticize and cite as an authority. I am still in the process of studying his thought but am gradually coming to believe that he has shown us how one can philosophize in the twentieth century: by seeking to fathom the universal nature of human existence even at the risk of reaffirming ideals cherished more in one culture than another. That he has managed to take this risk, forcing his readers to take it with him, is a measure of his astuteness and learning as a philosopher and a historian.

An earlier version of this study was presented May 10, 1974, at the Spring Meeting of the Regional Seminar of the Center for Chinese Studies, University of California, Berkeley. This seminar proved to be most useful to me in making me more aware of the issues I had slurred over than I could ever have become without the advantages of such a gathering. I also received valuable criticism while participating in a planning conference on early Ch'ing thought organized by Professor Wei-ming Tu under the sponsorship of the American Council of Learned Societies and held in Berkeley, California, in August, 1975. I also benefited greatly from participating in the Regional Seminar in Confucian Studies that Professor Tu organized in 1975–1976 at the Center for Chinese Studies, University of California, Berkeley.

I am especially grateful to the East Asian Institute, Columbia University, for sponsoring publication of this study and to Professor Nathan for his empathy and help. Ms. Winifred I. Olsen of the Institute also was most helpful. At Columbia University Press, special thanks are due to Mr. Bernard Gronert, Executive Editor, and Mr. Leslie Bialler, Manuscript Editor. Ms. Linda J. Huggins and Ms. Dolores C. Swetland expertly typed much of the manuscript. The bottom line of my gratitude goes to my wife, Suzanne Kay Metzger, who helped me greatly in both the writing and the preparation of this book.

T. A. M.
Del Mar, 1977

Table of Contents

Table of Contents

Table of Contents

Escape from Predicament

Introduction

DESPITE fears of lapsing into Spenglerian generalizations, the macroscopic discussion of the culture of late imperial China on the eve of modernization is still very much alive. References to the "value system," "spirit," "worldview," or "ideology" of the imperial society abound in the literature on China. Some such concept is needed as an analytical base line not only by Chinese thinkers charting the direction of their country's development but also by Western students trying to determine the continuities and discontinuities of Chinese modernization. John K. Fairbank has recently remarked that in the People's Republic of China today, "The unity of the Chinese world-within-a-world is like a religious faith."[1] Surely we have to describe this "faith" and its historical origins as best we can if we are to understand the course of Chinese history. Consequently we cannot in this instance enjoy the academic luxury of confining scholarly efforts to precisely delimited subjects and should rather try to make as much sense as possible out of the amorphous welter of perspectives and data currently available.

Lately scholars have approached this subject using the concept of "political culture," which usefully directs our attention to the connections between cosmology and attitudes toward authority.[2] The notion of authority cannot be separated from ideas defining the relation of the self to the cosmos and to the group or community.[3] At the same time, the extent to which ideas about authority left the self with the possibility of challenging inherited norms is also a crucial issue. Max Weber was primarily responsible for raising it. He taught us to ask whether the culture of any historical society provided the spiritual "leverage" with which to transform the social order or to import foreign transformative ideologies. Thus attitudes defining the modalities of change as well as the desired moral order are central to any political culture.

In this whole discussion, a major role has been played by Weber's brilliant and still unparalleled attempt to put Confucianism

3

in cross-cultural perspective. His thesis was that Confucianism "reduced tension with the world to an absolute minimum. . . . Completely absent in the Confucian ethic was any tension . . . between ethical demand and human shortcoming." To a'large extent he explained this lack of moral tension by adducing the Confucian view that "human nature was disposed to [be] ethically good," a view in terms of which "the individual necessarily lacked an autonomous counterweight in confronting this world."[4] This thesis is reflected in S. N. Eisenstadt's conclusion, based on extensive study of the secondary literature, that despite some transcendence "in principle," the "stagnative . . . nontransformative. . . . Confucian ideology" did not focus on a moral order differentiated from the political status quo.[5] Lucian W. Pye holds similar views.[6] Weber, however, was writing without the guidance of scholars who since his time have made Confucian thought much more accessible to modern minds. His idea that Confucianism largely lacked a sense of "tension with the world" meshed with the increasingly influential modern Chinese scientistic image of the Confucian tradition as "stagnant," but his understanding of the Confucian views about human nature and the moral life was simply mistaken, a truly monumental example of *hao-li-chih ch'a ch'ien-li-chih miu* (if one is off by the slightest fraction to begin with, one ends up nowhere near the target).

Partly diverging from Weber, a new view has now been put forward emphasizing that if the Confucian personality lacked "tension with the world," it still was characterized by moral tension in that it was dominated by an anxiety-ridden need to depend on social superiors for authoritarian guidance. This thesis, however, put forward almost simultaneously by American and Chinese behavioral scientists, has been challenged especially by those with a humanistic approach to Chinese history.[7] It is hard for them to reconcile it with the views of leading Chinese scholars who have argued that a morally assertive "spirit" was basic to Chinese history.

b. THE BACKGROUND OF MODERN CHINESE
INTELLECTUAL HISTORY

At this point it is clear that the macroscopic discussion of Chinese culture has become entangled not only with the discrepancies between the humanistic and the behavioral models of behavior but also with philosophical and ideological controversies which, in twentieth-century China as well as the West, have deeply affected various current interpretations of the traditional Chinese culture. The complexity of these issues can hardly be exaggerated. Hao Chang has recently pointed out that many Chinese intellectuals facing the problems of our century have been concerned not only with devising strategies of modernization but also with solving perennial and universal existential problems of suffering and meaning.[8] Their very sophistication in so doing creates still another dimension of difficulty for us. Extensively and self-consciously drawing on cosmopolitan intellectual resources to develop critical perspectives on their own situations, many of them came to share some of the very analytical horizons in terms of which we propose to study them. For instance, Ho Lin, a well-known idealist philosopher and friend of Fung Yu-lan (1895–), completed a little book in Kunming in 1945 reviewing the development of Chinese philosophy since K'ang Yu-wei (1858–1927).[9] He thus gave his views on various issues still with us today, such as the "cosmopolitan" character of much modern Chinese thought,[10] the need for a generous spirit of constructive criticism applied to all philosophies right and left,[11] the tendency of Chinese intellectuals unconsciously to adopt attitudes which they consciously claim to be rejecting,[12] the unmet challenge of simultaneously probing the depths of both Chinese and Western thought,[13] the dangers of gross cross-cultural comparisons,[14] the validity of intellectual history in the face of the Marxist critique, and the integrity of metaphysical knowledge in the face of the positivistic attacks mounted by the Vienna circle.[15] Reading his acute remarks on such matters, we are confronted with a process of intellectual reflection any peculiarly Chinese aspects of which are hard if not impossible to identify. This refusal of Chinese intellectuals to cooperate with our analytical efforts by staying conveniently culture-bound, if indeed they ever were, makes it most difficult for us to analyze them as delimited cultural objects exhibiting certain delimited historical influences. Moreover, their thought has typically dealt with issues interconnected in exceedingly complex ways, that is, the nature of the given world in its cultural history and geography, the epistemological and ontological underpinnings of this

5

world, the ethical and political goals which Chinese should select, and the tactical means needed to pursue these goals.

Confronted with such a complex subject, we can nevertheless discern two major trends in modern times. Joseph R. Levenson once characterized them as "the progressive abandonment of tradition by iconoclasts and the petrification of tradition by traditionalists."[16] A different formulation, however, can be attempted: one can speak of an often bitter and radical rejection of China's cultural and institutional heritage and of a transformation of the traditional commitment to it. Yet only in recent years have more Western historians come to realize that by concentrating on only the reaction against tradition, we fail to fathom the attitudes involved in both trends.

What is more, these two trends cannot be conceived of as distinct, compartmentalized developments. This point is vividly suggested by the phenomenon of conversions moving in opposite directions, such as that of the philosopher Fung Yu-lan, who embraced the Marxist attack on China's tradition about a decade after completing his profound attempt to develop a systematic, modern worldview grounded in the philosophy of Chu Hsi (1130–1200),[17] and that of the philosopher Yin Hai-kuang (1919–1969), who turned to traditional ideals after spending years scouring the anthropological and sociological literature of the West for arguments demonstrating the pathological nature of the Confucian order.[18]

The scientistic May Fourth rejection of the Confucian order,[19] which deeply influenced Yin's important book *Chung-kuo wen-hua-te chan-wang* (An Appraisal of Chinese Culture and its Prospects), published in 1966, is still very much alive, whether in Mao's Marxism or in the careful research of behavioral scientists like Yang Kuo-shu and Li I-yüan, both of the Academia Sinica on Taiwan, who in 1970 and 1971 organized a seminar dealing with the question of Chinese personality patterns. It resulted in a major symposium volume published in 1972. Although acutely aware of the need to avoid identifying "modern" personality patterns with peculiarly Western ones, they are forced by the very nature of their disciplinary literature to evaluate China's traditional patterns according to the norms of "modern" behavior formulated by American behavioral scientists like Alex Inkeles, and they often use terms like "authoritarian" and "particularistic" to type traditional behavioral traits as pathological or at least undesirable today. Their conviction that a "modern man" is gradually but inevitably displacing "traditional man" in China as elsewhere makes difficult any humanistic attempt to turn back to their tradition as a source of moral values needed in contemporary life.[20]

Such an attempt, however, has been and is still being made by prominent Chinese intellectuals. Yet their work also has involved a radical departure from this tradition. Generally speaking, they have rejected what can be called institutional Confucianism and Confucian fundamentalism (see chapter 5), and especially the imperially sponsored position of the Confucian school, going back to the Early Han period, as the only source of true learning. To be sure, even in imperial times Confucian scholars continuously distinguished between the true understanding of Confucius' Way and the false Confucianism with which it had become entangled. However, the modern adherents of Confucian philosophy have given, perhaps, an unprecedented emphasis to this distinction, sifting through the impure ore of their past to extract a "spirit" of morality which could serve for the future. Thus they have to some extent shared the May Fourth insistence on "opposing the authority of tradition,"[21] and, looking to a "new," critically developed body of learning drawing on the resources of various Chinese as well as Western schools, they have largely accepted the ideals of science and democracy, as well as highly Westernized versions of cultural geography and world history.

They have, however, sought to transform rather than eliminate the Chinese commitment to traditional ideals. Searching for a "new philosophy," they have nevertheless viewed this philosophy as based on traditional ideals and behavior patterns, which they have glorified. Perhaps, as some suggest, they have been motivated by a "religious faith" in these ideals or by a sense of moral obligation to save their ancestral traditions from being destroyed by the tide of Westernization.[22] Levenson has viewed their insistence on the high "value" of their traditional culture as expressing an "emotional" attachment lacking adequate intellectual justification, and Yin Hai-kuang, influenced by Robert N. Bellah's typology of value orientations in developing countries, once analyzed them as advocating a form of "neotraditionalism" which could "soothe the nostalgia of the uprooted Chinese intellectuals" and "defend the status quo as far as possible."[23] Even more cynically, we can view them as unconsciously determined to recover the traditional status, privileges, and power of the Confucian scholar class by demonstrating that even in a fully modern, industrialized world, their specialized skills in the fields of philosophy and history are indispensable for establishing the moral foundations of national power. At the same time, to use William James's and Arthur O. Lovejoy's terms, they can be seen as "tender-minded" intellectuals searching for a sense of "metaphysical pathos" with which to handle the stresses of existence, reacting against the "tough-minded" engineers of Westernization.

Yet why should we insist that their outlook was based more on ulterior motives or "emotion" than those of other intellectual camps? Could anything be more emotional than the "bitter hatred" of the traditional order expressed by May Fourth partisans proposing to "strike [it] down"? Tradition-oriented thinkers have also been "intentionally" concerned with objective problems. It is clear that they accepted a central premise of Neo-Confucian thought, namely that the understanding of ontological questions is an urgent precondition of morality; that they were confronted by a momentous coincidence, the fact, namely, that the ontological question of the relation between the cosmos and the flow of human consciousness was central to both Neo-Confucianism and German idealism; and that they were greatly heartened by the hope that this coincidence, intricately connected to the question of science, would lead to a new understanding of this ontological issue and thus to a new spirit of moral and political renewal (see chapter 5).

Not that all these generalizations apply with equal force to all those intellectuals contributing to this transformation of the commitment to traditional ideals. As Ho Lin points out, some like Ouyang Ching-wu (1871–1943) and Hsiung Shih-li (1885–1968) dealt with the above ontological question drawing mainly on the resources of Buddhist thought and of the idealistic Lu-Wang wing of Neo-Confucianism. Others, like Wang Ching-an, Chang I, and Chang Tung-sun, contributed mainly through their expertise in German thought. T'ang Chün-i, as shown in chapter 2, was among those who could draw on the resources of both groups. With a methodology reminiscent of Kant's "transcendental deduction" and Husserl's phenomenology, he inferred the existence of a morally conscious cosmos from the concrete facts of moral experience.

The philosopher Fung Yu-lan, on the other hand, was too impressed by pragmatism and the neo-realism of Bertrand Russell to accept such a "mystical" view of the cosmos. The "real" world, for him, was made up of mere "phenomena" which could not form a single continuum with man's moral consciousness. Yet Fung still had to show that the "sublime" in life had an objectively universal foundation. Like the logician Chin Yüeh-lin, he found it in the logically universal *raison d'être* or category which one can abstractly infer from the existence of any phenomenon. Influenced by Buddhism and Spinoza, he felt morally transformed by this vision of a purely "formal" realm of categories, displaying things in their "most complete forms" and transcending any selfish attachments. Then, by arguing that Chu Hsi, with his notion of "principle," had almost grasped the nature of this purely formal realm, Fung could analyze the whole history of Chinese philosophy as gradually moving toward this understanding, and simultaneously he could use this understanding as the foundation for a moral and political philosophy applying to the tumultuous conditions of China and the rest of the world in modern times. If the task of a philosopher is to inspire us while making sense of the complexities of history and cultural interaction, Fung Yu-lan, with his limpid style, his vast learning, his gift for analysis, and his moral idealism, was quite a philosopher.[24]

Scholars in the West are only beginning to digest the contributions of this whole group of humanists. In evaluating them, I would tentatively make four points, which are discussed further below. First, they have created one of the great moments in world intellectual history and have yet to win the reputation they deserve. Second, although their thought owes much to the Confucian tradition, they have been heavily influenced by what Hao Chang calls China's "intellectual transition." Third, partly because of this fact, they have presented an interpretation of Neo-Confucianism which, as history, is illuminating but not inductively balanced. Fourth, they have not been convincing in their varied efforts to vindicate Neo-Confucian epistemology. Nevertheless, they may well have succeeded in showing that the essential ideals of the Confucian tradition are as noble, as pertinent to the modern world, and as epistemologically defensible as those of any other tradition.

This multifaceted movement reconsidering the relationship of China's traditional "spirit" to the issues of modernity crystalized fully at National Southwest Associated University in Kunming, the intellectual capital of wartime China, just as Chinese intellectuals were turning in increasing numbers to Marxism as an answer to the continuing economic and political crisis of their nation. Yet this tradition-oriented movement to some extent was sympathetic to the idea of socialism and of massive social reorganization, as can be seen from the thought of the influential Fung or of the learned eccentric Shen Yu-ting (see chapter 5, section n). Their differences with the Communists were less over ultimate ethical and political goals than over epistemological and ontological issues, cultural history, and the question of the class alignments and tactics needed to realize these goals.

c. BASIC METHODOLOGICAL CONSIDERATIONS

Certainly both of these crosscutting intellectual trends—the rejection of tradition and the transformation of the commitment to it—have biased the major Chinese contributions to the literature on the traditional culture. This is only to say that the polemics of the twentieth century have partly shaped the views of Chinese scholars analyzing the Confucian tradition, often leading them either to condemn it or glorify it. Yet even though entangled in their own historical situation, these scholars have often interpreted this tradition with unique expertise and insight. Therefore, however interesting it may be to analyze their historical situation, we cannot afford to ignore their insights. While Stuart Hughes treated Max Weber as an historical figure exhibiting certain intellectual tendencies of his day, Talcott Parsons treated him as one expert among others on the question of the structure of social action.[25] Both perspectives are valid. Similarly, in this book I focus not on the historical influences that shaped the views of experts like T'ang Chün-i but on the insights their works offer us regarding the subject of their expertise, that is, the shared cultural orientations of late imperial China.

Further study of these shared orientations, I believe, calls for some methodological innovations in order to try to pull together the insights of different disciplines while avoiding their biases. Growing out of the two Chinese trends just discussed as well as more familiar Western tendencies, the current literature touching on these orientations can be divided into five approaches, those of the Neo-Weberians, the humanists, the anthropologists, the behaviorists, and the intellectual historians. By Neo-Weberians, I mean behavioral scientists who have pursued Weber's interest in the shared orientations of imperial China's educated classes. Leading examples are Li I-yüan, Yang Kuo-shu, Solomon, Pye, Eisenstadt, and, to some extent, Yin Hai-kuang. Humanists, such as T'ang Chün-i, Fung Yu-lan, and Donald J. Munro, have also analyzed these orientations, but from a philosophical standpoint. (In chapter 3, section a, I try to explain the difference between the cultural and the philosophical approaches.) The anthropologists' village studies have shed great light on shared orientations in China, but not on those of the educated classes, since they largely ignore orientations expressed in historical documents. By behaviorists I mean those historians and social scientists who believe that only quantifiable or overt behavior is a proper object of detailed study, and that cultural orientations, although important, can be understood in simple and general terms. Many modern China historians, notably the Fairbankian school, have leaned in this direction. Finally, the intellectual historians are deep into the relevant materials, but because of their commitment to the genre of intellectual biography and their frequently philosophical bent, they have neglected the question of shared cultural orientations. The late Joseph R. Levenson's seminal approach to China's modern intellectual history was based on a uniquely synoptic style which, like Casals' rubato, cannot be profitably imitated by others. Studying materials he partly had not yet reflected on, I have to join scholars like Hao Chang who have disagreed with his basic conclusions.[26]

In this book, I try to build on the heritage of the Neo-Weberians and the humanists. Although these scholars loosely assume that there was enough cultural homogeneity in imperial China to allow the use of concepts like "national character," "modal personality," and "cultural spirit," this assumption is at least heuristically valid.

It would be hard to reject it when leading Chinese social scientists, whose competence stems from both professional training and personal experience, continue to make it.[27] Moreover, my assumption is narrower and more closely aligned with specific historical materials than theirs, since my argument applies only to the political culture of the educated elite during the Ming-Ch'ing period (1368–1912) and is supported by a review of the complex intellectual and institutional conditions of that period (see chapter 3, sections a and x, and chapter 4).

Moreover, the Weberian emphasis on the educated elite also is justified. F. G. Bailey has recently written that "The anthropologist has two tasks: discovering what people think and value, and explaining what situations lead them to these thoughts and values."[28] The educated in China also were people, and influential ones at that. Nor is the Weberian school peculiar in emphasizing the behavioral importance of intellectual or religious currents. Even an historian like Lucien Bianco, who stresses the material conditions of the rural masses, writes of "the intellectual origins of the Chinese revolution." Indeed, echoing Marx's own paradoxical view that the effect of religious ideas on behavior is as powerful as that of opium, Chinese Marxists have typically been in the vanguard of those holding that intellectual currents exert a great influence on political action. For instance, after becoming a Marxist, Fung Yu-lan held that in modern China, the combination of "the corrupt philosophical thought of feudalism" with "the philosophical thought of the corrupt Western bourgeoisie" proved to be a "most effective tool" of political control for the forces of "imperialism and feudalism."[29] Indeed, the behavioral importance of intellectual currents seems to be doubted only by American positivists playing academic hardball in their ivory towers, and the realistic statesmen these tough-minded intellectuals look up to are often wise enough to shudder at the stroke of a pen. Moreover, as discussed in chapter 5, the traditional emphasis in China on "correct thought" as the basis of morality has led to an especially close relation between intellectual movements and political behavior. Certainly the intellectualized aspects of China's political culture did not comprise all of it, but if we are to grasp what the educated classes of late imperial China "thought and valued," we have to understand in all their complexity the attitudes discussed in this book.

Yet while attempting to build on the contributions of the Chinese humanists and the Neo-Weberians, I criticize them methodologically on a number of points, which are developed mostly in chapter 3, section a. First, the vast range of materials available for studying value orientations has yet to be exploited. Materials from institutional and bureaucratic history, used in chapter 4, are one example. Not every norm was realized as an actual organizational procedure, but every administrative procedure necessarily expressed a normative orientation.

Second, the philosophical, humanistic approach leads us to focus just on the moral ideals of historical actors instead of on all their ways of defining reality, including their own frailties and the other dissonances of life. Because Neo-Confucians were interested in figuring out how to reach their goals, not in analyzing their own way of thinking, their criterion for distinguishing between valuable insights and clichés should not be adopted by anyone wanting to understand them. Modern scholars, however, have very largely accepted the Neo-Confucian sense of cliché, failing to analyze what Neo-Confucians took for granted. We rather should learn from the anthropologists' fascination with clichés as the verbalized symbols of shared cultural orientations. Otherwise many of us Westerners will remain unfamiliar with the clichés making up the context of Neo-Confucian ideas, not to mention figuring out how these clichés formed the pattern of Neo-Confucian thought as a whole. Certainly many of these clichés are familiar to many Chinese-born intellectuals, who often can easily sense their meaning and context. Yet they too cannot remain aloof from the need for a balanced analysis of Neo-Confucian thought patterns, cliches and all. Only with such an analysis can they evade the strong tendency in modern China to condemn or glorify Neo-Confucianism in a one-sided, ideological way. ("Neo-Confucianism" is defined on pp. 51–52.)

The third methodological point, which applies especially to Weber and the Neo-Weberians, is that the shared orientations of an educated class cannot be understood without analyzing that counterpoint of ideas traditionally studied by intellectual historians. It is here, I believe, that we have to combine the wisdom of the intellectual historians with that of the Chinese humanists, the Neo-Weberians, and the anthropologists. We are often told that Neo-Confucians shared some belief or other, but what they disagreed about was as important to them. The main methodological premise of my book is a neglected truism: we understand a group of people best by understanding what they worried about. Nothing tells us more about a set of shared orientations than the way it defined the issues of controversy. Neo-Confucian arguments are often analyzed to determine whether they were logically or experientially valid, but I analyze them to obtain a closer understanding of what Neo-Confucians argued over, what their shared points of uncertainty and concern were.

Therefore I suggest looking at Neo-Confucianism as a widely shared "grammar" defining the problems of intellectual struggle by positing a discrepancy between the goal of life and the given world. Sharing this grammar, Neo-Confucians differed in terms of their solutions for these problems. When we use this standpoint, their shared assumptions and their controversies are clearly related to each other; their intellectual concerns are put into the context of shared cultural orientations; their cultural orientations are understood as living thought, not as a static set of beliefs; and the tensions of their intellectual struggle become clearer.

True, even with such a grammar, one still commits that cardinal sin of the Neo-Weberians and the humanists, reifying Chinese culture as a single, homogeneous entity. Yet the specter of Spenglerian *Geisteswissenschaft* has intimidated us too much, and the exaggerated positivistic demand for behavioral specifics has diverted attention away from the meaning and the context of ideas. As always, one has to seek a path avoiding equally the dangers of *k'ung-t'an* (empty talk) and *chih-li* (disconnected details presented without a sense for the whole to which they belong). If historical phenomena always exhibit the complexity of the heterogeneous, they also involve the complexity of the homogeneous, such as that of a shared language or intellectual "grammar." Neither kind of complexity can be usefully ignored. To describe an ethos in all its complexity is not to oversimplify intellectual attitudes but to elucidate them by putting them into context.

d. AN OVERVIEW OF THE ARGUMENT

Apart from these methodological considerations, my argument substantively differs in various ways from prominent views currently put forward by philosophical humanists, Neo-Weberians, intellectual historians, and modern China historians.

It begins with the notion that humanistic and philosophical accounts of the moral meaning of Confucian life indicate a *psychological* pattern of gratification and self-assertion which served as a counterweight to those anxieties described in the behavioral literature on dependence. For this point I rely greatly on Martin M. C. Yang's theory of familism and on T'ang Chün-i's concept of Confucian self-fulfillment. In chapter 3, however, analyzing Neo-Confucianism as a "grammar," I argue that it involved a "sense of predicament" filtered out of the current interpretations of Neo-Confucianism, including T'ang's. Because other intellectual historians writing on Neo-Confucianism have been less interested than I in specifying a shared cultural "grammar," it is hardly surprising that my view of this movement differs in some respects from theirs. Because of this difference, I have presented the evidence for my conclusions in some detail.

Our next problem is how to relate this sense of predicament to the anxiety stressed in the theory of dependency as well as to that "spirit" of Confucian self-fulfillment emphasized by T'ang. This question is discussed in chapter 4. In that chapter I also seek to relate the above factors to orientations which, as I argued in *The Internal Organization of Ch'ing Bureaucracy*, served as routinely expressed administrative norms. The result, summed up in the last chapter, is the thesis of an "ethos of interdependence." This thesis revolves around the interplay between the sense of anxiety and that of autonomy or self-fulfillment. We seem to be dealing with a modal personality pattern according to which control over anxiety did "depend" on a power perceived as outside the immediate ego, but to a large extent this power was mentally projected not onto social superiors but onto a transcendent source, that is, it was internalized in the self rather than projected onto other social roles. Therefore I speak of interdependent acts of moral self-assertion rather than a "dependency social orientation."

When this ethos of interdependence is described in terms useful for those studying cultures in a comparative way, a number of points can be made. The pattern of Confucian self-assertion and interdependence can be grossly contrasted with Western individualism, but we cannot describe it unqualifiedly in terms of dependence, the repression of emotion, the abhorrence of aggressive behavior, lack of self-esteem, lack of a notion of legitimated protest, familism, collectivism, authoritarianism, and particularism. It ascribed to the self powers godlike in Western eyes, yet it simultaneously involved an anxious fear of moral failure and a desire to subsume the needs of the self under those of morally legitimated groups. The importance of a shared, "correct" doctrine articulating the common moral purpose of this interdependence is also distinctive, as is the tendency for such doctrines to be "ideological" in the sense of Daniel Bell, that is, to assume that norms can be closely deduced from verifiable givens with complete objectivity.[30] Echoing the theme of interdependence, such doctrines also postulated an ontological sense of oneness, of human thought and the material world as fully and noumenally united. Partly promoting a sense of tension between moral ideals and the status quo, such thought cannot be called "stagnative." Such are some of the points I try to make in discussing the two issues raised at the start of this introduction: what was the character of those late imperial orientations defining the desired moral order and the modalities of change?

Finally, also in the last chapter, I argue that in twentieth-century China this ethos of interdependence has positively influenced not only conservative thought but also transformative and even revolutionary movements, including Maoism. The fact that these movements have to a large extent denounced the Confucian tradition as corrupt and invalid does not prove that this tradition has failed to affect the ideals they have embraced. After all, the tendency unconsciously to accept some of what we consciously reject is common throughout the world, and its presence in China has been observed by Chinese scholars also. This is a platitude, but one the implications of which relative to modern Chinese history still require much study. From this standpoint, there is far more ideological continuity in China between the modern and the premodern periods than has been recognized in most studies by historians. The recent work of Don C. Price effectively challenges the common tendency to view the growing understanding of the West as the cutting edge of modern Chinese intellectual history.[31]

From this standpoint too, our view of the basic direction of modern Chinese thought changes somewhat. To whatever extent a crisis of "cultural identity" or "cultural despair" has occurred, when we take into account the "sense of predicament" basic to Confucian thought in late imperial times, we cannot but recognize that the leading Chinese thinkers in the modern period have come to express a new optimistic confidence in the capacity of Chinese society to realize its goals. Whatever the lines of ideological continuity with the past, the rise of this optimism, crosscutting the various ideological camps right and left, has constituted a major point of discontinuity.

That is, the developing Chinese decision at the turn of our century to modernize was not simply based on the discovery that certain Western methods were superior to native ones. Rather, these Western methods proved enormously appealing just because they seemed useful for solving agonizing problems and realizing social ideals with which Confucians had long been preoccupied. This is merely to say that, as Ralph Linton pointed out, cultural diffusion is a two-way street and so depends on both the availability of ideas to import and the intensity of the indigenous impulse to import them. Neither side of this transaction can be taken for granted. The Chinese mind was not a *tabula rasa* reaching out for instruction from the outside. My argument is that, to a large extent, it was the indigenous, intense, centuries-old desire to escape from a metaphysical, psychological, political, and economic predicament which led many Chinese enthusiastically to devote their lives to the overthrow of traditionally revered institutions and the adoption of strange and foreign ways.

To be sure, the shortage of wealth and power in China was perceived as part of this predicament, and it was partly the search for wealth and power which influenced many to turn to the West. But if we agree that Confucian thought deeply affected the thinking and ideals of many Chinese on the eve of modernization, we can legitimately inquire into the cultural definition of reality found in this mode of thought. As we do so, we find a psychologically deep-rooted sense of predicament, dissatisfaction, and existential dissonance going far beyond the instrumental worries about wealth and power, and we also find personality and social ideals to which Chinese in modern times have kept remarkably faithful. Of course, the radical transformation of Chinese civilization in modern times cannot be explained purely in intellectual or cultural terms. At the very least, however, we should fully describe the intellectual aspects of this transformation, taking into account without bias those indigenous transformative impulses which did exist.

Obviously, the more we look into the traditional base line from which modernization proceeded in twentieth-century China, the more we shall have to adjust our understanding of that mix of continuities and discontinuities which modernization has involved. Certainly much of this mix has long been understood, and no one would deny that with the influx of Western ideas about nationalism, political participation, science, technology, and economic development, China to a large extent broke with its past. Yet we must still ask to what extent the transformative impulse to make this break paradoxically depended on indigenous intellectual resources, what cultural patterns have persisted unbroken, and to what extent this break left Chinese intellectuals metaphysically and psychologically floundering in a state of disorientation and despair. The common theory of an almost complete break made on the basis of Western ideas and leading to a crisis of cultural despair seems to be untenable as we consider more carefully the base-line orientations of modern China, and as we remember that the leading ideologues of modern China have been more concerned with refuting their opponents than with providing their international scholarly audience with a diagram elucidating the nature and the sources of their ideas. In the tracing of intellectual influences, the horse's mouth is not necessarily our best source. The often Manichaean mental set of historical actors struggling amidst violence, catastrophe, and humiliation to reshape their world is bound to produce biases of the sort discussed above. As Western students, we must try somehow to wend our way between the Scylla of such biases or blind spots and the Charybdis of our own relative ignorance.

e. REMAINING METHODOLOGICAL POINTS

With this line of argument, I do not intend to try to do justice to Max Weber's sociological comparison of the religious experience of Confucians with that of the Puritans. While Weber sought systematically to contrast these two kinds of religious experience, my focus is not primarily comparative, and while Weber was interested in the broad question of religion, my discussion merely concerns certain widespread orientations involving the issues of tension, anxiety, dependency, and autonomy. Although Weber's position on the question of tension is relevant to my discussion, I am trying here to review this position of his along with those of a variety of other scholars, and my focus is on certain major Chinese contributions to this problem area. Throughout, but especially in the first four chapters, I try to relate the anxiety described by the dependency theorists to the spirit of autonomy emphasized by humanists like T'ang Chün-i, two themes outside Weber's work, which was necessarily limited by a variety of factors, especially the inadequacy of the information available to European scholars half a century ago. In trying to evaluate and build on the scholarly work revolving around these two themes, we do not merely criticize Weber's and Eisenstadt's still influential view of late imperial orientations as "stagnative." Rather, we seek positively to help lay the foundation for an alternative conceptualization of these orientations.

I should also make explicit the great importance I attach to Richard H. Solomon's theory of a "social dependency orientation," which, strikingly paralleled by the views of Chinese behavioral scientists like Tseng Wen-hsing and Hsü Ching (see chapter 1), has shed enormous light on one of the two themes noted above. To some extent, my book is an attempt to respond to Solomon's. Although a review I wrote of his book did pay tribute to aspects of his discussion of dependency and authoritarianism, I was then so preoccupied with trying to define the limitations of his contribution that my final evaluation was one-sided and overly harsh. Without his systematic and rich discussion of the problem of anxiety, my thesis here would never have been put forward, and it will be years before really comprehensive and sensitive formulations can be advanced to describe the orientations that are the subject of his book as well as mine.

I think of orientations as words with a structured context (apart from whatever else they may also be). Consequently in describing them, I try both coherently to unfold this context and to bring to the reader's attention the key Chinese expressions involved. When a romanized Chinese word or set of words is followed in my text by one or more English words in parentheses, the English is an exact translation. When the English is in quotation marks and is followed by romanized Chinese in parentheses, the English is usually an exact translation except for a syntactic difference; occasionally, it is just an exact translation, thus presented for stylistic reasons.

CHAPTER ONE

Dependency and the Humanistic Theory of Chinese Familism

To put the issue of anxiety and dependency into context, we can turn to a recent discussion in Taiwan academic circles about the nature of traditionally inherited socialization patterns within the Chinese family. This discussion is in a 1972 symposium volume edited by Professors Yang Kuo-shu and Li I-yüan. In this volume's "Looking at the Chinese Character from the Standpoint of Personality Development," an article by Tseng Wen-hsing, Lecturer in Psychiatry at the Medical School of National Taiwan University, one finds an emphasis on the concept of dependency similar to that of R. H. Solomon.[1] Influenced by Erik H. Erikson, Tseng bases his discussion on his own life experience, his practice as a psychiatrist, the Chinese and Western scientific literature, and data from other sources such as children's stories and teaching materials. He divides a Chinese person's life into eight chronological stages and holds that various practices at each stage bring about: "oral," food-associated feelings of dependence on other members of one's solidarity group; a sense of unclear boundaries between one's ego and other egos;[2] and virtually unquestioning respect for the authority of those on whom one depends. Obeying the latter, one learns to avoid the sanction of "shame" by repressing spontaneous appetitive and physical outbursts, by following a demanding work ethic, and by treating others according to a complicated code of etiquette involving the norms of "yielding" and "reciprocity." Forced to restrict his quest for direct gratification, the individual suffers from strong if repressed feelings of frustration and resentment, as well as, presumably, a lack of self-esteem.

Tseng's account reminds us that although there was a turning point around the age of six when the child "suddenly" was subjected to more severe treatment, strictness began as early as one and a half years, when a child about to touch something was likely to hear "Don't move!" In the past, adults from time to time would even tie such an infant's hands and feet so as to restrain his movements and thus guard against his growing up "naughty." Tseng leaves not the slightest doubt that he prefers the way in which "Westerners" allow their children to grow up "independent, masters of themselves," while the typical Chinese felt frustrated as he waited for years to obtain "position and power," with which he then restarted the cycle of control and repression.[3]

Hsü Ching, a psychiatrist at Keng-hsin Hospital, has a similar account, which dwells still more on the elements of bitterness and frustration. The "oral dependent type" "feels a bitter hatred in his very bones" for those on whom he depends but who do not satisfy his needs. Parents thus hate children who disappoint them, and clinical experience shows that the need absolutely to obey their parents arouses in young children "strong feelings of burning hatred and dissatisfaction." Using the concept of "reaction formation," Li Mei-chih suggests that the "abnormal" and "extreme" stress on filial piety in traditional times reflected the "repressed hostility" children felt toward their parents.[4]

Tseng's view of the character-forming effects of socialization was directly criticized in the seminar, especially by Li I-yüan, who pointed out that the causal sequence involved had not been experimentally verified; that Tseng's impressionistic description lacked any "standardized" framework allowing more precise comparative propositions; and that Tseng had failed to weigh the effects of childhood socialization against the effects of other experiences on the formation of character.[5] Yet if doubts were thus raised about the relative and causative importance of this whole syndrome of dependency, the discussions directly dealing with Hsü Ching's and Tseng Wen-hsing's papers were positive; no one questioned either the existence or the ultimate importance of this syndrome. This remained for Martin M. C. Yang with his sociological version of what is generally regarded as the received humanistic wisdom about Chinese "familism."

In comparing Yang's humanistic approach to the psychological one above, one finds different assumptions about behavior. The central issue, I believe, is whether behavior is essentially a matter of the ego's quest for direct gratification, that is, its quest for survival, appetitive satisfactions, wealth, power, and prestige; or whether the ego *also* has basic desires for certain intangible values, namely knowledge of a sense-making cognitive and moral order, involvement in feelings and symbols intimating transcendence of death, a sense of moral worth and the associated pleasures of extending feelings of affection toward others, and feelings of solidarity, including the opportunity to devote oneself to one's group. The psychological approach interprets family life largely according to the former assumption; the humanistic, according to the latter. More specifically, the psychological approach assumes that while the ego's quest for direct gratification is basic, the structure of this quest varies culturally, and the socialization practices of a particular culture predispose an individual to accept those culturally structured patterns of deprivation and gratification with which he is presented. This approach seems to assume that the above-listed intangible values alone cannot provide real gratification. Alone, without accompanying increments of direct gratification, they can only hide frustration.

Yang insists on a humanistic approach. In analyzing any "national character," one should focus on those virtues consciously emphasized generation after generation, not on those "dispirited" forms of behavior which "pessimistic persons" always dwell on in times of national turmoil, i.e. frustrations and anxieties. Not unconscious feeling but *ch'ing-ts'ao* (morally articulated feelings) are his subject-matter. "National character" is "the spirit of a culture," says Yang, using a favorite term of Chinese humanists. It is a "mass faith" derived from a "religion, [system of] ethics, or philosophy of life" the "thought" of which originally arose in the minds of great teachers like Confucius or Martin Luther. This level of conscious thought, of *ch'ing-ts'ao*, not just the ego's quest for direct gratification, yields those various intangible goods mentioned above. Yang especially emphasizes that *ch'ing-ts'ao*

1. Dependency

can "reduce the anxiety, fear, and grief connected to death" and can satisfy a desire felt by all "civilized" people to live a social, cultural, and moral life on a "high level."[6] Therefore, even if, as Li Mei-chih asserts, the child in his family lacked "any status to speak of" (*ti-wei*),[7] he could still find gratification in terms of the *ch'ing-ts'ao* of his life situation as a whole.

To put it still another way, if one holds that the child was prevented from developing feelings of "self-esteem," what is one to make of the common ethical emphasis on having a "deep sense of respect" for one's own "self" as a moral being, a notion emphatically expressed by words like *tzu-tsun, tzu-ai,* and *tzu-chung*? Hsün-tzu (third century B.C.) said that "The person who has benevolence is one who has true respect for himself." Yang Hsiung (53 B.C.–18 A.D.) said: "*Tzu-ching* (reverence for one's own person) is the supreme realization of *li* (the rules of moral propriety)."[8] The reader might object that such concepts and the *ch'ing-ts'ao* emphasized by Professor Yang were merely part of the rhetoric of family life and did not effectively relieve the frustrations of those in subservient roles. Yet how is one empirically to decide this question either way? It is significant that Yang's account of Chinese family life, based on an intimate knowledge of many facts and on his credentials as the author of a classic village study, was not challenged as excessively idealized in the seminar where it was discussed.[9]

Besides emphasizing the more intangible gratifications in Chinese family life, Yang's analysis suggests that these gratifications and the more material ones were inextricably intertwined, and in effect he challenges the emphasis on dependency as one-sided. Let us take up his main points, which I here present with a little elaboration.

Did children feel that they were "dependent" or that they were entering a relationship of interdependence? The theme of interdependence had already arisen when the dependency theorists brought up the idea of *yang-tzu fang-lao* (raising children against the hardships of old age).[10] Obviously to feel dependent is also to perceive oneself as turning into one on whom others depend. And in Confucian terms this process of growth was one in terms of which one depended not only on one's models but also on one's own efforts (*kung-fu*). Children also gave pleasure to their parents by actively extending feelings of gratitude to them, as summed up in that central concept of filial piety, *kan-en pao-te* (to feel gratitude for favors received and seek to reciprocate).[11] It is significant that the basic concept of *yang* (to care for) applied equally to the nurture of children and the sustenance of aged parents.

The process of submitting to authority not only was painful and frustrating but also involved important feelings of gratification. The traditional ethical rhetoric did not seek to gloss over that parental harshness deplored by modern psychologists. As the *I-ching* says: "Those in a family have a severe ruler, that is, the father and mother."[12] However, we need to keep in mind the *ch'ing-ts'ao* connected to "serving" (*shih*) one's parents. "Serving" was not necessarily a state of humiliating subservience. "Serving" not only expressed feelings of gratitude but also was perceived as displaying that humility salient in the character of a sage. As the historian Wei Cheng-t'ung pointed out, Mencius described the sage emperor Shun as having "exhaustively practiced the true way of serving kinsmen."[13]

Moreover, contrary to Hsü Ching, parental authority was morally bounded, not "unlimited."[14] Parents held up their ancestors, not themselves, as models with which their children should identify. Yang argues that traditionally Chinese generally "identified with" their idealized ancestors, vivid accounts of whose virtues children often heard on occasions of both relaxation and moral admonition.[15] Not their own will but the generalized, stereotyped ideals which they transmitted legitimated the authority of parents. Thus even in the family there was some differentiation between moral ideals and the actual persons of those in immediate authority, a differentiation so vital to Chinese political thought. Similarly in the world of scholarship, authority was interwoven with respect for the past, as illustrated by the "unwritten law" that "in writing commentaries one may not contradict the classics, in speaking, one may not contradict the commentaries."[16] Indeed, what else is traditionalism but norms governing *all* living generations?

Certainly a child was painfully shamed into learning the behavior patterns viewed as right by those in authority, but we should also take into account the feelings he had regarding both the transmitters and the content of this learning. The child felt grateful to and vividly "identified with" the former,[17] and he felt that what he learned was valuable to him since it would turn him into a person of moral cultivation. The goal of putting aside the ego's quest for direct gratification, summed up in Confucian ideals like *k'o-chi* (overcome self-centeredness) and *tan-po* (indifference to personal advantage), has been endorsed even by Westernizing admirers of individualism like Yin Hai-kuang.[18] Socialization, in Yang's eyes, was a relation between *shih-hua-che* (the one who extends the possibility of moral development) and *shou-hua-che* (the one who receives instruction about moral development).[19]

Moreover the work ethic, the learning of which was part of this transformation, made sense, especially in an economy of great scarcity. Learning the habits of *ch'in-chien* (industriousness and frugality) was a reasonable way not only to please one's parents but also to obtain personal gratifications. By *chieh-ch'i-li* (exerting oneself to the utmost) in productive work, the child could express the inexhaustible gratitude he felt toward his parents, avoid shame, and obtain not only admiration but also, eventually, material gratifications for himself.

It is important to see that the process of submitting to authority not only involved the intangible gratifications mentioned above but also coincided with the ego's quest for direct gratification. Yang notes the desire of Chinese parents to brag about their children's successes. Unsuccessful children were tragically blamed by their parents for being "unfilial."[20] Yet if the child's success was his parents', it surely was his also. Preserving his own physical well-being, getting married, and raising children satisfied some of the son's own desires for pleasure, position, and participation in a mortality-transcending continuum. Yet these acts simultaneously accorded with Mencius' injunction: "There are three ways of being unfilial: leaving no posterity is the worst." Similarly, no act was more filial than realizing a goal for oneself—say a *chü-jen* degree— which one's ancestors had pursued in vain.[21]

While the partly painful process of being subject to authority also involved direct gratifications, conversely the partly pleasurable process of exercising authority over one's children was interwoven with a painful sense of responsibility. The painful severity with which a father instilled the work ethic into his children involved not only his desire to experience the pleasures of domination but also his fear that his children would fail to adopt this work ethic and thus break off his ancestral line, letting it fall into the yawning historical pit of eternally unremembered souls. In such a situation, he himself would be guilty of the gravest impiety toward his ancestral line. His exercise of authority, therefore, was itself an anxiety-ridden continuation of his subservience to the desires of his parents and ancestors. The struggle for survival and a morally meaningful existence was a fearfully dangerous enterprise, especially in a world of great economic scarcity and general uncertainty. The attainment of high status was no escape from these fearful dangers.

Precisely because the anxieties of responsibility and the gratifications of solidarity were thus interwoven and experienced by both those in dominant and those in subservient positions, the theory of a sharp contrast in the life cycle between the frustrations of subservience and the pleasures of domination seems simplistic and mechanical. This contrast no doubt existed, but only within the context of a more general psychological transaction: only by assuming the fearful responsibilities of family life could the individual feel that he was obtaining both the material and the intangible goods of life.

Yang does not deny that Chinese family life led to many abuses of authority and consequent personal tragedies, but he feels that much of it was in fact shaped by the ethic he describes.[22] No Erik Erikson, he did not try to elucidate the complex interplay between conscious and unconscious factors in Chinese family life, but neither did anyone else in the seminar, and I do not believe the conscious *ch'ing-ts'ao* he described can be reduced to other psychological factors without arbitrarily making psychological assumptions.

Although the issues of socialization Yang raises will eventually require a fuller psychological and sociological analysis, he plausibly suggests that anxieties stemming from various kinds of deprivations and frustrations were interwoven with more pleasurable feelings, especially the intangible gratifications of active participation in a morally meaningful, mortality-transcending continuum.

CHAPTER TWO

Tăng Chün-i's Concept of Confucian Self-fulfillment

a. INTRODUCTION

T'ANG CHÜN-I's masterful *Chung-kuo wen-hua-chih ching-shen chia-chih* (The Value of the Spirit of Chinese Culture), completed in 1951, also makes clear the importance of the more intangible gratifications, especially the ego's sense of possessing moral worth as a vital part of an awe-inspiring cosmic flow of empathy, and the satisfactions derived by the ego from cognitively understanding this cosmic process.[1] In this context T'ang forcefully develops a concept of Confucian self-fulfillment. Indulging in a kind of Spenglerian *Geisteswissenschaft*, T'ang is interested in philosophical ideas. These, his analysis presupposes, articulate a primordial paradigm of mental life which is more general than the norms of intercourse between different social roles, and which determines or somehow underlies these norms as well as other cultural characteristics. Admittedly, in all such matters behavioral questions are raised which cannot be answered simply with literary sources, but, conversely, attitudes expressed in influential literary sources also have to be weighed.

T'ang, currently Professor of Philosophy at The Chinese University of Hong Kong, is a major figure in that intellectual movement described in the introduction as seeking to define a new kind of commitment to the ideals of the Confucian past. Consequently it is not surprising that he is concerned to show that because the "value" of China's traditional "spirit" is "as high as possible" in some respects, the Chinese need not humiliate themselves by adopting a "self-deprecating, admiring attitude" toward the West.[2] Moreover, his adversary analysis of Western culture is at best acute and almost never empathetic. For instance, instead of deploring the Chinese failure to emphasize the role of athletics in education, T'ang criticizes the Greeks' Olympic games as illustrating an unfortunate Western tendency to differentiate culturally significant activities from the routines of daily life.[3] His simplistic view of the Greek preoccupation with "purely intellectual rationality" demonstrates that the rule of *hao-li chih ch'a ch'ien-li chih miu* (off by a fraction in the beginning, far off the mark in the end) applies not only to Westerners studying Chinese thought.[4] Yet one can be defensive about something one really believes in. The genuineness of T'ang's intellectual commitment to the universal validity of Confucian values is obvious, despite his definite tendency toward that defensive posture *vis-à-vis* the West which Levenson identified as a major aspect of modern Chinese thought.

Because it is heavily influenced by a particular school of Neo-Confucianism (Lu-Wang) and by modern Chinese trends, T'ang's exegesis of human experience is not necessarily typical of Chinese thought generally. Indeed, in a crucial sense, it differs from the Neo-Confucian exegesis (see chapter 3, section k). Moreover, T'ang's book is neither popular nor philosophically rigorous. Arguing that man through his moral experience has knowledge of the ultimate, noumenal reality of the cosmos, T'ang brushes aside Kant's doubts about the possibility of such knowledge instead of systematically showing how they can be disposed of. This task was left to Mou Tsung-san, who, in his *Chih-te chih-chüeh yü Chung-kuo che-hsüeh* (The Intuition of Noumenal Reality and Chinese Philosophy), completed in 1969, defended the Neo-Confucian assumption that such intuition is possible by examining Kant's arguments in great detail (he used the Norman Kemp Smith translation of the *Critique of Pure Reason*) (see below). Yet although much more sensitive to the epistemological difficulties involved, Mou's defense of the Neo-Confucian position is substantially the same as that developed in T'ang's much earlier work (which itself acknowledged Mou's contribution in this regard). The great advantage of T'ang's work is that, spending less time on Western doubts, it nevertheless provides a richly detailed and comprehensive interpretation of the Neo-

Confucian position within an analytical framework easily accessible to those accustomed to modern ways of thought.

b. CHINESE AND WESTERN CULTURE

In a masterly comparative discussion which roughly makes a few broad points based on far-reaching scholarship and profound reflection, T'ang shows how prevalent Chinese and Western views have differently treated basic mental phenomena like feelings of empathy, feelings of a self-centered kind, the decisional capacity, and abstract thought.[5] Feelings of empathy perceived as "good" and as different from feelings of a selfish kind have been recognized in Western as well as Chinese thought; T'ang cites the Christian idea of a "believing heart" and of "love."[6] The mainstream of Confucian thought, however, differs from Western thought in focusing on these feelings as basic, rational, integral to human nature, and directly part of an ontologically ultimate reality which is "good." Thus a major Confucian theme is the interconnectedness of *ch'ing* (feelings), *li* (principle), and *hsing* (man's ontologically ultimate, heaven-conferred nature), and the idea that *hsing* is "good." In Western theories of the mind, on the other hand, these empathetic feelings typically play a secondary role, are contrasted with man's rational capacities, and do not directly stem from a good, ontologically ultimate reality. Thus T'ang notes that, in contrast to the word *ch'ing*, the English concept of "feeling . . . leans toward what is felt subjectively," that the idea of "sentiment" is in tension with that of rationality, that "emotion" connotes "being excited," and that Heidegger's concept of "mood" is too specialized to have general cultural significance.[7] Of course Freud's concept of unconscious desires places the world of feeling still further away from rationality, and Freud's idea that erotic feelings are directed even toward one's parents and siblings strikes T'ang as "utterly fantastic" (also a common Western reaction in the 1940s).[8]

Generally Western theories focus not on such empathetic feelings but on what the Chinese call *yü*, i.e. feelings of a self-centered kind, as with the emphasis of Locke and the utilitarians on "the pursuit of pleasure."[9] Where Western theorists speak of "responding" or "adapting" to the "environment" in order to satisfy the "desires of the mind," Chinese thinkers speak of *kan-ying* (responding empathetically) to things or *kan-t'ung* (empathetically pervading with one's response).[10] Another aspect of the mind is its decisional capacity. Western theories, with their stress on "free will," have focused on it, but while Chinese thinkers fully conceptualized it they never quite regarded it as such a key aspect of mental life.[11] Similarly Chinese thinkers have paid much attention to abstract concepts, which they generally refer to as *nien*, but they lacked anything like Plato's and Aristotle's emphasis on man's "reason" and his rational "capacity to understand universal, eternal 'concepts' or 'forms'" as his fundamental nature, or the Kantian interest in analyzing the variety of abstract concepts and the principles in terms of which they are connected.[12]

T'ang also explains how the Chinese found the allegedly right paradigm of mental life, and in a Spenglerian way he analyzes a large variety of societal and cultural patterns allegedly connected to differences between the Chinese and Western paradigms. Suffice it to say that he sees the Western fixation on the "rational" aspect of mental life as leading to a view of reality whereby the ultimate units of existence are distinct entities which are "external" relative to each other, are interrelated in terms of instrumental action rather than interchanging empathies, and are ultimately in conflict.[13] The struggle to compete with others and overcome nature therefore became decisive in the West.

The Chinese with their *shih-tsai-kan* (deep sense for the real) found a more holistic approach, he says.[14] They could "discuss mental life and human nature directly in terms of the mind's inner knowledge of its own experience."[15] The traditionally central imagery of water flowing is basic to T'ang's epistemological analysis here. In analyzing the nature of reality, we need to "flow along together with the processes of transformation."[16] Therefore we have to avoid "being stuck in any particular, fixed form of response" (*chih*), and we have "emphathetically to interact and feel one with things without anything obstructing or any artificial clinging to and seeking to keep static the inherently moving" (*chih-cho*). The Western fixation on rationality is such a "clinging," preventing an authentic encounter with "experience." Reflecting the influence of

Wang Yang-ming, this use of the *chih-cho* concept lies absolutely at the heart of T'ang's epistemological and cross-cultural analysis.[17]

The paradigm of mental life which, T'ang holds, was realized to varying degrees in the experience of much of China's population since Han times[18] can be summed up as the participation of the self in a noumenal flow of empathy. Instead of a Humean self cut off from the cosmos except for a flow of fragmentary sense impressions, T'ang describes a self that shares feelings of empathy with the cosmos's immanently ordered processes of transformation. Trying as a philosopher to prove that this Chinese concept of the self is based on a systematically verifiable understanding of the universal nature of experience, T'ang presents an exegesis of experience which can be divided into six steps.

c. THE EXEGESIS OF EXPERIENCE

First, the ultimate subject of experience, *wu-jen-chih hsin* (the conscious self), *chih-chüeh* (has an intuition or is directly aware of) *tang-hsia ch'eng-hsien* (that which appears in the immediate present). Second, the conscious self *t'ung-shih chien-chih* (simultaneously knows both) this new given and things stored in its memory from previous experiences, that is, it carries on a process of comparison and categorization involving *li* (general principles).

Third, the self "does not use what it has stored from the past to harm what it is about to receive," that is, its process of comparison and categorization is completely objective, allowing it to be in undistorted contact with the new given. In the view of Hsün-tzu, which T'ang accepts without even the hint of a quibble, the mind can simultaneously "store" memories and be "empty" in its unprejudiced receptivity to current experience. As Hsün-tzu put it with magnificent simplicity, we can *chih tao* (know the way of action which is inherent in the cosmos and which people should follow).[19]

T'ang is thus totally unimpressed by that powerful Humean tradition of doubt about the human capacity to formulate values as objectively verifiable propositions. Paradoxically, T'ang's (and Hsün-tzu's) awareness that one's views can be easily warped by self-interest is very strong. Because of the strength of selfish desires and the tendency to rationalize these desires through a one-sided fixation on some abstract doctrine (*chih-cho*), one must learn to view one's own ideas with suspicion and to be constantly on guard against "holding onto one view while arbitrarily rejecting a hundred others."[20]

This emphasis on doubting the validity of one's own views, however, is not so radical as the Humean one. From T'ang's standpoint, enough moral effort can produce an outlook which is "empty" of distorting preconceptions, and historically "men of ultimate wisdom" did in fact provide succeeding generations with rather clear, written guidelines of moral action fully expressing this "empty" outlook. Thus T'ang himself can be confident that in modestly "synthesizing the positions of China's earlier men of wisdom and clearing away some difficulties,"[21] he is probably presenting his readers with objectively valid views. Consequently, whatever the difficulties may be, it is practical for one to attempt to base one's society on moral values the objective, universal truth of which is demonstrable, that is, on what Bell calls an "ideology."

From the Humean standpoint, however, moral effort itself is based on historically and culturally conditioned preconceptions. A sense of doubt and openness based on this one allegedly universal fact therefore replaces the martial determination to establish an ideology. When Hu Shih once looked for such a radical sense of doubt in Confucian thought, the closest he came was Lü Tsu-ch'ien's (1137–1181) view that "It is not easy clearly to understand what is good, and it is not easy to examine into true principle."[22]

What is the given reality which the self can thus objectively apprehend? Citing philosophers like Whitehead and Bergson to refute the Humean view that "fragmentary sense impressions" constitute man's primordial contact with experience, T'ang holds that the idea of such impressions is only a rational construct used to describe experience, and that experience in its primordial, immediately given form reveals itself as "the movements and transformations of things. . . . internal to which are. . . . order and laws," including that of "cause and effect." Contrary to Kant, therefore, these "things" are not just phenomena known to our senses but are "things-in-themselves," i.e. noumena.[23]

Fourth, the conscious self empathetically responds to the "things" it perceives. Going back to concepts in the *Li-chi* and the

Classic of Changes, the key phrase here is *kan-wu erh hou tung* (stirred by things and then moving). When this response takes the form of the self's moral feeling of compassion for suffering objects, this compassion is intentionally related (to use the phenomenological term) to its object and is not due to a subjective "association" by the self with painful experiences in the self's own past, as some psychologists hold.[24]

Fifth, the self also is "directly aware" that this feeling of empathy with other things is not produced by and confined to the self but rather is "given" to the self by the objective noumenal world itself ("heaven"), in which this feeling of empathy inheres just as it does in the conscious self.[25] T'ang's meaning here, conforming to Confucian tradition, is that this relation of mutual empathy is shared by the conscious self even with animals and purely material objects like stones.[26] T'ang adds that "sense impressions" arise only "after" this "shared feeling of empathy," thus again refuting Humean empiricism.[27]

Since empathy is thus shared, the ultimate unit of experience can be called *chiao-kan-chih-chi* (point at which empathies are interchanged), although in T'ang's thought, as we have seen, noumenal "things," including the "conscious self," are also treated as ultimate units of existence. In a Whiteheadian way, the very nature of a "thing" is viewed by T'ang as "including" the "changes" in it arising from the interchanges of empathy it experiences.[28]

T'ang generously ascribes to these interchanges a number of objective characteristics. Suspicion of reification is not something he learned from Whitehead, and he does not hesitate to believe that words like "the virtue of heaven" not only express some "metaphysical pathos" (as Lovejoy would have it) but also have objectively existing referents.[29] His central point is that, properly viewed, objective reality is something gloriously full of "value."

These points of interchange, in the first place, fully exist in the way that "common sense" assumes that the world exists. Chinese thinkers have never experienced doubts about the reality of the commonsense world, according to T'ang.[30] Each of these interchanges is inherently "concrete," "particular," and "unique."[31] The "flowing forth" of these occasions of interchange is inherently "inexhaustible" and "endless," exhibiting the "creativity of endless renewal."[32] The ambiguity of the word *sheng* (to live, to produce) is vital here, expressing the idea that the flow of these occasions is inherently living, even as it extends to purely material objects. Besides life, "freedom" is implied, since these interchanges can allow for "change" free from the "mechanical control" of either "habits" accumulated in the past or "force" applied from "the outside world."[33] (This notion of freedom is thus connected to that of absolute objectivity.)

Because each interchange of empathies brings the self out of itself, has a context of inexhaustibility, and is inherently subsumable under universal categories, the adjectives "transcendent," "universal," "limitless," and "encompassing" can be applied to it. T'ang is particularly fascinated by the convergence of concreteness and universality,[34] and from this "encompassing" vision he derives what can be called a pathos of immensity involving ideas like "long-enduring," "great broadness and substantialness," and "sublime."[35] This sense of something immense, living, inexhaustible, and transcendent is then reified through the notion of "the empathetic awareness of heaven (*t'ien-hsin*), the nature of heaven, the virtue of heaven."[36] Finally, since "heaven" is thus found in each occasion, all occasions are seen to be of equal value, each, monad-like, embodying all the value in the universe: "Not only is every person a 'supreme ultimate,' each thing that happens is a 'supreme ultimate.'"[37]

In this light, the concept of a noumenal flow of empathy involves a kind of Panglossian optimism. Because the flow of occasions is inherently one of interpenetrating empathies, it precludes the ultimacy of conflict or opposition, including any gap between subject and object.[38] Even political and familial obligations are regarded as "essentially" compatible, despite those tragic times when they actually are not.[39] The existence of suffering is fully acknowledged, but the experience of suffering, although so basic to the Mencian concept of empathy, is never used as an ultimate paradigm of existence. So common in the West, that agonizing over the idea that the march of history has inevitably cost the lives of innocents is foreign to T'ang: "In all human activities, in all the situations of life, one can see and empathetically grasp the positive value involved."[40] The ultimate meaning of suffering is simply that it creates in men the desire to eliminate it.[41] The moment of succor, not the moment of need, is primordial, and the teleological meaningfulness of life, its "value," is unproblematic. It is highly significant that despite his impressive knowledge of European thought and his true brilliance as a thinker, T'ang is utterly immune to that sense of angst, of absurdity, of meaninglessness, of nothingness-closing-in so basic to modern existentialism. His philosophy has the cheerfulness of a kind of metaphysical YMCA. It expresses that *le* (joy) which Mencius spoke of with regard to the feeling of being one with the cosmos.

As a sixth step in his exegesis, T'ang shows how empathetic responses take different forms, constituting moral life in all its variety.[42] Furnishing a moral basis for particularism, the most important distinction is that between the empathetic feeling of gratitude toward those who gave life to the self, in terms of which one filially serves parents (whether or not they are suffering), and the feeling of empathy with suffering objects, which, as the basis of moral obligation toward nonkinsmen, implies indifference toward one's fellow citizens when they are feeling fine.

d. MORAL AUTONOMY

Moral life, however, is not just *kan* (feeling empathy for), it is also *ch'eng* (bringing to completion). As the *Chung-yung* indicates, one "brings to completion oneself and the things of the world" (*ch'eng-chi ch'eng-wu*).[43] Moreover, one has a "responsibility" to do so. There is a shift here from merely experiencing feelings of empathy to acting on them, to self-assertion. This is a crucial issue. Without exploring this question of self-assertion, one cannot even try to clarify questions like individualism, collectivism, authoritarianism, and interdependence.

In the first place, as has already been indicated, Confucian thought makes *wu-hsin* (the conscious self) the agent of moral action. This is plain whether we look at the *Chung-yung*'s concept of *ch'eng-chi ch'eng-wu* or the famous eight steps of the *Ta-hsüeh*, which depict the self as first obtaining knowledge about "things" and gradually putting the whole world in order. In both cases, the locus of moral action is the self's unmediated contact with "things," that is, with the natural and social cosmos as a whole, not just with mankind, not to mention just with one's family or the state. As T'ang puts it, "all the different kinds of relationships between human beings . . . equally cluster around the character of the individual as spokes do around the hub of a wheel."[44] Filial piety is crucial for T'ang precisely because it is a vital expression of the individual's moral empathies, indispensable to the process of "completing oneself." In no way does "serving" one's parents mean that their moral empathies supersede one's own. Parents are just "things" relative to the "self," and one's sense of gratitude for the gift of life is primordially directed toward the cosmos itself, only derivatively toward one's parents. In filial piety, says the *Classic of Filial Piety*, nothing is more important than *p'ei-t'ien* (matching heaven in virtue).[45]

While the self is thus the ultimate agent of moral action, it also has immense, godlike power available to it to carry out its moral mission. It is true that when T'ang tells us that "each thing that happens is a 'supreme ultimate,'" we tend to lose sight of man as "the truly spiritual being among the ten thousand things" (that popular phrase from the *Shu-ching*).[46] But T'ang also points out that "man," indeed every individual, is the source of a unique moral energy vital for the proper functioning of the cosmos. Although the energy to produce life (*sheng*) is peculiar to the cosmos, the cosmos lacks *li* (energy used in moral efforts), which is what an individual should "exhaustively" expend in order to "bring to completion both himself and the things of the world."

T'ang's interpretation of man's potential moral power in Confucian eyes seems unproblematic. For Confucians, man in his ordinary condition has available to him a power which the Judeo-Christian tradition reserves for god. Because man draws on sources of moral power "given" to him by "heaven," man is not god. But man is godlike because he is the sole existing vehicle of that moral assertion needed to put the world right. Other aspects of human experience, already mentioned, also contribute to the godlike quality of Confucian self-assertion: a feeling of oneness with "heaven," involving a pathos of immensity; the direct experience of a noumenal, Panglossian world free of grounds for angst and teleologically unproblematic; an intellectual ability to know this world, both as fact and as value, with complete objectivity; and the ability, based on utilizing man's unique moral energy with complete intellectual objectivity, to achieve a society free of the distortions of self-interest.

As one reflects on these godlike qualities, the importance of T'ang Chün-i's emphasis on the question of the "distance" between man and the divine in early religious thought becomes clear. I am aware of no evidence or consideration contradicting his view that this distance was great in the Judeo-Christian tradition and small in the Chinese tradition.[47] The Chinese were not just created in the image of God; they could "match heaven." It was in "matching heaven" that the self exhibited those godlike qualities described above.

e. EMOTIONAL AND VIOLENT SELF-ASSERTION

Thus striving to be one with heaven, the morally assertive self typically expressed itself in terms of the Confucian work ethic, with its stress on *ch'in-chien* (industriousness and frugality). But it was also oriented toward actualizing itself through opposition to corruption in the world. Without this backdrop of widespread moral decay, including the debilitating forces of selfishness within the self, Confucian thought makes no sense at all. This obvious point has been obscured by the sociological myth of traditionalism and by the ingenious speculations of Max Weber, who was mistaken in his view that Confucian thought precluded a sense of radical struggle against the forces of evil in oneself and the world and thus provided no ideological "counterweight" for change. Very briefly, he did not know that Confucians recognized the great power of bad material desires (*yü*), despite their tendency to believe that man can also overcome *yü* by drawing on a heaven-conferred power of goodness within himself (see chapter 3, section n).

Confucian thought thus did focus on universalistic ideals differentiated from the existing structure of authority, and it did legitimate protest. Nor was it authoritarian insofar as that word connotes "blind submission to authority." Expressing a common Confucian standpoint, T'ang says that human action lacks "the character of morality" when it does not "issue from the self" and merely consists of "carrying out the orders of others, following the conventionally accepted sayings of the past, or copying the behavior of others."[48]

To be sure, the travails of moral assertion play a much smaller role in T'ang's thought than they did for many Confucians in imperial times. T'ang, as I argue in the next chapter, glosses over the sense of predicament which informs Neo-Confucian discussions of the self's floundering efforts to tap the moral power within it. Brushing aside the then-experienced agonies of intellectual uncertainty, oppressively used imperial power, bureaucratic corruption, gentry and merchant oppression, and economic misery, T'ang has an extravagantly idealized picture of the traditional period as a time when "the greatest possible amount" of social, religious, intellectual, and political "freedom" was realized; when husband and wife, calling each other "lord" and "minister" respectively, treated each other with "deep respect"; and when the virtues of "filial piety and loving concern" pervaded social and political relations.[49] The character of the imperial society as T'ang describes it is more like that of The Three Dynasties as perceived by Confucians in imperial times than that of the imperial society as perceived by those who lived in it.

Nevertheless, T'ang is fully aware of the Confucian emphasis on pursuing moral ideals differentiated from the status quo, on "opposing current customs," on "disassociating oneself from *hsiang-yüan* (hypocrites who seek a reputation for prudence and morality while going along with the immoral trends of the day)."[50] With its famous *loci classici* in *Lun-yü* and *Mencius*, this basic concept of *hsiang-yüan* implied the importance of autonomy because it was explicitly correlated to the idea that one had to be ready to challenge the morally polluted world of conventional opinion and established authority. T'ang dwells on this theme in his discussion of the various exemplars of traditional morality. He describes *hao-chieh* (men of outstanding character and ability) like Liu Pang as "overcoming the wrongness of ten million persons with the rightness of one." Other ideal types of personalities, such as *hsia-i-chih shih* (valiant men devoted to justice) and *ch'i-chieh-chih shih* (outstanding men of unshakable integrity), were similarly perceived as determined to act right however opposed by men of high status and even public opinion.[51] This autonomous spirit is expressed in the *Li-chi's* concept of *t'e-li tu-hsing* (to stand and act independent of any moral support from others).

This spirit, it should be noted, was infused with emotional force, as can be seen from the frequent use of *ch'i* (flow of aroused feeling, spirit) in words like *ch'i-ku*, *ch'i-ko*, *chih-ch'i*, *i-ch'i*, and *ch'i-chieh*, which all involve the idea of an emotionally aroused sense of moral strength and courage. "Outstanding men of the purest integrity . . .

washed away the moral filth of heaven and earth, their blood fired up, their manner like a cold wind." "How can there be a sage who does not get angry?" asked Chu Hsi.[52] Moral effort (*kung-fu*) was discussed by Confucians in terms of *li* (effort), which directly involved the materially emotive aspects of personality designated with words like *ch'i* and *ch'ing* (feeling). To say that Confucianism "condemned expressions of emotion" implies some arbitrarily restrictive definition of emotion, not to mention confusion over the distinction between *ch'ing* and *yü* (selfish desires). Of course, feelings of empathy, so basic in Confucian morality, are also emotional. If the emotional expression of private urges was condemned, emotional fervor in the pursuit of right was not. Should we regard as exotic the emotional fervor that has characterized virtually all political movements in modern China, especially, we are told, those of the "traditionalists"?

Moreover emotional action could be violent. In terms of the *hao-chieh* ideal and other concepts, violent conflict and war were viewed by Confucians as a legitimate tool of political action. T'ang regards all the personality ideals above, including that of the *hao-chieh*, as different phases of one spirit,[53] not as involving some antithesis between Confucian values and those more overtly activistic attitudes often found among the secret societies and sometimes viewed as forming an "antisystem" within Confucian society. Consequently Mao's well-known admiration of the *hao-chieh* ideal did not of itself mark any break with Confucian values. The Confucian spirit may seem foreign to the notion of "struggle" (*tou-cheng, fen-tou, fen-chan, chan-tou*), so widely used in the twentieth century by Marxist, liberal, and Kuomintang writers as a paradigm of political action (see chapter 5, section p). Yet the idea of *fen-jan yung-chüeh chih chih* (a goal determined on in a fearless, hotly aroused way) is basic to Chu Hsi's notion of self-cultivation and refers to a state of mind similar to that of "struggle." This idea was echoed in words like *fen-mien* (acting with utmost zeal and energy) commonly used in the Ch'ing bureaucracy as part of its pervasive emphasis on *li* (effort) conscientiously put into one's duties.[54] It is clear that the idea of being "aroused," brushing aside "fears and anxieties," was integral equally to that of moral courage and that of zeal in routine work. Admittedly, the idea of "struggle" refers more than does this

Confucian sense of resolve to outwardly martial behavior. Some may insist that Lu Chiu-yüan's (1139–1193) call to "burst out of the net" of immoral constraints was little more than a Walter Mitty-type fantasy, in contrast to T'an Ssu-t'ung's (1865–1898) inspiring call to "burst out of the net" of traditional social bonds.[55] Even so, the idea of violent struggle against an externally binding, immoral force was an important image of moral action rooted in the Confucian tradition.

f. THE PROBLEM OF INDIVIDUALISM

Yet if the pattern of Confucian self-assertion precludes any simplistic emphasis on fear of aggressive behavior, suppression of emotion, dependency, familism, or collectivism, it is still very different from "individualism," which T'ang, like most scholars, views as opposed to Confucian ethics.[56] Because it is difficult for us to conceive of a social system which lacks individualism and yet stresses self-assertion, some scholars have simplistically described Chinese culture as collectivistic and innocent of any emphasis on the importance of the individual. To clear up this prevalent misunderstanding, we should try to distinguish between different forms of self-assertion, even though this whole issue is still as yet a most amorphous one.

Looking at the matter on the level of metaphysical symbols, we can easily see one distinction involving the issue of godlike power discussed above. In the Confucian tradition, the value of individual assertion lies in those qualities perceived as divine, while in that prominent Western tradition associated with thinkers like J. S. Mill and the Romantic movement, the importance of the individual lies exactly in that peculiarly human condition perceived as different from divine omnipotence. One implication of this is that where Confucians admired the individual's ability to actualize a feeling identical in all individuals, individualism in nineteenth-century Europe prized his "differentness," as Arthur O. Lovejoy put it.[57] T'ang acutely notes that "Although Confucius and Mencius deeply respected the individual, what they respected . . . was his ability to become one in feeling with that ultimately benevolent nature and that heart of benevolence shared by all men." In describing a man who was a model of behavior, T'ang says, Confucian biographers were interested in his acts as expressions of a general spirit of morality, not at all in the biographical circumstances and experiences out of which these acts had developed.[58] Every one of the godlike characteristics noted above is virtually the opposite of those "all-too-human" characteristics associated with the experience of the self in the thought of nineteenth-century Romantic individualism. Admittedly, the sweaty imperfections of people as they actually are are foreign equally to the creativity prized by the Romantics and the godlike qualities valued in Confucianism. Yet it is striking how T'ang, with all his glorification of the "concrete," is oriented toward a moral transformation abolishing the frailties of ordinary people. Certainly his humanism does not express a simple liking and zest for people as they actually are. It was Will Rogers, not T'ang Chün-i, who said "I never met a man I didn't like."

Connected to this largely symbolic distinction between godlike and ungodlike self-assertion is a fundamental difference in *ch'ing-ts'ao* (morally articulated feelings). Following T'ang, we can say that empathetic feelings played a central role in that psychic process of self-assertion which Confucian thought legitimated. Conversely, this process involved a cultural tendency to repress or neglect other psychic patterns which seem to appear prominently in Western individualism.

In stressing an empathetic confluence of the ego's feelings with those of its solidarity group, Confucian thought was endorsing what the psychiatrist Hsü Ching deplores as "a sense of unclear boundaries between the self and others."[59] Moreover, although different from passivity, the Confucian view of empathy as a response to things coming into one's experience (*kan-wu erh hou tung*) specified a rhythm of experience in which the self, however actively it pursued its goals, left the initiation of action to forces outside it. At the same time, the legitimated feelings of empathy with which Confucian self-assertion was infused were socially positive emotions oriented directly to the needs of others rather than to the ego's quest for direct gratification. They were the emotions of social interdependence.

To be sure, ego gratification in Confucian eyes was vital. In no culture has the individual been more anxious about the allocation of honor, about that painful question of who "acts respectfully" (*tsun-ching*) toward whom, the bitterness of which informs so much of Mao's writing about class relations. It is no accident that the feelings of the living were so often spared by channeling the flow of honor toward the dead. As T'ang makes clear, however, because the ethics of gratitude so dominated social relations, one could not directly pursue maximization of one's own gratifications without being viewed as an immoral person (*hsiao-jen*). Rather, the benefits one enjoyed were those conferred on one by others, and one reciprocated by conferring benefits on them, even the ultimate, yearned-for tribute of "worship."[60] Self-assertion, therefore, was intertwined with interdependence. It is in this context too that we can understand that tendency toward indirect, Machiavellian, and devious strategies of behavior which political scientists are increasingly regarding as a major aspect of China's inherited political culture. Scheming to advance his own interests in terms of an ethical code that emphasized the receiving of benefits from others rather than the direct pursuit of self-interest, a person was likely to use subtle cues and indirect methods to elicit behavior favorable to him while still appearing to conform to the ethics of interdependence. Yet such interdependence in all its complexity is still different from that emphasis on submission to the "unlimited authority" of others found in the theory of dependence.

Conversely, this Confucian psychic process avoided or repressed that individualism marking off the psychological space of the ego with clear boundaries, locating the initiation of action within these boundaries, explicitly emphasizing idiosyncratic creativity, and allowing a more emphatic and open articulation of the ego's quest for direct gratification. Moreover, even in the case of artistic geniuses, those "unfettered natures" (*pu-chi-chih ts'ai*) viewed as ignoring conventional morality, this Confucian outlook seems to have shunned idiosyncratic, anomic emotions not oriented toward the needs of others.[61] A prominent theme in the Romantic search for individuality and "differentness" has been a glorification of even evil sentiments, a "positive valuation placed on darkness and disorder in the soul," Yeats's "foul rag and bone shop of the heart." Writes Philippa Foot: "he who will accept only order and clarity deludes himself."[62] Nothing could be further from the Confucian spirit than this somewhat Dionysian outlook.

Our two forms of self-assertion, therefore, each imply that the other is pathological. On the one hand, Confucian thought can be criticized as suppressing exactly those psychic processes which constitute an authentic sense of self. Max Weber's position is the classic version of this criticism. Confucianism, he held, did not allow that "inward aspiration toward a 'unified personality,' a striving which we associate with the idea of personality."[63] From this standpoint, my term "Confucian self-assertion" is merely a semantic trick. On the other hand, from T'ang's standpoint it is Western individualism which, with its clearly bounded ego unabashedly pursuing direct gratifications, distorts human experience and blocks *ch'eng-chi* (the completion of the self). This deplorable Western outlook, T'ang suggests, is based on a mental act of "holding onto" (*chih-cho*) rationalized egotistic desires which cut into and interrupt the natural "flow" of empathy. From this Confucian standpoint, nothing is more grotesque than the Western admiration for great entrepreneurs who "struggle[d] untiringly and uninterruptedly for the sake of their own individual achievements." Similarly, Western philosophers proposing to create their own philosophical systems instead of reflecting on the thoughts of the past were perceived by many Chinese as preposterously preoccupied with self-glorification.[64] Because there is no obvious way to arbitrate such conflicting positions on the nature of virtue and mental health, anthropologists like Li I-yüan and Francis L. K. Hsu feel a need for theories of human behavior avoiding that bias toward Western individualism which they detect in Western theories of personality.[65]

g. AUTONOMY AND AUTHORITY

Whatever the different forms of self-assertion, however, T'ang's concept of Confucian self-fulfillment, referring to the ability of the self to act autonomously by rejecting group pressures, is based on abundant documentation. That this concept was a common one throughout the imperial period cannot be doubted. True, there were strong tendencies toward collectivism and authoritarianism. Among other factors, the claims of authority were buttressed not only by the Confucian emphasis on asserting feelings of gratitude toward morally deserving superiors but also by a strong presumption that these superiors were intellectually capable of articulating objectively valid norms of moral obligation. Since an objectively valid moral code, published and in print, existed in the form of the classics, it merely remained for superiors to claim that they could clearly and specifically apply it to current conditions. To be sure, awareness that such claims were false was routine, and reference to the current emperor as a "sage" was merely a form of institution-alized insincerity. However, partly because someone advancing counterclaims was vulnerable to the charge of pursuing self-interest, translating awareness of immorality into an effective challenge to those in authority was difficult. Thus in each of the innumerable arenas of social interaction into which the society was divided, the flux of moral claims and counterclaims often constituted a con-sciously painful drama of oppression and frustration. The despotism of the emperor was mirrored in the actions of innumerable persons in innumerable milieus who "used naked power to dominate others" (ch'eng-pa) or "accumulated wealth unrestrained by any feelings of benevolence" (wei-fu pu-jen). These patterns of oppression can be viewed as both aggravated and mitigated by that tendency toward Machiavellian behavior noted above.

A crucial point must be noted, however. Where some influential sociological analyses of Confucian society have gone wrong is in describing these tendencies toward authoritarianism out of context, failing to point out that they were part of an ongoing psychological drama of competing moral claims. Nor did the quashing of political dissent necessarily mean the repression of the psychological pro-cesses of self-assertion. Quashed in one arena, the court for instance, an individual could still assert himself in others, such as those of local office, local society, the academies, and family life, or even in some lonely military outpost to which the emperor had banished him and where the soldiers and officers reverently and legally flocked to him as their teacher. There was always room for one teacher or despot more. More basically, R. H. Solomon's view that quashed dissenters simply "swallowed" the anger aroused in them by their oppressors ignores the ch'ing-ts'ao (morally articulated feelings) often involved. From the standpoint of Confucian ideals with Bud-dhist and Taoist connotations, one could also respond to this ordeal by shifting from a yang-like stance of *k'uang* (impetuously self-confident action in the outer world) to a yin-like stance of *chüan* (withdrawing from worldly concerns and preserving one's purity of character).[66] Surely it is gratuitous to reduce this character ideal to an "oral" way of managing anger. Moreover, as discussed in chapter 4, the Confucian ideal of moral autonomy was an integral part of the behavioral situation in the bureaucracy.[67]

Its behavioral implications, however, are not our main concern at this point. We first have to make clearer its intellectual context so that we can better understand the actual feelings and psychological realities it involved.

CHAPTER THREE

The Neo-Confucian Sense of Predicament

a. METHODOLOGICAL CONSIDERATIONS

T'ANG'S analysis elucidates the Confucian belief that the individual can and should summon a godlike flow of moral power within himself, but this belief was paradoxically combined with a fearful realization that he would be unable to do so, trapped in a fundamental predicament. The awareness of this predicament has been filtered out of the leading modern interpretations of Neo-Confucianism, but it was taken for granted traditionally.[1] Expressed largely in the form of clichés, it served as an overarching "definition of the situation" or "grammar" of action in terms of which Neo-Confucians, at least since the twelfth century, carried on their discussions. One might say it constituted some of the rules of the game in terms of which different thinkers succeeded in distinguishing themselves or were regarded as mediocrities. In other words, what was controversial for Neo-Confucians was not the fearful predicament they found themselves in but the formulae of enlightenment they advanced to get out of it. Yet while Neo-Confucians thus focused on these formulae, we who want to understand their orientations as a whole have to analyze that sense of predicament which they referred to only in passing. To compare the formulae of enlightenment offered by Chu Hsi to those of Wang Yang-ming (1472–1529) without first understanding their common awareness of predicament is like trying to follow a game of baseball without first understanding its rules.

To describe such an overarching "grammar," it is necessary to study the clichés of Neo-Confucianism, the *chia-ch'ang pien-fan* (everyday fare) of the Neo-Confucian dinner table, to use Mou

Tsung-san's term.[2] This task has not been carried out in the past. Scholars have rather tended to select out those ideas interesting by modern philosophic tastes and to neglect the others as epiphenomenal. My rule is that if an expression is habitually used and can be logically and naturally associated with other such expressions, it constitutes a basic idea, not an epiphenomenal one.

Modern assumptions about what is a phenomenon, what is only an epiphenomenon, what idea has "value," what idea lacks it, obviously pose a problem for those interested in how historical persons actually thought. To check the influence of these assumptions on our interpretation of Neo-Confucianism, I have tried not only to collect inductively all the words making up the basic jargon of Neo-Confucianism but also to describe the elementary perceptions of human life given expression in this jargon. By elementary perceptions I mean those presumably found in any way of thought, that is, perceptions regarding the goal of life; the actual, given conditions of life in terms of which one has to struggle for this goal; and the means available for this struggle. In trying to collect all ordinary verbal expressions defining this framework of action, we have, I believe, an objective standard of analysis which serves as a counterweight to our own preconceptions, although of course it does not allow a complete escape from the trap of subjectivity.

Besides having perceptions regarding these elementary aspects of life, people also make claims about them. I define a perception as a concept representing a fact, ideal, criterion, or problem the reality or validity of which is taken for granted by all participants in a particular arena of communication. Roughly speaking, a perception is almost necessarily a cliché. A claim is an idea the truth of which is doubted and disputed within such an arena. In Neo-Confucian thought, controversial claims about how to realize one's goal were often called *shuo* (doctrines). For instance, a student might ask about the validity of Chu Hsi's *ko-wu-chih shuo* (doctrine regarding the investigation of things). Expressing doubt, the particle *kai* (it is reasonable to say that) was often used to introduce a claim. To support a claim, one looked for "corroboration" (*cheng-chü*). By contrast, the idea of "heaven" as part of the given world was a perception, not a claim. A Neo-Confucian did not occupy himself trying to find "corroboration" for the idea that "heaven" existed.

Similarly, the idea that *hsing chi li* (the heaven-conferred nature is principle), originally a claim advanced by Ch'eng I, came to be largely unproblematic for Neo-Confucians, while *hsin chi li* (mind is principle) remained a controversial claim.

From the philosophic standpoint, one would be interested in what these two ideas mean, what philosophical theories (materialism, monism, etc.) they are examples of, and to what extent they are logically and experientially defensible as true. For us historians, on the other hand, the extent to which a proposition was controversial and exciting for its historical audience also is a central issue. Without understanding what this audience was worrying about, we cannot understand its state of mind and its cultural orientations. It is in terms of the problem of controversy that the tools of the intellectual historian pry at the concerns of the social scientist. Consequently this distinction between perceptions and claims is indispensable.

Whether or not the great Confucian thinkers were right in looking down on the mediocre ones, the clichés used by all Neo-Confucians amounted to a profound worldview. Robert Musil was making a point often neglected by intellectual historians when he said that "I am thoroughly convinced that personal accomplishment means a hardly perceptible alteration of the spiritual riches which one takes over from others."[3] Yet even if these clichés lacked philosophic "value," they necessarily expressed widespread orientations comprising a "definition of the situation" with significant behavioral implications. Otherwise they would not have been clichés. To look into such orientations is a way of examining the psychological makeup of a widespread personality type just as surely as is using attitude surveys, which anyway cannot be used in historical research. A way of thinking, even if expressed in terms intelligible only to those with education, must articulate and partly satisfy basic psychological needs if it is to absorb the intellectual energies of an elite class generation after generation, and to mesh with fundamental cultural symbols and institutions, as Neo-Confucianism did.

Admittedly, to describe Neo-Confucian orientations is not to describe as a whole the political culture shared by the educated classes of late imperial China. Although the Western term "Neo-Confucianism" is sometimes used to denote all Sung (960–1279) trends seeking to revive the ideals of Confucius, it has more usually and more narrowly been used to denote that spiritual movement for which Huang Tsung-hsi (1610–1695) used the generic term *li-hsüeh* (the study of principle),[4] and which Li Chih (1527–1602) denounced as *tao-hsüeh* (the study of the true way).[5] As such, "Neo-Confucianism" would embrace primarily two schools, that of Ch'eng I (1033–1107) and Chu Hsi, and that of Lu Chiu-yüan (1139–1193) and Wang Yang-ming. (Mou Tsung-san separates out a third line of thought, that of Ch'eng Hao [1032–1085], Hu Wu-feng [1100–1155], and Liu Tsung-chou [1578–1645].)[6] One also has to keep in mind that in the Ming-Ch'ing period, the Ch'eng-Chu school was both a living intellectual movement and the official ideology of the state, though the important differences between these two forms have yet to be analyzed.

From this standpoint, at least eight patterns of thought should be distinguished from the Neo-Confucian. Much further research is required to explain how the relations between all these partly overlapping patterns changed over time, and how these changes were related to the far-reaching socio-economic developments of the Ming-Ch'ing period. First, there was a well-established tendency to emphasize Confucian ethics, erudition, and cosmology while avoiding the emphasis of *li-hsüeh* on the "inner," metaphysical search for oneness with heaven. The influential Sung scholars Ou-yang Hsiu (1007–1072) and Ssu-ma Kuang (1018–1086) are examples of this.[7] Second, Sung thinkers emphasizing *kung-li* (political achievements and material benefits) inclined toward Legalism and resisted the Neo-Confucian focus on the pure morality of "the true king."[8] To some extent, this semi-Legalist outlook blended in with that of Neo-Confucians as the latter gradually qualified the radical idealism of the eleventh century and adopted a political outlook which can be called "moderate realism" (see section v). The recurring emphasis on *ching-shih* (concrete study of governmental institutions) can also be viewed in this context. Third, partly growing out of Neo-Confucian metaphysics, the T'ai-chou school of the sixteenth century was also influenced by the ideals of the rather un-Confucian knight-errant tradition. While T'ai-chou thinkers like Li Chih may have developed a new sense of self and community which was more individualistic and egalitarian than that of Neo-Confucians, they also seem to have expressed attitudes traditionally widespread among the less educated. A specialist in crisis ethics interested in physically heroic behavior, Li Chih resembled peasants more than Neo-Confucians in lacking any anxious desire to find a formula which would save the whole world. His ethical heroism resembled that of the late Ming Tung-lin movement, which largely condemned him.[9] Fourth and fifth, the influence of Buddhism and Taoism has to be considered.[10] Sixth, Ch'ing scholars attacking the "empty talk" of Sung and Ming times had a problematic relation to Neo-Confucianism, but, as recent studies have argued, this Ch'ing movement at the very least was rooted in Neo-Confucianism (see section x). Seventh, one also has to consider individuals who differed from Neo-Confucians in that they seem to have satisfied their spiritual needs by studying the details of the natural world or savoring the artistic delights of civilization. We may call this trend Confucian secularism. Figures like Fang I-chih (1611–1671) or P'u Sung-ling (1640–1715) come to mind.[11] Neo-Confucians seem to have been accurate in regarding such secularism as a major trend. Like Puritans dourly gazing at the revels of the Restoration, they complained that the "writing of flowery compositions developed and those indulging in it were regarded as elegant. . . . Students of the world found themselves in a theater where a hundred plays were being presented, as it were. . . . They emulated one another in novelty and ingenuity."[12]

Besides these seven trends, it is important to keep in mind the popular culture, which itself partly coincided with some of these trends. Martin Yang has stated that in imperial times, except for an "extremely limited" number of persons enjoying higher education in the academies, "establishing a family, managing it, and maintaining it became the most important matter in the lives and activities of the Chinese [,outside of which] . . . there was almost no other matter of importance."[13] This familism was intertwined with economism, that is, the explicit exhaltation of private economic goals, such as the "wealth" and "status" which Chinese peasants pursued through "industriousness and frugality." Their economism is reflected in Wu Ts'ung-hsien's theory that many of the traditional norms and strategies of Chinese peasants stemmed from their central belief that the amount of wealth in the world cannot be increased, only redistributed.[14] This syndrome of familism and economism actually amounted to a comprehensive philosophy which can be basically distinguished from the Neo-Confucian in terms of the self-image of the moral agent, his goal, and his arena of action.[15] Just like many modern Chinese intellectuals, Neo-Confucians had a snobbish contempt for people who "busied themselves with property" (*wen-she ch'iu-t'ien*), but this economism was part of a crucial set of cultural orientations shaping the lives of those Chinese who in fact carried China's economy on their backs. If most Chinese were *hsiao-jen* (mean-minded persons), as Chu Hsi claimed, they nevertheless participated in the significant cultural processes of their society. We should also note that this popular culture partly meshed with the "moderate realism" characterizing much Neo-Confucian and bureaucratic thought. Indeed, the norms repeatedly referred to in bureaucratic communications also constituted a cultural pattern (see section v and chapter 4).

Yet having raised the problem of distinguishing Neo-Confucianism from other, partly overlapping trends, a question further discussed in section x, we still have no reason to challenge the widely held view of Chinese scholars that Neo-Confucianism dominated not just the intellectual world but even the society of late imperial China. In the words of Wen Ch'ung-i, an anthropologist with the Academia Sinica on Taiwan here discussing the development of China's "value orientations," "From the Sung through the end of the Ch'ing is the period of Neo-Confucianism."[16]

A final methodological point has to be raised in order to help the reader relate my thesis to the wealth of insights found in the two volumes edited by Wm. Theodore de Bary, *Self and Society in Ming Thought,* and *The Unfolding of Neo-Confucianism.* In my study, the Neo-Confucian grammar is regarded as a verbalized, culturally conditioned set of perceptions and claims, but de Bary's profound approach raises doubts both that the verbalized aspects of Neo-Confucianism were central to it, and that Neo-Confucianism can be accurately described if we thus reduce it to a culturally peculiar state of mind. The Neo-Confucian tradition, writes Professor de Bary, "even more than a set moral code or philosophical system, was a life-style, an attitude of mind, a type of character formation, and a spiritual ideal that eluded precise definition."[17]

Therefore the "metaphysical superstructure" of Neo-Confucianism, to which my study pays so much attention, was not its central aspect.[18] De Bary sees Neo-Confucianism as bringing to late imperial China "an enlarged, more expansive view of what it means to be human."[19]

If, at the risk of oversimplification, we try to reduce this approach to a set methodology, four premises emerge. The first is that it is possible to have a spiritual understanding of human existence on a universal level. When de Bary says that Neo-Confucianism taught people "what it means to be human," it is hard to reduce his view to the idea that Neo-Confucians helped people better to realize a peculiarly Chinese personality type. Second, knowledge on this universal level of spirit or morality often cannot be fully conveyed in words. This point has been made systematically by T'ang Chün-i in his general study of philosophy.[20] Third, Neo-Confucianism, particularly the Lu-Wang school, was just such a form of partly ineffable knowledge about the universal human condition, and, moreover, some of the thinkers in this tradition consciously made the very point that moral knowledge is more experiential than verbal. Fourth, to describe such a tradition, one should focus less on its verbal expressions, more on the kind of conduct it encouraged, and certainly not on its "metaphysical superstructure."

Like almost any viable humanistic methodology, this approach leads to an antinomy. We cannot deny that Neo-Confucianism was based on an experiential "spiritual ideal that eluded precise definition." Yet Chinese thinkers were very verbal and often consciously valued words. Chu Hsi glorified the sage's ability to speak (see section o), and he once remarked that "Even if it is through unverbalized comprehension that one comes to know something about principle, there still is not anything that one cannot tell others about."[21] Lü Wan-ts'un (1629–1683), a follower of Chu Hsi, said: "Whether or not a person understands the principles of life can be determined only from his spoken and written words. . . . I would say that spoken words are the sounds of the mind, while written words are the writing of the mind."[22] Wang Yang-ming, it is true, favored ineffable knowledge more than Chu Hsi. Characteristically, he once said of a point that "it must be grasped in terms of the ultimate substance of one's own mind and cannot be made clear in words."[23]

3. Sense of Predicament (a)

However he was extremely fussy about the use of words and indeed depended on verbal, ontological propositions to try to win students over to his understanding of things. He once rejected the saying that the object of learning was "simply mind and principle"; the conjunction "and," he felt, was misleading.[24] He also said: "When the words of a person lack coherence and order, this is enough to see that his mind has not been preserved."[25]

Moreover, even if what Neo-Confucians meant went beyond their words, their words still expressed a part of what they meant, and indeed that part most accessible to us today. All their verbal expressions, therefore, can be treated as clues revealing some of their state of mind. Furthermore, even if one agrees that Neo-Confucians were more interested in a spiritual mode of existence than in propounding metaphysical theories, their innumerable metaphysical statements can still be regarded as symbols expressing the kind of spiritual mode they were aiming at. Nor need we necessarily accept the theory that their words failed to express their meaning. If some philosophers today emphasize that moral knowledge goes beyond words, others will tell us that our language provides us with the categories through which we filter our experience. Indeed it is hard to reject the latter point when we consider the comprehensive ontological assumptions implied by the verbal expressions which Neo-Confucians habitually used.

At the same time, almost any moral tradition can be regarded as simultaneously confronting universal questions and expressing culturally peculiar assumptions. In a sense, this point is not disputed. In T'ang Chün-i's thought, for instance, these peculiarities are attributed to differences in the geographical and economic conditions of the different emerging civilizations in ancient times. For T'ang, however, these primordial conditions in the Chinese case turned out to stimulate the development of a true sense for universal human reality (*shih-tsai-kan*), which coincided with existentialism and other post-Kantian trends in the West. As he put it in about 1959, "Eastern philosophy" has focused on the question of man's ethical "character" and has approached it in "an internal way, interested in actual practice, [not theory,] grasping particulars on their own terms, [not in general terms,] and finding an ineffable corroboration for its understanding of ultimate principles. This is what Western existentialists call existential thought or existential reflection."[26]

This way of looking in different philosophical traditions for insights into the universal spiritual "value" of human existence has had a great influence on Western students of Neo-Confucianism. It is a welcome relief from the attempts of a Fung Yu-lan or a Hou Wai-lu to analyze Chinese philosophy as a series of speculative, cosmological theories partly coinciding with Western ones, whether Marx's materialism, Kant's idealism, or Bertrand Russell's neo-realism. Nevertheless, so long as one's discussion is restricted to intellectual convergences of any kind, the tendency to ignore culturally peculiar ways of thought is powerful indeed. No Chinese reader could guess from T'ang's account that through "existential reflection" Neo-Confucians arrived at "intuitions" (*chih-chüeh*) alien to those of Western existentialists. Finding within themselves through "existential reflection" the expandable presence of a divine, transcendent force pervading the cosmos, Neo-Confucians felt a Mencian "joy" antithetical to the existentialist sense of being "absurdly" thrown on the brink of nothingness. Along with this perception of the divine, Neo-Confucians emphasized a number of ontological, epistemological, ethical, and social ideas which are summed up in chapter 5 as forming an "ethos of interdependence," and which similarly were alien to the individualistic background of existentialism. "Existential reflection" in the West has often involved that openness to the emotional and sexual vagaries of the introspective life which can be traced back at least to Rousseau and which was foreign to the more Apollonian spirit of Confucianism. Confucians would have regarded as *yin* (disgustingly licentious) the pleasure Rousseau received as a boy from spankings administered by his nurse, but they would still more have been mystified by his desire as an adult to confess to such a thing in print. Conversely, what could be more mystifying to a Heidegger or a Sartre than the desire to be a "sage" who "controls heaven and earth"?

Perhaps "existential reflection" can eventually lead to some one, universally authentic understanding of the human condition. Yet even in Mou Tsung-san's rigorous examination of "intuition" as a way of grasping universal reality, we are left at best with the general understanding that our moral experience is part of a self-aware noumenal reality, a sort of *hsü-ling ming-chüeh* (intelligent awareness in its pure, naturally given, cosmically indivisible form, empty of any consciously specific concepts or sensations) (see section d). An actual way of life, however, is exactly a cluster of "specific concepts or sensations" forming, say, an ethos of either interdependence or individualism. Yet Mou gives us no criteria by which to determine which cultural cluster of specifics most authentically represents this consciousness beyond all specifics. Without such criteria, how can we look in different philosophic traditions for the one, authentic understanding of human morality? An anthropologist could just as well study different societies by looking in them for traces of the one authentic mode of social existence.

There are no epistemological obstacles, however, to treating a philosophic tradition as a view of human reality which can be described as a whole, warts and all. *Shih she-me, chiu shuo she-me* (Whatever something is, that's what you say it is), to quote Yin Hai-kuang somewhat out of context. Bluntness, after all, is the ultimate mark of respect. To describe a way of thought as a whole is not to lapse into cultural relativity but to express respect for what really does have universal "value," namely, the human quest for "value" itself, in all its particularity and vulgarity. Nor need we be disappointed with this outcome. If our studies fail to reach the conclusion that Confucian philosophy brilliantly led the way toward some one truth, aren't we really freeing ourselves of yet another nationalistic myth satisfying the egotistic craving for fixed, self-serving doctrines (*chih-cho*)?

While we cannot just look for universally authentic insights in Neo-Confucianism, neither can we just look for noble ideals, culturally peculiar or not. This point would be obvious to a behavioral scientist, but since it runs against established tendencies in the study of Chinese thought, I should discuss it here.

To be sure, the particular ideal of humanity expressed in a philosophical tradition is an absolutely central question, one that we, in our miserable age of positivism and hedonistic nihilism, have often lost track of. Ideals guide our conduct in the most intimate ways. Had the Greeks not made the astounding discovery that the wise man asks questions rather than "transmits" (*shu*) truths, the life of mankind would be unspeakable today. Similarly, it is not surprising that when Fung Yu-lan and T'ang Chün-i sought to vindicate the ideals of the Confucian tradition, they shed enormous light on the history of ideas, even if some of us cannot embrace these ideals. Much can also be learned from de Bary's view of "Neo-Confucian spirituality" as emphasizing a "reverent attitude toward life," "a natural and spontaneous joy in life," "unselfish service of others," and "constant effort and self-discipline."[27]

Conversely, we are all familiar with the ordinary ways in which life is unsatisfactory. To dwell on them would hardly distinguish any philosophy. When we go to a travel bureau, we do not expect to be given a street map of our home town. The very point of moral philosophy is to teach us how to grasp the more profound structures in our experience and find what T'ang Chün-i calls "spiritual value."

Yet the bad or ordinary world referred to in any moral philosophy is not simply a given fact. On the contrary, it is a culturally colored inversion of our ideals. When it is viewed as either a moral or an immoral process, the world is not a raw fact but a set of perceptions shaped by value judgments and intellectualized passions. Nothing is more distinctive in a body of thought than the way it defines the frailties of the subjective self, the terms of the moral struggle, and the evils of the outer world. Nor can one agree that there was no moral struggle for those philosophers who defined evil as an illusion or who sought, like Wang Yang-ming, to negate the distinction between the potential and the actual good (see section r). Whatever his philosophical strategies, no thinker can posit a desirable state of existence without perceiving realities clashing against this ideal.

Therefore we have to pull together the many passing references in Neo-Confucian writings to that dissonant reality perceived as threatening to disrupt the process of self-realization. These references were part of a culturally peculiar conceptualization of the given world, which in turn has to be related to the way Neo-Confucians defined their ideals or goals. Only by understanding the relation between their goals and their perception of the given world can we understand their sense of predicament and the meaning for them of the claims they advanced about how to escape from this predicament. As we will see, the schools of Chu Hsi and Wang Yang-ming differed mainly in terms of these "claims." Their "perceptions" regarding their goals and the given world were largely, though not entirely, the same.

The Neo-Confucian goal can be variously described as "self-cultivation," the achievement of "sagehood," or realization of "the oneness of heaven and man." Yet while these indigenous concepts are accurate enough, they blur together a variety of meanings and psychological nuances that have to be separated out for the benefit of outsiders trying to understand the state of mind they involved. We can also describe this goal as the achievement of those godlike qualities listed in chapter 2, but if we go back to the Chinese texts in an inductive way, we can obtain a still closer understanding allowing us to be more aware of the elusiveness inherent in this goal, which was viewed as something people constantly failed to reach. To realize this goal was to avoid various *pi* (morally corrupt ways) of thinking and *ping* or *ping-t'ung* (harmful shortcomings).[28]

Still another approach is found in T'ang Chün-i's monumental *Chung-kuo che-hsüeh yüan-lun* (Studies on the Foundations of Chinese Philosophy). Here he holds that "Generally in all these [Neo-Confucian] matters of moral effort, the main point was directly or indirectly to eliminate the material desires adulterating the ether of materialization with which one was endowed."[29] Such a view reduces the Neo-Confucian goal to an ethical or spiritual concern meaningful to us moderns and shared with various spiritual movements the world over. Yet this ethical concern, discussed below under the heading of "moral purification," was only one part of the Neo-Confucian goal. Above all, Neo-Confucians could not have been satisfied with mere personal moral purity, since they were driven by the need to find the "sage's" power to set the whole world right. To understand their historical situation, therefore, we have to look at all the ideas they used to describe what it was they desired.

Their goal, in the first place, was something one had to apprehend in a "living" way. Certainly, unlike ours, imperial China was a traditional society in which ancient sages had achieved total wisdom, but their wise ideas could not be mechanically transmitted the way, say, that one's salary was handed over. The contemporary generation not only had to absorb these ideas through "living" intellectual efforts but also had to express them with a new degree of urgency and clarity. Following Lu Chiu-yüan, Wang Yang-ming was especially bold in insisting that one has to reject the views of even Confucius if in one's own mind one finds them to be wrong.[30] Yet Chu Hsi had a similar emphasis. For instance, he held that in establishing *li* (rules of moral propriety), it was necessary to have *huo-fa* (living rules), just as the ancients had had. Only when filial piety was practiced by one grasping its total cosmic context did it become a *huo-wu* (living thing); otherwise, it was "dead."[31] The meaning of "living" here can be seen from Hsieh Shang-ts'ai's (1050–1103) statement that "what is living is *jen* (benevolence), what is dead is not *jen*."[32] A principle was "living" when its truth was directly experienced in a fresh, immediate way through one's own efforts (*tzu-te*). One could not *yin-hsi* or *yin-hsün* (indiscriminately, without thought accept what was handed down from the past).[33] Chu Hsi held that one had to make decisions "relative to the question of what to doubt and what to believe in the accounts handed down from the past."[34] Otherwise, one could not be *jen*.

c. TOTAL MORAL PURIFICATION AS A GOAL

This "living" condition involved moral purification, that is, rising above the licentiousness of "the birds and the beasts"; realizing man's inherently noble status as *wan-wu-chih ling* (the spiritually active being among the ten thousand things); completely eliminating *ssu* (selfishness) or *yü* (selfish material desires); and thus avoiding a destructively competitive spirit of *erh-wo sheng-fu* (do you or I win?), as Wang Yang-ming put it.[35]

This theme of moral purification was intertwined with another one which, for want of a better word, can be called "totalism." The vocabulary of this totalism was constantly used. The emphasis on "seeking absolute purity and oneness" (*wei ching wei i*) was compared to making "rice absolutely pure and white."[36] One "exhausted all one's strength" (*chin, chieh*) "exhaustively to understand principles" (*ch'iung-li*) and to realize virtue in its ultimate, supreme sense (*chi*). Thus one reached "the extreme of sincerity" (*chih-ch'eng*), the "final good" (*chih-shan*), but one's moral efforts had to proceed "constantly," "without the slightest interruption." Otherwise, Wang Yang-ming said, "one falls into the difficulty of being off by a fraction at the beginning and nowhere near the target in the end."[37] One had to have a mind "purely one with heavenly principle," so that "at no time and no place would one not be in accord with heavenly principle." Chu Hsi said: "If one relaxes for an instant, the mind will be caught up in the flow of material concerns, and there will be no way to recover the lost ground."[38] The "most minute trace of a selfish idea" had to be eliminated.[39] The cliché comes to mind of the scholar who studied "forgetting to eat and to sleep." The obsessive concern with "exhaustively" making moral efforts is illustrated by Chu Hsi's joke about the scholar who put two bowls next to where he sat: "Every time he had a good thought, he put a white bean in a bowl. Every time he had a bad thought, he put a black bean in the other bowl. At first there were many black beans and few white ones, but later there were many white ones, and few black ones. Still later, there were no more black ones at all, and finally, he had no occasion even to use white ones!"[40] Hopefully avoiding such a "dead method," as Chu Hsi called it, one had "constantly to envelop and nourish one's spontaneously good feelings (*han-yang*), constantly examine oneself to distinguish incipient good feelings and eliminate selfish ones (*hsing-ch'a*)."[41] Chu Hsi also said: "When principle is actual, there is no interruption in its realization. In their teachings, the sages just wanted to save people from such an interruption."[42]

The pathos of this totalism also made meaningful the Neo-Confucian term for ultimate being, *t'ai-chi* (the supreme, ultimate point which can be reached). Chu Hsi's view that this "supreme ultimate" is part of every individual existent connoted the totalistic quality of ultimacy ascribed to all moral life. Even the very idea of *ts'un* (preserving) the presence of heaven in one's daily life connoted the totalistic watchfulness needed to cling to something on the verge of being lost. The anxious fear of "losing" this presence is obvious in Chu Hsi but was just as basic to Wang Yang-ming, who referred to the fact that most people had "lost" it and spoke of "exhaustively realizing the filial piety found in one's mind, fearful that the minutest bit of selfish desire might be mixed in."[43] The very repetitiveness of a book like Wang Yang-ming's *Ch'uan-hsi-lu*, which so often says the same thing not even in different words, is a direct result of this anxious need for a totalistic, endlessly repeated moral effort.

This totalism was also illustrated by the ritualism of a Yen Yüan (1635–1704), which has been vividly described by Wei-ming Tu: "Indeed, he was so ritualistic about the way he dressed, ate, walked, and talked that every transgression was faithfully recorded as a warning for future action. He even insisted on putting down his evil thoughts before they materialized."[44] Yen Yüan's attention to ritualistic details was not necessarily typical of Neo-Confucianism, but his driving impulse "exhaustively" to eliminate the minutest trace of selfishness was.

T'ang Chün-i has vividly expressed this totalism as part of his own moral faith: ". . . having in the immediate present temporarily obtained that unending purity and oneness definitely does not guarantee having it in the future. Thus this continuity can ultimately be interrupted, and this purity can ultimately be adulterated. If a person in this situation thinks of the possibility of interruption, this very thought can bring about a break, and if he thinks of the possibility of adulteration, this thought itself is already a morally adulterated thought."[45] Contrary to T'ang, however, it is not self-evident that this totalistic approach is universally valid. What is clear is that it made obvious sense to Neo-Confucians as an integral part of their goal as a whole.

d. TOTAL COGNITIVE CLARITY AS A GOAL

Chu Hsi said: "Sincerity comes out of thinking."[46] Although moral purification revolved around *ch'ing* (feelings), it was inextricably connected to a cognitive process, to the ideal of total, rationalistic knowledge of ultimate reality. While explicit about this connection, Neo-Confucians did not inquire into its validity. Like their totalism, their rationalistic bias was pervasive and appeared to them as no more than a reflection of reality. It was not accidental that they were fascinated with "principle," which since Chou times almost invariably connoted a rationalistic type of knowing, such as the knowledge that physical objects appear smaller when farther away.[47]

3. Sense of Predicament (d)

After all, even the very idea of "feeling," as they defined it, included the cognitive "sense of right and wrong" (see section k). Far from any Dionysian enthrallment with the emotions, they looked always for a moral order derived from knowledge about the nature of things.

Thus the vocabulary of cognitive clarity pervades Neo-Confucianism. Most basic were *ko-wu* (investigate things) and *chih-chih* (broadening knowledge to the utmost). These two terms from *The Great Learning* were sometimes abbreviated as *ko-chih*. Other connected terms were *tao wen hsüeh* (pursuit of inquiry and study), *po-hsüeh* (broad learning), *tu-shu* (study through reading), *shen-wen* (examining and inquiring), *wen-pien* (making inquiries and seeing distinctions), *ming-pien* (clearly making distinctions), *ssu* (thinking), *ssu-pien* (thinking and seeing distinctions), *shen-ssu* or *chin-ssu* (thinking with utmost care), and *lun-shih* (discussing affairs).[48]

Wang Yang-ming, not only Chu Hsi, shared this commitment to cognitive clarity. True, Ying-shih Yü has argued that Wang epitomized the "anti-intellectualism" rampant in the Ming period. I believe, however, that application of this term to any Neo-Confucian is problematic (see chapter 5, section g). At any rate, Yü uses it only to refer to Wang's opposition to scholarly study (*hsüeh, tu-shu*) divorced from a focus on moral purification and practice, not to any opposition to *ssu* (thinking). Despite Wang's references to the ineffability of knowledge, he emphasized verbalization (see section a). He frequently talked as though doctrinal clarity was the basis of morality, and his concept of linkage was in fact an awesomely conceptual construct (see section u). Calling for a total synthesis of thought and action, Wang nevertheless emphasized the role of thought within that synthesis: "Generally, in learning doubts are bound to arise. So one asks questions. Questioning is learning, and it is also practice. More doubts arise. So there is thinking. Thinking is learning, and it is also practice. Still more doubts arise. So one draws distinctions and sifts through things. Such sifting is learning, and it is also practice. The distinctions being clear, the thought, careful, the questioning, thoroughly detailed, and the studies, sound, one then continues the effort without stop. That is what we call earnest practice."[49]

In their search for cognitive clarity, Neo-Confucians sought a certain architectonic grasp of things. "Thinking," especially for

Chu Hsi, was needed to develop an adequately generalized moral stance in terms of which one could cope with the complexity of the cosmos and the empire. Just being sincerely selfless in one's daily behavior was not enough. Such simple fulfillment of the norms of the local community was contemptuously regarded by Chu Hsi as "no more than the ethics of an ordinary fellow from some rustic, backward village, of a woman of model behavior." Such virtue was not a "living thing."[50] Chu Hsi said: "Everyone has some knowledge. Sons know filial piety, fathers know loving compassion. It's just that their knowledge is incomplete. . . . that a ruler should be benevolent, a subject, loyal, a father, lovingly compassionate, a son, filial—these principles are extremely obvious. But matters like yin and yang, the heaven-conferred nature, what heaven has decreed, the manifestations of the contracting and expanding ether of materialization—are not these matters indeed subtle?"[51] Following obvious moral impulses might be an adequate foundation for familial ethics but not for one seeking to "deal with the affairs of the empire."[52]

Seeking this broader outlook, one subsumed the details of moral life under abstract categories. Familial and political virtues were subsumed under more universalistic ones (the four metaphysical principles of *jen, i, li,* and *chih*).[53] Then a further effort at abstraction was made by using a few highly generalized moral concepts, especially *ching* (reverence), *ch'eng* (sincerity), and *jen* (benevolence). As a preparatory virtue, *ching* crosscut all the various forms of moral expression, just as did *ch'eng*, which served to indicate one's moral goal. At the same time, beginning with Ch'eng I, *jen* was seen as *pao* (enfolding within it) the other three metaphysical principles of *i, li,* and *chih*.[54] By grasping *jen*, one simultaneously realized all the more specific virtues, such as filial piety, and experienced oneness with the cosmos.[55] From another angle, *li* (the rules of moral propriety) were reduced to an aspect of *li* (principle). They were "the outward forms with which heavenly principle is adorned," or "the outward forms with which benevolence is adorned." Chu Hsi explained them in terms of a generalizing concept, the idea, namely, that specific rules are needed to guide human action. He also somewhat patronizingly referred to them as useful in "teaching."[56] The details of *li*, therefore, the specific rituals with which Hsün-tzu was so absorbed in his chapter on *li*, were placed at a mental distance from *wu-hsin* (the mind of the self). Being located in *ching-chieh* (the realm of concrete things and affairs), they hardly constituted that *ta-t'ou-nao-ch'u* (most important aspect) of things on which Neo-Confucians were focused (see below).[57]

Cognition was important also because action required *chun-tse* (standards).[58] More specifically, the image of *pien* (distinguishing between) things and feelings was basic to this rationalistic approach to morality. The fear of confusing one thing for another was prominent. It was particularly important to distinguish with utter precision between the good and the bad ideas that arose in the mind, since full moral success was a matter of building on an inner foundation of unadulterated moral feeling (see section u). "Off by a fraction at the beginning, nowhere near the mark at the end" was a significant saying going back at least to Han times and used by both Chu Hsi and Wang Yang-ming in this context.[59] This emphasis on making precise distinctions, therefore, reflected totalism, the idea of morality as something flowing out of a "source" (see sections c and j), and the view that moral distinctions are objective givens.

To "distinguish between" things, moreover, light was needed, and the image of light was also basic to this emphasis on cognition. Chu Hsi used the analogy of the "bright light" shed by a "candle."[60] To understand was to "see" (*chien-te*), avoiding the state of "being mentally in the dark" (*hun-mei*). Thus one could "distinguish in a brightly clear way" (*ming-pien*) between different points so as to clear away "doubts" (*i*) and determine what to "believe" (*hsin*). This emphasis on light is reminiscent of Hsün-tzu's reference to the mind as *shen-ming-chih chu* (that which controls through the spiritual force of its brightness).[61]

Yet having distinguished between things, it was necessary also to see how they were connected to each other. The goals of cognitive clarity and linkage, therefore, were connected (see section f). Moreover, both these goals were part of the pattern of totalism. Nothing could be really understood unless everything were encompassed. Chu Hsi observed: "One may say that *chih-chih* (broadening knowledge to the utmost) [that basic goal mentioned in *The Great Learning*] is in its original sense a vast and great matter. One must be able to explain things so that their inner and outer characteristics are encompassed and joined together. Only then will one have accomplished this goal."[62]

Thus searching for total understanding, one avoided views which either *p'ien-nei* (one-sidedly emphasized the inner, mental life) or *p'ien-wai* (one-sidedly emphasized outer things), and so one's views were not *p'ien-hsia ku-chih* (one-sidedly narrow, stuck in an obstinately unmoving position). One similarly rejected *ch'ien-chin* (shallow) views as well as views only partially true because they were *p'i-lou* (unsophisticated and vulgar), not to mention views that were completely false (*wei, hsieh*). Thus eventually "there is nothing one does not know."[63] This imperative of totality, of "exhausting" one's energies in learning, of understanding things by *chi* (penetrating to their deepest point), was an inescapable part of the Neo-Confucian goal, although it did not necessarily connote command of all kinds of detailed information.

The Neo-Confucian's emphasis on cognition was invariably combined with the insight that since the capacity to have awareness and think intelligently was itself not the product of human intelligence, it existed as a cosmic given. This *chih-chüeh* (purely natural consciousness) had, they further assumed, a kind of spiritual or even magical quality, for which they used ancient terms like *ling* (spiritually free), *ming* (bright), *shen* (buoyantly empathetic spirit), and *hsü* (empty of all particular concepts or feelings).[64] Thus Chu Hsi said, "The spiritually free aspect of existence is just the mind."[65] Neo-Confucians also assumed that this "purely natural consciousness" was indivisible throughout the cosmos. This idea was a correlate of their belief in the organic oneness of the cosmos and in the mind's transnatural power to control the cosmos (see section o). Although this indivisibility was particularly emphasized in the Lu-Wang tradition (see section r), Chu Hsi himself said that, despite the difference between "the human mind" and "the mind of the *tao*," "there is only one mind, when the matter is fully discussed."[66]

The process of seeing connections and distinctions, therefore, had to be carried on beyond the horizon of any normal empirical understanding. One could not rest until one had grasped the *ta-t'ou-nao-ch'u* (most important aspect) of the world as a whole, and with this final act of understanding one penetrated and merged with the inner essence of the cosmos, "the mind of the *tao*." The goal of knowledge could not have been defined in a more Sisyphean way.

e. COHERENCE, CONTROL, AND FIXITY AS GOALS

Cognitive clarity was connected to a feeling of coherence. The *hsü* (order, proper sequence) which Confucians since at least Tung Chung-shu wanted in their political procedures was paralleled by a need for an inner sense of control. For Chu Hsi in particular, inadequate knowledge involved a sense of *tsa-ch'u* (things appearing helter-skelter), of *wu-t'ung-chi* (being without unified order), or *i-hsiang fen-fen* (mental images in confused turmoil). This sense of cognitive disorder involved the idea of being out of contact with the ultimate basis of the cosmos, of *chih-li* (disconnected bits perceived without a sense for the whole to which they belong). It also involved a fearful, anxious sense of being powerless and subject to hostile forces, a feeling frequently referred to as *k'ung-chü fen-jao* (fearful feelings of confusion and disturbance) or *k'ung-chü yu-lü* (fears and anxieties). Chu Hsi warned against having *tsa-luan fen-chiu-chih hsin* (a confused and troubled mind). He described such feelings using the imagery of stormy water. Not to be guided by the "mind of the *tao*" was to be like a "boat without a rudder . . . entering stormy waters."[67] He similarly described the anxieties he felt while trying to find "the equilibrium of imminent issuance" (see section 1).

In this context of anxiety, the idea of control was central. Chu Hsi said that one "must cause the mind of the *tao* constantly to be the ruler of one's person, its orders always obeyed by one's human mind."[68] Similarly, Hu Chü-jen (1434–1484), a follower of Chu Hsi, spoke of "a ruler within the self."[69] At least for Chu Hsi, the problem of establishing self-control in the face of powerful anxieties was connected to the perception of *shih-shih wu-wu* (the realm of affairs and things) as powerfully and constantly tending to "overcome" (*sheng*) the self. As Wu Yü-pi (1391–1469), another follower of Chu Hsi, put it: "One may well say that if one's person and one's mind lack a sense of being securely in place, then in one's daily life one will just be constantly preoccupied and upset by considerations of personal advantage and disadvantage." To avoid being thus "overcome by outside things," Wu urged constant study through reading.[70]

This need for an inner "ruler" exerting control in the face of a force threatening to "overcome" the self was a widespread feeling which can be traced back to aspects of Chou Taoism, Chou Confucianism, and the Neo-Taoism of the third century A.D. It was reflected in the Neo-Confucian idea of a *chu-tsai* (lord) ultimately controlling existence.[71] It was expressed in Chu Hsi's desire to "master the ten thousand things" and "encompass heaven and earth."[72] It can also be seen in Ch'en Hsien-chang's (1428–1500) idea that a person with a proper understanding of "principle" would realize that "I have established heaven and earth, the ten thousand transformations flow out of me, and all of space and time is with me." (Ch'en's point probably also referred to Lu Chiu-yüan's idea of the cosmos as an indivisible mind.)[73]

This sense of mastery often involved the notion of a fixed counterweight with which to "respond to changes in the world of affairs" (*ying shih-chih-pien*). This counterweight, like Mencius' *pu-tung-hsin* (mind unperturbed by outer pressures), had to be something unshaken by the maelstrom of experience. *Hsün-tzu* similarly speaks of being *ting* (fixed) as a precondition of being able to *ying* (respond to things).[74] In Chu Hsi's terms, a *ting-li* (fixed principle) was needed to handle *wan-pien-chih fen-yün* (the helter-skelter disorder of the ten thousand changes).[75] Otherwise, one was like "a boat without a rudder," like someone "riding a horse, drifting about, without a place to return to."[76]

Admittedly, this stark contrast between raw events and the spiritual poise needed to meet them was resisted by Wang Yangming, who stressed that one must never in one's mind dissociate phenomenal happenings from the ultimate good (see section r). He also challenged the idea of fixity as an aspect of ultimate being (see section u). Nevertheless, he still believed in a kind of inner spiritual fixity and mastery, and he largely shared Chu Hsi's perception of "affairs and things" as involving a disruptive kind of turmoil which had to be overcome. First, he shared with Chu Hsi the traditional perception of experience as stimuli coming into the mind from the outside to which one responds. The ancient, interconnected ideas of the mind as a "mirror" passively "reflecting" outer stimuli before it responded, of *ying-pien* (respond to changing events), and *kan erh hou tung* (be aware of an event and then respond) provided a definition of experience shared by these thinkers, whatever their differences.[77]

Second, Wang Yang-ming's metaphysical bias and his decisive turn into the mind connoted the usual need for a spiritual foundation free from the turmoil of events. For Wang, as for Chu Hsi, the mind's *pen-t'i* (ultimate substance), to which one had to return to attain *chung* (equilibrium), could not be conceptualized without using the idea of transcending the turmoil of happening (*ching, chi-jan pu-tung, wei-fa*) (see sections m and u).

Third, Wang was explicit in noting a quality of fixity and mastery connoting Mencius' "imperturbable mind." He repeatedly referred to a *chu-tsai* (lord) as an ultimate part of the mind and the cosmos, and he saw this "lord" as *ch'ang-ting* (unchangingly, permanently fixed) amidst "the thousand changes and the ten thousand transformations." Wang added, "If there is no lord, this *ch'i* (ether of materialization) will simply run wild. How can the mind not be caught up in hustle and bustle?"[78] However immanent the *tao* was in the turmoil of the phenomenal flow, this turmoil still remained as something to be dissolved.

f. LINKAGE AS A GOAL

The sense of coherence, mastery, and fixity depended on cognitively conceptualizing the way in which all things were linked to each other to form a coherent whole. The importance of this issue is evident from two facts: while linkage was enunciated as a goal, a great deal of Neo-Confucian thought can perhaps be best understood as efforts to elucidate linkage (see sections t and u). This was the main question over which the two Neo-Confucian schools split. The Ch'eng-Chu school felt that by not recognizing the evil in the mind, the Lu-Wang school could not eliminate the condition preventing the full convergence of mind and principle and so remained mired in the mind without "exhaustively grasping principle." The Lu-Wang school felt that by focusing on this gap between evil and principle, the Ch'eng-Chu school "divided mind and principle in two" and so eliminated the mental foundation on which this convergence depended.[79] Both schools, however, took for granted that mind and principle were ultimately one and that without a cognitive grasp of how this was so, one could not become truly moral.

The way in which Chu Hsi conceptualized linkage was deeply affected by his feeling that seeing cognitively specific boundaries and connections was an essential part of understanding "things." As Ch'ien Mu has emphasized, Chu Hsi favored solving the problem of oneness by "seeing the distinctions in things without losing track of their oneness, seeing the unifying veins passing through things without losing track of the distinctions involved."[80] Chu Hsi conceptualized linkage as *kuan* (to pass a thread through things), using the term in Confucius' saying that "as for my way, it is threaded on one principle."[81] He once used the image of "a string" on which "many scattered cash coins" could be threaded.[82] He also stated that "on the true principle found in one mind can be threaded all the true principles that exist."[83] Referring to the general goal of knowledge, he spoke of the need to "arrive at that point at which things are joined together (*kuan-t'ung-ch'u*)."[84] Conceptualizing the relationship between the metaphysical and the sensory realms, Chu Hsi characteristically said that "heavenly principle" required an *an-tun-ch'u* (point at which it can be securely put down): "When it is not put down just right, selfish desires appear."[85] In a slightly different vein, Chu Hsi said that without *ch'i* (the ether of materialization), *li* (true principle) would "lack a place to be attached" (*wu-kua-ta-ch'u*).[86] Similarly, in seeking to set one's thoughts right, one looked for a *chih-cho* ([place to] hold onto), a *cho-mo-ch'u* (point where one can get a hold), a *cho-shou-ch'u* (place where one can get a grip, a point of purchase), or a *hsia-shou-chiao-ch'u* (a place where one can find a grip and get some footing).[87] Avoiding any *chien-ko* (interval or gap between things) or *feng-hsi* (open seam) was a similar image.[88] It was necessary clearly to see the *chiao-chieh-ch'u* (the boundary, the point of intersection) between "heavenly principle and human material desires."[89] Because *tao-hsin* (the mind of the *tao*) and *jen-hsin* (the human mind) were "confusedly mixed up within the space of a square inch" (i.e. in the human mind), it was necessary to "examine into this space where they both were and distinguish them clearly."[90] Only after thus mentally separating it out could one use *tao-hsin* as the "ruler" of one's person and thus "overcome the selfishness of human desires." With this cognitive grasp of boundaries and linkages, one obtained knowledge in terms of which "outer surfaces and the insides of things, the inner and the outer, all are completely joined together." One thus passed from a muddled mix-up festering with selfishness to a clarified oneness.

This emphasis on linkage was backed by a considerable variety of statements in the classics and other ancient sources speaking of "oneness," cosmic and otherwise.[91] Nevertheless, the concern with finding formulae of linkage pervades Neo-Confucianism in a way entirely foreign to Chou or Han thought. Neo-Confucians regarded their work as essentially elucidating the texts of the classics. But where Chou Confucianism was to a large extent focused on making clear the ethical principles of the *chün-tzu* (true gentleman) and on bringing the all-powerful *chün* (ruler) into a system of moral-political cooperation with the *chün-tzu*, both these roles are peripheral in Neo-Confucianism.[92] It focused rather on the *sheng-hsien* (men of ultimate wisdom), who, along with moral purification, were able to realize the coherence of the cosmos by conceptualizing its patterns of interlinkage. Of course, Han Confucians also were interested in showing how all aspects of existence were linked to form a symmetrical whole. Indeed Neo-Confucians seem generally to have accepted the main Han formulae of linkage, whereby all aspects of existence could be grouped into sets of qualities or things, which in turn respectively "matched" (*p'ei*) each other. It was obvious to Chu Hsi also that benevolence, righteousness, the rules of moral propriety, and moral understanding respectively "matched" spring, summer, autumn, and winter, as well as metal, wood, water, and fire, just as the Han scholars had pointed out.[93] But where for Han scholars this "matching" was an unproblematic exercise adequately describing obvious rules in terms of which the universe cohered, Neo-Confucians saw the problem of linkage as a complex puzzle and, as we shall see, struggled constantly with a variety of conceptual devices to solve it.

Sung Neo-Confucians, therefore, differed from Chou and Han Confucians not only in making more explicit the idea of the oneness of heaven and man but also in regarding this oneness as an unsolved problem.[94] Nor is this surprising when one considers the interven-

ing impact of Buddhism. According to Chu Hsi, the Buddhists regarded the realm of concrete experience (or, more precisely, *ch'i* [the
ether of materialization]) as *cha-tzu* (dregs, worthless leftovers).
Chu Hsi charged that this view "broke off and extinguished moral
relationships."[95] Whether or not he accurately gauged Buddhism's
moral implications, his assessment of its ontological position is
sound enough.

Chou and Han Confucians and Taoists had not questioned the
organic wholeness of ultimate being and concrete experience.
Whether in the *Tao-te-ching* or the cosmology of, say, Tung Chung-
shu, the process of "birth" was viewed as relating the "things" of
experience to "heaven" or the *tao* (true way), and the interplay of
yin and yang similarly brought "things" into contact with ultimate
being. On the other hand, given the basic teaching of the Buddha
that "birth is suffering" and that the proper human goal is to escape
from the realm of "suffering," it was only natural that Buddhists
in China, to a large extent at least, rejected the idea that the process
of birth was a glorious one bringing "things" into unity with
ultimate being. Birth rather meant conditioned existence
(*saṁskrita*). Thus tainted rather than hallowed by the process of
birth, "things" were also subjected to a new doubt by Chinese
Buddhists, since their reality was questioned. Chih Tun (314–366),
a famous Buddhist monk active in the capital of the Eastern Chin
dynasty, played an important role in making clear that the old
organic connection between "things" and ultimate being was
problematic. He did this simply by using *li* (principle) instead of
tao or *t'ien* (heaven) to denote the realm of ultimate being. As
frequently used in a variety of Chou and Han texts, *li* had various
meanings, such as the principle or reason involved in a particular
physical fact or political institution.[96] With this sort of abstractness, *li* did not connote the organic wholeness of all cosmic processes, as did *tao* or *t'ien*. Consequently when Chinese Buddhists
dismissed the theory of yin and yang, put aside the organic relation
between *tao* and *wu* (things), and instead used *li* (principle) and
shih (affairs, happenings) to conceptualize the distinction between
the ultimate and the merely phenomenal levels of existence, the
problem of disconnection between these two levels was immediately
apparent. As Kenneth Ch'en says, "In the writings of the Buddhists

from the fourth to the tenth centuries, li as the absolute was regularly opposed by shih, mundane events or facts of empirical experience. Later on, the Neo-Confucians took over this pair, keeping li in the sense of the absolute truth, but opposing it with ch'i, vital energy or matter."[97]

While Buddhism thus made the problem of linkage central and acute by appearing to postulate a chasm, it was also crucial in defining the dangers which Neo-Confucians perceived as attending the quest for linkage. Chou Confucians lacked the deep Neo-Confucian concern with avoiding overly general ideas appearing "empty" of any connection to the experiential world, just as they lacked the complementary concern with avoiding formulations overly immersed in the details of this experiential world and thus giving one a feeling of *chih-li* (dealing with disconnected bits of reality without grasping the root of things). Neither kind of formulation could demonstrate the interpenetration of the metaphysical and the experiential realms. Therefore even if one can refute the thesis that Buddhism positively supplied the main metaphysical formulae of Neo-Confucianism, the effects of Buddhism can be seen in the agenda of issues and criteria of validity shaping Neo-Confucian thought.

At the same time, Buddhism complicated the problem of linkage by drawing a new degree of attention to an area of existence where linkage also had to be demonstrated. This was the flow of feeling and consciousness in the "mind." Chu Hsi suggested that it was Mencius who deserved credit for shedding light on the nature of the mind, but, as Ch'ien Mu points out, Neo-Confucianism's elaborate analysis of the mind reflected the influence of Ch'an (Zen) Buddhism; Confucians since Han times had focused rather on ethical, practical, and political affairs.[98]

Ch'ien Mu's remark is most significant. De Bary has written that the influence of Buddhism lay in "the deepening of Neo-Confucian spirituality."[99] One is reminded of Fung Yu-lan's remark that "Li Ao [d. ca. 844] and all the Sung and Ming Neo-Confucians ... wanted to cause men to achieve a sort of Confucian Buddhahood by means of Confucian methods."[100] Whatever the particular spiritual qualities involved, the spiritual condition of the mind thus was defined as an issue emphatically differentiated from specifically social and political concerns. The ontological problem of linkage itself was an issue transcending the particularities of the socio-political world. As the need to solve this problem merged with Confucius' injunction to have "no depraved thoughts," morality was partly based on a socially unspecific state of existence habitually denoted with a variety of terms such as *wu t'ai-chi* (unrealized supreme ultimate), *ching* (state of perfect rest), and *chi-jan pu-tung* (total stillness without any sensation of and response to objects). Such highly generalized notions, although partly based on the classics, particularly the *Classic of Changes*, also reflected the common Buddhist tendency to reduce institutional and family life to mere *shih* (happenings) in the unreal realm of material desire, and to discuss the spiritual life without even referring to social virtues like *jen* (benevolence), not to mention filial piety, *li* (the rules of moral propriety), and *chih-tu* (governmental institutions). This tendency toward the transcendent is reflected also in the central Neo-Confucian emphasis on subsuming the socially specific virtues, that is, the "five relationships," under the universalistic, generic virtues of *ching* (reverence), *ch'eng* (sincerity), and *jen* (benevolence) and on putting the phenomenal world of moral particulars at a mental distance by referring to it as a "realm."[101] This differentiation of the mind from specifically social concerns was also in accord with the Buddhist emphasis on the moral fragility of the mind as an organ dominated by egotistic cravings and false notions about what is real.[102]

This focus on the "mind," moreover, meshed with the traumatic effects of Wang An-shih's (1021–1086) alleged failure. Chou and Han Confucians had optimistically perceived the "outer" realm of political and economic affairs as immediately responsive to directly political measures instituted by a Confucian prime minister, such as the appointment to office of only "superior" men, the identification of which involved no cognitive problems whatsoever, the lowering of taxes, and the stopping of all unnecessary killing. For this reason, the political roles of *chün-tzu* and *chün* were of supreme importance to them, as just mentioned. Wang An-shih and other Confucians in the eleventh century had shared this Mencian faith, as Ch'ien Mu has so eloquently argued, but after the failure of Wang An-shih's reforms, Neo-Confucians came generally to perceive this "outer" realm as unmalleable, as drained of any inherent power to "renew" itself without prior progress in the "inner" realm of the mind.[103] Where rulers unwilling to institute obviously good policies had been the enemy in Mencius' eyes, the enemy for Chu Hsi and Wang Yang-ming was overwhelmingly that "inner" force within "the mind" of the Confucian subject leading to moral corruption.

Conversely, where Chou and Han Confucians had been largely unanimous in ascribing to the "king" and his *chih-tu* (governmental institutions) the power to transform society, Neo-Confucians gradually came to agree in regarding *wu-hsin* (the mind of the self) as the prime vehicle of this power (see chapter 5, section e). This change in Chinese thought was certainly impregnated with the influence of Buddhism. Indeed one can conveniently distinguish Neo-Confucianism from other kinds of Confucianism by regarding it as a mixture of this emphasis on "the mind of the self," a total zeal to exploit the transformative powers of this mind, the organismic cosmology of Tung Chung-shu, and the ethics of Confucius. Just because it was "the mind," not "the king," which was the prime vehicle of hope, the mind's capacity to elucidate linkage became crucial.

Facing the task of linkage, Neo-Confucians to some extent simply reasserted the old Confucian belief in the organic wholeness of the cosmos and in man as a moral agent with the transnatural power to solve all cosmic problems. While Hsün-tzu had glorified "the true gentleman" as having the power to "put in order heaven and earth" (*li-t'ien-ti*), Chu Hsi noted: "One may say that when the affairs of the world are at some point not just right, they are set right by the sage."[104] Discussed in section o, the transnatural power of the human mind, a Confucian idea foreign to the Buddhist concept of the mind, was part of the Neo-Confucian assumption that man had the capability to solve the problem of linkage. Yet this capability had to be exercised by actively elucidating the linkage between the metaphysical and the experiential realms, that is, between *li* (principle), *hsin* (mind), and *wu* (things).

It was just this elucidation which repeatedly seemed inadequate, with the result that linkage continued to appear as an unsolved problem. One might say that the success of Neo-Confucianism lay in defining the rules of the cosmic game, not in supplying the winning formula. It was the posing of a problem, not the presentation of a solution, that changed Chinese culture in Sung times. Defining hopes was a more cunning ideological tactic than presenting any easily punctured theory claiming to satisfy them. If man's cosmic power was to be actualized, he had to grasp that formula of linkage which even Confucius had not clearly formulated. Chu Hsi said: "Whenever one looks at the principles of things, one must see them clearly in terms of their most important aspect (*ta-t'ou-nao-ch'u*). The various segments below are just the scattered manifold of this principle. For instance, when Confucius taught, he just explained matters one by one; he never discussed this ultimate aspect of things. . . . The words of the sages did not originally form a connected whole (*kuan-chü*). It was the Ch'eng brothers who for the first time by formulating such a connected whole arrived at the concept of *ching* (reverence) as a way to teach men."[105] Yet the task of "forming a connected whole" was still a largely unrealized goal.

g. COSMIC AND POLITICAL POWER AS A GOAL

With both moral purification and the cognitive grasp of linkage, one achieved that state of existence celebrated by T'ang Chün-i as participation in a limitless, inherently good flow of noumenal reality. The stock phrase was "to be one with heaven, earth, and the ten thousand things," a formulation which was especially popular in Ming times but which even Chu Hsi accepted on principle, although he objected to its vagueness.[106] With this sense of oneness, a person acted not under social or political pressures but above them, as an agent of the cosmos: "One acts to carry on realization of the will of heaven and earth, one transmits the truths of heaven and earth."[107] Even more, it was as an agent of the cosmos that one was able to transform the entire social and political world. One thus retrieved a cosmic spirit hidden beneath the accumulated moral debris of history (*chi-pi*) and enabled mankind to begin afresh. This was the Neo-Confucian paradigm of revolutionary action. Perhaps Chang Tsai (1020–1077) put it most eloquently: "To establish a mind for heaven and earth; to establish heaven's decree for

3. Sense of Predicament (g)

the people; to continue the tradition of learning which the sages established but which subsequently was not transmitted; to open an era of perfect peace lasting for the next ten thousand generations."[108] Having realized one's goal, one no longer merely "obeys heaven and follows what is decreed"; rather one realizes that "what heaven has decreed is up to me."[109]

Even more, the theme of power over the cosmos was clear, at least in Chu Hsi: "Man is the mind of heaven and earth. When man is not present, there is no one to control heaven and earth."[110] This sense of cosmic power, as already indicated, was connected to the desire for "mastery," and in Chu Hsi's thought it also was related to the image of the sage as one who is not only pure of heart but really does bring political harmony and economic well-being to the empire. Chu Hsi did not lose sight of the sage's role as one with "great power" (ta-li-liang) to set right the physical environment of the whole world: "Heaven is able to bring things into being, but ploughing and planting depends on man. . . . The sage assists in the transforming and nourishing processes of heaven and earth. If there is something not right in the affairs of the world, it is set right by the sage."[111]

Wang Yang-ming de-emphasized this sense of power over the cosmos and the empire. He was farther than Chu Hsi from the radical optimism of the eleventh century, when the hope of totally reforming the "outer" political realm was so alive. Wang's complicated ontological position, discussed below, led him to reduce the significance of questions not directly concerned with the moral condition of the individual. He said that to be a sage, the only thing that mattered was "being purely one with heavenly principle."[112] This view put the sage's role as the reformer of the empire into the background. A similar impression was left by his statement that "the effort to investigate things is to be carried out just with reference to one's person and mind," and that "there are no things outside the mind."[113] He even specifically divorced the question of sagehood from that of "outer" success when he held that "the effective abilities of a sage can be either great or small, just as the weight of a piece of gold can be heavy or light."[114]

Moreover, his famous idea that "knowledge and action are one" implied that the actions of the sage as ruler are not a central con-

cern for the moral individual. Knowledge and action were one for
Wang in the sense that understanding filial piety necessarily meant
acting in a filial way. Yet Wang had to admit that Confucius, who
had never succeeded in establishing the proper governmental institutions, nevertheless "understood the principles of all the under-
takings and achievements of ancient emperors and kings."[115] The
fact that this example of knowledge without action failed to jostle
Wang's faith in the unity of knowledge and action can be explained
only by the inference that when Wang spoke of action, he was thinking primarily of personal ethics, not of the rectification of the empire.

Wang's thought thus seems to be connected to that declining
interest in the complete ideal of sagehood which de Bary has seen
in the trends of the seventeenth and eighteenth centuries.[116] Yet
Wang himself remained ambivalent. He still took most seriously
the famous eight steps of the *Great Learning*, which included "bringing peace and order to the empire." He could not avoid the world-
encompassing burden of *jen* (benevolence): "The man of *jen* regards
himself as forming one body with heaven, earth, and the ten thousand things. If one thing fails to find its proper place, this shows that
my *jen* has not been exhaustively realized in one way or another."[117]

Underlying this difference between Chu Hsi and Wang Yang-
ming is the fact that, as Benjamin Schwartz has pointed out, Confucian thought generally wavered between the poles of self-cultivation
and political action. In *Mencius*, for instance, there is a combination
of enthusiasm for political reform and the feeling that the moral
individual has reached a final state of contentment independent of
any outer progress: "The true gentleman finds joy in three things,
and bringing the empire under the sway of virtue is not among
them." Similarly, Wei-ming Tu and de Bary have shed light on that
Neo-Confucian serenity transcending any dependence on the practical outcome of one's actions. Nevertheless, just as basic as this
serenity was the emphasis on compassion (*jen*), which necessarily
involved a desire for the power to "relieve the people of their suffering." To us, perhaps, compassion and serenity in this sense contradict each other, but not to Neo-Confucians, who liked to speak
of "moving while at rest." Paradoxically, then, Neo-Confucians did
not particularly desire cosmic and political power, but they still
aimed for it in a most serious way.

h. JOY AND SOCIAL ONENESS AS GOALS

This oneness with the cosmos also involved a physical, emotional sense of well-being. As Ch'eng Hao said, by overcoming the sense of existing as a "thing" "set apart from and opposed to" (*tui*) the other "things" of the world, one achieved the "great joy" Mencius had referred to, a feeling which included relief from those "fears and anxieties" mentioned above. Such "joy" was also basic for Wang Yang-ming. There was an emotional need for dissipating social friction and distance. Ch'eng Hao explicitly noted the parallel between the lack of *jen* (benevolence), with its sense of cosmic disjunction, and the way medical books referred to paralysis as a state of "not being *jen*."[118] Such hints suggest that further study could reveal more clearly the soma-metaphysical aspects of the Neo-Confucian goal. At the same time, besides this emotional sense of well-being, realization or even just pursuit of this goal carried with it pleasurable feelings of social superiority (see section p).

Furthermore, the oneness achieved by the individual in his relation with the cosmos was realized also in his relation to the community. True, Neo-Confucianism respected the hierarchical and familistic values expressed in the basic idea of "the five relationships." However, it also leaned toward the universalistic, utopian ideal of *ta-t'ung* (great oneness of all people), which was found in the classic *Li-chi* and later taken up by modernizers like K'ang Yu-wei. Indeed Wang Yang-ming's vision of the ideal society shares much with Mao Tse-tung's. Wang says:

> In the mind of the sage, heaven, earth, and the ten thousand things form one body. He regards all the people of the world as his brothers and children, no matter whether they be distant or near, outside or inside his family. He has no desire but to make their lives secure and complete, to teach and care for them, in order to follow his idea of being one with the ten thousand things. . . . At the time of Yao, Shun, and the Three Dynasties . . . . those in positions of responsibility desired only to be one in heart and virtue with those they employed in order together to bring peace and security to the people. They looked to see if a person's ability matched his task but did not regard high posts as more important than low ones. . . . Those who served them similarly desired only to be one in heart and virtue with them in order together to bring peace and security to the people. If one's task suited one's ability, one spent all of one's life doing heavy work without regarding

it as arduous and felt content with lowly work and odd jobs without regarding them as mean. . . . A single spirit flowed through everyone, a common purpose and feeling permeated everyone, and there was no distinction between other people and oneself, no gap between things and the self.[119]

i. GOAL AND GIVEN WORLD

The goal of Neo-Confucians, therefore, was to obtain a living, immediate, emotionally soothing, and elitist sense of cosmic oneness and power by achieving moral purification together with a comprehensive cognitive grasp of the cosmos as a coherently linked whole. With this state of mind, one would realize social oneness and put the whole world in order. Thus one avoided existing in a "dead," "bad," self-centered way, cognitively disoriented by the helter-skelter of happening, feeling out of contact with ultimate reality, subject to anxious feelings of powerlessness and aimlessness in the face of powerful forces threatening to "overcome" one, and so unable to realize social oneness and to save the world.

Trying to reach this goal, Neo-Confucians perceived themselves as acting in a particular ontological arena, in a particular given world of actual forces, the nature of which, like that of their goal, was widely accepted as a cliché "definition of the situation" and was thus presupposed by rather than subject to the intellectual controversies of Neo-Confucianism from the Sung through the Ch'ing periods. This given ontological setting can be best understood in terms of the interplay of three processes which, though interconnected, each had a distinctly different character. First, there was a good cosmic force bringing the spatio-temporal world into being and making possible realization of the above goal. Second, there was a bad cosmic force generating the negative phenomena noted above. Third, there was a process in terms of which the contest between these two forces was decided. This process itself consisted of an ongoing, partly competitive relationship between two partly distinct forces, the ultimate will of the cosmos (*t'ien-ming*) and the human will, which could intervene in the cosmic process, bringing to full realization the good force and preventing realization of the bad one.

How to use these resources of the will was the question Neo-Confucians argued most about, but we will better understand their controversies if we first analyze their essentially shared perception of the interaction between these three processes.

j. THE GOOD COSMIC FORCE AS A GIVEN

To begin with the good cosmic force, we are here dealing with nearly all the cosmological inventory of Neo-Confucianism. It can be broken down into four parts. First there were a number of terms which, if not unqualifiedly denoting things which existed *hsing-erh-shang* (above the realm of ordinarily experienced forms), could at least be regarded as especially relevant to discussion of this metaphysical realm. These were terms like *t'ien* (heaven), *tao* (the way of action which inheres in the cosmos and which should be followed), *yin* and *yang* (the negative and positive cosmic forces), *t'ai-chi* (supreme ultimate), *li* (principle), *so-i-jan* (the reason) underlying a concrete thing, and the *hsing* (heaven-conferred nature) of a concrete thing. At times Chu Hsi posited a "lord" as somehow "above" "heaven," and Wang Yang-ming also spoke of a "lord" (see section d).

Second, there were terms that either directly referred to *hsing-erh-hsia* (the realm of ordinarily experienced forms) or referred to a level of reality very close to the latter. These were terms like *ch'ing* (feelings), *hsin* (mind), *ch'i* (ether of materialization), *hsing-ch'i-chih chung* (amidst the realm of ordinarily experienced forms and the ether of materialization), *ch'i* (concrete thing), *hsing-hsiang* (concrete forms and appearances), and a number of terms denoting the "things" and "affairs" of ordinary experiences, such as *wan-wu*, *wan-shih wan-wu*, *shih-shih wu-wu*, and *ch'ien-t'ou wan-chien*. *Wan-wu* (the ten thousand things) included natural and artificial "things," such as *tien-chang* (governmental institutions); the "affairs" of "history" and the present; and the self—*wu-shen* (the self) or *wu-hsin* (the mind of the self)—as well as people in general.

To be sure, this distinction between the metaphysical and the experiential did not amount to a rigorous dualism. Even with Chu Hsi, this distinction was always combined with a strong belief in the immanence of the metaphysical in the experiential, and like all Neo-Confucians, he frequently used a number of categories in terms of which this distinction was bridged or blurred, such as *t'ien-ti* (heaven and earth), *t'ien-ming* (what heaven has decreed), and *jen* (man).

One cannot exaggerate the importance of the category "heaven and earth." Basic already in the classics, this concept has generally been treated by modern scholars as a cliché not worth remarking on. Its significance lies in the fact that as a cliché blurring together the metaphysical and experiential levels, it expressed a widespread perception of these levels as organically united.[120]

Even more, those Neo-Confucians, like Wang Yang-ming, who inclined toward monism avoided referring to the *I-ching's* blunt distinction between *hsing-erh-shang* and *hsing-erh-hsia* and described both as just different aspects of the same thing.[121] Yet whether a distinction between two different levels or two different aspects of one thing was at stake, a distinction of some sort between two different modalities was invariably made by all Neo-Confucians. Moreover, their frequent references to a whole spectrum of ontological dyads (see below) cannot be separated from their perception of these two modalities. Neo-Confucians generally viewed these two modalities as constituting an objectively real cosmos, but they did not conceptualize this reality in commonsense terms. Rather, various ideas inclined them to view the cosmos as a kind of monad, that is, a whole fully present in each of its parts.[122]

Third, while all the above terms had a nounal quality, another set of terms was used to denote that process of motion which overlapped the metaphysical and the experiential realms. Most metaphysical was the pair *ching* (state of rest) and *tung* (movement). Largely manifest in and totally pervading the level of ordinary experience, shifts from *ching* to *tung* constituted an "endless cyclical process" (*hsün-huan pu-i*).[123] To "move" was to "issue forth" (*fa*), an idea applied especially to the movement of "feelings." Similarly, the beginning phase of *tung* could be regarded as a process of *fa-yung* (issuance in experience), the return to *ching*, as a process of *shou-lien* (withdrawing back into oneself). As a whole, these dynamics were referred to as *i* (change), *pien* (transformation), or *hua* (transformation). The image of flowing water was used by Chu Hsi to conceptualize this process, which thus involved a "flowing forth" (*liu-hsing*, *liu-chuan*), the *kun-kun-chiang-ch'ü* (rushing along like currents of water) of "things and affairs." Chu Hsi said "The point out of which principles come is just a source," using a word also meaning "the source of a stream."[124] The "water in a well fed by a spring" was compared by Wang Yang-ming to the inexhaustible spirit of life in the cosmos.[125]

Fourth, with these various metaphysical and experiential elements in motion, certain dyadic relations were apparent. One cannot exaggerate either the frequency with which these dyadic concepts were used or the lack of controversy which attended them. Although a few of these dyads have caught the attention of scholars, their use was so commonplace that sinologists have not previously thought it worthwhile to collect them and note that their meanings clustered together to express a single moral-ontological distinction widely taken for granted. The most important among these dyads numbered more than ten, including *tao* (true way) and *ch'i* (concrete thing); *t'i* (substance) and *yung* (function); *pen-t'i* (ultimate substance) and *fa-yung* (issuance in experience); *ch'un* (pure) and *tsa* (impure); *chi* (consciousness without sensation of outer things, total stillness) and *kan* (sensation of outer things); *nei* (inner) and *wai* (outer); *wei* (almost imperceptible in its subtlety) and *hsien* or *chu* (fully manifest); *shih* (beginning) and *ch'eng* (completion); *ch'ang* (unchanging and permanent) and *pien* (changes); *pen* (basis, root) and *mo* (derivative aspects); *yüan* (source) and *liu* (flow from a source); and phrases like *pen-jan-chih-miao* (the finest essence of the ultimate basis) of something, which could be contrasted to *so-ch'eng-chih-chi* (the concrete possibility to be realized).

In virtually all these cases, the first concept of the pair denoted a condition which was both desirable and difficult to find in the ordinary course of experience. It was the ordinary condition of people to be alienated from the *tao*, to "lose" their "ultimate substance," to fail in "returning" to the "unchanging" "beginning," "root," or "source" of things, and to lose adequate contact with that "pure," "almost imperceptible" level of consciousness which was "within" them and free of disturbing perceptions. Conversely, the "fully manifest" world of "concrete things," "implementation," "issuance in experience," "impure" "sensations of outer things," and changing, derivative circumstances was usually an unsatisfactory world which was ordinarily and easily found in our experience. One surely did not have to struggle to "return" to it! Even in those philosophical trends seeking to maximize the feeling that the *tao* can be found only in phenomenal happening—Wang Yang-ming said "the *tao* is happenings, happenings are the *tao*"—a distinction was always drawn between the aspects of experience barren of the *tao* and those elusive ones tinged with the *tao*.

As is made clear in the next section, this idea of the dyads was an integral part of a single vision of process expressed also by the notion of the mind's oscillation between imminent and accomplished issuance (*wei-fa* and *i-fa*) and based on that fundamental paradigm of oscillation between the states of rest and movement noted above. In this vision of process, which was universally shared by Neo-Confucians, ordinary reality somehow stemmed from an elusive, underlying reality which was the locus of the absolute good and of the life-giving and transformative power inherent in the cosmos. Conversely, the ordinary flow of experience stood in constant danger of slipping out of contact with this underlying reality, and moral effort was needed to prevent this slippage. Even the Confucian concept of the polity was affected by this vision of cosmic process.[126] Certainly the Neo-Confucian perception of the mind was based on it.[127]

k. THE NATURALLY GIVEN PHASES OF THE MIND

The Neo-Confucian concept of the mind of the individual is most complicated. The mind was, first of all, something which controlled bodily forces. It was, as Chu Hsi said, "the master of the person."[128] Therefore, it had to be an aspect of the ether of materialization. Yet it also was an aspect of *hsü-ling ming-chüeh* (intelligent awareness in its pure, naturally given, cosmically indivisible form, empty of any consciously specific concepts or sensations) (see section d). As such, it had to be "the purest and liveliest part of the ether of materialization," as Chu Hsi put it.[129] Thus viewing the material as inherently conscious, Neo-Confucians evaded that dichotomy between mind and body so basic in the West since at least Descartes, and they could use "mind" and "ether of materialization" in an almost interchangeable way which has bedevilled Marxists trying to divide them into "idealists" and "materialists."[130] At the same time, the mind existed at a double cosmic intersection, that between the metaphysical and the experiential levels, and that between the

3. Sense of Predicament (k)

good and the bad cosmic forces. Moreover, the "mind" also incorporated a capacity to act on and transform this intersection. To present more clearly the Neo-Confucian model of the mind's workings, I have divided these into the given phases of the mind and the given intervening will.

Neo-Confucians mainly combined three ideas from the classics to develop their definition of the mind's phasic life. First, they accepted the idea that all life consisted of oscillation between *ching* (state of perfect rest) and *tung* (movement). Second, Chou Tun-i analyzed these two phases in the mind by respectively equating them with two states mentioned in the *Classic of Changes, chi-jan pu-tung* (total stillness without movement) and *kan erh sui t'ung* (aware of an outer object, one then empathetically pervades it through one's response). Chou Tun-i also drew attention to this classic's concept of *chi*. K'ung Ying-ta, the famous T'ang commentator, had explained this *chi* as something "poised between existence and nonexistence," and Neo-Confucians used *chi* to denote the mind's incipient movement.[131] *Chi* means "incipient, almost imperceptible phase in the movement of something," and it also connotes the heaven-tinged phase of total rest preceding any movement.

Third, Ch'eng I drew attention to the issuance of the feelings as described in chapter 1 of the *Doctrine of the Mean*, saying this passage described the Confucian way of cultivating the mind.[132] In this chapter, the quest for the *tao* is identified with the attempt to apprehend a transcendent reality which one can neither "see" nor "hear." The reader is then informed: "*Chung* (inner equilibrium) is what one calls the state in which the feelings of delight, anger, grief, and joy *wei-fa* (have not yet issued forth). *Ho* (harmony in one's actions) is what one calls the state in which these feelings have *fa* (issued forth) and completely hit the golden mean."

We should also remember that this idea of issuance accorded with that of the ontological dyads (see section j), especially the pair "inner" and "outer." Issuance meant making an inner quality outwardly manifest and operative (it certainly did not mean injecting an outer quality into the inner life). Conversely, to realize the "equilibrium of imminent issuance" was to "rectify things at their root and purify them at their source," as T'ang Chün-i puts it.[133]

The movement of the mind, therefore, occurred in terms of "responding" to "things" which (themselves "moving") "came" (*lai*) to the self, so that Chu Hsi could speak of *shih-shih wu-wu chieh yü wu-ch'ien* (coming before me, affairs and things come into contact with me).[134] The response to this contact consisted of *kan* (the sensation of something outside to respond to) and the subsequent *fa* (issuing forth) of the four *ch'ing* (feelings), "delight and anger, grief and joy." These emotions permeated all human action: "What affair in the world does not involve delight and anger, joy and grief? . . . How can there be a sage who does not get angry?"[135] Thus involved in the flow of emotion, one was in the phase of experience called *i-fa* (already issued, accomplished issuance). *Wei-fa* (not yet issued, imminent issuance) referred, I would say, to the moment just after some *kan* (sensation of outer things) had occurred but the feelings had "not yet issued forth" in response. When a feeling was still poised between imminent and accomplished issuance, it appeared as a *chi* (incipient, almost imperceptible phase in the motion of something). Chu Hsi once conceptualized this phase as *chi-wei-chih chi* (the point at which incipient feelings are almost imperceptible in their subtlety).[136] Just preceding the sensation of an outer object and imminent issuance was the *chi-ch'u* (point of total stillness). Also called *chi-jan pu-tung* (total stillness without movement), it coincided with *ching* (state of total rest) and *hsü-ling ming-chüeh* (intelligent awareness in its pure, naturally given, cosmically indivisible form, empty of any consciously specific concepts or sensations).

Five phases, therefore, were distinguished as forming a pseudo-temporal sequence: total stillness, sensation of an outer object, imminent issuance, incipient issuance, and accomplished issuance. It was in terms of this sequence that the mind existed at a double cosmic intersection. That is, this sequence had an origin which was both good and metaphysical, and which coincided with at least the first three phases. Passing through the last two phases, one not only came into the experiential realm but also was exposed to the danger of succumbing to the bad cosmic force.

It is important to sort out the terminology associated with the good origin of the feelings. How "heavenly principle" impinged on the feelings was a subject of debate, but that it did was not. Chu Hsi said: "When we inquire into the source from which the principles

3. Sense of Predicament (k)

of the world have come, there is no badness. How can delight and anger, grief and joy ever be bad in the form which they have when just on the point of being issued?"[137] In their incipient form, these four feelings could be classified as four types of *tuan-ni* (incipiences). These were Mencius' *ts'e-yin* (compassion), *hsiu-wu* (the sense of shame and hatred of evil), *tz'u-jang* (sense of self-abnegation), and *shih-fei* (sense of right and wrong).[138] Apparently only Liu Tsung-chou made a point of conceptualizing the relation of the four feelings to the four incipiences, holding that each of the latter was a "transformation" of one of the former.[139] Mencius had respectively matched the four incipiences with four human virtues (*jen* [benevolence], *i* [righteousness], *li* [propriety], and *chih* [moral understanding]), and Neo-Confucians in turn argued over whether or not the distinction between the four incipiences and the four virtues should be interpreted dualistically. Chu Hsi, for instance, took a dualistic position, holding that the four incipiences were the experiential aspects of moral life, while the four virtues referred to their corresponding metaphysical aspects (*li*).

Besides the four feelings, the four incipiences, and the four human virtues, the idea of the four "heavenly virtues" mentioned in the *Classic of Changes* (*yüan*, *heng*, *li*, and *chen*) could be used to characterize the spontaneous flow of moral feeling, which could also be equated with man's *liang-hsin* (spontaneously moral mind) or his *liang-chih* (spontaneous moral knowledge) (these two terms were from *Mencius*). Whatever the terminology, this good cosmic force as it welled up in the self was not just a source of moral standards and moral power, it also carried a note of authority, an imperative to obey these standards. In contact with heaven, one was also in the presence of "what heaven has decreed" (see section p).

In the world of Neo-Confucians, the existence of this good cosmic force could almost not be doubted. It is significant, however, that Chu Hsi did explicitly reject the theory that good behavior stemmed not from such spontaneously moral feelings but from enlightened self-interest—a "calculative selfishness."[140]

The problem was how to obey this heavenly imperative, how to keep these incipient feelings on course. As indicated above, this was the problem of *fa erh chieh chung-chieh* (the feelings issue forth and all hit the golden mean). To the extent that *chung-chieh* occurred, one had attained the goal virtue of *ch'eng* (being true to heaven, sincerity), i.e., one had maintained over time conformity with the *li* (principles) reflected in the four "incipiences."

We should be quite clear about the way this phasic life of the mind was a perceived reality for Neo-Confucians. An example is the following from Liu Tsung-chou's writings: "At the time of total stillness without movement, man's four *te* (virtues) of delight, anger, grief, and joy are present of themselves and are not lost in non-existence. Similarly, when one is aware of an outer object and pervades it empathetically through one's response, these four virtues do not become mired in existence."[141]

By referring to the four incipiences as "virtues," Liu was subtly claiming that the four "heavenly virtues" (*yüan, heng, li,* and *chen*) were identical with these incipiences, thus rejecting Chu Hsi's emphasis on the contrast between heavenly principle and concrete feelings. Such a use of *te* (virtue) can also be found in Wang Yang-ming. As "virtues" which did not become "mired in existence," the four incipiences were not entangled in the immoralities of accomplished issuance and so retained the quality of "equilibrium" which they had had "at the time of total stillness without movement."

The claim in this passage, therefore, was that by recognizing the character of the incipiences as "heavenly virtues," one understood and thereby preserved that unity of the mind otherwise broken in the phase of accomplished issuance. On the other hand, in this passage Liu did not need to claim that there existed a "time of total stillness without movement"; that the four incipiences existed; that there existed a time of "being aware of an object and empathetically pervading it with one's response"; that the latter phase involved the danger of becoming "mired in existence"; and that a special intellectual effort was needed to prevent a breach between the phases. All these matters were perceived as given facts defining the terms of the moral struggle. In other words, except for his interpretation of *te*, this passage was pure cliché and referred to the same perceived realities that were confronted by all Neo-Confucians.

At times, the linkage problem posed by the existence of the mind's naturally given phases was viewed as the gravest sort of issue and was at the heart of discussions about how to carry out *kung-fu* (efficacious moral efforts). This was the case to a large extent in the Sung period. Ch'eng I focused on this issue and left behind a variety of apparently contradictory statements. Partly out of these, two different approaches were developed: that passed on by Hu Wu-feng to his student Chang Nan-hsüan (1133–1180); and that passed on by Yang Kuei-shan (1053–1135) and Lo Yü-chang to Li T'ung (1088–1163), Chu Hsi's teacher. Chu Hsi, as discussed below, spent a troubled decade trying to resolve the difference between these two approaches.[142]

If Lu Chiu-yüan regarded discussion of these phases as derailing the process of self-realization from the start, Wang Yang-ming only briefly touched on this possibility and repeatedly referred to the phases to make clear what he meant by self-realization. True, Wang's discussion of *kung-fu* was not directly focused on the problem raised by the phases. Yet this was because he, like Chu Hsi after 1169, was confident that this problem had been solved, not because he did not perceive the phases as the given field of moral effort. Even more, to the extent that Chu Hsi and Wang Yang-ming felt that the problem of the phases had been solved, they fundamentally agreed on the nature of this solution, and the concepts they respectively emphasized, especially *ching* (reverence) and *liang-chih* (spontaneous moral knowledge), were distinguished precisely by the supposed capacity to solve this problem. In other words, it was largely this capacity which made these key concepts especially important for Neo-Confucians (see sections l and m).

Indeed the nervous oscillation of Neo-Confucians between different "claims" about how to bridge the phases would have made no sense at all had Neo-Confucians not perceived the phases as real. In the seventeenth century, a new view on how to bridge this gap appeared, as thinkers like Liu Tsung-chou took a position reminiscent of Hu Wu-feng's and Chang Nan-hsüan's. This new view, in turn, lay at the roots of what is sometimes regarded as Ch'ing "naturalism" or "materialism" (see section x).

The neglect of this phasic aspect of the mind in the current literature is largely due, I would suggest, to the impact of modern philosophical trends on the study of Neo-Confucianism. True, the terminology of the phases is often found in translations of Neo-Confucian texts, philological or historical studies, and basically traditional analyses of the problems of Neo-Confucian philosophy, such as Ch'ien Mu's. However, in studies trying to make sense out of Neo-Confucianism in terms of more modern philosophical perspectives, one finds no clear account of the phases.

Intent on extracting from Neo-Confucianism a kind of Platonic ontology based on the idea of *li* (principle), Fung Yu-lan entirely ignored the distinction between imminent and accomplished issuance in his two-volume history, which has had such a great influence in the English-speaking world. He also ignored it when he sought in his *Hsin li-hsüeh* (A New Philosophy Based on the School of Chu Hsi) to construct a neo-realist ontology meeting the critical standards of modern philosophy. Hou Wai-lu, in his Marxist polemic against the "idealism" of Neo-Confucianism, says that Chu Hsi reduced ethics to the "consciousness of an individual's subjective self." Hou then briefly adduces the "mystical" distinction between imminent and accomplished issuance as an example of Chu Hsi's analysis of this consciousness.[143] Like Fung's, however, Hou's discussion of Neo-Confucianism entirely revolves around the familiar cosmological concepts listed in section j.

T'ang Chün-i shows that the "inner" life of moral struggle, not cosmology, is the key to Neo-Confucian thought. Indeed, in his more technical and historical analysis of Neo-Confucian thought, he shows how important the distinction between the phases was. Neo-Confucians, he explains, believed that it was possible through "study" to realize that totally natural manner of the sage, who, as Chou Tun-i put it, is "empty of all but the presence of the cosmos when in the state of rest, and when in movement does what is right in a totally direct way." Consequently, how to reach this "equilibrium of imminent issuance" was a "most urgent, most profound, most serious, and most difficult question. It was a problem common to all the Sung and Ming Neo-Confucians, and it ran through the historical development of Sung and Ming Neo-Confucian thought. . . . If it was not possible to answer this question satisfactorily, there ultimately was an aspect of sagehood which could not be learned."[144]

In his less historical, more philosophically systematic work, however, T'ang barely mentions the phases. His philosophical thought leads him away from the framework of the phases, because his main point is that Neo-Confucianism gave an existentially valid account of human experience as the inherently dynamic life of moral empathy. Thus, as discussed in chapter 2, primordial reality for T'ang is a state of movement. The ultimate unit of existence is *chiao-kan-chih chi* (the point at which empathies are interchanged), and this interchange in turn reflects the ceaselessly dynamic creativity of the cosmos (*sheng-sheng pu-i*). T'ang himself tells us that when, in about 1940, he finally was able to see beyond the neo-realist view of metaphysical concepts as static abstractions, what especially persuaded him was Mou Tsung-san's insight that "it is as movement that the life of pure reason is increasingly realized."[145] Indeed, the leitmotiv of his thought in the next decade was *kan erh hou tung* (aware of an object, one moves in empathetic response). Conversely, in the exegesis of experience which emerged from this decade, the study discussed in chapter 2, the ideas of *chi-jan pu-tung* (total still-ness without movement) and *ching* (state of rest) play no role at all,[146] and neither does that of the phases. The idea of the phases, after all, is merely a construct referring to the transition from still-ness to movement. Without an emphasis on stillness, the distinction between the phases has no significance.

Neo-Confucians, however, while referring to the idea of *chiao-kan* (interchange of empathies), did not regard it as primordial. What was primordial for them was rather the transition from total stillness to the state of *chiao-kan*. That is, both poles, *chi-jan pu-tung* (total stillness without movement) and *kan erh sui t'ung* (aware of an object, one then pervades it through an empathetic response), were important to them. Even more, if either pole of this transition had primacy for Neo-Confucians, it was the pole of stillness, as illustrated by Wang Yang-ming's view that *shou-lien* (collecting one's spirit inward) has primacy over *fa-san* (issuing it forth).[147] As we will see when discussing Wang Yang-ming, the Neo-Confucian emphasis on this pole was connected to a metaphysical bias not shared by T'ang. Seeking not just moral purity but the power to transform the world, Neo-Confucians had to look for this power in the metaphysically "still" "source" of movement, since any power found in the experiential realm of movement was bound to be only partial and insufficient. Given their focus on this transition from stillness to movement, the distinction between the phases was nat-ural and indispensable for them.[148]

Events since the nineteenth century, however, have radically altered the Chinese view of transformative processes. The advent of new technological and political means rapidly promised transformation of the "outer" world (see chapter 5). As a result, no longer pressed to look for this transformative power in an "inner," transcendent realm, Chinese philosophers could abandon their quest for the metaphysical "source" of movement and so their preoccupation with the state of *chi-jan pu-tung*. This phase was no longer the key to cosmic potency, which now could be defined as a primordial, externalized dynamism. As Hao Chang has shown, just such a turn to the idea of cosmic dynamism marked the thought of K'ang Yu-wei, T'an Ssu-t'ung (1865–1898), and Liang Ch'i-ch'ao (1873–1929) in the 1890s.[149] By the 1930s, this idea of an externalized dynamism manifested in the physical world and in world history was widely accepted as fact. It was just in these years that T'ang also took this fact for granted as he went through an intensely creative struggle to articulate the "spirit" of Chinese culture in a way overcoming the skepticism of a largely scientistic audience and satisfying the ideological needs of a modernizing nation at war. Hence his determination to prove that Neo-Confucianism was not an untenable metaphysical system going beyond the truths of concrete experience. His philosophically systematic interpretation, however, does not do justice to his own historical account of the Neo-Confucian preoccupation with the ligature between concrete experience and the transcendent source of transformative power.

1. CHU HSI AND THE GIVEN PHASES OF THE MIND

As Ch'ien Mu's lavishly documented discussion shows, no issue in Chu Hsi's thought was more central and abstruse than that based on the distinction between imminent and accomplished issuance. Chu Hsi agonized for over a decade (roughly 1158–1169) over the problem in self-cultivation based on his perception of this distinction, and his solution of this problem was a decisive moment in his life comparable to Wang Yang-ming's moment of enlightenment in 1508.

The distinction between imminent and accomplished issuance was so important to him because it involved a problem that had to be solved before *chung* (inner equilibrium), an aspect of "sincerity," could be attained. The problem was how to "make the principle of *chung* manifest in outer actions," as Chu Hsi put it.[150] A particularly clear formulation of this dilemma is found in Chu Hsi's famous letter written in 1169 to "the gentlemen of Hunan" announcing his final solution of this problem: "Yet one cannot search for the feelings before they have issued forth, and once they have, there is no way to arrange them [so as to realize the equilibrium they had before they were issued]."[151] At the same time, to lose this equilibrium was to break up issuance as a unified process and so to break that contact with heaven always found in the beginning of every cycle of issuance. Therefore, realizing equilibrium in the phase of accomplished issuance was a way of restoring linkage, and the vocabulary of linkage permeates the Neo-Confucian discussion of the problem of issuance. For instance, Chu Hsi once remarked in the course of one of his earlier attempts to deal with this problem that with the solution he was then proposing, one "could just about be joined together with the whole substance of the great basis of things and the supreme *tao*, returning to the beginning."[152] Chang Nan-hsüan criticized one of the Chu's formulations on the grounds that with it, "one fell into the difficulty of regarding [imminent and accomplished issuance] as two things." Chu Hsi then proposed another formulation hopefully overcoming just this difficulty: "The feelings on issuing are just going, and when not yet issued, they are just coming. Thus there is no point of interruption, no gap, no cutting off. How can one point to anything else [outside this unity] and give it a separate name?"[153] As we will see, restoring the unity of issuance was exactly what Chu Hsi was seeking when he came to emphasize "reverence."

Ch'ien Mu has traced in great detail how Chu Hsi's thought about the problem of imminent and accomplished issuance went through three main periods. The first began in 1158, when he became Li T'ung's student. The second was the time during which his thinking moved toward that of the Hunan school, headed by Chang Nan-hsüan; the climax of this period was a visit of two months with Chang in Hunan during the fall of 1167. During this visit, Chu Hsi abandoned Li T'ung's view and adopted Chang's. The final period began in about 1169, when through a new effort to grasp Ch'eng I's position, Chu found enlightenment, brought Chang over to his new approach, and thereafter held to it with only minor adjustments. Ch'ien Mu vividly describes how the death of his teacher Li T'ung in 1163 filled Chu with anguish as he felt torn between the desire further to penetrate and vindicate Li's teachings and his growing affinity for Chang Nan-hsüan's opposite approach, which meshed with doubts he had had all along about Li's views. In an Eriksonian way, the anxieties of a maturing scholar interacted with the feelings of predicament necessarily accompanying this attempt to filter the traces of the transcendent out of the morally polluted concreteness of accomplished issuance. When Chu Hsi in 1169 felt he had solved this problem, he comforted himself with the thought that he had finally grasped the meaning of his dead teacher and had brought it into a deeper understanding to which Li T'ung also would have subscribed had he been alive.[154]

As Ch'ien Mu tells us, when coming to study with Li T'ung in 1158, Chu Hsi suspected that *chung* (inner equilibrium) had to be sought through moral effort in "daily affairs."[155] This view was supported by one of Ch'eng I's ideas, namely that the "mind" must be considered in terms of accomplished issuance.[156] If so, the "mind's" search for *chung* must be directed at the "daily activities" of accomplished issuance. Indeed even Li T'ung stressed such moral effort in daily activities.[157] Drawn to this view, however, Chu Hsi had difficulties from the start with Li T'ung's other idea, that one should "through quiet sitting without verbalized thoughts and through the purification of the mind try to see the material manifestations of delight and anger, grief and joy before they are issued."[158]

This method connoted the common idea of *shou-lien* (inwardly collecting one's spirit). In about 1166, Chu Hsi looked back on Li's teaching and described him as holding that one "should through transverbal comprehension grasp in his mind the reality found in the incipient motion between imminent and accomplished issuance." We have to remember that such an idea was more plausible to Confucians than to us because they so commonly thought of the knowing process as a way of somehow placing oneself within the thing known (*t'i*). Nevertheless, Chu Hsi added: "In the past, although I heard this, I was unable to fathom its meaning. Considering the matter today, I am for the first time beginning to realize that this doctrine absolutely has to be utterly right, but when all is said and done, one cannot in one leap arrive in this realm."[159]

This affinity for Li's position was expressed in about 1166, just one year before Chu Hsi visited Chang Nan-hsüan for two months in Hunan. Then, in 1167, after much discussion, Chu vacillated again, rejected Li's position, and embraced Chang's.[160] Largely received from Hu Wu-feng, Chang's doctrine was in the direction of Ch'eng I's notion that the mind is a matter of accomplished issuance. Chang, however, went further. He suggested that accomplished issuance is all that exists, that it is an indivisible process, and that in its very indivisibility it comprehends the equilibrium of imminent issuance. To apprehend equilibrium, therefore, was to revise and broaden our understanding of accomplished issuance, looking in it, so to speak, rather than behind it for *chung*. The advantage of this view was that by locating *chung* in a completely manifest form of experience, it not only directed moral effort toward the proper Confucian business of "daily affairs," rather than to the unworldly realm of Buddhism, but also raised hopes that *chung* could be more easily apprehended. The next year, in 1168, Chu Hsi wrote four famous letters to Chang Nan-hsüan describing his struggle to revise his understanding of accomplished issuance. The first letter, for instance, reads in part:

From the time one has life, one has some kind of knowledge. Affairs and things come into his life, and he responds to and is in contact with them without a moment's rest. His thoughts are changing continuously until he dies. Essentially this state of affairs does not come to a halt for even an instant. Thus it is for the whole world. Yet sages and superior men have spoken of what is called the equilibrium of imminent issuance and the state of total stillness without movement. How can we reasonably suppose that they regarded the concrete flow of daily affairs as accomplished issuance and a temporary interruption of this flow, some point lacking contact with affairs, as the time of imminent issuance? When I tried to think of it in this way, I only found moments without awareness, during which false and dark notions would clog up my mind, hardly the substance of pure consciousness responding to things. Moreover, as soon as I became conscious of any feeling just at that subtle moment of incipience, then this consciousness itself was just a recurrence of accomplished issuance, not what is referred to as total stillness. One may say that the more I sought it, the less I could see it. So I withdrew from this course and looked for it by examining daily affairs. I considered the fact that any case of becoming aware of an object and empathetically pervading it with one's response, that is, any instance of becoming conscious of something after coming into contact with it, can reasonably be regarded as an indivisible whole. In its inexhaustibility, the process of responding to things is the concrete possibility in terms of which the will of heaven is realized and things come into being without end. Even as things arise and are destroyed ten thousand times a day, the ultimate substance of total stillness is never anything but totally still. What is called imminent issuance is simply like this.

Chu Hsi goes on to say that since "the true essence of heavenly principle" is thus constantly manifest, the "student should thereupon apprehend it and hold onto and preserve it."[161] This notion of "first apprehend, then preserve and nourish" was a hallmark of Chang's Hunan school and also of Hu Wu-feng's approach.[162]

Chu Hsi in 1167 was convinced that Chang's path was the right one, but within two years he had changed his mind, "suddenly doubting [his] own understanding" while trying to explain his view to his student Ts'ai Chi-t'ung (1135–1198).[163] Clearly, he felt some guilt over rejecting his dead teacher's doctrine. He also felt that in concentrating on the search for "the incipiences of moral feeling" in the phase of accomplished issuance and giving up any attempt to grasp his feelings at their source, he was losing his spiritual strength. Describing his symptoms, he complained of "often feeling anxious and disturbed, lacking a kind of purity and oneness, a kind of deep, latent, inner wholeness, and in speech or actions, constantly hurried, responding without a sense of reserve, and lacking an easily poised, dignified manner with an aura of inner depth. One may say that just being off by a bit in one's views can lead to such harm. This is a matter one cannot but closely examine."[164] Feeling "as though tossed about on vast billows and great waves, unable to anchor oneself for an instant," he had lost that sense of fixity and mastery mentioned in section e. At one point, he had sought to capture Chang's idea of the indivisibility of the phases by suggesting we should think of them as one process of motion which first appears as a coming, then as a going. Now, around 1168, he repudiated this idea as "just putting one into a turmoil of hectic movement without any way of recovering one's balance."[165] Beset with doubt, he turned again to Ch'eng I's writings.

3. Sense of Predicament (1)

He "had not read more than a couple of lines when the ice broke up [and the truth became clear]."[166] The solution dawned on him as he considered Ch'eng I's view that "the effort to maintain reverence joins the states of movement and rest at their point of intersection" in the light of Ch'eng's seemingly contradictory remarks about imminent and accomplished issuance. Chu Hsi had wondered how Ch'eng could advocate "preserving and nourishing the feelings before they are issued" while also saying that "those who are good at observing them see [the incipiences of good moral feeling] after they have issued forth."[167] Chu Hsi now realized that both functions could be carried out only if one's mind were filled with "reverence," because "the moral effort which we carry out when thinking of the word 'reverence' pervades and joins together the states of rest and movement."[168] As Ch'ien Mu puts it, it was only when Chu Hsi arrived at this new understanding that "for the first time he was able jointly to attend to the two aspects of imminent and accomplished issuance in the mind."[169]

This emphasis on reverence, which became the hallmark of the Ch'eng-Chu school, was based, therefore, on the view that this state of mind had a special capacity to overcome the breach between imminent and accomplished issuance, and that this capacity stemmed from a transcendence of the distinction between rest and movement. Still more, in this transcendence, the state of reverence only accentuated the given constitution of the mind. That the mind similarly bridged the phases was a point which Chu Hsi found in Chang Tsai's writings and which he now used to complement and reinforce his notion of reverence. Chang Tsai had said that the mind "controls the heaven-conferred nature and the feelings." Writing in about 1181, Chu Hsi said: "One may look at the heaven-conferred nature as substance, the feelings, as function, while the mind is what passes through and joins both of them."[170] Similarly, in a letter to Chang Nan-hsüan written after finding his final answer to the problem of the phases, with which Chang agreed, Chu said that the nature of the mind remained the same irrespective of any oscillation between the states of rest and movement.[171]

The perception of accomplished issuance as the given field of moral effort, therefore, necessitated conceptualization of a transtemporal link as the only way to repair the breach between the transcendent force always in us and the ordinary flow of experience. Conversely, our dependence for linkage on such recondite ideas, difficult, as Chu Hsi himself admitted, to make clear in words, not to mention defend,[172] precisely signified the fragility of this linkage.

m. WANG YANG-MING AND THE GIVEN PHASES OF THE MIND

When one thinks of how Lu Chiu-yüan and Wang Yang-ming explicitly tried to reduce all philosophical problems to the simple task of spontaneously expressing one's humanity—"proudly be a man" was the way Lu put it[173]—it is difficult to see how something so far-fetched as this distinction between imminent and accomplished issuance was of any real importance to either of them. If we believe that their spirituality converged with modern humanistic perspectives, then this distinction could have been no more than a literary metaphor or an anachronistic residue of some older, mystically cryptic way of thinking. Moreover, Lu Chiu-yüan sought to persuade people not to think in terms of this distinction. He said that "in all that fills the mind and issues forth, nothing is not principle." Although Lu, like Wang, actually did not identify principle with everything in the mind, he felt that the presence of principle in the mind was so overflowing and accessible that one could not regard it as confined to the phase of imminent issuance, and so one should not focus on some problematic gap between accomplished and imminent issuance.[174]

Yet Lu's view was hardly a denial that the problem of morality was connected to the process of issuance. It rather was an attempt to solve this problem through more confidence in the overflowing presence of principle within the process of issuance, as T'ang Chün-i's interpretation of Lu's thought also suggests.[175] Still more clearly, in Wang Yang-ming's *Ch'uan-hsi-lu*, which was the "embodiment of Wang Yang-ming's philosophy . . . indisputably the most important Chinese philosophical classic since the early thirteenth century,"[176] self-realization appears as a particular kind of mental process which cannot be identified and described without using this distinction between the phases. Out of some seventeen passages in *Ch'uan-hsi-lu* using this distinction, there is only one with any hint that it might be misleading. But even here Wang explicitly noted that these two phases actually existed. His point was only that in the quest for inner oneness or linkage, one had to grasp the interpenetration of these phases, and this might be difficult when scholars "discussed them as separate."[177] That the phases were perceived by Wang as a real aspect of the mind can be shown in a variety of ways.

First of all, we should note that Wang was deeply attached to chapter 1 of the *Doctrine of the Mean*, the locus classicus of the phases (see section k). Many if not most of the references below from *Ch'uan-hsi-lu* are connected to this chapter. Apart from Wang's devotion to this ancient text, however, it is clear that Wang's use of the distinction between imminent and accomplished issuance formed a logically integrated concept without which his position could hardly have been verbalized. Visualizing issuance as the procedure whereby the transcendent was infused into ordinary emotions, he not only repeatedly conceptualized the transcendent as an issuable thing but also defined the transcendent virtues as qualities emerging in the course of issuance. Moreover, he sometimes used the concept of issuance when trying to make himself clear on basic questions, such as the investigation of things.

Wang emphatically shared the metaphysical bias of Neo-Confucianism and believed that to "be human" was to realize a transcendent quality. Sometimes calling this state *tao-hsin* (mind of the *tao*), he identified it as something "not mixed in with what is distinctively human." If one's mind was "correct," one's consciousness became one with this "mind of the *tao*."[178] Similarly, Wang spoke of aiming for a mind which "purely is heavenly principle,"[179] of "recovering the original condition,"[180] or of realizing "the ultimate good," which he identified as "the mind's ultimate substance."[181] In using such essentially interchangeable terms, Wang, as we shall see, was preoccupied with the task of elucidating the character of the purely metaphysical realm, quite apart from the question of linking this realm to the experiential one. For him, not only was this realm unadulterated by "what is distinctively human" and beyond what can be "seen" and "heard," it was also explicitly beyond any spatio-temporal distinctions and even beyond the distinction between good and evil (see section u below). Therefore to call it "transcendent" is unquestionably correct.

Admittedly, in Neo-Confucianism the transcendent could be regarded as either a cosmos existing largely outside me or an indivisible cosmic consciousness of which my mind was a part. The latter was Wang's position. Certainly he emphasized that the transcendent had to be regarded as an aspect of human experience. One of his most vigorous remarks to this effect was that "happenings are the *tao*, the *tao* is happenings."[182] As we shall see in section r, Wang's basic position on linkage was to try to dissolve any discrepancy between the potential good and actuality. Thus boldly claiming that "the mind is principle,"[183] that "the mind is the *tao*,"[184] and that the average person actually is a sage,[185] Wang insisted that moral effort is "easy,"[186] and that people therefore should follow their impulses with more "self-confidence."[187]

Nevertheless, whatever the complexities in Wang's view of the transcendent, he had in mind a quality of existence so elusive that the average person, as he said, had "lost" it. As discussed in section r, he was fully aware of the prevalence of evil and repeatedly referred to it. His insistence on referring to a transcendent state as one's emotional goal reflected his totalistic view of morality as something completely incompatible with any trace of selfish desire.

Having recognized Wang's need to define morality as a transcendent or highly elusive state, we must now note his equally basic insistence that this state had fully to permeate our actual emotions: "Except for human feelings and the changing affairs of human life, there are no happenings. Are not delight, anger, grief, and joy human feelings? So far as the changing affairs of human life go, I just mean everything from seeing, hearing, speaking, and acting to the questions of wealth, high station, poverty, low station, misfortune, calamity, and crises of life and death. These changing affairs also are just a matter of human feelings. The important thing in this regard is just to realize *chung* (inner equilibrium) and *ho* (harmony in one's actions)."[188]

If, however, one were to exhort people to bring a transcendent feeling into their ordinary emotions, one needed to visualize and verbalize the procedure through which this could be done. For Wang, as for other Neo-Confucians, no concept of such a procedure was available except for the interrelated ideas of "issuing," "moving," and "responding," although there were a few supplementary terms like *piao* (outwardly manifested), which could be used to

describe the transcendent in its experientially realized form. Apart
from the examples below, the reality for Wang of this process of
"issuing" is nicely illustrated by his view that "Generally in the
case of spirit, virtue, words, and actions, the important thing is
shou-lien (drawing one's spirit inward); the *fa-san* (issuing forth)
of it is just done as something which cannot be avoided. This is so
in the case of heaven, earth, man, and things."[189]

Given this process of issuing, the transcendent was repeatedly
referred to by Wang as something available to be issued. Thus if
one understood the "mind's ultimate substance," one understood
wei-fa-chih chung (the inner equilibrium of imminent issuance).[190]
Knowledge of "heavenly principle" was similarly identified with
grasping *wei-fa-chih chung*.[191] The latter phrase was repeatedly
used by Wang in similar contexts.[192] Wang's living concern with
understanding the transcendent as something poised on the verge
of being "issued" is also demonstrated by the fact that he not only
took seriously but also agreed with Ch'eng I's and Li T'ung's famous
views on how to apprehend the feelings in the phase of imminent
issuance, arguing that these two views converged.[193]

While the transcendent thus had the potentiality of being issued, just how it appeared in the process of issuance and movement
was a central question. A good example is the following exchange
between Wang and Lu Yüan-ching. The thrust of some of Lu's
questions in a letter to Wang was to raise doubts about the possibility of conceptualizing linkage between the mind's phases by pos-
tulating an interpenetration transcending any temporal sequence.
Lu suggested, first of all, that the idea of a transtemporal interpenetration of movement and rest could not be valid if movement were
identified with selfish material desire, and the state of rest with
"principle." After all, selfish desire and principle were mutually
exclusive. Wang agreed with this, not even bothering to answer
the point directly.

Lu then went on to ask whether the state of rest could be identified with the mind's "point of total stillness and absence of sensation of outer objects" as well as the condition of "no involvement
in daily affairs," while movement could then be equated with "being
aware of an outer object and, responding to it, empathetically pervading it" together with the condition of "involvement in daily

affairs." Wang agreed they could. If so, Lu said, movement and rest would be two distinct states, and the idea of their interpenetration again would not make sense.

Wang's answer to this was to defend the notion of interpenetration by pointing to another concept, *liang-chih* (spontaneous moral knowledge), as an aspect of the mind which, unlike the dichotomies above, was indeed beyond any distinction between movement and rest. Wang's point was that while "spontaneous moral knowledge" was the "mind's ultimate substance," the latter in turn was outside the contradiction between movement and rest because it was "the moment between the states of movement and rest."

While Chu Hsi, therefore, had emphasized reverence as the mental state with a transtemporal dimension bridging the phases, Wang Yang-ming brought the notion of spontaneous moral knowledge into the spotlight by ascribing the same capability to it.[194] This important point of convergence between the two philosophers was complemented by their agreement that "the ultimate substance of the mind" also had this transtemporal dimension, and by the fact that Wang still partly accepted Chu Hsi's view of reverence. Referring to the connected ideas of being "cautious" and "fearful," which came from the *Doctrine of the Mean*, T'ang Chün-i notes: ". . . although Wang in discussing 'being cautious and fearful' had doubts about Chu Hsi's view on this, Chu Hsi actually did not differ greatly from Wang in regarding the state of 'being cautious and fearful' as pervading imminent and accomplished issuance."[195]

Lu then went on to suggest that if the phase of imminent issuance were "prior" to that of accomplished issuance, "there would have to be pauses in the realization of ultimate sincerity." Since "sincerity" was definitely something achieved in one's outward actions, that is, in the phase of accomplished issuance, one would have to abandon it momentarily whenever realizing the "prior" state of "the inner equilibrium of imminent issuance." Wang completely agreed with this reasoning. Since it was absurd to posit a desirable interruption of sincerity, imminent issuance could not be "prior" to accomplished issuance.

Lu, however, raised a more serious difficulty in locating the phase of imminent issuance. If imminent issuance did not exist "prior" to accomplished issuance, did it then exist "in the phase of accomplished issuance, controlling it"? Wang agreed it did. In that case, Lu said, it was not clear to him how the distinction between imminent and accomplished issuance was related to that between rest and movement: "Are imminent issuance and accomplished issuance both mainly a matter of rest? Or is imminent issuance rest while accomplished issuance is movement? Or are they both without either movement or rest? Or do they both involve both movement and rest?"

Wang had two answers to this problem. First, although agreeing with it, Wang did not regard the theory that imminent issuance was "in" the phase of accomplished issuance as his main way of relating these two phases. He preferred another alternative also mentioned by Lu, namely that the relation between accomplished issuance and imminent issuance as the ultimate substance of the mind was the transtemporal, trans-spatial one of "an indivisible whole without any before or after, inner or outer." This again converged with Chu Hsi's position, as discussed above. From this standpoint, the relation of imminent issuance to the distinction between rest and motion was no problem. Imminent issuance was simply identified with the transtemporal "ultimate substance of the mind," which, as we have seen, was "the moment between the states of rest and movement." Consequently, Lu's attempt to correlate imminent issuance with either movement or rest instead of to this "moment" was wrong.

Wang, however, also tried to show that imminent issuance was "in" the phase of accomplished issuance. He defended this idea by noting that it did not mean that "in the phase of accomplished issuance there is still another phase of imminent issuance [besides the original phase of imminent issuance with which this particular issuance cycle began]." Trying to pin down this almost incomprehensible point, which perhaps was persuasive just on account of its almost unfathomable subtlety (*wei*), Wang again fell back onto the prominent Neo-Confucian claim that the distinction between movement and rest could not be applied to this matter.[196]

The very shakiness of Wang's abstruse argument, similar to that of his assertion that a "thing" is "that to which an intention pertains," was complemented by the crude, commonsense vigor of Lu's objections. This in itself is a significant historical fact showing that Wang's views about linkage within the mind, like Chu Hsi's, were indeed "claims," not "perceptions." Certainly the convoluted subtlety of Wang's thought was hard for many scholars to reconcile with the straightforward manner displayed by Confucius in the *Lun-yü* and made Wang vulnerable to the charge of engaging in *k'ung-t'an* (empty talk) and leaning toward Buddhism, which indeed was leveled against him by the seventeenth century.

Our main point here, however, has been to show that for Wang, self-realization was a matter not only of realizing a transcendent quality but also of showing specifically how this realization could occur in a mind continuously going through the phases of imminent and accomplished issuance, or, more precisely, the five phases noted above. Just because the moral self was perceived as something realized through these phases, to understand the eight Mencian moral impulses and virtues listed above (benevolence, righteousness, and so on) was to know at what point they emerged in the course of these phases. Without this perception, the following interchange would make no sense: "Lu Yüan-ching asked: 'Do [the four virtues of Mencius,] benevolence, righteousness, propriety, and moral understanding, get their names from the fact that they refer to qualities found in the phase of accomplished issuance?' Wang Yang-ming said, 'Yes.'"[197] Similarly, the importance of these phases as a basic reality was reflected in the tendency to use them as points of reference when explaining the differences between various kinds of moral effort: "The cultivation of one's person is more on the side of accomplished issuance; the rectification of the mind is more on the side of imminent issuance."[198] Wang also referred to the phases to clarify his favorite theory regarding the investigation of things. Rejecting the idea that such investigation should begin with cognitive inquiries into objective matters, he explained: "A person must just realize the ultimate substance of his own mind. If he does so, then concrete implementation [the correlate of substance] will be found right in the midst of this. If he nourishes this substance so that he really has the inner equilibrium of imminent issuance, then naturally he will have the harmony in action that goes with hitting the golden mean after the feelings have issued forth."[199]

Finally, unless we understand Wang as dealing with the perceived reality of these phases, it is impossible to make sense of Huang Tsung-hsi's account of the development of Wang's thought in three stages, which allegedly occurred after Wang in 1508 finally left behind the temptations of Buddhism and Taoism. Huang was probably the greatest expert on Ming thought writing in the seventeenth century.

In the first stage, roughly 1508–1517, Wang saw moral development as a sequence and put priority on nourishing the mind in the phase of imminent issuance. He regarded outward action as the subsequent part of this sequence: "He regarded quiet sitting without verbalized thoughts and purification of the mind as the goal of study. Only after one had attained the inner equilibrium of imminent issuance could there be the harmony in actions that goes with hitting the golden mean after the feelings have issued forth. In general, whether in seeing, hearing, speaking, or acting, the main thing was to draw in and collect one's spirit, while issuing it forth was just something to be done as unavoidable."

In the second stage (roughly 1517–1522), Wang had overcome this sequential approach, seizing on Mencius' concept of *liang-chih* (spontaneous moral knowledge) as a dimension of the mind equally present in all phases, and perceiving a transtemporal unity dissolving these phases and so making all aspects of moral activity interchangeable. Huang Tsung-hsi paraphrased him as follows:

> After his time in Kiangsi, he exclusively emphasized the five words "fully realize spontaneous moral knowledge." Attaining the unverbalized comprehension of ultimate reality did not depend on quiet sitting. Realizing the ultimate substance of the mind did not await a special program of mental purification. One should not look to special training or reflection. Heavenly standards, rather, were to be found directly in one's everyday actions. Clearly, spontaneous moral knowledge is the inner equilibrium of imminent issuance. There is no imminent issuance as something else prior to this knowledge. Spontaneous moral knowledge is also the harmony in actions which goes with hitting the golden mean. Accomplished issuance is not something else existing besides this knowledge. With this knowledge, one naturally gathers inward one's spirit. There is no need to make a separate effort to do this. With this knowledge, one naturally issues forth one's spirit in action. Action is not something done after getting this knowledge. Gathering one's spirit inward is just the substance aspect of the process of sensing an outer object and responding to it. It is a case of movement in the state of rest. Issuing forth one's spirit is just the function aspect of the state of total stillness. It is a case of rest amidst movement.

3. Sense of Predicament (m)

Certainly this passage expresses a sense of oneness dissolving any distinctions between the phases of the naturally given mind. Such oneness was exactly the goal of all Neo-Confucians, including Chu Hsi—what I have referred to as linkage. My point here, of course, is not that Wang perceived these phases as simply a fact to be experienced. On the contrary, he experienced them as a problem which was part of the given world. One had to find both a concept and a way of acting in terms of which accomplished issuance would no longer exist as a distinct state pulling one away from the inner equilibrium unchangingly present in the phase of imminent issuance. Exactly because it could fill this function, the recondite concept of a transtemporal dimension realized through *liang-chih* (spontaneous moral knowledge) was crucial for Wang. Had the problem of self-realization not appeared to Wang and his audience as a question of conceptualizing a transcendent unity threatened by the cycles of issuance, his emphasis on *liang-chih* would not have caused the excitement it did. Wang could hardly have aroused any interest by just agreeing with Mencius that we all should put to use a conscience received from heaven.

In his third and final stage (roughly 1522–1529), Wang, according to Huang, spoke and acted simply out of a fully spontaneous oneness with his "original mind" and apparently at that point had no more need to refer to any theoretical explanations.[200] Such oneness, one might argue, precluded any concern with the inherited discussion regarding the phases of the mind. Yet his concern with oneness or linkage was still explicitly dominant and connoted the disruptive tendency he had overcome. Apart from awareness of this disruptive tendency, what meaning could the image of Wang as a spiritual hero have had for his audience? I do not believe that any historical experience of spiritual poise can be understood apart from the dissonances filtered out to achieve this poise, in this case, the perceived tendency of the mind to follow a cycle of issuance often leading to selfish desire. Nor can it be understood without taking into account the religious belief facilitating spiritual poise, in this case, the belief that the divine can be fully concretized because it is something inherently available to be "issued."

In any case, whatever the nature of Wang's final beatific state, the distinction between imminent and accomplished issuance

remained a basic Neo-Confucian topic. Thus it continued to verbalize the feeling that although the divine could permeate the mind,
that part of the mind most commonly accessible to us was prone to
pull us away from the divine.

n. THE GIVEN FORCE OF EVIL

This pull was powerful. We have just noted that in the eyes of both
Chu Hsi and Wang Yang-ming, it was so powerful that we could
regain the "lost" ground of imminent issuance only with the help
of metaphysical acrobatics contradicting our commonsense understanding of temporal sequence. Indeed, the tension between "good"
and "bad" was central to Neo-Confucianism, a point misunderstood
by Max Weber and often overlooked by scholars focused on the
theme of "harmony."

For many Neo-Confucians, the martial terminology of conten-
tion was basic in this regard. Sometimes describing this tension as
a struggle between *li* (principle) and *ch'i* (ether of materialization),
Chu Hsi suggested that the former was "weak," the latter "strong."
Chang Tsai saw it as a struggle between *te* (virtue) and *ch'i*, raising
the question of which was *sheng* (victorious over) the other. Chu
Hsi similarly said of *ch'i* and *te-hsing* (the virtuous, heaven-conferred nature) that "each can either be victorious over or defeated
by the other."[201] Looking at this struggle from another angle, Chu
Hsi said: "All there is in the case of a person is *t'ien-li* (heavenly
principle) and *jen-yü* (human material desire). If this one is victorious, that one withdraws. If that one is victorious, this one withdraws. In this process there is no possibility of circumventing this
principle of advance and withdrawal."[202] Chu Hsi also worried that
"what heaven has decreed" so often led to evil (see section p), and,
like Wang Yang-ming, he saw history as dominated by the tendency
for "human material desires" to "flow forth unchecked every which
way." As discussed in section r, Wang Yang-ming also emphasized
the existence of evil, and he frequently referred to the unqualified
contradiction between heavenly principle and material desire:
"Heavenly principle and human material desire cannot coexist."[203]
Nothing was more basic for Wang than the idea that "If you expel
human material desire, you will recognize heavenly principle."[204]
Unlike Wang, Lu Chiu-yüan felt that if one thus contrasted heavenly

principle and material desire, one would lapse into the mistake of regarding principle as separate from the mind. However, Lu did not object to the condemnation of "material desires," only to the idea that "man is material desire" in contrast to the purity of heaven.[205] His view of the self as dangerously poised between "good" and "evil" was as emphatic as anyone's, and he once said that the central issue in history was whether *li* (true principle) controlled *shih* (the powerful force of circumstances) or vice versa.[206]

Above all, this perception of rampant evil informs much if not all of the Ming and Ch'ing historical and bureaucratic writing, insofar as this writer has studied it. Nor should we in this context overlook the typically Manichaean quality of modern Chinese political perceptions, whether Marxist, liberal, or conservative. Praising Chinese and Indian philosophy for avoiding the more abstract concerns typical of Western thought, T'ang Chün-i has written that from the standpoint of the former, "what is important for man is eliminating troubles, moral pollution, all evils, not abstractly inquiring into their origins."[207] Thus even for T'ang, the need to define human existence as a struggle against evil supersedes the suspicion that such a definition may moralistically distort realities. In the thought of Yin Hai-kuang, an outstanding liberal philosopher with an excellent grasp of American social science, one finds exactly the same Manichaean sense of "struggle" against evil (see chapter 5, section p). The case of Maoism is too obvious for comment. Without doubt, this modern Manichaeanism was rooted in traditional perceptions.

True, the "flow" of evil, however pervasive, was not inexorable. The possibility of suddenly dissipating it was tantalizingly real. In a way puzzling to us Westerners, Neo-Confucians stressed the power of evil while still in an almost contradictory way regarding evil as something inherently prone to dissipate. Though sometimes regarded as excessive by Confucians, Mencius' often euphorically optimistic faith in the possibility of making the actual world totally good never died out. If the world was a fabric stained by evil, this fabric was eminently washable. One could indeed "wash away the moral filth of heaven and earth" (*hsi-ti ch'ien-k'un*). Yet at the same time the recurring failures to do so proved that the force of evil, whether or not inexorable, was immense.

3. Sense of Predicament (n)

What, according to Neo-Confucians, accounted for this tendency toward evil? Certainly, given the metaphysical bias noted above, it is clear that Neo-Confucians associated evil largely with the experiential realm. Yet Westerners are generally accustomed to philosophical traditions blaming the existence of evil on the radical separation of concrete experience from a transcendent, metaphysical realm embodying the absolute good. If on the contrary the absolute good is physically immanent in the concrete self, how can evil arise in the latter? Yet it did indeed "flow forth." One might then reason either that Neo-Confucians did not hold to a position of immanence or that the fact that they did so was somehow irrelevant to their concept of evil. A closer look, however, leads to a different conclusion.

On the one hand, whatever their preferred formula of linkage between the metaphysical and the experiential realms, Neo-Confucians did most definitely hold to what we would regard as a position of immanence. Thinkers like Wang Yang-ming, whether taking the concrete flow of consciousness (*hsin*) or the ether of materialization as ultimate reality, were emphatic about the immanence of the metaphysical in the experiential and ascribed to Chu Hsi a false dualism. So did those who, like Liu Tsung-chou, Huang Tsung-hsi, Wang Fu-chih (1619–1692), Yen Yüan (1635–1704), and Tai Chen (1723–1777), regarded metaphysical reality (*tao*) and concrete things (*ch'i*) as inseparable.[208] Yet even Chu Hsi said that "True principle is not a distinct thing; it inheres in the ether of materialization." He held that both evil and the absolute good were found in both the metaphysical and the experiential realms. The *chi* (incipient, almost imperceptible phase) in the motion of heavenly feeling existed in the experiential realm, and, conversely, the *chi* of evil existed in the metaphysical.[209] Therefore, contrary to Fung Yu-lan, I would say that in the Confucian framework it was impossible to equate the fundamental distinction between "good" and "bad" with that between the metaphysical and the experiential realms, arguing, say, that *pen-t'i* (ultimate substance) is "good," while *fa-yung* (issuance in experience) is "bad."[210] Indeed it was exactly this immanence of the ultimate good in the experiential realm which accounted for both the potentially enormous power of goodness in the actual world and, conversely, the peculiar dissolubility of evil.

On the other hand, there are degrees of immanence. Indeed, had Neo-Confucians believed in total immanence, their very concept of evil would have been impossible. On the contrary, they held to an idea of incomplete or even elusive immanence, which is only another way of saying that the conceptualization and full realization of linkage was an acute problem for them. More specifically, Neo-Confucians blamed the existence of evil on three factors: the individual's bad choice freely arrived at; the universal weakness of the human will; and an inherently degenerative force immanent in the very flow of existence and constantly threatening to "overcome" (*sheng*) the self. Because of these basic perceptions, more specific theories about the genesis of evil were by no means central to the *Problematik* of Neo-Confucianism.

Most important, it was a cosmic shortcoming, not human action, which was responsible for the miserably weak condition of those much-vaunted moral feelings, the constant welling up of which excited so much admiration. They were nothing but *tuan-ni* (incipiences) or *chi* (incipient, almost imperceptible phases in the motion) of concrete feelings. After all, even Neo-Confucians like Lu Chiu-yüan and Wang Yang-ming, who liked to think of the overflowing presence of "principle" in the mind, could not take exception to the *Shu-ching's* statement that "The mind of the *tao* is almost imperceptible in its subtlety."[211] Conversely, there was nothing "incipient" about the experiential flow of selfish desires, which, exactly opposite to moral feeling, were incipient only on the metaphysical level. This issue of relative power was analyzed by Chu Hsi, who said that on the metaphysical level, "it is very easy for heavenly principle to be victorious over human material desires," while on the experiential level, "it is on the contrary very easy for human material desires to be victorious over heavenly principle."[212]

What accounted for the elusiveness of the good cosmic force? The famous Neo-Confucian phrase *pien-hua ch'i-chih* (morally transform one's material substance) suggests that evil was inherent in the ether of materialization, and Chu Hsi could refer to a "bad [portion of the] ether of materialization." But had they pressed this argument, Neo-Confucians would have been forced back into a Buddhist-like view of the "mind" and the "feelings" as evil "dregs" (*cha-tzu*), since the mind and the feelings were regarded as aspects of the ether of materialization. As Mencians believing in the trans-natural power of the mind, they had to find another view. Their answer was a formula ascribing the origin of evil to the combination of certain circumstances which of themselves were either moral or amoral. This approach reflected their "radical" concept of evil as something generated by given circumstances antecedent to partic-ular human efforts and yet allowed them to feel part of a good cosmic force.

Connected to the problem of linkage, a lack of fit between the metaphysical and experiential realms, aggravated by the frictions of movement and certain amoral deficiencies in the ether of materi-alization, was what Chu Hsi pointed to as the source of evil and selfishness. He suggested: "One may say that heavenly principle essentially lacks selfish human desires, and that these are produced as a result of the discrepancies involved in the concrete realization of heavenly principle as it flows forth."[213] Similarly, the ether of materialization was that on which principle was "put down." When not "put down just right, selfish material desires appear." Pre-sumably the fact that much *ch'i* was inherently "muddy," "uneven," and "not of good quality" made it difficult for principles to be "put down just right."[214] Moreover, although the idea of *tung* (movement) did not per se connote evil, Chu Hsi was uneasy about concrete movement. He said: "How can yin, yang, and the five elements ever be morally incorrect? It is only when there is the rushing to and fro of things that impropriety arises."[215]

When linked to the basic image of water, the susceptibility of movement to disorder was still plainer: "The mind can be compared to water. Water of itself is still and clear but with unceasing wind and waves, it really becomes shaken and full of movement. Only after the wind and waves stop can the mind in its essence once more be at rest."[216] The idea of water moving also connoted a quality of slipperiness contributing to the elusiveness of those incipient feelings in which "heavenly principle" was reflected. Chu Hsi used the slippery beads of mercury in an illuminating simile: "One must first see a heavenly principle in front of one and then act accordingly. This is just the point where difficulties arise. If one does not succeed in putting down this heavenly principle, it's like having an empty thing. One tries over here to put it down, but there's no way to do it. One tries over there, but there's also no way to do it. One tries over here, but perhaps it will fall and break. One tries over there, and again it could well fall and break. If one speaks of this heavenly principle in a vague, wavering way, it is like a piece of mercury which one cannot pick up as it rolls back and forth."[217]

Similarly, the feelings and thoughts one had to "control" (*chih*) seemed inherently prone to resist control: "Someone asked Chu Hsi: 'When trying to make my mind pure and still, I often am disturbed by the way my thoughts go.' Chu Hsi answered: 'This is just because you fail to concentrate on perceiving the oneness of things. The human mind always has this difficulty.' ... Someone asked: 'There are false thoughts and correct ones. Obviously false and vulgar thoughts are not too difficult to control. But I just do not know how to control those many petty thoughts the meaning of which is hard to determine.' "[218] Such uncertainty about how to "control" oneself naturally led to "fears and anxieties."

Finally, we should note that at least to some extent the existence of evil was seen as willed by the cosmos. As Ch'ien Mu puts it, "But the fact that true principle must be attached to the ether of materialization and that this ether with which everything is endowed is necessarily incapable of being even, this is a matter of what heaven has decreed."[219] Just because evil was ultimately a product of the cosmic will, which was viewed as just outside the limits of the cognitively fathomable, Chu Hsi could feel comfortable with the fact that he could explain its existence only with awkward suggestions. That he thus ascribed to evil an ultimately transcendent basis again shows that, contrary to Weber, he had a "radical" concept of evil as something necessarily erupting out of the cosmos into human experience.

o. THE INTERVENING HUMAN WILL AS A GIVEN

However the matter was phrased, and there was no completely lucid way of putting it, no one could assert that for "feeling" to turn into "selfish desire," a great and painful effort was required. It rather was terribly easy and indeed completely natural, despite any ontological priority ascribed to the "incipiences" of moral feeling.

113

3. Sense of Predicament (o)

Indeed, despite their agreement with Mencius that man could tap the powerful sources of heavenly goodness, many Neo-Confucians has a perception of the flow of feeling which Mencius lacked, since they emphasized its almost irrepressible tendency toward evil. While Mencius had said that "man's nature is naturally good just as water naturally flows downward," Chu Hsi used the image of flowing water to describe the power of evil desires: "Material desires are like a stream of flowing water overflowing its banks." He also used the image of *po-t'ao* (stormy waves) to describe chaotic feelings.[220] Chu Hsi was aware that his view of human nature was darker than Mencius'. According to him, Mencius had failed to take into account the evil effects of man's material constitution, his *ch'i-ping* (that portion of the ether of materialization with which each thing is endowed) (see section p).[221] Probably Chu Hsi's emphasis on the fragility of the mind as an instrument of moral effort, which Lu Chiu-yüan and, to a lesser extent, Wang Yang-ming struggled against, reflects the influence of Buddhism.[222] In any case, given the power of selfish desires, it was plain that without some intervening force applied with difficulty and pain, the flow of feeling could not hit the "golden mean."

This intervening will was perceived by Neo-Confucians as largely different from the spontaneous process of issuance. Regarding this will as a part of the "mind," Neo-Confucians never systematically analyzed it, probably because such an analysis, though psychologically interesting to us, would not have struck them as relevant to the pursuit of their goal. As a result, some modern scholars have neglected this pervasive volitional aspect of Neo-Confucian thought.

Two common dichotomies illustrate the difference between what we call the naturally given phases and the intervening will. The distinction between *pen-t'i* (ultimate substance) and *fa-yung* (issuance in experience) connoted the naturally given phases, while that between *pen-t'i* and *kung-fu* (efficacious moral efforts) connoted the intervening will. Put together, these two distinctions form a triangular model which nicely sums up the Neo-Confucian concept of the mind.

We have seen that the naturally given mind consisted of "feelings" which constantly "issued forth" passing through five phases.

Something in the mind, however, was perceived as controlling the feelings, directing them toward either one of the two forms of accomplished issuance, the golden mean or selfish desire. Thus Chu Hsi liked Chang Tsai's formula that "the mind controls [that process of issuance involving man's] heaven-conferred nature and his feelings."[223] Similarly, Wang Yang-ming saw in the mind a capacity for acting on the flow of feeling: "When a good thought arises, recognize it and make it pervade the mind. When a bad thought arises, recognize it and stop it. It is the mind's ability to decide on its goal, a heavenly intelligence, which enables one to know thoughts and stop them or make them fill the mind."[224]

This capacity for "control" can be broken down into roughly four mental characteristics which were repeatedly referred to. First, there was a cognitive and expressive capacity, by which I mean something partly resembling what Munro calls an "evaluating mind."[225] The mind had the capacity to "think" and to turn its thoughts into words communicated to others. The ability to "speak" was crucial especially for Chu Hsi. He frequently made his points by referring to the way one may or may not "speak" of something: "However, to be clear, one cannot but speak of [*ch'i* and *t'ai-chi*] as separate things." Ch'eng I, Chu Hsi said, had "discussed" *li* and *hsing* in an unprecedented way. If one "speaks of this heavenly principle in a vague, wavering way," one cannot understand it, and one's moral cultivation will at the least be impeded. Above all, "Heaven and earth are unable to speak. They ask the sage to appear and speak on their behalf."[226] It was only by "speaking" that the intellectual could clarify the patterns of linkage in the universe. This explicit glorification of speech seems absent in Wang Yangming, but the emphasis on cognitive and verbal clarity was central for Wang as well (see sections a and d).

Besides this cognitive and expressive function, the "mind" also had the power of volition. Although the word "free" did not exist, the idea of free will was entirely plain and heavily emphasized. There could be no moral efforts unless one were *k'en* (willing) to exert them. Therefore Chu Hsi said that "the capacity to choose a goal is the deep part of the mind," enabling a person "not to go down another road but rather go down this road."[227] The basic term here was *li-chih* (determine one's goal). If "sin" was not used in this context, *tsui* (crime, guilt, state of deserving punishment) was: "If one does something bad, one's given constitution is not guilty. It is simply a case of the person himself wanting to do something bad."[228] Wang Yang-ming also said that "establishing one's goal" was important and that one had to "be willing" (*k'en*) to pursue one's goal.[229]

To choose one's goal was to choose to *cho-li* (exert oneself) in pursuit of it: "[Other problems can be solved,] but if one's goal is not established, then there just is no way to exert oneself."[230] Perhaps because of his desire to make moral effort seem "easy," Wang did not use *li* (effort) as much as Chu Hsi. Nevertheless, Wang could not avoid this concept, which had been basic since *Lun-yü*. He said that to grasp the distinction between "heavenly principle and selfish desire" in all its "subtlety," one "must constantly exert oneself (*yung-li*) to examine oneself, overcome egotism, and master one's feelings; only then can one gradually gain some moral understanding."[231] He also said: "If now one wants to rectify the mind, at what point in the ultimate substance does one make a moral effort (*kung*)? It must be at the point where the mind is in movement that one exerts oneself (*cho-li*). When in movement, the mind cannot be free of what is not good. Therefore it is just at this point that one must exert oneself."[232] Wang similarly pointed to the "painfulness" involved in "holding fast to one's goal."[233] We should also remember that this same *li* (effort) was a central value in the Ming-Ch'ing bureaucracy, the documents of which frequently referred to officials who "did not exert themselves" (*pu-li*), or who "vigorously exerted themselves in the performance of their duties" (*ch'u-li*).[234]

In Neo-Confucian minds, "effort" was a perceived reality which, for all of its importance, was taken for granted and was not regarded as a category requiring analysis. Similarly, modern scholars have taken great pains to figure out what Neo-Confucians meant by "mind," "feelings," "establishing one's goal," "the heaven-conferred nature," and so on, but they have never singled out "effort" as a category. Yet since "effort" was an idea central to the Neo-Confucian picture of how the mind worked, we have to see how this idea was related to the other ideas making up this picture.

Since "feelings" were spontaneous, "effort" was not the same as "feelings," whether the feelings spontaneously emerging from the phase of imminent issuance or the feelings of accomplished issuance turning into selfish desires. (It was more involved in those feelings moving successfully toward the golden mean.) Nor, obviously, was "effort" perceived as identical with the mind's first phase of total stillness or with the act of volition (*li-chih*) itself. As an aspect of the Neo-Confucian picture of the mind, therefore, "effort" was *sui generis*. Like the rest of the mind, it was a form of the ether of materialization, but if it was a sort of material force able to shape the flow of "feeling," what energy was available in the mind beyond the "incipiences" of moral feeling which "issued forth" and the "material desires" which "flowed every which way"?

Only one answer is available, and it is a significant one from the psychological point of view: fear. Fear was an emotion which was frequently referred to, easily perceptible, conveniently available in almost limitless supply, and different equally from selfish desire and the "incipiences." Although listed in the *Li-chi* as one of "the seven feelings," it was excluded from the Neo-Confucians' standard list of the four feelings, since, like "material desire," another on the list of seven, it could not be easily regarded as part of the emotional basis of Mencius' four incipiences.[235] Yet it played a pivotal role. It was readily available in the phase of accomplished issuance as those *k'ung-chü yu-lü* (fears and anxieties) which one sought to overcome, but it also was integral to the process of exerting effort.

Our clue is the martial terminology associated by Chu Hsi with the idea of *li-chih* (determining one's goal). Some of the words used have been basic also in the contemporary jargon of "struggle," words like *fen* (aroused with a fiery enthusiasm) and *fen* (simmering anger). Study was a matter of *fa-fen* (to feel fiercely aroused). One had to be like "soldiers in battle formation. As soon as the sound of the drum being struck is heard, they know that if they don't kill the bandits, they will be killed by them. How can they still not advance?" One thus had to act with a "goal determined on in a courageous and fiercely aroused way, fearful of doing anything shameful." Chu Hsi used a phrase from the *Shih-ching* to describe the behavior of the "true gentleman": "Proceeding with a sense of fearful caution, like one at the edge of a deep abyss, like one treading on thin ice."[236] Similarly, in a passage basic to both Chu Hsi's and Wang Yangming's concept of *kung-fu* (efficacious moral effort), the *Doctrine of the Mean* emphasized the need to be "cautious" and "fearful" in order to apprehend the *tao*. Closely connected was the emphasis on *ching* (reverence). Going back especially to Ch'eng I, *ching* was a kind of preparatory virtue, a way of getting spiritually set to pursue moral cultivation. Emphasizing *ching* and the need to avoid "being muddled and lazy," Chu Hsi spoke of "constantly using that mental riding whip [on oneself]."[237] Alluding to *ching*, Wang Yang-ming said: "If one uninterruptedly strives to be cautious and fearful, then one's contact with heavenly principle will be constantly preserved . . . and the ultimate substance of the mind, intelligent awareness in its pure, naturally given form . . . will not be lost amidst fears and anxieties."[238] Chu Hsi similarly mentioned "fearing that selfish intentions may find an opportunity to arise."[239] Finally, the "totalism" discussed in section c was inseparable from this fear: just because one was ever fearful of moral failure, one never dropped one's guard.

Considering the pervasive theme of totalism, the pivotal role of fear, and the frequently used image of flowing water, one dimly perceives a single gestalt made up of mutually reinforcing mental elements. While the image of flowing water conveyed the idea of a total, uninterrupted continuum reflecting the universe as constantly regenerating itself (*sheng-sheng pu-i*), so the idea of "stormy waves" fearfully brought to mind the danger of drowning, and the constant fear of drowning in turn implied the idea of a constant, uninterrupted flow of efforts to save oneself. Somehow the interplay of these three themes generated euphoria as well as a sense of dread. On the one hand one's own moral efforts could not but be fear-ridden and ineffective so long as they turned on nothing but one's own lonely *li* (effort). On the other hand, at some point, like a floundering swimmer finding a *cho-shou-ch'u* (a point at which one can get a hold), one received support from that good cosmic force constantly if faintly welling up in one.

The vital need to establish this juncture between the good, powerful cosmic force and the floundering self's intervening will is reflected in Chu Hsi's view that the decision to pursue morality (*li-chih*) tends to be meaningless unless one decides to try to tap this ultimate cosmic force, that is, to become a sage: "Unless one has the idea that one must necessarily reach the level of the sage or superior person, one's moral efforts will just be a worthless repetition of study routines inherited from the past."[240] But by tapping it, one obtained the *ta-li-liang* (great power) of the sage, which enabled one to "do" whatever "heaven and earth failed to do."[241] Chu Hsi was well aware that the unique power ascribed to man appeared incongruous: "Man together with heaven and earth forms a trinity. A person ought to ask himself: 'Heaven being so high, the earth being so thick, how can my little body, seven lengths of blood and breath, form a trinity with them?'" The answer was that only man had the capacity to effect the moral juncture described above. Because of this capacity, Chu Hsi was moved to say: "Man is the mind of heaven and earth. When man is not present, there is no one to control heaven and earth."[242]

This idea of establishing a juncture between the intervening will and an ever-beneficent cosmic force reminds us that the Neo-Confucian concept of the mind cannot be interpreted in purely humanistic, not to mention naturalistic, terms. While the external cosmos was seen as tending organically to unite ultimate being and experienced events, the mind had a diffuse, transnatural power to bring this tendency to full realization. That is, the ethical activity of the individual could cause vast changes in the social and physical world. Whether or not the idea of this transnatural power was taken literally by all Neo-Confucians, they at least emphasized the pathos of this power, and so clung to the terminology which allowed them to visualize and symbolize it.

This point should be carefully considered, especially because it seems to be one on which Neo-Confucianism differed from the main thrust of Chou Confucianism. Since H. G. Creel, scholars have adduced evidence supporting the view that Confucius, Mencius, and Hsün-tzu analyzed the moral life in humanistic or pragmatic terms. Even in *Mencius*, it is possible to interpret the assertions about the vast and speedy social effects of personal morality as a kind of practical optimism about the tendency of people to admire morality and to rally to a benevolent leader. Although Mencius saw morality as a process of recovering one's true being, which in turn was rooted in the ultimate nature of the cosmos ("heaven"), and although this recovery for him involved an emotional sense of power, it is hard to argue that this power was viewed by him as having transnatural effects. Similarly, *Hsün-tzu* is often viewed as offering a humanistic or naturalistic analysis of the mind, although I would argue that Hsün-tzu did partly define the mind in transnatural terms.[243] Since the empire had not yet been unified, it was possible for Chou thinkers like Mencius to have such euphoric hopes about the benefits which would naturally and practically flow from unification that ascribing any transnatural powers to the unifying king would have been superfluous.

A more distinct idea of transnatural power can be seen in the *Doctrine of the Mean*, a classic written perhaps in the second century B.C. Chapter 22 states: "Only those in the world who have reached the extreme of sincerity can exhaustively realize their heaven-conferred natures. If one can exhaustively realize his heaven-conferred nature, then he can exhaustively realize that of other people. If he can exhaustively realize that of other people, then he can exhaustively realize that of things. If he can exhaustively realize that of things, he can assist in the transforming and nourishing processes of heaven and earth. If he can do the latter, then he forms a trinity with heaven and earth." The greatest Han Confucian, Tung Chung-shu, who lived in this century, certainly emphasized transnatural processes, especially the causative relation between the king's virtue and the play of yin and yang in the physical world. This theory meshed with popular beliefs. Even in Ch'ing times, many educated persons believed that the failure of a provincial governor to practice benevolence or excessive harshness in the administration of criminal justice could cause a drought (see chapter 4, section e).

So far as I know, Neo-Confucians did not challenge this heritage of Han organismic theory about the causative interaction of cosmic and ethical processes. They did differ from Tung Chung-shu, however, in that gradually, by the twelfth century, they lost his faith in "the king" as the central figure in this moral-cosmic drama. Yet in turning to *wu-hsin* (the mind of the self) as the prime agent of transformation, they were by no means willing to abandon that capacity for manipulating cosmic forces which Tung Chung-shu had ascribed to the emperor. As a result, they had to suggest how such a transnatural capability, which the awesome "son of heaven" might plausibly claim to have, could be found in the mind.

3. Sense of Predicament (o)

It was the need to solve this problem which was partly responsible for the persistent Neo-Confucian tendency to mix the terminology of ethics with certain ideas particularly hard for modern
minds to digest: the emphasis on consciousness as indivisible
throughout the cosmos and as alive with a semi-magical force (*shen*,
ling) (see section d); the pervasive assumption that all events, including my thoughts, consist of the interplay of yin and yang and of
ceaseless oscillation between the states of rest and movement, thus
ever returning to this indivisible point of consciousness; and the
idea that this state of rest, "total stillness," and "imminent issuance" is integral to the outcome of the moral struggle, that is,
ch'eng (sincerity) and *jen* (benevolence). These ideas made it
possible for Chu Hsi to assert that the "manifest efficacy" of an
individual's moral effort was so great that if one could achieve
moral perfection, the entire material cosmos would also be perfect
(see section r). Possibly this idea was not always taken literally, and
Chu Hsi was not saying that one should directly strive for the
attainment of *kung-li* (political achievements and material benefits). He was, however, expressing the crucial Neo-Confucian
feeling that through moral effort one could hope to obtain the
sage's vast, materially transformative power, as described in the
Doctrine of the Mean. The pathos of this power therefore was
integral to the Neo-Confucian's sense of identity and process of
self-realization.

Two complementary critiques also suggest that Neo-Confucians
perceived a transnatural power within the mind. First, the idea of
access through the mind to the power of heaven was precisely what
Neo-Confucians said they missed in Buddhist discussions of the
mind, just as they said they missed the idea of an organic connection
between ordinary experience and ultimate being (see section f).
Thus T'ang Chün-i points out that the founding fathers of Neo-
Confucianism (Chou Tun-i, Chang Tsai, and Shao Yung) all believed
that "we Confucians base ourselves on heaven," while "the Buddha
based himself on the mind."[244] In other words, the Buddha failed to
see that through the mind he could draw on the power of heaven.
Similarly, Chu Hsi said: "I regard mind and principle as one. The
Buddha regarded them as two." That is, the Buddha failed to see

that despite its fragility, the mind incorporated access to the metaphysical foundation of the cosmos. Actually, it seems clear that this Neo-Confucian critique of Buddhism was as accurate as such a cross-cultural comparison can be.[245]

Conversely, it was precisely this idea of the sage's transnatural power over the concrete world which Fung Yu-lan identified as the major fallacy of Neo-Confucian philosophy. Developing a neo-realist position that metaphysical concepts like *li* (principle) or *ch'i* (ether of materialization) are purely "formal" or "logical," Fung held that metaphysics could "cause people to grasp the highest realm" but in no way "increased knowledge of or the capacity to affect the actual world." Fung went on: "The mistake made by most Chinese philosophers in the past was not that they developed a form of learning without concrete substance but that they were not themselves aware, or did not make clear that their learning was without concrete substance. They tended to hold that the sage, solely relying on his being a sage, had the greatest possible knowledge of the actual world and the capacity to control the actual world. Even if some of them did not make this mistake, the words with which they described the sage could cause others to make it."

It is true, as Fung notes, that there were doubts about the existence or scope of this transnatural power, and Fung feels that Wang Yang-ming partly, but only partly, avoided this fallacious concept of the sage.[246] The scope of these doubts, however, is a difficult issue. As mentioned in sections g and v, Wang Yang-ming in an ambiguous way participated in a tendency to deemphasize the goal of total control over the polity and the cosmos and to focus on personal ethics. Yet self-realization for him still could not be conceptualized apart from the process of becoming one with an indivisible cosmic mind in terms of which any distinction between evil actualities and the potential good was dissolved (see section r). With his metaphysical bias, furthermore, Wang emphasized not only the need to realize one's authentic existence but also the identity of this "ultimate substance of the mind" with the ultimate reality of the cosmos as a whole. This identity was a point he came back to again and again (see section u). Nor should we overlook the fact that for Wang, this ultimate reality also explicitly included the

outer cosmos as organically shaped by the forces of yin and yang.[247]
If we suppose that Wang Yang-ming was primarily interested in the
existential quest for authenticity and did not seek to fill himself
with an indivisible cosmic force which as a "lord" pervaded and
controlled all things, we refuse to take him at his word.

The intervening will was thus characterized by not only a
volitional capacity but also a cognitive and expressive capacity, the
use of fear to generate moral energy, and the transnatural ability to
tap the beneficent, transcendent cosmic force impinging on the
naturally given mind and organically shaping the world outside.
Finally, the various activities generically regarded as *kung-fu*
(efficacious moral efforts) can best be seen as aspects of this intervening will. They certainly differed from the naturally given
phases, and all were ways by means of which one acted on both the
"inner" process of issuance and the "outer" world in order to hit
the golden mean after one had chosen to do so.

The three ways of doing this were spiritual nurture, cognitive
study, and practice. It is significant that although teaching, writing,
and the propagation of the true doctrine were regarded as needed
activities, they were not central to *kung-fu*. The problem of creativity is complex, but in terms of its explicit program, Neo-Confucianism did not call for a creative will bringing new ideas into the
world. Confucius' rule of *shu erh pu tso* (transmit the past, not
create) pervasively held, and Wang Yang-ming, like Mencius, had
to apologize for his extraordinary ability to articulate the truth.[248]
It was especially this downgrading of *explicitly* creative activities
along with the emphasis on spiritual nurture which distinguished
the Neo-Confucian tradition of education and moral training from
that familiar to us in America today.

A prime characteristic of spiritual nurture was the totalism
discussed in section c. One totalistically engaged in two kinds of
mental effort: a repressive, expulsive, and destructive effort (*k'o-
chi, ch'ü jen-yü, p'o*), and a positive effort to seek out, see, preserve,
inwardly collect, nourish, fill up, and pile up (*ch'iu, ch'a, ts'un,
shou-lien, yang, ch'ung, chi*). The latter is particularly hard for us to
understand. What did one "expand to the point it filled everything"
(*ch'ung*)? The answer was obvious only to a Neo-Confucian, who
took for granted that "heavenly principle" existed in his mind as

an expandable physical presence vibrant in his living "ether of materialization," an "inner equilibrium" available to be "issued." One "filled" one's mind with what was about to "issue forth," just as Mencius' *hao-jan-chih ch'i* (vast, overflowing inner vital force) "filled up heaven and earth." Simultaneously the repressive or destructive aspect of spiritual nurture also hinged on this perception of a heavenly presence, which would "expand" of itself as the selfish desires *pi* (covering over and hiding) it were *p'o* (smashed).

Since this endeavor to "preserve heavenly principle" was an attempt to achieve *wei-fa-chih chung* (the inner equilibrium of imminent issuance), spiritual nurture merged with recondite reflections about how it might be feasible to apprehend feelings in their phase of imminent issuance despite the fact that feelings were easily visible only in their phase of accomplished issuance. These frustratingly subtle reflections about the feasibility of apprehending "inner equilibrium," as discussed in sections l and m, were part of the quest for linkage, and they sometimes led to the idea that this apprehension would be a kind of seeing with the mind's inner eye. Thus connoting the pursuit of such an elusive vision, the distinction between imminent and accomplished issuance was particularly useful in reminding students that the goal of spiritual nurture was a quality of sincerity so excruciatingly rarefied and transcendent as to be almost unattainable. Seeking this vision by simultaneously "nourishing" the inner presence of "heaven," intellectually grasping the transtemporal conditions of linkage, and "expelling selfish desires," Neo-Confucians often felt that periods of quiet meditation carried out in a sitting position would help them.[249] Indeed, the very absence of physical movement and involvement in affairs was often associated with metaphysical "stillness," even though both Chu Hsi and Wang Yang-ming tended to reject this association. It was only because heaven was thus perceived as a living force within the mind that these routines of "quiet sitting" made sense. The facts of spiritual nurture corroborate T'ang Chün-i's view that Neo-Confucianism was based partly on a culturally peculiar religious belief in the nearness of the divine to the human (see chapter 2).

One further aspect of spiritual nurture is suggested by Wang's idea of "self-confidence." The volitional aspect of the mind involved the freedom to find the proper mix of reverence and temerity with which one would "seek" the "heavenly principle" within the mind. Thus Ku Hsien-ch'eng (1550–1612) criticized the school of Wang for "lack of inhibition" and that of Chu Hsi for "excessive self-restraint."[250]

The terms used to denote this process of spiritual nurture included *hsing-ch'a* (examine one's flow of feeling), *ts'un-yang* or *han-yang* (preserve or envelop and nourish one's heaven-conferred nature), *chin-hsin* (exhaustively realize the ultimate substance of the mind), *chih-hsing* (know one's heaven-conferred nature), *chü-ching* (dwell in the spirit of reverence), *tsun te-hsing* (reverently realize one's virtuous nature), and *ch'eng-i* (make intentions sincere).

While spiritual nurture was largely a matter of expanding and expelling, cognitive study was a matter of extending the pure awareness mentioned above (*hsü-ling ming-chüeh*) (see section d). Since this pure awareness necessarily coincided with one's *chi-ch'u* (point of utter stillness) and so with "heavenly principle," or better, "the mind of heaven," cognitive study had to coincide with spiritual nurture, not just for Wang Yang-ming. Thus *ch'iung-li* (exhaustively know principles) connoted both cognitive study and spiritual nurture.

Cognitive study, however, was largely directed at the objects in one's life. Even for Wang Yang-ming, it was a way of relating to *wu* (things). Even if the "outer" was redefined as something "inner," what *appeared* as the "outer" had to be dealt with as an object of moral action. The "outer" remained there, whether as an objectively existing "thing" or "that to which an intention pertains" (Wang's formulation). Through cognitive study, one wanted to understand the function of a thing and the principle which one should follow in acting with reference to it, but a broader, totalistic kind of knowledge also was desired, as discussed in section d. As for "practice," this simply meant putting into effect one's knowledge and realizing one's intentions (*li-hsing*).

One could thus employ a variety of tactics in exercising one's will and trying to realize the goal of Neo-Confucians, but this process was endangered because the mind, for all its godlike potentiality, was inherently fragile and vulnerable. Above all, its functioning was a spasmodic, pain-ridden, contingent process in comparison to the two great, immanent forces of morality and chaos, which constantly flowed of themselves without any conscious or painful effort. The "mind" was inherently subject to *ping-t'ung* (harmful shortcomings), and it existed in "a state of danger," as the *Shu-ching* put it. It was compared to "water" easily churned by "wind and waves."[251] In its cognitive capacity, whereby all the principles of the cosmos could be "set forth" (*chü, pei*) in it, the mind was compared to a "mirror" which "can reflect things as they come," but this very simile suggested the passive vulnerability of the mind to any and all troubling outer stimuli, a thing perfectly designed to be victimized by *shih-shih wu-wu* (affairs and things) and their unremitting onslaught. This aspect of passive vulnerability was in turn connected to the fundamental paradigm of mental action as expressed in the formula *kan-wu erh hou tung* (to be stirred by things and then move).[252] Moreover, the mind was viewed as inherently susceptible to unconscious bias, "frequently without knowing it lapsing into the selfishness of material desires by inclining toward that which one one-sidedly favors."[253]

It is important to remember that Confucians did not ascribe misunderstanding only to selfishness. They saw a persistent tendency toward muddled thinking, to be taken in by "empty talk," a shortage of that intellectual capacity needed to trace out the complexities and subtleties of linkage. As Mencius had pointed out, it was unfortunately necessary to "argue" for the truth because there was no other way to "correct the minds of people," who otherwise would believe "false doctrines." Hsün-tzu also was intensely concerned with how to "dispel the darkness of misunderstanding." For both Mencius and Hsün-tzu, the only way to overcome "false doctrines" was intellectual propaganda; without it, no amount of economic or environmental improvement could make society moral. For all their "anti-intellectualism," no one was more exasperated by the prevalence of false ideas than Lu Chiu-yüan and Wang Yang-ming. This intellectual sluggishness aggravated various basic conditions viewed as impeding communication of the *tao*. It was just because of all these vulnerabilities that the mind was dependent on some outer source of moral power (see chapter 5, section e).

3. Sense of Predicament (p)

All in all, the Neo-Confucian perception of the "mind" cannot but be described as complex, profound, culturally peculiar, and pregnant with psychological implications, but we need to view it as a whole rather than isolating a few aspects, such as the capacity for evaluation or for realizing oneness with heaven. As I have argued in sections k, l, m, n, and o, Neo-Confucians perceived the mind as consisting not only of a phasic flow of feeling dimly stemming from a good cosmic force and gravitating toward a bad one but also of an intervening will, which they saw as a vulnerable, fragile organ with a variety of capacities, namely, a volitional capacity, a cognitive and expressive capacity, a capacity to use fear to generate "effort," and a capacity to draw on the good cosmic force by directing this effort into the processes of spiritual nurture, cognitive study, and practical action.

p. THE COSMOS AS A GIVEN WILL

Still another aspect of the functioning of the mind has to be considered, however. Did not the concept of *ming* or *t'ien-ming* (what heaven has decreed) suggest that the human will was not only vulnerable but also impotent if not even dominated by forces external to it and robbing it of its very capacity for self-determination? Burdened with "what heaven has decreed," did it really have the potentiality to intervene effectively in the struggle between "good" and "bad" and thus to determine which would be "victorious" and so "to control heaven and earth"? It did indeed, or at least it did to a crucial extent, but not without confronting a force often pitted against it and thus aggravating the predicament stemming from its own deficiencies. Again following Ch'ien Mu's discussion of Chu Hsi's views, we can here make clear the basic points involved in this very difficult issue. Wang Yang-ming, ever intent on nourishing our "self-confidence," barely discussed the question of "what heaven has decreed," at least not in *Ch'uan-hsi-lu*. However, his few comments on this question show that his perception of *t'ien-ming* was similar to Chu Hsi's.[254]

The Neo-Confucian category of *ming* has proved the hardest to fit into my analysis. Not even explicitly mentioned in much of the Neo-Confucian writing about central cosmological and ethical questions, it is also largely passed over in modern Chinese interpretations of the Neo-Confucian "spirit." One is almost tempted to compare it to a stranger who has stumbled into a gathering where he really has no functional role to play. Yet this category was involved with virtually every facet of the Neo-Confucian *Problematik*, as is clear from the particular analysis of this *Problematik* developed in this study. First, it was involved in both the goal and the perceived given situation of Neo-Confucians; realization of the goal meant obeying "what heaven has decreed." Second, when we sliced up this given situation into a good and a bad cosmic force, we similarly found that the idea of *ming* pertained to both forces, giving to the cosmic flow of goodness the aura of a moral imperative and at least partly serving as the ultimate source of evil. Finally, in now looking at the Neo-Confucian conceptualization of the process deciding the contest between good and evil, we again encounter *t'ien-ming*, this time as the one deciding factor competing in a complex and unclear way with the human will. As we now examine this contest, we should keep in mind that for Neo-Confucians the concept of *ming* was as peculiarly abstruse as that of the intervening human will, its existential antipode. To list the various objects in the universe and to expatiate on their modes of possible integration was a relatively feasible task, however tricky, but to elucidate the nature of those forces with the purpose and the power to bring about or disrupt this integration was somehow to try to peep behind the ontological scenery, to try to see what was going on backstage behind the existential drama. At this point, only dark hints were available: "In considering things and affairs, one must trace them back to that source from which they have come; there we find what heaven has decreed."[255]

Somewhat more specifically, to the extent that the metaphysical and experiential character of a specific "thing" and the particular course of events associated with it were given to it rather than brought about by it, that thing was encountering "that which heaven has given. . . . that which comes to be without anyone bringing it about." With its aura of authoritativeness, this given was compared to an imperial order, and Chu Hsi analytically broke it down into a number of dimensions. He himself usually posed the problem by distinguishing between two dimensions, seeking to

align the issue of *ming* with the distinction between the metaphysical and the experiential realms (*li* and *ch'i*). That which each
particular thing "received" as its "endowment" (*ping*) from each
of these two realms constituted its *ming*, for Chu Hsi. However,
the experiential dimension itself involved a further basic, though
blurred, distinction. Yet whether we view them as three or two,
all these dimensions were regarded by Chu Hsi as ultimately one,
as "what heaven has conferred."[256]

The first dimension consisted of the external circumstances of
life: the individual's economic position, social status, and longevity.
Viewed cumulatively, such individual circumstances made up the
trends of an historical period and thus involved the particular place
occupied by a ruling house on its dynastic cycle. These external
circumstances were regarded as resulting from the particular portion of *ch'i* (ether of materialization) with which a thing had "been
endowed." For instance, the unfortunate fact that so many evil
rulers had failed to die young was due to their having "wholly
obtained that kind of *ch'i* resulting in long life." What particular
portion of the ether of materialization was "bestowed" on an individual thing was determined "accidentally," without any "intention"
on the part of heaven, and without any "ordered sequence," except
for a vaguely conceptualized pattern perhaps similar to our "wheel
of fortune." Chu Hsi spoke of a *ting-shu* (fixed point in a sequence
made up of a given number of phases) involved in the way that one's
endowment of *ch'i* determined the critical external circumstances
of one's life: "Of course heaven and earth don't say 'I want in
particular to produce a sage or superior man'! The production of a
sage or superior man is based just on the fact that in the given
number of phases through which the ether of materialization passes,
a particular phase is reached (*ch'i-shu*), and all the required elements
just happen to converge. So when the sage is born, it's only as
though heaven did it intentionally." It was in this sense that Chu
Hsi referred to one's fate as *ch'ien-ting* (predetermined).[257]

These external circumstances, Chu Hsi like to say, constituted
ming "from the standpoint of that which one happens to encounter,"
as distinguished "from the standpoint of that with which one is
endowed." Actually, as just indicated, this distinction was blurred,
since one's "endowment" determined what one "encountered."

3. Sense of Predicament (p)

Nevertheless, Chu Hsi did repeatedly distinguish between external circumstances and one's internally endowed capacity to "respond" to them, that is, one's native intelligence and moral bent. This internal capacity was what he had in mind when he referred more narrowly to one's *ch'i-ping* (particular portion of the ether of materialization which a thing has received). This involved the famous question of the "clearness" or "muddiness" of one's *ch'i-ping*.

This given internal capacity or talent can be regarded as our second dimension of *ming*. If the first dimension already suggests a fatalistic outlook, the second does so even more. Pushed to its logical extreme, Chu Hsi's theory held not only that external questions like one's station in life were decided by a cosmic force rather than by one's own strivings but also that this cosmic force determined the quality of one's internal response to these external events. At least to us, this view seems to negate the rationale of *kung-fu* (efficacious moral effort). Said Chu Hsi: "Whether there is or is not an adequate response to that which is encountered in all cases stems from the way one's portion of the ether of materialization differs from those of other persons in terms of thickness or thinness, clearness or muddiness." Whether or not one managed to fulfill one's moral obligations was a matter of one's heaven-decreed "endowment," Chu Hsi reasoned, omitting in this immediate context any reference to *kung-fu*.[258]

Before weighing the psychological force of this fatalistic or deterministic concept, however, we must consider a third dimension of "what heaven has given." While the first two dimensions were associated entirely or largely with "the ether of materialization," this third dimension was purely metaphysical in character. It "comes out of true principle," and it is "that true principle with which a thing is endowed." That is, it was identical with man's moral norms viewed as imperatives, not just standards to be followed if one so wished. *Ming-chih-cheng* or *cheng-ming* (one's true fate) was Chu Hsi's characterization of this dimension. *Ming* in this sense was not something predetermining one's external situation and the scope of one's moral efforts but something one "reached" through moral efforts, that is, by "exhaustively understanding true principle and realizing one's heaven-conferred nature."[259]

But how was this dimension of *ming* reconciled with the idea that the character of one's experience, morally and materially, was determined not by one's striving to "reach" something but by the nature of one's "given" constitution? The answer is that, at least with Chu Hsi, Confucians were easily satisfied with an imprecisely formulated concept of mixed causation. Although external circumstances like longevity were repeatedly regarded as determined by "heaven," Chu Hsi could still quote Chang Tsai's view that even this question of longevity might be affected by human efforts.[260] Chu Hsi even said that one should try to "not accept" tendencies stemming from one's *ch'i-ping*.[261] When Yao decided to transmit his throne to Shun rather than to his "bad" son, a situation that "originally was bad in its meaning was turned by him into something good." Thus a sage could "assist in heaven's and earth's processes of change and growth" (a phrase from the *Chung-yung* which Chu Hsi used in this context).[262] Chu Hsi gave another example of mixed causation: "With regard to someone who gets killed in the course of acting unethically, this certainly involves action of his own choosing, but it is also predetermined. One may reasonably say that in the bad ether of materialization with which he was endowed there was that which brought about this outcome."[263] Given such openings for the role of choice, Chu Hsi could elsewhere leap to the conclusion that "whether or not I incur guilt is purely up to me."[264] Most important, just who had "bad *ch'i*" was uncertain. I have seen no evidence that the typical Confucian suffered from the suspicion that his own *ch'i-ping* was "bad" to the extent that a Calvinist suffered from the fear that his predetermined fate was damnation. "Bad *ch'i*" precluding moral cultivation was something to be perceived in others, particularly uneducated people and criminals. "My" possibilities were summed up by Mencius' view that "the sage and I are of one kind," a statement which filled Chu Hsi as a youth with "joy."[265]

Since one could, therefore, exercise his will to pursue virtue, it was one's duty to do so. In doing so, one "obediently followed" what Chu Hsi called *cheng-ming* (one's true fate), i.e. *ming* in our third sense. Conversely, one should "not accept" what Chu Hsi called the "morally misleading" aspects of *ming*, those first two dimensions above in terms of which one's external experience and internal capacities were determined by heaven. At the very least, one "should not inquire into what is decreed," that is, one should not adduce these two dimensions as an excuse to evade one's moral obligations.

Yet at the same time, there was a moment when moral striving coincided with "obeying heaven" by "accepting" these very tendencies or events stemming from one's "endowment" of *ch'i*. It was here that our three dimensions of *ming* logically and emotionally merged into one. In those situations where moral action and painful consequences came inextricably together, one still acted morally, thus simultaneously exercising one's will and accepting one's painful fate: "One merely looks to see what righteousness requires; if it calls for death, then one must die." Fate here was accepted not as an excuse to avoid moral exertion but as the painful price of moral exertion. In the pathos of this moment, moreover, even the idea of a painful price was not truly relevant, because any conflict between what one desired and what was necessary was dissolved. This pathos, often associated with the heroic Tung-lin scholars of late Ming times, was fully captured by Chu Hsi: "The sage does not think in terms of enduring some unavoidable evil." Only in this moment did one *chih-ming* (know what has been decreed) in all its fullness and apparent contradictions. This fatalism of the moral hero was worlds away from the fatalism of the moral failure, which Chu Hsi disgustedly referred to as an "immoral, lax outlook, what is called obeying heaven and following what is decreed."[266]

We have already noted how this moment of moral heroism coincided with the goal of realizing oneness with heaven and a sense of control over events. The connotations here of social superiority should also not be overlooked. One who failed to cultivate himself morally and was "unable to become learned" would be entirely subject to the tendencies of his natural "endowment" (i.e. the first two dimensions of *ming*) and could only "obey heaven," but one who "strengthened himself" (*tzu-ch'iang*) with "learning" and moral cultivation would find that "heaven's decree is up to me" and could even "establish heaven's decree."[267] This point illustrates how the elitist feeling of scholars that they could shape a malleable cosmos contrasted with the feeling of subjection to unmalleable cosmic forces, which at least Chu Hsi ascribed to the masses, and which indeed does seem to have been an aspect of the peasants' worldview, as suggested by the well-known peasant saying *k'ao-t'ien ch'ih-fan* (depend on heaven for one's livelihood).

What we have called the distinction between the fatalism of the moral hero and the fatalism of the moral failure was a major issue for Chu Hsi, and this fact has important cultural implications. It shows that the Confucian psychology of moral effort did in fact have to compete with a fatalistic outlook, and the force of this fatalism should not be underrated. Any reader of Ch'ing bureaucratic documents constantly encounters complaints about laxness, about officials who "deal with things in a lax, superficial way" (*hsü-ying ku-shih*), "regard official orders as mere pieces of paper" (*shih-wei chü-wen*), and "merely follow accepted ways, excessively tolerant of bad behavior" (*yin-hsün ku-hsi*). It is highly significant that in the bureaucratic rhetoric of at least the Ch'ing period, this stress on acting in an energetic, thorough way was as prominent as that on eliminating "selfish" interests. Similarly, in modern times Hu Shih inveighed against Mr. More-or-less, a type of person who never tried to do anything thoroughly and accurately. Both a behavioral trend and a central ethical issue, such laxness was explicitly connected by Chu Hsi to fatalistic beliefs. He referred to officials who felt "it is not necessary to want to emulate Yao, Shun, and the Three Dynasties," and to scholars who felt that "in cultivating one's character, it is not necessary to reach the level of Confucius and Mencius." Such people held that "if one just does ten or twenty percent of something, that's also satisfactory." It was just this kind of attitude which Chu Hsi referred to as an "immoral, lax outlook, what is called 'obeying heaven and following what is decreed.' " Moreover, even if it outraged Confucians, this outlook could perhaps be legitimated in Taoist or Buddhist terms. Such legitimation must have intensified its behavioral influence.

Yet it is another thing to say that this "lax, immoral outlook" dominated the behavioral situation and so nullified the Confucian stress on will and sense of moral tension. Why should we give it greater behavioral weight than the Confucian denunciations of it and the numberless pages of Confucian writing about *kung-fu*? That it never became an intellectually respectable, legitimated outlook within the Confucian arena of discussion, which was culturally central, certainly limited its behavioral force. If a Confucian sought to enjoy elitist feelings of spiritual and social superiority, he could not consciously embrace this fatalism of the moral failure. Neither could the example of Confucius be persuasively associated with such fatalism. The habitual association of the idea of *ming* with that of *hsing* (heaven-conferred nature), illustrated by the very common term *hsing-ming*, indicates that it was difficult if not impossible to disassociate the connotations of "what is decreed" from the imperatives of moral striving. Indeed in at least some of its most ancient connotations, *ming* seems to have had exactly this moral meaning.[268] The idea of *ming* never became one shunned and feared by Confucians as undermining the spirit of moral engagement, as did a number of other concepts, such as Hsün-tzu's idea that one's given "nature" is "bad," views of the "heaven-conferred nature" which seemed "empty," or those late Ming T'ai-chou views claiming that the goodness of one's given nature extended even into the realm of material desires (*yü*). On the contrary, even those seventeenth-century scholars emphatically focused on the need for *kung-fu* naturally used the idea of *ming* to reinforce this emphasis of theirs.[269]

Yet although the idea of *t'ien-ming* thus validated the importance of the intervening human will, it also underlined the predicament within which this will found itself. Since it limited the human capacity to decide the contest between good and evil, Chu Hsi's statement that "man" can "control heaven and earth" was at best an oversimplification, an enthusiastic utterance ignoring the power of "heaven." Heaven existed not only as a source of moral power, an imperative to use this power, and an object to be controlled through the use of this power, it also could thwart the use of whatever moral power the self was able to muster. Locked into this unending encounter with something unpredictably elastic and awesomely immense, the self oscillated erratically between the status of a victim and that of a demigod. The self had immense capabilities, but they could be exercised only in a slippery cosmic arena.

q. CHU HSI AND WANG YANG-MING

The problem faced by Neo-Confucians, therefore, was how to devise some combination of spiritual nurture, cognitive understanding, and practice through which they could tap a beneficent but elusively transcendent cosmic force and realize their immense goal of world harmony, while contending with their own weaknesses, the evils of society, and a cosmic will often undercutting their own endeavors. Merely summing up this situation which they perceived as a given fact suggests that they had managed to define life as an agonizing predicament with virtually no route of escape. Their sense of predicament becomes clearer still, however, if we look at the positions they advanced to solve their problem and notice the difficulties which these positions entailed in their own minds. In arguing that they had a sense of predicament, my main piece of evidence is the distinction in their own minds between what was obviously real and what was much more open to doubt. Their goal, the need to pursue it, and the forces blocking this pursuit were real; the efficacy of the solutions they proposed to each other was open to grave doubt. Consequently their goal necessarily appeared to them as unrealized, and their struggle to realize it had a Sisyphean quality.

Although Marxists like Hou Wai-lu hold that intellectual divergences in late imperial China were due to either the "factional character" of the academic establishment or to class interests,[270] these divergences themselves have to be understood more fully before their various nuances can be related to the shifting mosaic of societal trends, which also are still far from clear. Certainly sincere intellectual disagreements were bound to arise as Neo-Confucians tried to figure out how to solve the virtually insoluble problem they had generated for themselves. The two main approaches—those of Ch'eng-Chu and Lu-Wang—had overlapping roots in the same intellectual matrix of the eleventh and twelfth centuries. Ch'eng Hao, Ch'eng I, Hsieh Shang-ts'ai, Yang Kuei-shan, and Hu Wu-feng all had views reflected in the seminal thought of both Chu Hsi and Lu Chiu-yüan.[271]

Ch'ien Mu has shown that the Ch'eng-Chu and Lu-Wang schools cannot be adequately distinguished in Fung Yu-lan's way as, respectively, the "school of principle" and "the school of mind"; both were very concerned with both concepts.[272] Both Fung and T'ang Chün-i have noted that another distinction also is misleading, the idea, namely, that Ch'eng-Chu put "the pursuit of inquiry and learning" first, while Lu-Wang put "reverently realizing the virtuous nature" first. Fung and T'ang both note that Ch'eng-Chu, not only Lu-Wang, emphasized "reverently realizing the virtuous nature," that is, spiritual nurture. T'ang adds that they differed over how to carry out spiritual nurture.[273] A similarly useful point, made by Fung Yu-lan and developed by Yü Ying-shih, is that Ch'eng-Chu emphasized the pursuit of learning (cognitive study) much more than Lu-Wang.[274]

Yet one wonders whether either one of these approaches comprehensively sorts out all the major differences involved or makes clear which differences were seminal, which, derivative. I would suggest that both these issues—the character of spiritual nurture and the place of cognitive study—can be clarified by putting them within the context of an overarching problem, that of realizing the goal of linkage.

r. CHU'S AND WANG'S CLAIMS ABOUT THE
RELATION OF THE METAPHYSICAL
TO THE EXPERIENTIAL

In elucidating the patterns of linkage, Chu Hsi and Wang Yang-ming began with different assertions about the primordial relation between the metaphysical and experiential levels. As Ch'ien Mu has emphasized, Chu Hsi believed that there was a clear contrast between these two levels. One could not slur over the *Classic of Changes'* distinction between "what is above experiential forms" and "experiential forms."[275]

Wang Yang-ming, on the other hand, sought to ignore this distinction, and, so far as I recall, it is not even mentioned in *Ch'uan-hsi-lu*. In this, Wang followed a tendency traced by Fung Yu-lan to Ch'eng Hao.[276] Although never failing to admit that we are confronted by these two modalities, Wang nevertheless struggled to reduce them to a passing distinction, sometimes evoking the image of a single, multifaceted entity. For instance, he held that "*li* (principle) is the order in the ether of materialization, while the ether of materialization is principle actively realized."[277]

Overriding this distinction from the *Classic of Changes*, according to Wang, was an indivisible cosmic consciousness. True, the indivisibility of "pure consciousness" (*hsü-ling chih-chüeh*) was obvious to Chu Hsi as well (see section d). Chu Hsi, however, characteristically emphasized the contrast between the meta-physical *tao-hsin* (mind of the *tao*) and the experiential *jen-hsin* (human mind), holding that "the human mind must always obey [the mind of the *tao*]."[278] Echoing Lu Chiu-yüan, Wang disagreed with Chu's alleged implication that there were two minds.[279]

As evoked by Lu and Wang, the pathos of an indivisible con-sciousness enclosing all existence had Confucian connotations. They were thinking of *jen* (benevolence) as a force pervading the cosmos, of the idea that "all good is present" in morally pure feeling, and of the idea that this feeling, identical in whomever it appeared, was shared by the self with all sages.[280]

Yet this idea that "my mind is the cosmos" also had roots in Ch'an Buddhism,[281] and it indeed resembled Berkeleianism. More-over, since there was no intractable reality outside it, this indivisible mind was an indivisible will, and any distinction between the potential good and actual evils was really the result of a refusal to exercise this will. It is striking that even Chu Hsi expressed this thought: "One may say that that heaven, earth, and the ten thou-sand things ultimately are one with me. If my mind is correct, then the mind of heaven and earth is also correct. If my ether of material-ization is free of all deviant tendencies, then heaven's and earth's ether of materialization will also be free of all deviance. Thus the manifest efficacy [of moral effort] reaches such a point! The highest achievements to be reached through learning, the sage's brilliant ability to deal with affairs, these in the last analysis do not depend on outer conditions."[282]

That even Chu Hsi could thus assert the primacy of the will indicates how basic for Neo-Confucians was the belief in the exis-tence of an indivisible cosmic consciousness (*hsü-ling ming-chüeh*). However, this theme was emphasized more by Lu Chiu-yüan: "How is there anything impeding this principle in the cosmos? It is you yourself who makes it sink down and buries it."[283] Similarly, Wang, as we have seen, sought to collapse the distinction between the potential and the actual with various statements, such as "mind is principle" and "the people filling the streets are all sages" (see section m). Certainly the Lu-Wang attempt to dissolve this distinc-tion was Buddhist in inspiration and alien to Chou and Han Confucianism.

3. Sense of Predicament (r)

To be sure, this attempt remained ambivalent. Lu and Wang were fully aware of the existence of evil. In particular, Wang Yang-ming as well as Chu Hsi perceived a dyadic ontological situation, including the distinction between imminent and accomplished issuance in the mind, which turned pursuit of the good into pursuit of something elusively transcendent. They both accepted the *Shu-ching*'s idea that "The mind of the *tao* is almost imperceptible in its subtlety," as did Lu Chiu-yüan.[284] Chu and Wang both associated the ether of materialization with a kind of morally chaotic turmoil that had to be mastered (see section e). They both urged students to be constantly "fearful" that the selfishness associated with this turmoil might reappear, and even Wang noted that "When in movement, the mind cannot be free of what is not good" (see section o). They both saw the world, especially the "outer," historical world, as a moral wilderness dominated by "human material desires," which often "covered over" (*pi*) the "mind's ultimate substance," and they both lamented the moral and doctrinal degeneration of mankind after the misty beginnings of history during the Three Dynasties.[285] They both were exasperated by the difficulties which even their own students had in obtaining that true understanding on which any moral regeneration depended. Responding "with a sigh" to one of Hsü Ai's objections, Wang Yang-ming said: "The view you mention has been obscuring the truth for a long time. How can one bring about enlightenment with just one word! Yet I'll now try to discuss this matter along the lines of your question."[286] Although Wang liked to say that moral effort was "easy," it surely did not appear easy to him in this case. In fact, it was not easy in the sense that following material desires was easy. On the contrary, it depended on grasping a recondite view of linkage which Wang himself was barely able to articulate (see section u).

Chu Hsi, however, soberly emphasized this gap between the potential and the actual, going on at length about the difficulties of moral effort, the existence of evil, and the sources of evil.[287] He put repeated emphasis on the *Shu-ching*'s statement that "The human mind exists in a state of danger, while the mind of the *tao* is almost imperceptible in its subtlety." He explained the matter thus: "The human mind turns to selfishness with ease but only with difficulty to devotion to the public good. Therefore it exists in a state of danger. The moral consciousness of the true way is hard to grasp clearly and easy to be in the dark about. Therefore it is almost imperceptible in its subtlety."[288]

s. CHU'S AND WANG'S CLAIMS ABOUT
SPIRITUAL NURTURE

With these different views of the gap between the potential good and actual evils, Chu and Wang had different opinions about how to carry out the spiritual nurture needed to close this gap. Should one begin by accepting the reality of potentiality, that is, the presence of heavenly principle in the mind? Or should one begin by recognizing the reality of those evil actualities impeding realization of the potential good, that is, selfish impulses? To make a wrong choice at this point was precisely a case of being "off by a fraction at the beginning, and nowhere near the mark in the end."[289] Because Neo-Confucians believed that the presence of heaven was physically in them, and that it could be "expanded" to the point that all their goals would be realized, they could not afford to be wrong about this issue. Moreover, the very nature of these alternatives seemed to exclude any simple compromise. No one could just bluntly recommend simultaneously expelling selfish desires and sensing the inherently limitless power of heaven; these two actions inherently collided. If there was such a middle path, as Wang Yangming apparently thought, it could be traced only through exceedingly subtle reflections.

Wang thus followed Lu Chiu-yüan in believing that once one sensed the presence of principle in one's feelings one could "have confidence in oneself" (*tzu-hsin*). This confidence, moreover, was reinforced by the idea that the problem of apprehending "the equilibrium of imminent issuance" was either false or solved (see section m). With this confidence, Lu thought, one simply "made one's original mind fully manifest."[290] Wang's similar idea of "fully realizing one's spontaneous moral knowledge," however, was an attempt to combine Lu's "self-confidence" with Chu Hsi's reverence. Wang often said that it was, after all, necessary to "expel human desires," using one's "spontaneous moral knowledge" to distinguish between them and heavenly principle. As T'ang Chün-i points out, moreover, Wang supplemented "self-confidence" with an emphasis on being "fearful and cautious."[291]

For Chu Hsi, however, spiritual nurture depended entirely on reverence. Apart from moral effort, he felt, the presence of principle in the feelings was so faint that one could not "confidently" begin one's efforts on a platform of feelings infused with principle. Rather, through reverence one could become more aware of heavenly principle as the standard one should aim at, one could repress selfish desires, one could grasp that transtemporal dimension of the mind in terms of which the equilibrium of imminent issuance could be extended into the phase of accomplished issuance, and one could constantly discriminate between the different impulses of the mind.

t. CHU'S CLAIMS ABOUT LINKAGE

Yet one could not begin to expand the presence of principle in one's feelings unless one knew how principle impinged on them. Intuition was not enough. With their rationalistic passion, Neo-Confucians necessarily insisted on a discursive theory as the basis on which "clearly to distinguish" (*ming-pien*) between principle and selfish desire. They also assumed that since not only principle but also consciousness were the same throughout the cosmos (see section d), this theory would deal with the cosmos-wide linkage between mind, principle, and things. Perplexing to us, the interdependence of spiritual nurture and cosmology was obvious to Neo-Confucians.

Asserting that the contrast between the metaphysical and the experiential must be respected, Chu Hsi sought conceptualizations of linkage which did justice to both these levels. He also was wary of conceptualizations lapsing into either *k'ung-t'an* (empty talk) or *chih-li* (disconnected details presented without a sense for the wholeness of things). This is illustrated by his criticism of the Ch'eng brothers: "Ch'eng I discusses *jen* (benevolence) in terms of being one with heaven, earth, and the ten thousand things, but this approach is too deep, it lacks something one can get hold of. . . . In learning, Ch'eng Hao holds that one must first know *jen*. His statement that the person with *jen* is indivisibly one with things is excellent. It's just that he discussed the matter in too broad a way, making it difficult for the student to enter into [the process of self-cultivation]."[292]

Chu Hsi thus looked for formulations avoiding the complementary shortcomings of *k'ung-t'an* and *chih-li* and delineating the seam between the metaphysical and the experiential. His method, almost totally alien to Wang Yang-ming, was to reflect on cosmological relationships in a flexibly discursive way, trying out a variety of formulae. As already noted (see section f), he like the formula "seeing the distinctions in things without losing track of their oneness, and seeing the unifying veins passing through things without losing track of the distinctions involved." Similarly, he put great weight on the formula "one and yet two." He said: "In general the relation between the mind and the heaven-conferred nature is rather like a case of being one and yet two, two and yet one. It is most important to grasp this point. . . . It is extremely hard to clarify the issue of the relation between the mind and the heaven-conferred nature. On the one hand, if one calls them two things, they are not two things. On the other, if one calls them one thing, they also are not one thing. But if a person thinks of one thing in the process of splitting into two, then one can say he understands the heaven-conferred nature. . . . Therefore to speak of yin and yang as one is correct, and to speak of them as two is also correct."[293]

Chu Hsi, like Wang, also insisted on the existence of relations transcending the commonsense world of time and space. As we have seen in section l, to overcome the rupture of the phases and turn the mind into an indivisible whole suffused with the transcendent quality of equilibrium, he advanced a concept of the state of reverence as dissolving temporal sequence. He also said that in the relation between a *li* (principle) and its corresponding thing, "there is no sequence of first and later to discuss."[294] Similarly: "If now someone were to say that on the yin and the yang there is another thing, formless and shadowless, which is the supreme ultimate, that would be incorrect."[295] Yet Chu Hsi simultaneously was forced to depend on the spatio-temporal concept of being "attached" or "put down" in order to explain the link between the metaphysical and the experiential (see section f).

Subsumption was another relational concept he used. Thus *jen* (benevolence) "enfolded" the three other moral principles of righteousness, propriety, and moral understanding (see section d). To say that two things were identical was often plausible so long as the two in question were both obviously on the metaphysical level. That "*hsing* (the heaven-conferred nature) is *li* (principle)" was one of the great formulae of linkage that Neo-Confucians turned to. Advanced first by Ch'eng I, this formula seemed to reconnect the world of ethics with that of metaphysical reality in the face of the perceived Buddhist challenge. Chu Hsi said: "In the whole history of thought after Confucius and Mencius, no one had seen this. Indeed since ancient times no one had dared to discuss the matter in this way."[296]

Other such examples using a simple copula were "the supreme ultimate . . . is merely a principle. . . . One can say that the *tao* is principle." Certainly this use of "is" (*chi*) was facilitated by the ambiguity of the term, which was not used in any rigorously logical way. For instance, contrary to logic, one could not deduce from the above propositions that the heaven-conferred nature is the true way. (Rather, Chu Hsi suggested that "the heaven-conferred nature is the form and the embodiment of the true way.") At times the copula *chi* was used in a deliberately extravagant and ambiguous way: "Benevolence is the mind. . . . Heaven is man and man is heaven."[297]

Besides subsumption and identity, the notion of a "beginning" could be adduced to formulate a relationship or link. Although yin and yang "lack any beginning," it was usually safe to point out that something must have a beginning. Therefore Chu Hsi could say: "The process of giving birth must have a beginning. This beginning is called the primal."[298] Similarly, almost anything had a *raison d'être* (*so-i-jan*). Therefore Chu Hsi could say: "This continuous occurrence of movement and rest must have some principle serving as its *raison d'être*, and this is what we call the supreme ultimate."[299] Virtually anything also had its *pen-t'i* (ultimate substance). Thus the indivisible consciousness of the cosmos (*hsü-ling*) could be linked to *hsin* (the mind) by asserting that it was the mind's *pen-t'i*.[300] Chu Hsi also once tried to use the basic dyad *t'i* (substance) and *yung* (function) to describe the relation between the supreme ultimate and the states of movement and rest: "I used to relate the supreme ultimate to the states of movement and rest by regarding the former as *t'i*, the latter as *yung*. But this way of putting it certainly had its problems. Later I changed it to say that the supreme ultimate is the finest essence of the ultimate substance of things, while movement and rest are the concrete opportunities to be realized. This tends to come near the mark."³⁰¹ Such formulations show how the given stock of perceived dyadic relations, listed in section j, facilitated the conceptualization of linkage.

In another instance also, the problem of using the *t'i-yung* distinction in a realm of relations outside the spatio-temporal framework came up: "Someone asked: 'Why in [Chou Tun-i's] explanation of the supreme ultimate does movement precede the state of rest, [with the result that] function precedes substance, and sensation of outer things precedes the state of total stillness?' Chu Hsi said: 'Admittedly if we talk of yin and yang, function refers to yang, and substance refers to yin. [Therefore if movement precedes the state of rest, we do have the strange result that function precedes substance.] However, the states of movement and rest follow each other continuously without any point of beginning or end, and yin and yang lack a beginning. One cannot here distinguish between what is first and what follows. . . . Thus ultimately before movement there again is the state of rest, before function, there again is substance."³⁰²

Coming to the most controversial problem of Neo-Confucianism, the triangular relationship between *hsin* (mind), *wu* (things), and *li* (principle) or *hsing* (heaven-conferred nature), Chu Hsi also once tried to find a solution using the *t'i-yung* concept: "Principle is found in all the ten thousand things of heaven and earth, but it is controlled by the mind. Since the mind controls it, its function indeed cannot be outside this mind. If so, then the substance of principle is in things, but its function is in the mind."³⁰³

Dealing with Lu Chiu-yüan's theory of the identity of mind and principle, Chu Hsi did grant that in the case of one who had realized the virtue of *jen* (benevolence), "mind is principle." (Lu Chiu-yüan's copula *chi* was rejected for the slightly less blunt *pien-shih*.)³⁰⁴ But apart from this limiting case, Chu Hsi struggled to find a formula of linkage different from that of identity using concepts like "in," "put," and "set forth": "Without the mind, principle would lack anywhere to be put. . . . principle is not a thing in front of one, it is in the mind. . . . To say that the mind puts to use all principles in a marvellous way is like saying it can put them into action. But the term 'put into action' is inadequate. Therefore one just uses 'puts to use in a marvellous way.' . . . Someone asked: 'In your

3. Sense of Predicament (t)

Mencius with Collected Commentaries you say: "The mind provides for the setting forth (*chü*) of all principles and responds to the ten thousand affairs." But here you say "puts principles to use in a marvellous way and controls the ten thousand things." Why is there this difference?' Chu Hsi answered: 'The phrase "puts to use in a marvellous way" is rather striking but not very sound. The phrase "provides for the setting forth" is sound.' "[305] Similarly, Chu Hsi liked Shao Yung's (1011–1077) suggestion that "the mind is the heaven-conferred nature's second or outer city wall," but this static metaphor was less useful to him than the concept of the mind which he took from Chang Tsai: "The mind controls [that process of movement involving] the heaven-conferred nature and the feelings."[306] Besides "control," with its connotations of political authority, Chu Hsi used analogies taken directly from the bureaucratic world to elucidate relations between ontological concepts: "Heaven is the emperor; what is decreed is like giving an imperial order to me; the heaven-conferred nature is like the official duties I have received, just as the duty of a district policeman is arresting robbers, the duty of a clerk is keeping records in order."[307]

Chu Hsi also made a major point of emphasizing the speaker's point of view as a factor determining which relational concept was the most appropriate in a particular case. Although wary of slipping into relativism, Chu Hsi did try to solve the problem of conceptualizing relationships partly by insisting that one must be able to move back and forth between different perspectives:

> I would suppose it is acceptable to say that the supreme ultimate has within it the states of movement and rest; this is to discuss the matter from the standpoint of substance. Or one could say that the supreme ultimate goes through phases of movement and rest; this is to discuss the matter from the standpoint of the concrete realization of things. . . . Someone asked: "Last night you said that the distinction between substance and function lacks a fixed point of application, that its application depends on one's standpoint. But if now one considers the ten thousand affairs as a whole and applies to them one large distinction between substance and function, then what?" Chu Hsi said: "But what is substance and function is given in a fixed way: if the present is substance, then what happens later [has to be] function; if this thing is substance, then its involvement in action [has to be] function." . . . In understanding what is written, one must grasp the meaning in a living way, one cannot remain fixed to a single standpoint. If we speak of

knowing relative to benevolence, then benevolence is substance, knowing is function. But if we are talking [just] about knowing, then knowing also has its own aspects of substance and function. . . . [In looking at such questions,] one must not discuss them holding on to just one view. One must rather revolve around them looking at them from different standpoints.[308]

To sum up, Chu Hsi used the ideas of oneness in diversity, of a transtemporal and trans-spatial relation, of subsumption, and of identity. Moreover, he explained linkages by referring to the universally accepted ontological dyads, by drawing analogies with actions and relations in the world of ordinary experience, by asking people flexibly to shift their perspectives, and by appealing to widespread feelings or beliefs about what was self-evident.[309] In holding that Chu Hsi regarded linkage as fragile and difficult to conceptualize, I can point as evidence not only to his emphasis on the difficulties of spiritual nurture and on the contrast he stressed between the metaphysical and the experiential levels but also to the fact that he struggled with so many formulae of linkage and that he sometimes advanced them in an uncertain way. Most important, we can sense a discrepancy between the character of his formulations and his own goal of cognitive clarity. By looking at one matter after another as an object of discursive understanding, Chu Hsi expressed a sober respect for external realities which was truly in the Confucian tradition and which Wang Yang-ming could not match. Yet how could such a discursive approach result in that essential understanding encompassing all "inner" and "outer" facets of existence which Chu Hsi himself aimed for? (See section d.) This was the point of vulnerability to which Wang referred with his famous story about futilely staring at a piece of bamboo to grasp its principle.

The contrast between Wang and Chu on this issue becomes clearer if we look not at Chu Hsi's ways of conceptualizing linkage but at what he sought to link. We find that in all cases he was looking for linkages between the naturally given aspects of the cosmos, including the naturally given phases of the mind. Thus some of his linkages were purely on the metaphysical level, such as those between the supreme ultimate and principle, between principle and the heaven-conferred nature, between the supreme ultimate and the states of rest and motion, or between the supreme ultimate and the forces of yin and yang. The others were between the metaphysical and experiential levels, such as those between the heaven-conferred nature and the mind, principle and the mind, imminent and accomplished issuance, the supreme ultimate and the ten thousand things, or heaven and man. Seeking to close the gap between the ideal and the actual, Chu Hsi was oriented toward the objects of thought and action, whether those of the "inner" or of the "outer" life.

On the other hand, the mind as subject, as an intervening will, was not regarded by him as part of the problem of linkage. Trying to think through the oneness of *pen-t'i* (ultimate substance) and *fa-yung* (issuance in experience), he did not dream of considering the oneness of *pen-t'i* and *kung-fu* (efficacious moral efforts). The distinction here can best be put as the difference between activities linking together objects on which these activities impinge and activities themselves constituting the link one is aiming for. For Chu Hsi, one carried out spiritual nurture, cognitive study, and practice so as to bring about the interlinkage of principle, mind, and things. He did not apply the vocabulary of linkage to these three activities of the intervening will themselves and just discussed them in a pedagogical way. That they be "done at the same time" was Chu Hsi's concern, not that the oneness of mind and principle was revealed in the very process of carrying them out. Thus he said: "As one preserves and nourishes one's heaven-conferred feelings, one must also seek to broaden one's knowledge to the utmost. As one seeks to broaden one's knowledge to the utmost, one must also vigorously carry out one's intentions in practice. Indeed, all of these must be done together at the same time. One cannot say he will today envelop and nourish his heaven-conferred feelings, tomorrow broaden his knowledge to the utmost, and the day after vigorously put his intentions into practice."[310]

u. WANG'S CLAIMS ABOUT LINKAGE

In the case of Wang, however, the intervening will itself was the main point or locus of linkage, not just the vehicle of *kung-fu* (efficacious moral efforts) directed at the naturally given cosmos. To show this, he argued that the activities of the intervening will—spiritual nurture, cognitive study, and practice—were one; that they in turn were one with the mind's *pen-t'i* (ultimate substance); and that the mind's "ultimate substance" was one with the ultimate structure of the whole cosmos. Later, Huang Tsung-hsi astutely described Wang Yang-ming as believing in the oneness of *kung-fu* and *pen-t'i*, an idea which Huang himself as well as various Tung-lin scholars embraced.[311] Western scholars have not in the past made clear this basic difference between Chu Hsi and Wang Yang-ming, but T'ang Chün-i, in partly different terms, has noted this development of a new way of thinking about the relation between the naturally given cosmos ("mind and heaven-conferred nature") and the intervening will ("efficacious moral efforts"):

> In previous chapters, I have discussed the views held by Chou Tun-i, Chang Tsai, the Ch'eng brothers, and Chu Hsi on the mind and the heaven-conferred nature but have touched only in passing on their views regarding efficacious moral efforts to realize the virtuous nature. Generally, these two topics were discussed separately by such scholars. They were, however, rarely discussed separately from the time of Lu Chiu-yüan and Yang Tz'u-hu on, coming down to Ch'en Hsien-chang, Wang Yang-ming, the various schools stemming from Wang, the Tung-lin school, and Liu Tsung-chou. In general, these latter scholars all held that there are no efficacious moral efforts outside of enlightenment regarding the mind and the heaven-conferred nature, and also that one cannot discuss what the mind and the heaven-conferred nature are like apart from the enlightenment of efficacious moral efforts. With these scholars, the discussion of efficacious moral efforts and the discussion of the mind and the heaven-conferred nature always converged, coming down to one word. This indeed began with Lu Chiu-yüan.[312]

It was in a cautious, partly indirect way, frequently shocking his audience and meeting objections, that Wang Yang-ming sought to solve the problem of linkage by elucidating the oneness within *kung-fu* and the oneness of *kung-fu* and *pen-t'i*. His subtle vision was and remains difficult to understand, though it was entirely coherent. He was not just talking as an activist when he said that "knowledge and action are one."[313] Neither was he just talking as a humanistic educator convinced that scholarship and moral development go hand in hand when he argued that "the investigation of things is the effort to make the intentions sincere," "exhaustively investigating principles is the effort exhaustively to grasp one's heaven-conferred nature," "the pursuit of inquiry and learning is the effort reverently to realize one's virtuous nature," "the extensive study of literature is the effort to restrain oneself with the rules of moral propriety," and "dwelling in reverence and the exhaustive investigation of principles are . . . one thing."[314]

Admittedly, Wang had a particularly vivid way of explaining how all such ways of cultivating oneself fed into one another. Yet the pedagogical meaning of the above statements was obvious to all Confucians. Had not Chu Hsi said that spiritual nurture, cognitive study, and practice must be "carried out at the same time"? Unlike Chu Hsi's, however, Wang's point involved an idea that was shocking, as shown by the reactions of his audience (Hsü Ai's [1487–1518] conversion experience is a typical example).

Nor was this the idea that if one could perfect spiritual nurture, cognitive study, and practice, one would recover the mind's "ultimate substance" and so realize the goal of linkage. Chu Hsi also had said: "In the case of one who has realized *jen* (benevolence), mind is principle," that is, the metaphysical and experiential levels converge.

Wang's point was rather that one could perfect these activities only if one understood the way in which they were linked with each other and with the mind's "ultimate substance." In other words what he kept driving at and what his audience found new and sensationally promising was the idea that if man was part of an indivisible cosmic mind, then the activities of his own intervening will must themselves be seen as part of this indivisible mind. Elucidating the cosmic pattern of linkage meant showing how *kung-fu* itself was an integral part of this cosmic mind. The will to achieve linkage was not something apart from the indivisible cosmic mind; it was itself the very point at which this indivisible mind was fully realized.

We have to remember that "confidence in oneself," which Wang regarded as indispensable for spiritual nurture, came from knowing that "heavenly principle" was present in one's spontaneous feelings as an overflowing indivisible mind. Yet great precision was needed just at this point (see section d). One could not but worry over confusing the boundaries of this presence with the influx of material desires, because one had to be sure that one's feelings retained their pristine purity. The constant "fear that selfish ideas may emerge" was correlated to a need to clarify one's feelings precisely at their very "source."

Consequently, without exactly understanding the constitution of this indivisible cosmic mind, one could not identify and sense its presence and so could not carry out spiritual nurture with "self-confidence." Wang's point that this constitution included the intervening will itself was therefore crucial. It was nothing less than a revelation which put familiar educational routines in a totally new light. Realizing that my moral exertions were themselves the life of the indivisible cosmic mind, I finally could authentically identify and sense the presence of this mind in me and so could exert myself confident that material desire had stopped leaking into my basic state of mind, and that heavenly principle, thus unobstructed, would "fill up" my whole being. Still more, the basic Mencian idea of "getting the truth for oneself" (*tzu-te*) in a "living" way was given new meaning (see section b). The reason one could not just mechanically accept a truth from others was that the very act of "getting it for oneself" was itself the substance of the cosmic mind. Chu Hsi had said: "In one's studies, one must just aim at an understanding which cuts to the core (*pien-pi chin-li*)." That was what Wang's concept seemed to do.

Wang's statements, therefore, were "shocking" because they constituted a new understanding of how principle was present in the mind and so promised to solve the problem of how to discover a solid platform on which to begin spiritual nurture. Consequently, the impact they had on Wang's audience cannot be divorced from the fact that they dealt specifically with the linkage between mind, principle, and things. Had Wang not been able to show that his approach could clear up the problem of this linkage, his position would, very simply, have had no significance at all for his Neo-Confucian audience.

For instance, arguing that "the investigation of things is the effort to make the intentions (*i*) sincere," Wang's entire emphasis was on showing that the oneness of principle and things can be grasped by viewing them as merely different dimensions of "intentions." His recondite demonstration went as follows. He could easily make the point that with sincere intentions, one was "preserving the heavenly principle" in one's mind. As part of the mind's naturally given phases, "intentions" necessarily arose out of one's "point of total stillness," which coincided with heavenly principle. Since "heavenly principle" was also associated with "things," "preserving heavenly principle" plausibly appeared to have some connection to "the investigation of things." Yet outer "things" and "intentions" still appeared to be different, as Wang's disciples repeatedly complained. The only way to overcome this doubt was to redefine "things" as aspects of intentions. A "thing," Wang said, was "that to which an intention pertains." To help this argument along, Wang noted that "things are affairs." Therefore a good example of a "thing" was "serving a ruler."[315] To be sincere in one's intentions regarding the serving of one's ruler was to "investigate things" in that particular case.

The link between "things" and "principles" was therefore conceptualized in a new way: both were aspects of "intentions." Had they not been, making sincere one's intentions could not have simultaneously been a way of investigating things. Conversely, what was exciting about the idea that these two kinds of effort converged was precisely the suggestion that it was through this convergence that the link between principle and things was realized. Had the oneness of principle and things not been the driving concern of Wang's audience, his emphasis on the convergence of cognitive study and spiritual nurture would not have appeared to them as an answer to an important problem. Similarly, when Ch'en Chiu-ch'uan (1495–1562) came to Wang perplexed by the idea that the "investigation of things" was the way to "make intentions sincere," Wang sought to convince him by arguing that "the person of someone, mind, intention, knowing, and things" are all just different aspects of "one thing," and he again based this view on the proposition that a "thing" is "an intention from the standpoint of that to which the intention pertains."[316]

Wang's answer to the problem of linkage was so complex, subtle, and controversial that he had trouble even articulating it. It was difficult enough to deal with doubts about the convergence of spiritual nurture and cognitive study and that of cognitive study and practice. Directly to suggest to his audience that spiritual nurture and practice were one (claiming, say, that *tu-hsing shih tsun-te-hsing-te kung-fu)* was impossible. It would have aroused still graver doubts: how could *shou-lien* (drawing one's spirit inward) be the same as *fa-san* (issuing it forth)? The tendency to regard these two as alternatives was almost irresistible. Still more, while Huang Tsung-hsi and his contemporaries could easily appreciate the idea that that "ultimate substance is what efficacious moral efforts come to," this bold identification of *kung-fu* with *pen-t'i* could not be openly emphasized in Wang's time.

Admittedly, Wang did explicitly formulate this identity. Using terminology from chapter 1 of the *Doctrine of the Mean*, he said that one should not separate *kung-fu* from *pen-t'i* by regarding the former as human effort (being "cautious and fearful") and the latter as a given transcending this effort ("what is not seen and not heard"). Ultimately, he said, one should realize that human effort and the givenness of being were the same: ". . . ultimate substance really is what is not seen and what is not heard but it also is being cautious and fearful."[317] Nevertheless, it was only in Wang's controversial four-sentence teaching that he managed to crowd into one concept all the different facets of linkage ranging from ultimate substance to spiritual nurture, cognitive study, and practice: "The absence of any consciousness of evil and [so] of good [as well] is the mind's ultimate substance. [To the extent that] there is a distinction between good and evil, this is the emergence of one's intentions [from the phase of imminent issuance]. Knowing good and evil is the spontaneous knowledge [grounded in one's heavenly point of total stillness]. To act by doing good and eliminating evil, this is the investigation of things."[318]

Wang's philosophy, however, his answer to the problem of linkage, cannot be understood if we pay attention only to his attempt to show the identity of man's ultimate being and his existential moral strivings. This is an idea which converges attractively with modern existentialism, but if we simply regard it as his one central point, we abandon our function as inductive scholars and arbitrarily dismiss as epiphenomenal another basic theme to which he often returned.

This theme does not converge with any serious modern idea and to our ears is no more than a series of flowery, tautological platitudes with no living meaning. For all his emphasis on morality as experience, Wang was overwhelmingly committed to the metaphysical bias of Neo-Confucianism. It was in terms of this bias that all Neo-Confucians, though particularly concerned with conceptualizing the link between the metaphysical and experiential levels, also repeatedly fussed with the problem of linkage on the purely metaphysical level. In this they followed Ch'eng I, whose proposition that "the heaven-conferred nature is principle" was the classic Neo-Confucian concept of linkage between two purely metaphysical relata. After we examine the way Wang dealt with this issue, we can ask why this issue was so important to him.

We are here far indeed from the world of Jean-Paul Sartre. For Wang, it was important to assert that the mind's "ultimate substance" was identical with "heavenly principle" and with the first phases of the naturally given mind, that is, total stillness and imminent issuance. Thus it necessarily had a flavor of virtue, summed up in the *Chung-yung's* idea of "the equilibrium of imminent issuance" and also expressed with ideas like "state of broadness and extreme impartiality," "heavenly virtue," "the supreme good," and "bright virtue."[319] Moreover, since the mind's phase of total stillness was one of pure awareness, "ultimate substance" could also be seen as participating in the indivisible consciousness of the cosmos as a whole (see section d). While "knowing is the mind's ultimate substance,"[320] "the ultimate substance of the mind is that which is called the mind of the *tao*."[321] Also called "spontaneous moral knowledge," this "knowing" could in turn be identified with "equilibrium."[322] As "knowing," moreover, "ultimate substance" could be regarded as "always shining."[323] As "shining," ultimate substance was "easily" perceivable, in contrast to the almost indiscernible "incipiences" Chu Hsi liked to talk about. At the same time, easily identifiable with one's *hsing* (heaven-conferred nature), "ultimate substance" could be seen as emerging out of "heaven" and thus imbued with heaven's creative capacity (*sheng, tsao-hua*). One with one's ultimate substance, a person was one with the whole organic cosmos of yin and yang.[324]

Wang echoed Chu Hsi in saying that this metaphysical reality transcended spatio-temporal distinctions. However, he also saw it as transcending the distinction between good and evil (since awareness of this distinction was based on ideas realized in the phase of accomplished issuance, the conscious desire to be good was not the ultimate foundation of morality).[325] Moreover, he embraced an emphasis on unbroken movement as a dimension of ultimate being, lacking Chu Hsi's distrust of movement and rejecting Chu Hsi's effort to conceptualize a tentative suspension of movement ("two and yet one"). Where Chu Hsi used *chih-cho* (hold) usually to indicate preliminary success in grasping the truth, Wang used *chih-cho* in a pejorative way with Taoist and Buddhist overtones when he said that one could not "*chih-cho* (hold onto) the *tao* as a fixed thing."[326] Similarly, he said that "righteousness and principle lacked any fixed location," and he resisted Chu Hsi's view of our moral standard as a *ting-li* (fixed principle). By using the idea of "making brightly manifest one's bright virtue," he conceptualized the achievement of morality not as reaching something "fixed" but as a realization of a continuously flowing process uninterrupted by any artificial "holding."[327]

Wang's metaphysics certainly reinforced his whole approach to linkage: if the indivisible cosmic will was pure activity, its identity with the intervening human will as moral activity was that much more plausible. Certainly Wang had to steer his audience away from Chou Tun-i's metaphysics. Although he did not reject outright Chou's way of spinning out the structure of the cosmos from the existence of a supreme ultimate majestically independent of any human mind, Wang had to see this structure as a "lost" dimension of my mind, not as something from which the existence of my mind was derived.

There is a more basic point, however. The significance of Wang's extensive metaphysical concerns lies in the fact that recovering the "mind's ultimate substance" would not have satisfied him at all had not this substance been the power of the cosmos itself. It was the cosmos—"heaven, earth, and man"—to which Wang, like all Neo-Confucians, was explicitly oriented. Like all Neo-Confucians, he "based himself on heaven," not just on the mind. The reality of heaven could not be denoted just with the term "the mind's ultimate substance," not to mention *jen-hsin* (the human mind) or *wu-hsin* (the mind of the self). Far from being thrust back into the privacy of his own soul, the individual had to depend on the cosmic force which had given birth to him. Wang had to claim that in carrying out self-realization, we were becoming one with the force of heaven itself. It was this point which he tried to establish again and again by interrelating "ultimate substance," "heavenly principle," "the mind of the *tao*," "heavenly virtue," and so on. For Neo-Confucians, to equate such things was not tautological, since these words denoted distinguishable aspects of reality.

What I call the metaphysical bias of Neo-Confucians comes down to the key point that for them, the individual was not a self-sufficient moral agent, and ethical purity was not enough. They needed to feel supported by an immense power transcending the immediate ego, and they wanted this power in order to transform the world. Even when they suspected it was unavailable, they still sought the pathos of this power.

In other words, along with their humanism, they believed that the mind had a transnatural power to control the cosmos. Said Ch'en Hsien-chang, Wang Yang-ming's foremost precursor in the Ming period: "If I understand principle, then heaven and earth are what I establish, the ten thousand transformations are produced by me, and all space and time is with me. With this handle in my hands, what else is there to worry about?"[328]

v. CHU AND WANG ON THE SCOPE OF PRACTICE
AND POLITICAL ACTION

As we consider the points over which Chu and Wang disagreed, it is partly impossible to say which were seminal, which were derivative. While Chu and Wang had basic differences about how to carry out spiritual nurture, these differences cannot be separated from Wang's view that because an indivisible cosmic mind dissolved the boundary between the metaphysical and the experiential, Chu Hsi was wrong to emphasize this boundary and the correlated contrast between the ideal good and actual evils. One may suppose that these differences were basic, and that it was because of them that Chu and Wang arrived at such different conceptualizations of the linkage between principle, mind, and things.

On the other hand, that Chu emphasized scholarly study more than Wang was a secondary difference. It was because Wang was concerned with the oneness of cognitive study, spiritual nurture, and practice as constituting the immediate existence of an indivisible cosmic mind that he had to reject scholarly study except as it directly merged with these activities. Even if we can call Wang "anti-intellectual," we still have to ask why he was. His aim was to do everything necessary to achieve oneness as he understood it. It is hard to discern any other motive for his de-emphasis of scholarly study.

At the same time, however, Chu's and Wang's differences regarding the distinction between the metaphysical and the experiential levels may itself have partly stemmed from another seminal difference, that concerning the mode of action in the outer world. From Sung times on, scholars were gravitating away from the radicalism of the eleventh century toward what can be labeled "moderate realism." This change developed largely as a response to political and bureaucratic conditions, but I would hypothesize that it in turn conditioned metaphysical tendencies.

Radicalism and moderate realism are inductively formulated ideal types.[329] From the radical standpoint, one sought to act on society from the center of the political arena, that is, by advising the ruler; from the moderate standpoint, one thought of acting as a local or regional official on one locality or institution. From the radical standpoint, political action, once based on the right principles, was easy and quick, because society was malleable. From the moderate standpoint, it was difficult and gradual, because society was not easily malleable. From the radical standpoint, one aimed for tight (*mi*) and total control of the society by the state; from the moderate, only loose (*shu*) and partial control. From the radical standpoint, the state directly mobilized the populace; from the moderate, it worked largely through mediating elites. From the radical standpoint, private property rights had to give way before the needs of the state and "the people"; from the moderate standpoint, they were often respected. From the radical standpoint, economically activistic state enterprises were often desirable (*yu-wei-chih cheng*); from the moderate standpoint, there were strong arguments against them. From the radical standpoint, laws were enacted and so gave rise to customs; from the moderate standpoint, lawmakers were wise to respect and follow changing customs.

3. Sense of Predicament (v)

From the radical standpoint, the state stressed fear, moral influence, or both in guiding the people; from the moderate, remunerative sanctions were emphasized, as the state often sought to elicit obedience by devising procedures making it more profitable to obey than to violate the law. From the radical standpoint, raising the moral tone of the whole society (*feng-hua*) was vital. From the moderate standpoint, hope was placed more exclusively on raising the moral level of the bureaucracy so that it could umpire the activities of a populace openly given to the selfish competition for profits (*chui-li*), and personnel policy within the bureaucracy was often given a higher priority than concern with "the people's livelihood." From the radical standpoint, political programs were formulated in general, macroscopic terms, and they were seen as according with either the principles of ancient dynasties or some abstract program (e.g. that of the Legalists). From the moderate standpoint, detailed analysis of particular institutions was emphasized, as was the need to study all history after the ancient periods in order to find analogies relevant to the present.

It is striking that radicalism as here described has been typical of modern Chinese thought, particularly Maoism (see chapter 5). It was also typical of Chou Confucians and Legalists, and it reached a climax with Wang An-shih's reforms.[330] Disappointment with their outcome underlay the subsequent shift to moderate realism, but radical ideals remained alive. Oscillation between these two modes, often leading to hybrid attitudes, was facilitated by the ambivalence integral to Confucian political thought, as argued elsewhere.

Basically radical thinkers like Ku Yen-wu (1613–1682) and Huang Tsung-hsi, who advocated fundamental, empire-wide reforms going back to ancient models like the T'ang system of taxes-in-kind, were criticized for "being unable to grasp changing circumstances and to adjust to current conditions."[331] Conversely, the radical criticism of moderate thought was based on the idea, stressed by the Tung-lin movement in the early seventeenth century, that one must "make clear right and wrong," fearlessly avoiding *hsiang-yüan* (hypocritically going along with current rationalizations of self-interest). Ku Hsien-ch'eng, the Tung-lin leader, was partly criticizing men with a healthy respect for the ambiguities of government when he referred to those who "fear that if right and wrong are distinguished too clearly, affairs won't proceed smoothly and harmoniously." Such people, he said, believed in *han-hu* (cautiously dealing with matters by not probing too deeply into basic issues) and felt that "there must be some wrong in what is right, some right in what is wrong."[332]

Rejection of *han-hu* was a simple application of Neo-Confucian morality to the affairs of the polity, but it led almost necessarily to longing for the *gemeinschaft* of the past and to suspicion of the whole Ming-Ch'ing trend toward a larger, more complex, more differentiated, and more commercialized society. After all, the latter lacked the social oneness Neo-Confucians sought. Consequently, in Neo-Confucian eyes, unlike those of an Adam Smith, such commercialization could not embody historically progressive and morally dynamic forces. For instance, Lü Wan-ts'un, a follower of Chu Hsi, said that those who believed it was impractical to return to the well-field system and the ancient Chou mode of feudalism were motivated only by their lack of *jen* (benevolence) and their selfish fear of endangering the material security of their families.[333] His view vividly illustrates the clash between Neo-Confucian principles and the economism endorsed by both the popular culture and the elite philosophy of moderate realism.

Yet Neo-Confucianism itself shared in the Confucian ambivalence toward ultimately immoral policies. For instance, Chu Hsi felt that the Legalist-inspired Ch'in dynasty was following inevitable historical trends when it abandoned the ancient model systems of the Chou dynasty, and he echoed Ssu-ma Ch'ien in praising this much-reviled dynasty for properly elevating the position of the emperor.[334] Furthermore, since both he and Wang Yang-ming emphasized the regeneration of the individual's morality as the prerequisite of progress, a radical attitude toward political reform appeared increasingly pointless.

The thought of both Chu and Wang, therefore, was ambivalently compatible with moderate realism, but Chu and Wang offered different rationales to the Confucian denied an opportunity to act in the center of the imperial political arena. Closer to the radicalism of the eleventh century, Chu Hsi still clung to the ideal of action directed outward and aimed ultimately at mastering the political world. Much of his thought meshed with this ideal: his emphasis on recognizing and closing the gap between the ideal and the actual; his focus on the naturally given cosmos, not the intervening will, as the locus of linkage; his emphasis on the scholarly investigation of the outer world and its history; his glorification of words, with which this knowledge could be communicated; his glorification of the sage's ability to "act" (*tso*), changing the outer world; and his view of the sage's cosmic power as inhering not in an indivisible mind but in an immense cosmos obviously large enough to include all the power needed to overcome the vast, "outer" flow of evil.

Wang's opposite approach illustrates the common and sound generalization that Ming thought turned "inward." His approach was peculiarly suited to the needs of a Confucian resigned to act only in his personal and local environment and to those of a society becoming so large and complex that localism increasingly appeared as an answer to the dysfunctions of centralization. Whether or not the "beginnings of capitalism" in Ming-Ch'ing China brought about a new sense of individualism, they did perhaps encourage a kind of spiritual localism effectively expressed by Wang Yang-ming (see section g).

w. THE NEO-CONFUCIAN SENSE OF PREDICAMENT

The Neo-Confucian sense of predicament is now clear. Whatever the great "revolutions" of Sung society as analyzed by modern scholars, the "outer" realm of political and economic affairs had been mostly drained of hope since the disappointment with Wang An-shih's reforms. Perceiving theirs as a society shaped largely by the selfish pursuit of profit and wrongly designed institutions, Neo-Confucians could labor conscientiously with a spirit of moderate realism but could not hope to realize their classic goal of social oneness, political order, and economic well-being.

Nevertheless determined to pursue this goal, they turned to the "inner" life of moral striving as a prerequisite, but here again, in the eyes of both the Lu-Wang and the Ch'eng-Chu school, they were confronted by a massive tendency toward moral failure based on inescapable cosmic conditions which they could all too easily sense in their own individual minds. The world, both in its history and in the present, was largely a moral wilderness. Whether we look at the views of Lu Chiu-yüan and his brother, those of the Ch'eng brothers, or Chu Hsi's, there is agreement that after Confucius and Mencius, more than a thousand years went by "without a true Confucian," and that only one or at best a few scholars had managed to recover the true learning during the Northern Sung (just who had was a point of disagreement among the above-named).[335] Like Wang Yang-ming, Chu Hsi saw himself as living in an age when "heterodox doctrines are rising up like a swarm of wasps,"[336] and he said that such evil doctrines in his day were more "difficult to refute" than they had been in the days of Mencius.[337] Referring to "the thousand differences of opinion and the ten thousand ways of thinking in our times," he felt himself to be living in a detestable marketplace of ideas.[338] Because "in terms of actual affairs . . . it is really very easy for material desires to be victorious over heavenly principle. . . . true gentlemen are always few, while the mean-minded are always numerous."[339] Chu Hsi also said that he had gradually come to learn that becoming a sage was "a difficult thing to do."[340] Most significant, Chu Hsi believed that because of the increasing complexity of life, becoming a sage was harder in his day than it had been in the past.[341]

Although Wang Yang-ming tried to divert attention from these painful realities by claiming that one must consider the potential as actual, this very claim was part of a recondite argument he found difficult to explain even to his own students (see section u). Moreover, repeatedly forced to contradict this claim, he too recognized most of those harsh realities emphasized by Chu Hsi (see section r). Above all, it is clear that statements about how to achieve linkage remained mere claims advanced in a context of doubt and controversy, while statements about the need for linkage and the factors impeding it expressed widespread perceptions of the world in its given form.

Yet the intellectual who was committed to the Neo-Confucian outlook could not respond to these "inner" and "outer" obstacles by abandoning his goal. This would have meant discarding his own actually irrepressible participation in the cosmic flow of morality, embracing a life of "fears and anxieties," giving up any claim to the *ti-wei* (status) of sagehood (as Chu Hsi revealingly referred to it),[342] forfeiting the rationale for his sense of identity as a charismatically superior person, and abandoning the hope of finding some way to realize the eight steps of the *Great Learning*. Moreover, any commitment but a complete one appeared as "dead" and futile.

The Neo-Confucian predicament, therefore, was a paradoxical alienation from a constantly accessible truth which had to be pursued. After all, Chu Hsi could complain about the moral wilderness he lived in and yet agree that "in all things there is heavenly principle, in all affairs there is benevolence."[343] Expressing this paradoxical sense of estrangement, Chu Hsi said: "The body of a person is heaven and earth. It is only because people are separated from the latter by material desires that they naturally do not see this idea. . . . In the world there is just one principle of good and bad. What is not good is bad, what is not bad is good. This principle is there for all men. It is just that they place themselves at a distance from it, not that it is distant from them."[344]

It is this sense of *chien-ko* (separation) from the ultimate meaning of the cosmos which has been filtered out of Neo-Confucianism by its great philosophical interpreters in our century. Presumably they view it as lacking "value" or as epiphenomenal, even though it involved a moving and persuasive definition of man as simultaneously frail and magnificent. But whatever the "value" of this perception in universal terms, we are interested in it as an historical fact.

Admittedly, in saying that Neo-Confucians had a sense of predicament, we are saying something about them that they would not have said. The wholeness of the cosmos was for them something ever there which had been perfectly understood by the sages and which they were now in the process of once again properly understanding. Continually trying to brush aside the problems impeding this understanding, they were intent on making increasingly evident this glorious oneness existing beyond any predicament whatsoever. We skeptics of the twentieth century, however, know little about any such oneness. All we know is that although Neo-Confucians were convinced that this oneness latently existed, they also felt that conceptualization of it was both a prerequisite of effective moral action and a continuing problem, indeed *the* problem of their lives. Standing back as outsiders looking at their state of mind, we can state as a fact that they had a fearful perception of their world as continuously failing to close the circle of this oneness, and that their philosophical endeavors were to a large extent aimed at finding a remedy for this continuing problem.

x. NEO-CONFUCIANISM IN THE EARLY CH'ING PERIOD

If this analysis of the ideas shared by the Ch'eng-Chu and Lu-Wang schools is right, we still have to ask to what extent these ideas were widespread in the Ch'ing period. Certainly Neo-Confucianism remained an important force throughout this period. As Wing-tsit Chan has recently shown, scholars explicitly following the Ch'eng-Chu school in early Ch'ing times were important. Moreover, the state vigorously promoted the influence of this school throughout the Ch'ing period. Ch'an speaks of the K'ang-hsi emperor's "adoration for Chu Hsi." Compiled in 1715, the *Hsing-li ching-i,* an official collection of writings from the Ch'eng-Chu school, was "published for use in all schools in the country."[345] Chu Hsi's commentaries on *The Four Books* were officially used in the examination system all during the Ch'ing period.

The relation of Neo-Confucianism to other Ch'ing intellectual trends, however, is a question still requiring more study. As mentioned in section a, Neo-Confucianism was part of a heterogeneous, developing intellectual situation with at least some eight other, partly overlapping tendencies. In particular, the two Neo-Confucian schools were explicitly attacked in Ch'ing times by highly influential scholars marching under the allied banners of "substantial learning," "Han learning," and "textual study." This movement involved a wide range of evidentiary studies, often philological or phonological, aimed at recovering the exact meaning of the classics and often combined with an ontology emphasizing the primacy of concrete fact. De Bary has aptly described this ontology as a form of "vitalism."[346]

Historians still do not agree on how to explain the rise of this movement. Some maintain that the "literary inquisition" of the Ch'ing dynasty scared scholars away from controversial subjects. Yet if the muting of dissent is to be blamed on the societal environment, one might also argue that the economic prosperity of the eighteenth century, partly stimulated by the government's *laissez faire* policies, tended to obviate the grounds for protest. Certainly there is an impressive consensus, led by scholars like Ch'ien Mu, that the passion for protest and the moral zeal of scholars declined in the eighteenth century.[347] "Moderate realism" was widespread and partly merged with Confucian economism and secularism, which in turn justified the pursuit of erudition for its own sake.

Other scholars trace the Ch'ing emphasis on evidentiary studies back to Ming scholars like Ch'en Ti (1541–1617) and Chiao Hung (1540?–1620). A third view stresses that, as a reaction to the difficulties of the Ming government, many scholars in the seventeenth century poured their energies into *ching-shih* (the concrete study of governmental institutions), and this tendency eventually turned into a focus on historical and textual studies.[348] Similarly, Ch'ing scholars blaming the fall of the Ming on the "empty" metaphysics of Neo-Confucianism preferred "substantial studies." Finally, it is clear that the rise of this movement must be accounted for also in terms of the inner development of Confucian thought.

From this standpoint, one has to consider the relation of this movement to Sung and Ming Neo-Confucianism. Professor Ying-shih Yü has recently analyzed this problem. Liang Ch'i-ch'ao and Hu Shih interpreted "Han learning" as a revolt against Neo-Confucianism, but the roots of Han learning in Neo-Confucianism are now widely recognized. Ch'ien Mu pointed out that the founders of Han learning in late Ming times "were all indebted to Sung learning," and Fung Yu-lan took a similar position. Yü Ying-shih has suggested that it was especially the search for the sages' authoritative answer to the metaphysical questions splitting the two schools of Neo-Confucianism which moved Ch'ing scholars to devote themselves to the philology of "Han learning."[349]

Moreover, Liu Tsung-chou's answer to the Neo-Confucian problem of imminent and accomplished issuance has been clearly connected by Ch'ien Mu to the "vitalism" of Huang Tsung-hsi, Wang Fu-chih, Yen Yüan, and Tai Chen. As is now widely recognized, modern accounts of these thinkers as moving toward "materialism" or "naturalism" are misleading. True, there is an element in their thought definitely similar to materialism, and they did reduce all existence to a kind of concrete, material reality. Nevertheless, if we look into their concept of this concrete reality, we find it stuffed with all the metaphysical and experiential items listed in section j as comprising the ontological inventory of Neo-Confucianism.[350] While Western materialists were taking God out of the objectively existing cosmos when they reduced it to mere matter and energy, Ch'ing vitalists were reducing all existence to a concrete reality teleologically infused with divine meaning. Far from rejecting Neo-Confucian ontology, they were still trying to solve the problem of linkage.

Their solution harked back to that of Chang Nan-hsüan and others, who argued that because principle and accomplished issuance formed an indivisible whole, principle and imminent issuance could not be regarded as somehow transcending accomplished issuance (see section l). Far from denying that we should occupy ourselves with the search for our heaven-conferred nature, Liu Tsung-chou wanted to facilitate this search by directing us to look for heavenly principle in our concrete feelings. Setting up a straw man, therefore, he denied that "imminent issuance is the heaven-conferred nature, and accomplished issuance is the feelings." He sought to clarify the problem with still another murky distinction: we should "discuss the heaven-conferred nature in terms of the feelings, rather than seek to see the heaven-conferred nature as something preserved in the feelings."[351]

A similar interpretation can be made of all the vitalist views. Moreover, as T'ang Chün-i points out, Huang Tsung-hsi's emphasis on "substantial" historical and institutional studies was connected to this very metaphysical point that principle existed only in the form of overt experience.[352]

Yet it is true that for Chang Nan-hsüan, being aware of the indivisibility of principle and overt experience was a way of finding the sage's "equilibrium of imminent issuance," while in Ch'ing times it rather tended just to legitimate all forms of overt experience as proper objects of detailed study. Indeed it partly became a way of reifying the experience of academic study as the *kung-fu* which themselves constituted the *tao*. In this way a formula used in the Neo-Confucian quest for sagehood and transformation helped rationalize a shift away from this quest toward a secular preoccupation with worldly pursuits.

3. Sense of Predicament (x)

The pathos of this shift, however, is still far from clear. Did those who abandoned the Neo-Confucian quest as chimerical feel themselves to be losing hope as well? Or, in realistically devoting themselves to family matters, local concerns, and scholarly details petty by Neo-Confucian standards (*chih-li*), did they still feel that they were living up to their mission as followers of Confucius? Certainly if the Neo-Confucian quest appeared chimerical to some, abandoning it did not necessarily dispel the gloom of predicament. Tung-lin figures like Kao P'an-lung believed that courage at the *kuan-t'ou* (moment of critical moral choice) was more important than elucidating the conditions of linkage, but the very glory of their integrity lay in their attachment to it in the face of the utter hopelessness of their cause. To what extent this hopelessness remained as the spiritual heritage of Ch'ing scholars living under Manchu rule is a crucial question.

At the very least, Ch'ing scholars remained acutely aware of the gap between the ideals of the *Four Books* and the moral wilderness which they perceived within and without. This awareness was integral to routine bureaucratic attitudes.[353] We also know that once they suspended the Neo-Confucian quest, there was nothing else in their lives until the late nineteenth century which they perceived as even remotely capable of closing this gap. It would seem, therefore, that without this quest, their sense of predicament could only have deepened.

We come back, therefore, to the question of their declining moral zeal. Useful in this context is Ernst Troeltsch's distinction between church and sect. He defined "the Church" as a religious group with a realistically flexible sense of morality harmonizing with the interests of the current political establishment, and he viewed the "sect" as a voluntary association based purely on a radical commitment to the goal of total spiritual purity, which stood in contrast with the morally compromised secular order.[354] More generally, one may say that intellectual groups can oscillate between periods of zealous determination to overcome the ills of the world and periods of accommodation to an unmalleable environment of persisting evils.

Admittedly, in the Confucian scene, church and sect tendencies were typically intertwined, as illustrated by the blending of Neo-

Confucian thought, secularism, moderate realism, and state Confucianism. Nevertheless, the Neo-Confucians' zealous pursuit of the goal of inner purity and outer moral transformation did set them apart as a sect in Troeltsch's sense. They were zealously determined to grasp linkage and the "equilibrium of imminent issuance" as the prerequisite of outer transformation. Time and again, Chu Hsi and Wang Yang-ming told their students that they had to "make up their minds" (*li-chih*) to achieve this goal, and the famous Neo-Confucian controversies invariably emerged out of the zeal of men dedicated totalistically to the pursuit of this goal, intensely hopeful that with just one more formulation of linkage, they would finally be able to realize it. Their "claims" all arose out of this zeal. This sect-like zeal seems to have declined in the eighteenth century, and Confucian scholars leaned more to the morality of "the Church." Ch'ien Mu's thesis that the scholars of the textual studies movement lacked moral dedication therefore remains a most important one.

If, however, we look not at the zeal with which Neo-Confucians pursued their goal but at the way they perceived their goal and the given world, then it is hard to distinguish their ideas from garden-variety Confucianism. Indeed, stripped of their zeal, their outlook was close to that of the bureaucracy's political culture. Nor is this surprising when we remember that all along we have been referring to Neo-Confucian perceptions which were verbalized in the form of clichés. Had these verbal symbols not expressed widespread, slow-to-change, psychologically deep-seated orientations, they would not have been clichés repeated century after century.

CHAPTER FOUR

Neo-Confucianism and the Political Culture of Late Imperial China

a. CULTURE AND CORRUPTION

IF we think of a political culture as a set of attitudes and motivations bringing about overt patterns of political behavior, we must first say that in imperial China, much political behavior was based on the realistic pursuit of material interests by men lacking much sincere commitment to Confucian principles. All political systems involve the kind of amoral, instrumental rationality which Weber called *Zweckrationalität* as well as the violation of societal norms by persons putting primacy on egotistic and particularistic needs. The massive phenomenon of Ch'ing bureaucratic corruption only confirms this observation. Even more, this corruption was legitimated in terms of some of the cultural patterns listed above, such as Confucian familism, particularistic economism, and Confucian secularism (see chapter 3, section a).

Yet corrupt officials are not peculiar to imperial China, and neither is the existence of a landowning elite exploiting the poorer classes. Much more distinctive are the kinds of political symbols, social ties, and organizational structures in terms of which these officials and landowners banded together to implement their interests and mobilize their society. To put it in another way, the dysfunctional patterns of self-interested corruption eroding the organizational effectiveness of the Ming-Ch'ing state were important, but they appear in a different light when we note the obvious contrast between the state's complex organizational routines and the organizational backwardness of the peasantry. Partly because the peasants had not internalized through education a shared ideology dissolving the cultural barriers between different localities, the gap between their organizational capabilities and those of the elite was usually large enough to ensure the empire's political stability. Therefore, while the dysfunctions of the state were often deplored by indigenous critics in revealing if hyperbolic terms, we also have to take into account the functional orientations in terms of which the state stemmed the tide of such dysfunctional behavior, sustained the flow of authority, and promoted the cooperation needed to realize its goals.

My approach to the question of political culture is influenced by Talcott Parsons' emphasis on shared values, which stems from the thought of Weber and Durkheim. It is not for me here to try to review the criticisms currently being leveled at Parsons. S. M. Lipset has noted that sociological theorists have as yet been unable to reconcile the Weberian "stress on values as the key source of action" with the Marxist emphasis on "the significance of interests."[1] This puzzle is certainly reflected in Chinese studies. In his study of Chinese political culture, R. H. Solomon observes that "The social and political orientations of the Chinese we had interviewed very strongly reflected the values of the Confucian tradition—even where the individual had not been formally schooled in classical Confucian literature."[2] Yet how did these values shape the behavior of individuals unscrupulously pursuing their own ends? Certainly unscrupulous Chinese—the majority of the Chinese population, according to Chu Hsi—were still "culturally conditioned," but to admit this is hardly to solve the puzzle of the relation between their culture and their behavior.

I would heuristically suggest that the more action is characterized by ties of cooperation and the more it takes the form of patterns stabilized over time, the more it depends on shared values. If the realistic pursuit of self-interest brushing aside moral injunctions can be said to characterize violent conflict and vertical class relations of exploitation, horizontal ties of organizational coordination between peers in a particular social class depend more on shared cosmological and ethical beliefs. Thus both the warp

168

and the woof of social action have to be considered. In particular, at least in imperial China, relations of trust needed to coordinate organizational activities were forged through a shared sense of moral outrage and self-justification, which in turn presupposed shared perceptions of the self and society as a moral drama. Without such shared orientations, the bureaucracy could not have functioned as a mixture of factionalism and crosscutting solidarities limiting conflict.

A comprehensive account of the late imperial political culture is not yet possible. What I will attempt here is an account of those shared, functional orientations facilitating bureaucratic cooperation. Although some of my analysis deals with obvious facts, the reader will see that my interpretation of the late imperial political culture differs from the views of the Neo-Weberians as well as the Chinese humanists (see Introduction). After discussing these orientations, I will describe some of the basic ways they directly molded overt political behavior.

b. THE CONVERGENCE OF INTERNAL AND EXTERNAL PRESSURES

Neo-Confucianism was closely connected to these orientations. True, I have argued that Neo-Confucians were a sect in Troeltsch's sense. By this, however, I referred to the fact that they not only perceived the mind as existing at the intersection of a good and a bad cosmic force but also were zealously determined to eliminate the bad one (see chapter 3, section x). Apart from this zeal, their perception of this perilous moral intersection was by no means peculiar to them. It rather was a widespread orientation which shaped the officials' image of themselves and their world.

Let us begin with half of this intersection, the Neo-Confucian view of the mind as so embroiled in a tendency toward evil and so beset with "fears and anxieties" that the *tao* appeared as "almost imperceptible in its subtlety." It is striking that this view accorded with the self-image of Ch'ing bureaucrats as the latter can be inferred from study of Ch'ing administrative practices and views. While the officials were confronted with an external barrage of official rhetoric and administrative sanctions defining them as moral failures, they themselves in their own minds perceived the very selfishness they were accused of succumbing to. The evidence for such a convergence of external pressures and internal tensions is convincing.

c. THE CONDEMNATION AND PUNISHMENT
OF BAD OFFICIALS

As supervised by the Board of Civil Officials, the Ch'ing system of administrative punishments was rooted in ideas and practices going back some eighteen hundred years. It called for sanctions like salary fines, demotions, and dismissals, while the officials' serious crimes were handled by the Board of Punishments. These administrative sanctions were so frequently inflicted that they were a routine aspect of official life.[3] Although modern scholars have sometimes held that these sanctions violated the Confucian sense of status honor, they actually were legitimated in terms of a "probationary ethic" based on clearly Confucian ideas.

For instance, the classic *Book of History* approved of *ch'u-chih* (demotion or dismissal and promotion), and no Confucian, I believe, ever challenged this idea. Even Mencius favored the dismissal of bad officials. Some Confucians went still further, approving of harsh, criminal punishments for bad officials. Some even believed that criminal officials should be punished more harshly than criminal commoners, because they had betrayed their obligation to serve as models of behavior.

Such ideas were complemented by the common opinion that most officials in fact were not *chün-tzu* (true gentlemen) above material considerations but rather *chung-ts'ai* (men of medium ability), who would act decently only if motivated by a proper mix of external incentives.[4]

A view of officials as men perpetually on the verge of moral failure was also expressed by the Ch'ing emperors in their denunciations of censors (the edicts in my sampling come from the period 1651–1745). These censors were the *k'o-tao* (censors of the Six Sections and provincial censors), and they had the responsibility of revealing the shortcomings of all persons in the government, including the emperor.[5]

It is a striking fact that the emperor was nearly always angry with them. When they boldly offered criticism, he was liable to suspect them of fishing for "the fine reputation of one who dares to remonstrate." On the other hand, when they avoided bold criticisms, the emperor at various times denounced them for failing to speak up at all, for discussing only trivial matters, for merely rehashing old stories, for acting on unsubstantiated rumors, for obsequiously trying to avoid upsetting him, for divulging imperial secrets, for vacillating, or for spreading rumors behind his back. He saw them as frustrating him in his anxious efforts to be totally informed, to reward and punish officials with perfect justice, and to relieve the common people of their continuing misery.

Through their shortcomings, the emperor charged, they were failing to carry out their basic moral contract with him. He had appealed "with a sincere mind" for information and criticism, but they had failed to "respond" to him with "a sincere mind."[6] In terms of openness and sincerity, they were supposed to "expose their livers and reveal their gall-bladders," but often they only "pretended to act in a public cause while actually seeking to further selfish interests." It was because they had failed to rectify their own characters that they were unable to pay the moral debt they owed the emperor for the favors he had bestowed on them. In some cases, losing all sense of moral proportion, they had even felt more obligated by the "small favors" they had received from ordinary persons than by the "great favors" they had received from him. Through such particularism, they had blocked the emperor's efforts to build up a polity in which "superiors and inferiors are one in their feelings." Denouncing such censors in 1736, the Ch'ien-lung emperor exclaimed: "How can they not feel shame here aware of the favors I conferred on them by special promotions and speaking in the presence of scholars who know what discussion by the pure really means!"[7]

To put it in another way, the emperor repeatedly charged his censors with having taken the wrong side in the moral struggle that was continuously being waged in the bureaucracy. Evildoers, an amorphous group with a totally fluid membership, were always present and were often referred to by the emperor in broad, un-specific terms as lurking "in the dark," "demon-like," pulling

171

strings behind the scenes in a "hateful" way. Evil practices had to be uprooted the way a doctor cured an "infected abscess" or "tumor."

Censors and other officials, therefore, were always morally on the spot. Would they join the tide of evil or help check it by "impeaching and correcting transgressors"? Without their help, the emperor, for all his virtue, could not succeed. Facing "ten thousand events daily," the emperor could not take Mencius' advice simply to depend on his own benevolence. Said the Yung-cheng emperor in 1726: "If one desires to rectify the minds of men and customary ways of behavior, one must begin with the efforts of the provincial censors and the censors of the Six Sections. But only if they themselves are free of selfish considerations can they then impeach those who aren't."[8] When the censors faltered, the emperor was often ready to "forgive" them, but he also "tirelessly warned" them to get rid of their "deceitful hearts," "cleanse themselves of their evil habits," and "morally renew themselves."

d. INTERNAL PRESSURES: THE ADMINISTRATIVE, PHILOSOPHICAL, AND PSYCHOLOGICAL EVIDENCE

The probationary ethic, however, did not consist only of the feeling that bad officials should be denounced and punished. This feeling applied to ego as well as alter, since the image of the bad official was generally internalized. This can be inferred from various administrative practices and terms, especially the fact that there was no strict normative line drawn between the status of an official and of a criminal. For instance, an official tried and sentenced could, even after actually serving a criminal sentence, resume his career as an official. Had the officials' self-image and sense of status honor been simply based on the rationale that they were men of honor above the vileness of criminal acts, they could not have formally and routinely accepted former criminals back into their midst. The emphasis on expiation also reflected this internalized sense of guilt or shame. One of the most common sentences was *tai-tsui liu-jen* (dismissal from office with retention of duties while carrying along one's guilt). Officials thus sentenced were said to be *hsiao-li shu-tsui* (exerting themselves to expiate their guilt). Moreover, it was explicitly recognized that such an inner sense of shame was needed if external sanctions were to work. Said one Ch'ing official: "Only when officials have morale and integrity can they be made use of. Such officials, when rewarded, appreciate why they are being encouraged, and, when punished, appreciate why they are being chastised."[9]

Thus basic to a "probationary ethic" expressed in bureaucratic documents, the idea that people tend toward evil would presumably have been expressed also in intellectual writings. When first considering this question, I could only speculate that this bureaucratic idea harked back to Hsün-tzu's theory that human nature is originally evil. At the time, I was influenced by the mistaken notion that Mencius' optimistic view of human nature dominated Neo-Confucianism. Actually, as we have seen, it was Neo-Confucianism itself which emphasized the power of selfish desires within every individual mind. Indeed, Chu Hsi pointed out that with this emphasis, he diverged from Mencius' optimism. (Neo-Confucians could reject Mencius' optimism while still depending on Mencius' view that what moral feelings the mind had emanated from heaven.) (See chapter 3, section o.)

Even more, the very timbre of the bureaucracy's moral rhetoric resembled that of the Neo-Confucian discussions of moral effort. As illustrated by the repeated denunciations of censors, officials, like individuals engaged in self-examination, had their motivations picked apart and were repeatedly criticized for lacking "sincerity" and succumbing to "selfishness."

True, some Ch'ing scholars defended "material desires" as part of one's heaven-conferred nature, but their intention was to work out a kind of vitalist position (see chapter 3, section x), redefining the locus of heavenly principle, not to legitimate selfishness. For instance, Ch'en Ch'ien-ch'u (1604–1677) argued that "heavenly principle must be seen in terms of material human desires. When one sees the point at which human desires are just right, that is heavenly principle." Huang Tsung-hsi wrote to him in 1676, insisting that material desire and selfishness cannot be thus distinguished and reiterating the standard Neo-Confucian view that "heavenly principle and human material desires are exactly opposite to each other." Ch'en's contrite answer to Huang was that he had only meant to clear away some misunderstandings of the day stemming from the Ch'eng-Chu school.[10] Similarly, Tai Chen held that "material desire is an aspect of one's given moral nature," but Tai's goal was *jen* (benevolence), and of course he held that being *jen* meant "not lapsing into selfishness."[11]

The feeling that people have shameful selfish desires, therefore, was basic equally to the probationary ethic, Neo-Confucianism, and the vitalist trend growing out of the latter in Ch'ing times. While we can infer from bureaucratic practices and rhetoric that this feeling was widely internalized, Neo-Confucian and other intellectual writings are themselves records of spiritual struggle appealing to an audience which had internalized it.

Still more, it seems clear that this feeling had a psychological basis in that syndrome of childhood socialization which is described in the literature on "dependency" (see chapter 1). First of all, this feeling involved a pattern of diffuse and free-floating anxiety. Chapter 3 has shown that the people seeking to solve the problems discussed in Neo-Confucian writings were people interested in overcoming painful "fears and anxieties," the existence of which in their own emotional lives took the form of a felt experience so pervasive and ordinary as to be completely taken for granted. Had they not been subject to this continuing feeling of anxiety, the way in which Neo-Confucian writings formulated the problems of life would not have made sense to them, and they would have turned to some other philosophy to verbalize their vision of reality.

True, these anxieties arose partly in response to specific, objective circumstances. Fan Chung-yen's (989–1052) famous injunction illustrates the tendency to worry about the empire's economic and political problems,[12] and scholars also worried about their own careers. Yet they were not just "greedy for material profits and official salary," to cite a favorite formula of Confucian morality. An obsessively anxious concern with the vicissitudes of one's worldly career can be detected in Chu Hsi's lament that scholars do not pursue their true studies with the same energy they devote to passing the examinations and obtaining office, "constantly thinking about [the latter] from the moment they get up in the morning." Chu Hsi also spoke of the need to "expel the desire to emulate those successful in worldly terms."[13] It was exactly these anxieties aroused by considerations of worldly "advantage and disadvantage" which Wu Yü-pi referred to as "being overcome by outer things."[14]

Even if not specifically concerned with personal advantage, Neo-Confucians were diffusely apprehensive about the competitive and threatening social reality which they perceived as existing around them. This diffuse sense of apprehension can be inferred from Chu Hsi's complaint about "often feeling anxious and disturbed, lacking a kind of purity and oneness, a kind of deep, latent, inner wholeness, and in speech or actions, constantly hurried, responding without a sense of reserve, and lacking an easily poised, dignified manner with an aura of inner depth" (see chapter 3, section 1). R. H. Solomon has vividly described a widespread Chinese tendency to fear and shun social situations involving "emotional tension, conflicting desires . . . and interpersonal hostility."[15] Certainly this fear is reflected in the pervasive Neo-Confucian emphasis on social oneness, in the search for a world in which one relates to one's social environment through a smooth flow of "interchanging empathies" (*chiao-kan*). Thus Ch'eng Hao deplored a society in which individuals are "set apart from and opposite to" each other, and Wang Yang-ming denounced the spirit of "do you or I win?"[16] In fact, however, this spirit was powerful in the imperial society, especially in the bureaucracy, and the fear of being engulfed in it was both a reflection of objective conditions and a projection of diffuse anxieties motivating individuals to avoid social confrontations. All these anxieties were simultaneously reflected in and exacerbated by the Sisyphean sense of predicament articulated in the Neo-Confucian vision of the cosmos. One is tempted to see a connection between this multifaceted anxiety and the great frequency with which Ch'ing bureaucrats fell ill, causing innumerable problems of personnel management for their bureaucracy.

Besides this diffuseness, the "fears and anxieties" of Neo-Confucians involved a psychologically suggestive association with the need to depend on a beneficent cosmic force. In Neo-Confucian eyes, the individual disconnected from this force could only flounder, helplessly subject to destructive anxieties and completely unable to achieve the desired inner sense of control, coherence, and fixity (see chapter 3, section e). One must suppose that this perception of the self as dependent on a beneficent outer force authoritatively determining right and wrong appeared plausible precisely to those adults who as children had been brought up to feel dependent on the moral guidance of authority figures, as described in the psychological literature on dependence (see chapter 1).

e. AUTONOMY AND CHARISMA

Behavioral scientists, however, have failed to enter deeply enough into the question of the perceived location of this authoritative power. They have wrongly assumed that this power always inhered in authoritative social roles. Had it done so, the Chinese would have been merely perplexed by Neo-Confucianism, since Neo-Confucian thinkers did not locate it in any of one's social superiors, whether one's father, teacher, or ruler. These roles and one's relation to them were entirely peripheral to the concerns of Neo-Confucianism, which consistently and without the slightest ambiguity located this power in the structure of the cosmos itself as something accessible without mediation to each individual will. From a psychological standpoint, then, this transcendent power was internalized within the concrete self, although distinguished from certain impulses within the self. The individual therefore could autonomously react to the cues of his social environment in terms of an introspectively decided process of moral struggle. It is in this sense that T'ang Chün-i correctly depicts the Confucian self as the one agent of the moral process, tapping godlike powers latent in the flow of its own mental life, pouring the resulting energy with emotional fervor into its arduous strivings, deciding whether the cues of its social superiors are morally legitimate or not, accordingly obeying these superiors or protesting against their actions (whether violently or not), and responding to environmental vicissitudes either by engaging in "bold action in the outer world" or by "withdrawing from worldly concerns and preserving one's purity of character." If this sense of autonomy was often perceived as lost in the turbulent flow of corrupt emotions, the struggle to assert it was also a continuous part of the behavioral situation. There is no other way to account for the fact that so many Chinese for so many centuries felt at home with the symbols of Neo-Confucianism. These symbols, therefore, represented real feelings which were not epiphenomenal.

4. Political Culture (e)

It is illuminating that the serious revival of Neo-Confucian thought in modern times has turned not on homilies about familism and the political order but on an effort to demonstrate the oneness of man and heaven. From the Neo-Confucian standpoint, there was a psychological need for a subjective sense of moral power perceived as immune to the contemporaneous structure of social and political authority, and in a philosophical milieu given to reification, this power had to be conceptually embodied in a thing like "heaven" which physically transcended this otherwise menacing structure. Indeed, without the feeling of being supported by this unmatchable counterweight, the Neo-Confucian individual lacked the ability even to conceptualize his own moral intentions and accept his role in a political order, authoritarian or not. The anxious need for authority, in other words, was a need for that kind of authority aligned with the imperatives of one's own autonomous moral sense.

This internalized sense of moral autonomy and transcendent power was connected to the political charisma traditionally claimed by scholars in their role as *chün-tzu* (true gentlemen). If charisma, as Etzioni suggests, is the "ability of an actor to exercise diffuse and intense influence over the normative orientations of other actors," it can be seen in the "reverential respect" (*tsun*) which even the authoritarian Hsün-tzu recommended as the proper attitude for a ruler to adopt when dealing with a scholar. Mencius arrogantly demanded still more, comparing his "righteousness" and "heavenly rank" with a ruler's mere "human rank." In this demand for "reverential respect," scholars were claiming a morally ultimate responsibility for the fate of the empire, a claim expressed particularly in the traditional ambition to occupy the *tsai-hsiang* (prime office) and use it as the fulcrum of moral-political transformation. The fact that officials, not just the emperor, were held personally responsible for evoking favorable responses from nature, such as rain, also illustrates the magical charisma with which their roles were endowed.[17] Certainly given their pathos of immensity (see chapter 2), a sense of oneness with heaven could make the scholars feel bigger and more powerful than the ruler.

Yet their charisma had a fragility bound up with the anxieties of the probationary ethic. Both the fear and the perception of moral failure in both oneself and others was constant. The rhetoric of bureaucratic organization turned entirely on this perception of the political arena as ever tending to corruption while yet constantly susceptible to moral effort and charismatic influence. Because of this perception, bureaucrats could retain their sense of identity as budding sages while making moral sense out of their often humiliating organizational situations. It was the combination of the sense of charisma and the probationary ethic which formed the bureaucrats' sense of responsibility.

The idea of existing at a perilous moral intersection was, therefore, extremely widespread. From the standpoint of Neo-Confucianism, the self could attain sagehood by tapping a beneficent cosmic force but still was embroiled in a tendency toward evil. From the standpoint of bureaucratic rhetoric, the official both possessed the charisma of the "true gentleman" and was a contemptibly weak being often driven by selfish desires. The fact that both these views applied to the same elite class reinforced their inherent affinity. They were indeed different aspects of a single class ethos. Moreover, the world itself, both in its present form and its history, existed at this moral intersection, according to the outlook routinely expressed in Ch'ing bureaucratic documents. I have elsewhere argued that the perception of this intersection was vital to the organizational flexibility of Ch'ing bureaucracy:

> The heart of the political process was thus perceived as an intersection where good and bad mingled in a partly unclear fashion. . . . Many Confucian officials felt that they themselves were riveted into this moral intersection, and they saw themselves as seeking to improve both themselves and the world around them. . . . Because they had this profound feeling of badness within and without and this uncertainty as to the best policies and organizational forms, they could feel morally comfortable working within a complex organizational structure of which they partly disapproved.[18]

f. AUTHORITY AS A TRIANGULAR PATTERN

The charisma in the official's role is particularly relevant to the question of political culture because of its connection to the problem of authority. If we consider only the probationary ethic, Ch'ing political culture can be simply described as authoritarian. After all, had not the Confucian officials internalized the transgressions with which their superiors charged them? This vertical flow of authority, however, was complicated by the charisma of the officials, which resulted in a triangular concept of authority: the sovereign authority of the *chün* (ruler) was balanced by the *chün-tzu's* (true gentleman's) role as the potentially ultimate vehicle of moral insight, and the authority of the classics overarched both these roles. Although the ruler was officially addressed as a "sage" by Ch'ing officials, this was a form of institutionalized insincerity. He too was perceived as existing at a moral intersection, and his need for criticism from scholars was repeatedly articulated as a ritualized aspect of his role.

g. THE *CHUN-TZU* AS A CAMOUFLAGED ROLE

This triangular concept of authority is clear from famous passages in the very *Four Books* which officially served as the foundation of education in the Ming-Ch'ing period. Yet the tense relationship between these two charismatic roles, the *chün* and the *chün-tzu*, is curiously ignored in most sociological discussions of Confucianism, which usually misrepresent Confucianism as "extoll[ing] the virtues of family life as the pattern of the state."[19] As an institutionalized situation, it is true, this dramatic confrontation between the *chün* and the *chün-tzu* was not synoptically defined and consciously emphasized as an ideal relationship, such as "the three bonds" or "the five relationships." The emphasis was rather on the parallel between the father–son and the ruler–minister relation (*chün-ch'en*), and these two standard sets of model relationships did not bring to mind the moral tension between the *chün* and the *chün-tzu*. This confrontation was thus excluded from the image of the ideal society, where, the ruler being a sage, there was no need for it. In this light, the *chün–chün-tzu* relation was less an ideal to which one was oriented than an arena of ethical adjustment.

Yet although the role of the *chün-tzu* was not an ultimate ideal, like that of the "minister" loyally following the dictates of a sage ruler, it still determined the self-image of that central agent of moral action, the scholar. The *chün-tzu*, in other words, acting as a "teacher," stood to one side as it were, directing the attention of people toward the hierarchical structure they should realize. Yet it was in terms of this admonitory act rather than these hierarchic roles themselves that the Confucian scholar defined his own social role and moral stance. In modern times too, it was taken for granted that this stance was merely an expression of universally obvious principles of moral integrity rather than any peculiarly Confucian role. For this reason, Chinese could continue to adopt it even while denouncing Confucianism and urging "total Westernization." The very obliqueness of this approach was a way of emphasizing authority and hierarchy without undermining morality, but it has also camouflaged the influence of Confucian morality on modern trends (see chapter 5, section c).

Given the common view that kinship ethics provided the only paradigm of authority in traditional times, we have to emphasize the contrast between the *chün–chün-tzu* relation and the father–son relation. Asserting himself as a *chün-tzu*, the scholar partly related to his *chün* as a son did to his father, but unlike any son, the scholar (at least in terms of his ideology) placed himself in the position of a "teacher" relative to his political superior, demanded "reverential respect" from him, and in addressing him leaned on a metaphysical counterweight (heaven), and acted as the spokesman of a constituency, that is, "the people." While the common people, at least in the eyes of some scholars, merely "follow what heaven has decreed," the scholar found that "what heaven has decreed is up to me," and he could even feel he was "establishing heaven's decree." Whatever these words mean, they express a confidence that one has an unsurpassed claim to moral insight. At the same time, "the true gentleman" was typically and explicitly related to his social superior in terms of a fragile bond full of mutual distrust and disappointment, culminating often in the final banishment of the social inferior and at least theoretically allowing for the legitimated execution of the superior. The bond between ruler and scholar was one which could be extinguished and then re-established with a peculiar flexibility, as when a high official was sentenced to death, had the sentence commuted, and then was reinstated at the top of the bureaucracy (a common phenomenon). Conversely, no father stood in danger of losing "heaven's mandate." This propensity toward distrust and mutual rejection as a normative, institutionalized condition had no analogue within the family. It was as though, along with the teacher–student relationship and a unique sense of political constituency and metaphysical potency, three familial experiences had been selected out and partly transvaluated to form the norms of a new social relation: the son's respect for his father's authority, the expulsion from his family of the wicked son, and the murder of the father by the son. This normative relation was as central as any other in imperial times, and in fact Confucian writers probably dwelt on it more than on kinship norms.

h. BUREAUCRATIC PROTEST

Granted, then, that the officials' sense of charisma involved a triangular concept of authority, we still have to ask how this concept molded overt bureaucratic behavior. Certainly it legitimated overt patterns of protest, as illustrated by the long, officially endorsed traditions of *chien* (remonstrance) and *ch'ing-i* (discussion by the pure), as well as by the Confucian idea of morally legitimate rebellion. Admittedly, Ming and Ch'ing officials failed to match the outspokenness of Sung censors, who sometimes critized the current emperor in language close to that of Huang Tsung-hsi's famous denunciation of despotism, a general critique which Huang wrote as a private scholar in 1662. In Sung times, for instance, officials frequently criticized the emperor for issuing orders bypassing the Prime Office, which had the authority to check all imperial orders for improprieties and impracticalities. In one protest against this irregular practice, a memorial written by Liu Fu around 1270, the emperor was sternly told that "The affairs of the empire ought to be carried out together with the empire; the ruler cannot regard them as his private concern." It is striking that Sung officials sometimes even refused to honor these irregular imperial orders.[20]

To speak out even less boldly in the Ming-Ch'ing period sometimes required extraordinary courage, especially during the reigns of unusually bloody tyrants like T'ai-tsu, the Ming founder (1368–1398). Yet officials with courage did come forth and invariably were admired by their peers for living up to the ideals of a shared tradition. Around 1376, for instance, T'ai-tsu unjustly ordered the executions of hundreds of officials. He felt that there was corruption in the widespread practice of bringing blank but already stamped fiscal forms from provincial offices to the Board of Revenue at the capital, where these forms could be conveniently filled in whenever the Board required corrections. Having the blank forms handy allowed the immediate preparation at the capital of a set of consistent reports from all the administrative levels involved, saving the time which otherwise would have been required to send mistaken reports back for corrections and stamping to the provincial offices. Most officials did not dare point out to the half-crazed emperor that this established practice was a matter of convenience, not corruption, but one Cheng Shih-li did. He also told the emperor that punishing people for a practice without previously making it illegal was unjust. (T'ai-tsu went ahead with his executions anyway.)[21]

A more famous example is that of the Tung-lin scholars, some seventy-five of whom presented memorials in 1624 denouncing the crimes of the emperor's favorite eunuch. Some of them shortly were executed, but the Tung-lin protests have remained as a sacred memory for Chinese to this day.[22]

In 1726, the censor Hsieh Chi-shih argued with the emperor in court, holding that one of the emperor's most trusted officials was corrupt. Accused at his trial of making unfounded allegations, Hsieh replied "Confucius and Mencius" when he was asked with whom he was acting in collusion. He explained: "I have read in the books of Confucius and Mencius that one should remonstrate in a sincerely loyal way. To see corruption and not attack it is to be disloyal." Convicted and banished to Mongolia, he calmly spent his time there surrounded by Manchu officers who revered him as their teacher. When he was reinstated as a censor in 1736, he promptly risked ridicule by requesting that his commentaries on *The Great Learning* and the *Doctrine of the Mean* replace those of Chu Hsi in the official system of education. Eventually he retired to his native place, peacefully living out his last years.[23]

Hsieh Chi-shih was extraordinarily self-willed, but we cannot conclude that arguing against the ruler's decision was a particularly momentous event in the Ch'ing period. That it did not necessarily arouse much attention is significant. Historians have barely noted the fact that in 1884, at least three officials memorialized asking the Empress Dowager to withdraw her order that the young emperor's father take part in the deliberations of the Grand Council; they strongly criticized her idea as out of accord with the "proper institutions of the state." She rejected their protest but not without asking that officials "excuse" this procedure as a necessary expedient.[24] Hsüeh Yün-sheng (1820–1901) is famous as the outstanding expert on penal law in late Ch'ing times. Few are aware that in 1896, as a president of the Board of Punishments, he twice insisted on his interpretation of the law when the Empress Dowager sought a lighter punishment for two palace eunuchs sentenced for resisting arrest by instigating a violent melee in which life had been lost. Hsüeh specifically rejected the legal reasoning of the empress. His biographer notes: "Knowing he would not bend in his adherence to the law, the ruler in the end followed his proposal." The very next year Hsüeh was transferred and slightly demoted on account of an unrelated problem which may nevertheless have reflected the empress's annoyance with his steadfastness. Yet he ended his career honorably and was praised on his death by the empress for his integrity in the administration of criminal justice.[25]

i. BUREAUCRATIC ESPRIT

Whether or not such a stoutly independent stance was typical, we have to keep in mind that the Ch'ing rulers explicitly encouraged it in that they publicly recognized their own fallibility and had a clearly articulated interest in promoting a spirit of adherence to the written regulations and the precedents of their imperial ancestors. Moreover, as has been argued elsewhere, they controlled their officials by relying not on the despotic use of terror but on a complex mixture of sanctions, including a major emphasis on striking a pose of extraordinary benevolence and empathy for the feelings of the elite. Officials, in turn, had numerous gratifying opportunities to strike a pose of obstinancy with little fear of severe punishment, and they did take advantage of them in both significant and trivial ways.[26] The crucial behavioral effects of the elite's Mencian tradition of charisma have to be seen within this complicated situation as a whole. They can be analyzed in terms of two interconnected themes, the esprit of the officials and the powerful universalistic tendency to respect the letter of the law. Damaged as it was, this universalistic esprit was the indispensable foundation of the bureaucracy's effectiveness, as the following considerations should make clear.

4. Political Culture (i)

However corrupt, the bureaucracy could not have functioned without some basic level of esprit, for which the common word in administrative documents was *ch'i* (inner flow of vital force, morale). Officials frequently worried about the *ch'i* of officialdom. *Ch'i* was part of a large number of ordinary words close to our "guts" or "backbone," and in bureaucratic usage it necessarily connoted the ideal of the "true gentleman" as well as the probationary ethic. Thus it harked back to Mencius's idea of a *hao-jan-chih-ch'i* (vast, overflowing inner vital force), which, as Mencius said, would "fill up heaven and earth" if properly "nourished," giving one the "unyielding strength" to hold fast to the *tao* with an "imperturbable mind." This "vital force" involved a gratifying sense of self-esteem. When Chu Hsi in his "teens read that passage in Mencius which states that the sage and the ordinary individual belong to the same category of beings, [his] joy too great for words." Every official was entitled to this joy, because in terms of its official rhetoric, the government believed in *tsun-hsien* (treating superior men with deep respect). This inner pride of the officials was regarded as a necessary part of the "courage" needed to carry out their duties, "exhaustively devoting themselves to their responsibilities and enduring the hardships and resentments involved," instead of "shirking their responsibilities," that most pervasively denounced of bureaucratic sins.[27] If this self-respect seldom led to direct defiance of the emperor, it frequently led to self-confident pronouncements about the merits and faults of various officials and policies, as is obvious from the flood of criticisms, proposals, and counterproposals found in memorials to the emperor and privately published essays.

Ch'ing officials would have been surprised by the modern psychological view that, because of their syndrome of "dependence," they lacked "self-esteem." While they habitually lamented the shortage of superior officials, whom they called *hao-chieh* (men of superior quality), they were also typically appalled by the surplus of overstuffed egos in their society, such as individuals who regarded themselves as destined to be sages, or former officials who, serving as private secretaries, were "discontented with their station" and so "inevitably" were apt to "presumptuously act like powerful persons" (*chao-yao*).[28] It was partly because this tendency toward arrogance was perceived as powerful that Wang Yang-ming's call

184

for "self-confidence" was criticized as unleashing dangerous urges. Some Chinese took the old Confucian idea of *tzu-tsun* (respect for oneself) all too seriously! Most important, had the officials lacked this Mencian esprit, the rhetoric of moral denunciation directed at them would have had no emotional bite and merely sounded foolish.

The sense of charisma thus was basic to the esprit needed to criticize policy and carry out the laws, just as the probationary ethic legitimated the punishment of officials who failed to perform their duties. This respect for the law, however, was reinforced by a variety of realistic factors powerfully inclining the behavior of the emperor as well as the officials toward universalism, that is, an emphasis on generalized norms of performance rather than ascriptive characteristics in the distribution of rewards and sanctions.

j. BUREAUCRATIC PRACTICE AND UNIVERSALISM

On the side of the officials, we have to remember that the ethical universalism connected to their charismatic image was complemented by the universalism in both the examination system and the system of disciplinary law (*ch'u-fen tse-li*). In the emphatically universalistic way it was written, the disciplinary law differed from the bulk of the penal law. Furthermore, while the system of avoidance shifted officials geographically so as to hinder the growth of particularistic ties, the very exigencies of organization required some degree of universalism, and the use of law proved desirable as a way of resolving bureaucratically internal disputes in a neutral, conciliatory way.[29]

Officials, moreover, were not only vulnerable to the disciplinary sanctions but also where placed in a bureaucratic structure ingeniously designed to maximize the crosscurrents of suspicion and denunciation, notably those between capital "staff" offices and regional "line" offices. To protect themselves, officials competed with one another in trying to prove to the emperor that they were faithful to the law. All too familiar was the stereotype of the mediocre official who protected his career by avoiding all risky actions and "sticking blindly" to the law (*chü-ni*). Frequently deplored was the conduct of the local magistrate who neglected the needs of his people because he was so preoccupied with trying to avoid administrative sanctions.[30] It is significant that much of the corruption took the form not of offenses against the law but of immoral manipulations in the finding of the law. Endlessly denounced were clerks and officials who looked for legal precedents justifying decisions in favor of their friends and clients. That interests were so often pursued in this way testifies to the great emphasis on the authority of the law. Although some laws were customarily ignored (*shih-wei chü-wen*), these typically were laws too difficult to enforce because of either their inherent impracticality or the inertia of a particular well-established custom. Where legal procedures were feasible and in the interest of powerful persons, the tendency to respect them was strong.

We have to keep in mind that even the scoundrel will seek the approval of his peers by carrying out many acts conforming to culturally defined ideals, and as he deviously and hypocritically acts to further his own interests, he will still seek to utilize culturally approved, legal kinds of social ties and organizational forms. What else is meant by that classic word for the most pervasive kind of elite immorality, *hsiang-yüan* (hypocritically following the fashionable moral opinions of the day)? Thus unscrupulousness and culturally conformist behavior are often mutually compatible.

Finally, respect for law as well as the ability to carry it out was furthered by a marked though limited tendency toward functional as well as regional specialization within the bureaucracy, which historians are now only beginning to study. For instance, although the "amateurism" of Ch'ing officials has been contrasted to the expertise of private secretaries, the line between officials and private secretaries was in fact blurred. As much as the shortage of expert officials, it was the moonlighting of officials as private secretaries which worried the emperors in the middle Ch'ing period. They denounced it in a series of edicts stretching over the period 1747–1847.[31]

k. UNIVERSALISM AND THE POWER OF
THE EMPEROR

There is no basis at all, then, for supposing that the officials' egotistic and particularistic drives were necessarily stronger than the universalistic pull of all these factors. At the same time, this pull was reinforced by the character of the emperor's office and interests. The emperor had immense power, which indeed did shape the behavior of the officials, and he necessarily used it with a fundamental interest precisely in the universalistic performance of bureaucratic duties. How else could he protect his throne and increase his power? No wonder, then, that the emperor publicly presented himself as one following the law. The *Ta-Ch'ing hui-tien* (Collected Statutes of the Great Ch'ing Dynasty) held that its laws were followed by both "the court and the people." In 1724 the Yung-cheng emperor heatedly rebuked some high officials for having failed to object to one of his orders which violated the regulations.[32]

Furthermore, the awesomeness of the emperor's position impeded particularistic entanglements with his officials, and his immense wealth usually made bribery impossible (bribery of the court in Tz'u-hsi's time was regarded as shocking). Respect for law was also furthered by the "appellate" structure of so much of the imperial executive process. Often, the Ch'ing emperor did not himself initiate proposals but merely responded to proposals made and criticized by officials in terms of legal precedents. Finally, the Confucian emphasis on law was not restricted to a few passing remarks in the classics. Rather, the fact that so much law, especially in the Ch'ing period, was conceptualized as *li* (precedent) merged respect for law with respect for the hallowed past and the revered decisions of the imperial ancestors. After all, this was a "traditional" society, but one in which traditional values consisted not only of particularistic norms but also of respect for the wisdom of the past.[33]

The behavioral impact of this whole syndrome of universalism and Mencian esprit thus becomes clearer when we realize that it stemmed not only from noble ideals but also from the endless resources of self-interest, arrogance, and power. The triangular structure of authority was based not only on moral values but also on an intricate web of norms and procedures serving the interests of the emperor as well as the elite.

IF, then, the Neo-Confucian emphasis on inner moral frailty meshed with the bureaucracy's authoritarian rhetoric of moral

denunciation, the Neo-Confucian perception of inner moral potentiality was crucial to the bureaucrats' sense of charisma, which in
turn led to a triangular concept of authority with basic behavioral
implications. True, as a working official, the Neo-confucian continually had to shift his focus from the goal of true sagehood to the
authoritatively ritualistic fiction of the current ruler's sagehood,
suspending any zeal to turn his charismatic status into that mission
of world transformation for which Neo-Confucianism called. Nevertheless, we should not exaggerate the contrast between the scholars'
idealistic philosophy of moral autonomy and the harsh authoritarianism they encountered in the bureaucracy. On the contrary,
their autonomous quest for sagehood involved an anxious feeling
of moral insufficiency that was basic to their probationary ethic
as bureaucrats, and the bureaucracy, for all its authoritarianism,
still depended on a diffused quality of esprit and charisma interwoven with the bureaucrats' self-image as budding sages.

1. AUTHORITY, MODERATE REALISM, AND RADICALISM

To present a fuller analysis of Ch'ing political culture, we would
have to relate this triangular concept of authority to all other
attitudes shaping political behavior, a task requiring much further
study. We should, however, touch on the obviously connected
issue of radicalism and moderate realism. As already discussed,
"radicalism" refers to the classically Confucian vision of society
as dominated by transforming impulses emanating from the center
of the political arena. "Moderate realism" refers to a less optimistic vision of politics in which the weakness of the center's
controlling impulses is recognized (see chapter 3, section v). That
is, in the radical view, the empire's ultimate center of sovereign
authority is morally invigorated, pursues policies conforming to
morally sound principles, arouses the enthusiasm of the morally
insightful, reshapes the whole society and economy, and thus successfully channels moral energies into the "outer world." Radicalism, therefore, was correlated to a vision of authority in which
the disjunction between *chün* and *chün-tzu*, that is, between sovereign authority and the charismatic class of morally insightful

persons, was minimized. To the extent that the center of the political arena was seen as morally reinvigorated, the sense of predicament could fade, and the totalistic effort to achieve moral purification could be turned from the "inner" life to the "outer" world.

On the other hand, in the case of moderate realism, to which Neo-Confucianism was closely connected since the twelfth century, the center of the political arena was viewed as morally enervated. Tung Chung-shu's idea of *wang-chiao* (the teachings of the king) as the salvation of society was merely a peripheral hope for Ming-Ch'ing Neo-Confucians. They remained "waiting for a visit" from such a king, to quote from the title of Huang Tsung-hsi's book denouncing despotism.[34] Thus turning to the "inner" life of *kung-fu* (efficacious moral efforts) and to limited political efforts in their local environments, they accepted the clear-cut disjunction between sovereign authority and moral insight as part of their fundamental predicament.

In terms of the triangular concept of authority, therefore, the perception of a disjunction between sovereign authority and moral insight mingled with the continuing hope that this disjunction could be dissolved. The difference between radicalism and moderate realism was correlated to the rising and falling of this hope. Fulfillment of this hope necessarily meant a morally vitalized center of sovereign authority capable of radically and totally dominating the "outer" political arena, while the inability to fulfill this hope tended to divert the attention of scholars away from this enervated center and the "outer" world to which it was linked through the system of territorial administration.

This is not to say that moderate realism, which dominated political thought in Ming-Ch'ing times, was necessarily the politics of despair. True, the perceived disjunction between moral principle and sovereign authority could not be overcome by the propaganda of those Ming and Ch'ing emperors who explicitly claimed that their rule conformed to "heavenly principle" or to the *tao*. Nor could it be overcome by the rising commercial prosperity of the Ming-Ch'ing period. Much as Confucians were concerned with "the people's livelihood," the improvement of this livelihood through purely economic developments impressed them no more than it has impressed liberals in Taiwan today. What Ming-Ch'ing

4. Political Culture (1)

Confucians generally perceived in their political and economic environment was at best that kind of amoral, inherently unstable success expressed by the ancient concept of "rule by the hegemon" (*pa*), a ruler unable to realize a stable and truly moral polity but nevertheless maintaining peace and order through a mixture of coercion and "trust."[35] Yet this kind of society did not plunge Confucian scholars into despair because it allowed them not only to achieve wealth and prestige but also to oscillate comfortably between the "inner" *kung-fu* which kept their ultimate vision alive and the aesthetic pleasures of secularism (see p. 53 above).

It was this delicate balance which was threatened by the impact of Western imperialism in the late nineteenth century. As the imperial state proved unable to maintain it, the Chinese were forced to think about how to redesign their political structure. Certainly many of them tried to reformulate the moderate realism of the Ch'ing period, looking for some institutional compromise facilitating both gradual modernization and the continuing efforts of intellectuals to build up their own moral stamina, broaden their learning, and point the way to utopia. Among others, however, the impact of the West revived the traditional zeal for total reform along with the radical hope of reshaping society through the transforming impulses of a political center truly grasping the ultimate principles of morality and the cosmos. For them, Huang Tsung-hsi's long wait was about over. Yet how could foreign ideas revive a traditional hope? This puzzle is the subject of the last chapter.

CHAPTER FIVE

The Ethos of Interdependence in an Age of Rising Optimism and Westernization

a. WESTERNIZATION

B<small>EGINNING</small> with the Opium War (1839–1842) and the Taiping Rebellion (1850–1864), the Ch'ing empire experienced a series of internal and external political shocks which gradually undermined its power. Simultaneously, a varied movement began to adopt Western ways in order to strengthen and modernize the nation. At first conscious only of Western military superiority, the Chinese elite within a few decades realized that this superiority had an economic, political, social, and cultural basis. By 1912, when the Ch'ing empire fell, there was a broad consensus that "The republic is universally recognized as the best form of state," and on March 11, 1912, the Provisional Constitution of the new republic was promulgated.[1] Yet China's political difficulties only deepened. The May Fourth Movement, which spread through much of the country from 1917 to 1923, expressed the idea that China had to break with the past in still more fundamental ways, replacing Confucian values with a devotion to "science and democracy." The slogan of "total Westernization" was popular for a time, and Marxism flourished amidst the ferment of this attack on the Confucian tradition. While the continuing efforts to restructure Chinese society increasingly merged with the revolutionary aspirations of the dispossessed, intellectuals who looked back to Confucianism for moral values were effectively ridiculed as opponents of modernization and allies of reaction. When the Chinese Communists established the People's

5. Optimism (a)

Republic of China in 1949, they were committed to a vision of nationalism, political participation, science, and economic growth which stood in sharp contrast to the traditional outlook. They then proceeded to carry out a revolution which redefined the international position of their country; radically altered the polity and its relation to the city, the village, the family, and the individual; transformed patterns of economic production and distribution; and changed interpersonal relations.

Thus the traditional interpersonal emphasis on hierarchy and deference was altered in possibly two ways. First, the suffrage of full ethical and personal dignity, previously restricted to certain elite groups, was largely extended to classes of individuals previously regarded as morally inferior or underdeveloped, notably females, the young, and those doing physical work, especially peasants. One might even say that extension of this suffrage was combined with a reformulation of the conditions of inequality, since to some extent the peasants and the young were newly defined as more moral than the old and the intellectuals. Mao's "populism" has indeed been revolutionary. Second, apart from this redefinition of the membership of the morally elect, relations between persons of full moral dignity developed in the direction of egalitarianism, although the Confucian version of this concept—relations between "friends" who are *chün-tzu*—was not necessarily hierarchical.

Besides this change away from the traditional pattern of deference, the lines of solidarity between groups have been redefined. We might say that the topology of interdependence has changed. As argued below, the new national pattern of solidarity, merging the moral empathies of the polity, the village, and the family to an unprecedented extent, seems to be connected to the enthusiastic feeling that the Chinese are now entering an era during which they will be more successful than previously in realizing their moral goals. Although these new lines of solidarity have been defined along with new lines of antagonism, these new antagonisms of class struggle are themselves perceived as part of a creative historical process continuously reaffirming and strengthening the solidarity of the morally elect masses.[2] At the same time, the practicalities of economic production, always basic to Confucian minds, have now been systematically emphasized to an unprece-

192

dented extent. Moreover the ferment of mutually reinforcing interaction between this new focus on practicality and the enthusiasms of a more egalitarian mass society can itself be regarded as dissolving traditional orientations. Certainly this momentous transformation as a whole largely ended Confucian fundamentalism (the belief that all truths were essentially realized in The Three Dynasties and expressed in the classics) and institutional Confucianism (traditional familism, gentry life, the examination system, the monarchy, and other governmental institutions like the tribute system).

No wonder, then, that it has been widely regarded by Western historians as based on "the death of the Confucian world view."[3] In Chinese intellectual circles also, there is broad agreement that this transformation, whether admirably or deplorably, has been opposed to the traditional cultural "spirit." To those Chinese modernizers who have seen themselves as "striking down" a tradition deserving "bitter hatred," the idea that this very tradition may have informed some of their own attitudes is preposterous, while to those scholars desiring a renewal of the Confucian "spirit," the idea that this "spirit" may have influenced the very movements seemingly bent on destroying it is equally unattractive.

b. THE INERTIA OF THE PAST

Only in the last few years have scholars begun to question this view of Chinese modernization as Westernization.[4] Certainly the new technology, the new organizational forms, and other manifestations of modernization are largely the result of Westernization. But what prompted the Chinese to adopt their particular kind of collectivism? Above all, what is the secret of their success? Educated elites throughout the Third World have appreciated Western forms of technology and organization, but the Chinese government has been able to implement these forms by mobilizing a largely peasant population of 800 million. This mobilizational achievement does not stem from any distinctive economic conditions since, in terms of per capita income, mainland China remains among the poorest nations in the world. Nor can it be explained as the result of China's exposure to cosmopolitan influences, which have also reached many other equally poor but far less mobilized countries in the Third World. Rather, as Ralph Linton has emphasized, cultural diffusion is a two-sided game, and "the real core of the problem of diffusion . . . [is] the reaction of the accepting group to the elements presented to it." To understand the motivational basis of China's reaction to cosmopolitan influences, we cannot but examine what Linton calls "those vital attitudes and values which lie largely below the level of individual consciousness" and which are "not susceptible to diffusion."[5] These attitudes include beliefs about the nature of authority, about the relation of the self to the cosmos and the group, and about the ultimate meaningfulness of social mobilization and transformation.

Historians, therefore, are beginning to reconsider the question of the inertia of such attitudes in China. With our missionary heritage, we Westerners have often assumed that rapid cultural conversion is feasible, and the similar idea of finding enlightenment in "one leap" goes back many centuries in China. Yet it goes against common sense to suppose that Confucian values could have faded so quickly. Whitehead's statement that all Western philosophy consists only of footnotes to Plato may have been a witty remark, but it points to the great inertia of old ideas in even the world's most dynamic civilization. As some Western textbooks would have it, the trauma of the Japanese victory in 1894–1895 was enough to dissolve cultural beliefs developed over some 3000 years, but Chinese modernizers complain to this day about the persistence of traditional attitudes, whether on the mainland or Taiwan. I believe that Chinese scholars today would generally agree with Wen Ch'ung-i, an anthropologist with the Academia Sinica on Taiwan, that "we Chinese are currently following the path of Western culture but have definitely not yet internalized it."[6] Indeed it is unlikely that the new forms of social and political organization which took root in modern China, finding acceptance among a very large part of even the illiterate population, could have done so had they not meshed to a considerable extent with some long-established traditional orientations. After all, propaganda expressing the ideals of liberal democracy was massive for more than half a century, but these ideals did not take root, and there is no shortage of close observers like Yin Hai-kuang who ascribe this failure partly to cultural incompatibility. If we accept this diagnosis, it is hard simultaneously to deny that cultural compatibility facilitated the acceptance of those ideals that did take root. Donald J. Munro, I believe, is close to the mark when he observes: "The unconscious historical legacy in Communist thought is made up of ideas about man or nature that were originally found in a philosophic setting but have, over the years, become unquestioned assumptions in the minds of educated Chinese."[7]

c. THE AMBIGUITY OF CHANGE

After all, discrete changes in doctrine and overt behavior do not necessarily reflect changes in psychologically deep-seated attitudes. It is one thing polemically to denounce "the three bonds" and "the five relationships," another to uncover and alter partly unconscious beliefs about the nature of authority and selfhood.

Moreover, the very obliqueness of the *chün-tzu* ideal made it possible for Chinese modernizers to remain possessed by this ideal while engaging in wholesale denunciations of the traditional order (see chapter 4, section g). Determined clearly to distinguish between old ways to be discarded and new ways to be adopted, they embraced the apparently obvious contrast between old Confucian ways and new Western ones, impetuously identified the entire range of Confucian attitudes with little more than the norms of filial piety, and projected onto Western thought that sense of moral autonomy on which they and their ancestors had in fact been bred. One such *chün-tzu* was Yin Hai-kuang. Yin was a highly sophisticated "liberal" and Westernizing admirer of "individualism" who merged the ideals of the May Fourth Movement with a deep interest in American social science. Yet he was repulsed by the Western notion of idiosyncratic individuality as an ultimate good and by the idea of democracy as an adversary system of interaction between a variety of interest groups, preferring rather to smuggle in under the labels of "individualism" and "freedom" character ideals virtually identical with the Mencian concept of moral autonomy. Indeed Yin often used phrases from *Mencius* (or the *Li-chi* phrase *t'e-li tu-hsing*) when trying to make clear the kind of character ideal Chinese must pursue if they are to overcome the shortcomings of their Confucian heritage. This position never even struck him as paradoxical. Insofar as he provided any explanation for it, he simply asserted that the generally unacceptable Confucian tradition did happen to include some worthy ideals. (In his very last years, he developed a much fuller admiration of the Confucian tradition.)[8]

Certainly when scholars hold that "the one theme in Mao's personality which stands in sharpest contrast to China's traditional cultural pattern is his strong element of self-assertiveness,"[9] they are laboring under a misunderstanding of what the range of this culture was, taking at face value Chinese rhetoric about the Chinese rejection of the Confucian tradition. Surely such rhetoric should be regarded as part of the history of Chinese thought rather than as an adequate analysis of it. Nor do the diffuse hatred expressed in much of this rhetoric and the violent class struggle associated with it demonstrate of themselves that basic cultural orientations have been rejected. Violent mass uprisings infused with hatred for a corrupt elite go back many centuries in the history of imperial China, but they generally constituted only breakdowns in political consensus and did not lead to the formulation of new moral and social ideals.

Intellectually, then, the rejection of the past has been basically marked by ambiguity, as suggested especially in the writings of Wakeman and Price.[10] Moreover, in Chinese history, eras of intellectual turmoil and change have usually clouded over persisting lines of consensus and of continuity with the past. Commenting on the polemics of the Chou period, the Han historian Ssu-ma T'an observed: "The ways of thinking in the world are very different and numerous but ultimately converge." Historians since Liang Ch'i-ch'ao have viewed the rise of Han learning in the Ch'ing period as simply a rebellion against Sung and Ming Neo-Confucianism, but the roots of Han learning in Neo-Confucianism are now recognized (see chapter 3, section x).

d. THE ETHOS OF INTERDEPENDENCE

The understanding of a change requires clarification of its base line. Only as the character of China's traditional orientations becomes clearer can their development in the twentieth century be fathomed. To explain China's failures in modern times, a focus on the economic and institutional problems of the last century was crucial. Suddenly, however, we have been confronted with the need to explain China's success, and the analytical framework developed to deal with her failures seems partly insufficient. Unlike the causes of failure, the roots of success lie less in economic than in intellectual history, and they reach back many centuries. Absorbed by the spectacle of the Chinese failure, we could easily accept the interpretation of her traditional orientations as stagnative, particularistic, authoritarian, and pathological. Any indigenous ideas not fitting in with this pattern could be dismissed as epiphenomenal rhetoric. Trying now to explain her success, however, we are beginning to see how this very rhetoric functioned as part of the behavioral situation, articulating and molding the sentiments of solidarity.

Trying now to analyze these sentiments, we can begin by putting together the insights already developed in different disciplines, as discussed in the previous chapters. Thus we can describe the traditional orientations as involving an ethos of interdependence. Along with Confucian familism, this ethos was a central part of the heterogeneous and dynamic cultural situation of late imperial China (see chapter 3, section a). It was strongly expressed in Neo-Confucianism, but it also was broadly diffused among at least the educated classes, as discussed in chapter 4. It can be described under five headings: an ontology of elusive immanence; an epistemology emphasizing the knowability of universal moral truth as an object of cognition and reasoning; a tendency toward "totalism" affecting ontological, epistemological, ethical, and social views; social norms involving a tension between notions of interdependence and authority; and a moral-psychological sense of living along a perilous divide between moral success and moral failure. To say that this ethos amounted to a comprehensive, continuing "religious faith" is not an exaggeration.

e. ELUSIVE IMMANENCE

By "immanence" I mean the religious belief that the cosmos is infused with a divine force, that this force is physically present "within" all "things," especially the self as "the most spiritual among the ten thousand things," and that the self can draw on this divine force realizing it fully. As T'ang Chün-i shows, the Confucian self was godlike, and it sought to realize a state of oneness with the divine. Otherwise it could not overcome anxieties and feel the pathos of control, fixity, and coherence. The religious or metaphysical bias in this standpoint is indicated by the fixation on the idea that full realization of the divine was a process of expanding an "inner" presence to the point that it permeated the "outer" world. From this standpoint, the opposite idea that one could in a Jamesian way find spiritual value in the "outer" world and then inject it into the "inner" self was unthinkable. Hence the constant emphasis on *shou-lien* (drawing one's spirit inward).

Since no "outer" social force or even religious figure could either interrupt or provide this inner contact with the divine, the self was autonomous. Since the potentiality for realizing oneness with the divine existed, the cosmos included a transformative power, which the sage could tap. The crucial implication that the human mind has a transnatural power to tap transformative cosmic forces is most clearly revealed in Fung Yu-lan's critique of traditional Confucian metaphysics, which he criticized precisely for positing such a human power (see chapter 3, section o).

We should add that while the divine was thus immanent in matter, conversely matter was a partly sublime, teleologically meaningful kind of substance. Consequently monistic attempts in China to reduce all existence to a form of matter had a spiritual connotation quite different from Western theories of materialism, which contradicted the idea that the cosmos was divine.[11]

Yet this divine existence of the self was constantly endangered. One cannot agree with Weber that the Confucian tradition lacked a "radical" concept of evil as flowing from ontologically ultimate conditions. On the contrary, due to primordial cosmic circumstances discussed by Chu Hsi, the divine was "almost imperceptible in its subtlety," whether in the "inner" arena of the "mind" or the "outer" one of "history." Both arenas were pervasively shaped by a dyadic view of reality according to which the "ultimate substance" of things was typically in the process of being "lost." Whether in the case of history or the mind, the full reality of the *tao* lay just beyond the pale of the easily remembered or perceived. Of course, the transmission of the Confucian doctrine did in fact encounter difficulties. These breaks in communication, however, came to form a historical pattern with the power of a myth reinforcing the *tao*'s inherent tendency toward elusiveness. Thus Confucius complained that he was unable to "corroborate" accounts of the Three Dynasties. The *History of the Han Dynasty* noted that "When long ago Confucius died, the transmission of his most profound ideas, which he had not openly expressed, ceased." Then in 213 B.C. the famous burning of books conveniently brought about 2000 years of doubt about which versions of the classics were the authentic ones.

Still more, the admitted lack of information about the "Three Dynasties" and the admitted vagueness of the classics were paralleled by the elusiveness of "heavenly principle" within the mind. The "traces" of sage institutions still found in the current polity were paralleled by the "incipiences" of heavenly feeling found in the mind. The concern with *p'ei-yang kuo-chia-chih yüan-ch'i* (keeping vigorous the original vital force of the state) was parallel to that with *ts'un-yang* (preserving and nourishing one's heavenly feeling). The term *pi* (corrupt practice) was used equally to describe what was happening in the mind and the political world, and the abundance of information about the evil, "hegemon"-dominated period of history after the sacred Three Dynasties was paralleled by the ease with which one could observe selfish impulses within the mind.

In particular, one has to emphasize the pervasive Neo-Confucian perception of the mind as caught in unending cycles of imminent and accomplished issuance. While this idea vividly expressed the feeling that the divine was concretely immanent in the self, it also defined the most easily accessible part of human experience as a form of morally alienated consciousness obscuring the presence of the divine. Only a people with a deep need to express the feeling that the divine is almost impossible to realize could have accepted the idea of the phases as an obviously accurate reflection of reality. This feeling was also expressed in the perception of linkage as an unsolved problem.

All these striking parallels and their logical relation to the idea that "the mind of the *tao* is almost imperceptible in its subtlety" have to be recognized as one of the most basic aspects of the Chinese worldview. It was hardly restricted to Neo-Confucianism. When

5. Optimism (e)

K'ang Yu-wei in the closing years of Ch'ing rule issued his great call for reform, he could base it on the immediately plausible lament that after 2500 years of Confucianism, the real meaning of Confucius' teachings still was "in the dark and unclear."[12]

Perhaps in any religion, the spiritual struggles of the self are supported and implemented by some kind of divine force inherent in the cosmos, but in Neo-Confucianism, this dependence was accentuated. If godlike power was available by tapping the force of the cosmos, the failure to tap it resulted in an impotent life of "fear and anxiety." Still more, since complete success in tapping it was a state just beyond the experience of ego, the person identified as "knowing the *tao*" almost necessarily was alter. Although the confrontation of the self with the cosmos was unmediated, the fully successful management of this confrontation was the achievement of alter, not ego. Not even Wang Yang-ming was regarded as a sage. Hence the unending importance of an authoritative body of writing overarching any living individual.

Yet alter was dead, and his words vague. Even more, some Chinese thinkers liked to accentuate the problem of communication by claiming that moral knowledge could not be transmitted in words. It was just this lapse in communication which endowed ego with a charismatic mission of interpretation even while staying oriented to the unattainable wisdom of alter.

For Neo-Confucians trying to realize the *tao*, its elusiveness was not a subject worthy of analysis. It was just an obvious and painful condition involving their own equally obvious weaknesses, about which they hardly wanted to boast. In this miserable situation, there was, as T'ang Chün-i would put it, nothing of "value." What did have "value" were the ideas they had on how to escape from this condition through moral cultivation, and these are the Neo-Confucian ideas which modern historians have generally selected as worthy of study.

With our Weberian interest in orientations generating "tension" between ideals and the status quo, however, we have to congratulate Neo-Confucians for what they were ashamed of. Having some cross-cultural base of comparison and knowing that what people think of as a fact is often a culturally conditioned idea, we view the agonizing elusiveness of the *tao* not as an unfortunate condition but as an idea expressing some of the very "tension" Weber was looking for. Driven by a simultaneously egotistic and altruistic need to change the world, Neo-Confucians needed a philosophy which made an unending need for change obvious and which glorified their "efficacious moral efforts" as a process of salvation on which the whole world depended. Had the *tao* suddenly become "manifest," their gratifying sense of charismatic mission would have lost its rationale. To suppose that they cared less for the prestige of this spiritual mission than for the pecuniary gratifications of bureaucratic life is to regard them as far more practical than they actually were.

We therefore have to reexamine Weber's influential statement that in Confucian China, "Tension toward the 'world' had never arisen because, as far as known, there had never been an ethical prophecy of a supramundane God who raised ethical demands. Nor was there a substitute for this in the 'spirits' who raised demands and insisted upon faithful fulfillment of contract."[13] In astutely recognizing the possibility of a "substitute" for prophecy, Weber helps us interpret the idea of the *tao*'s elusiveness. Like the Jewish tradition of prophecy, this idea posited a break between ordinary experience and ultimate value brought about not by ordinary, reversible historical events but by primordial circumstances which could not be altered by normal human endeavors. While in the Jewish tradition this break was caused by original sin, in the Confucian, it was caused by lapses in perception, communication, and understanding, although much blame was also put on the pervasive flow of "human desires." In Confucian China, the endless lament over these lapses in communication partly substituted for prophecy. Nor did the Jewish prophets necessarily outdo Confucian moralizers in the vehemence and sheer repetitiveness of their denunciations.

It should be noted that in ascribing a religious significance to Neo-Confucian beliefs about heavenly principle and its elusiveness, I am following the view of humanists like T'ang Chün-i, who holds that the Mencian idea of heaven stemmed directly from "the religious spirit of ancient China," and that the apparently secular Confucian emphasis on ethics actually expressed "the highest moral and religious spirit."[14] Moreover, these Neo-Confucian beliefs must be regarded as religious if one takes into account their inherently spiritual character (not to mention the influence of Buddhism), and considers them in terms of the systematic definitions of religion offered by social scientists like Robert N. Bellah and Clifford Geertz.[15]

True, these Neo-Confucian beliefs have been neglected in the Western literature on Chinese religion, which generally has avoided making use of any such systematic definition of religion; has ignored many manifestations of religious feeling in the written Confucian tradition; has usually focused on the popular beliefs about "gods, ghosts, and ancestors"; and, when occasionally turning to "elite religion," has been concerned more with cosmology and cults than with the inner spiritual life of the Confucian subject engaged in self-cultivation.[16] Yet it is clear that until we regard this inner life as a religious phenomenon, we shall not achieve a comparative understanding of the various forms of religion found in China.[17]

f. AN INHIBITED TRANSFORMATIVE IMPULSE

Certainly the primordial elusiveness of the *tao* indicated a Weberian tension between ideals and the status quo. Still more, Confucians generally posited the existence of a transformative power within the cosmos. Whether by "the king" or "the mind of the self," this power could be activated, in the sense that corrective human efforts could bring about a state of cosmic harmony eliminating the persisting comtemporaneous contrast between ideals and actualities. Can we then call Neo-Confucianism a transformative ideology? We can, but only with qualifications.

On the one hand, the self in its attempt to tap this transformative cosmic power did not exist in a "traditional" way as a being reverently imitating the practices of the past. Nor was it a being realized through "ceremonial and ritualist propriety," as Weber would have it, or through Fingarette's "ceremonial acts."[18] On the contrary, the self transcended the particularities (*chieh-mu*) of the existential "realm" (*shih-chien, shih-chieh, ching-chieh*). Influenced by Buddhism, Neo-Confucians had a need to derive their morality from a state of existence explicitly and systematically denoted by many terms lacking any specifically social content, such as *wu t'ai-chi* (unrealized supreme ultimate), *ching* (perfect rest), *chi-ch'u* (point of total stillness), *t'ien-li* (heavenly principle), and *sheng-sheng pu-i* (the ceaseless process of bringing into being). They similarly were insistent on deriving the socially specific virtues, that is, the famous "three bonds" and "five relationships," from the generic, universalistic virtues, *ching* (reverence), *jen* (benevolence), and *ch'eng* (trueness). Even more, this transcendence of specifically social bonds, including those of the family, was accentuated by the continuing interest of Neo-Confucians in Taoism and Buddhism. So many Neo-Confucians, indeed both Chu Hsi and Wang Yang-ming, felt drawn in their youth to these philosophies of transcendence, typically returning to the fold of worldly orthodoxy just in time to climb up the ladder of official distinction and reap the rewards of a Confucian old age.

Moreover, in the quest for morality, the self, not the polity, was viewed as the more likely vehicle. Neo-Confucians did not believe, as did Tung Chung-shu, the greatest Han Confucian, that *wang-chiao* (the teachings of the king) were the main bulwark against evil. The universalistic "inner" realm of the self appeared to them as far more promising than did the "outer" realm of the state. Neo-Confucians relegated the dissonances of social and political interaction to the realm of "accomplished issuance," which could never enter into one's incipient source of identity with heaven. In all these ways, their thought had a clear-cut, transformative tendency toward transcendence of the status quo.

On the other hand, the Neo-Confucian self also had a tendency to lapse into acceptance of the status quo and its norms. As just noted, the very elusiveness of heavenly principle within ego led ego to feel deference toward alter, and the state could capitalize on this deference, especially since the state's constant claim to be the organ of heaven's will could be explicitly challenged only by an individual with an extraordinary sense of personal moral achievement. Furthermore, although the idea of oneness with heaven was universalistic, this idea was intertwined with an emphasis on procreation, gratitude, and reciprocity as the universal ethical nature of heaven.

5. Optimism (f)

This particular vision of virtue directly supported the common norms of filial piety, loyalty, and intense respect for authority. Consequently, while the Neo-Confucian could easily envisage an ideal community vastly different from the status quo in terms of institutional procedures, moral purity, and the enlargement of the sphere of utmost solidarity (*ta-t'ung*), this ideal community and the status quo typically shared the same norms, that is, the principles of the family and the monarchy.

Furthermore, whatever the Confucian sense of tension with the status quo, it cannot be equated with those transformative orientations in terms of which certain groups in Western Europe modernized their societies in the eighteenth and nineteenth centuries. As Bellah has made clear, "the mere *presence*" of transformative orientations "is simply not enough if they exist passively side by side with [stagnative] elements . . . and are not pushed through 'methodically and systematically' to their conclusion as they were in Weber's paradigmatic case of Protestantism."[19] However crucial to the social structure, the moral tension I have focused on did indeed "exist passively side by side" with that partly legitimated "fatalism of the moral failure," and the "zeal" of Neo-Confucians could give way to other, less transformative intellectual trends (see chapter 3, sections p and x). In this regard, we cannot brush aside the consensus recently reached by a group of behavioral scientists in Taiwan to the effect that the Chinese traditionally tended to have a relatively passive attitude toward inherited mores, the social environment, and the natural environment,[20] although this generalization applies most clearly to the popular culture of ancestor worship, familism, and economism.

g. RATIONALISM AND TOTALISM

Besides this ontology of elusive immanence with its ambivalent implications for the development of a transformative morality, the ethos of interdependence involved the rationalistic epistemological position that knowing is the basis of morality and that the mind can know universal moral truth. The absolute sense of "right and wrong" was present as an emotional impulse. Since the divine was inherently a form of cognitive awareness, man's capacity to overcome all biases and embrace the one correct doctrine was not

204

doubted by Neo-Confucians, just as it has not been doubted in any of the leading modern ideologies, right and left.

True, as Fung Yu-lan once pointed out, Confucians valued *jen* (benevolence) more than *chih* (moral understanding). Whether applauding or deploring the fact, a cross section of modern scholars have agreed that Confucians put moral practice above the pursuit of theoretical truth for its own sake. Nevertheless, "thought" (*ssu, ssu-hsiang*) was indispensable as an aspect of morality.[21] Just as it could dissolve all prejudiced preconceptions, so "thought," especially elucidation of the oneness of things, was needed to dissolve selfishness. Even with the "anti-intellectualism" of a Wang Yangming, the stress on cognitive clarity as an indispensable condition of morality was central. A morality based purely on a faith or moral sentiment contrasted with reasoned knowledge was alien to Neo-Confucianism, which invariably, as T'ang Chün-i has emphasized, viewed *ch'ing* (feelings) in the context of *li* (principle). Whatever the hostility to *hsüeh* (scholarly study), this stress on cognitively grasping the ontological basis of morality precluded the rise, within the context of Neo-Confucianism, of any anti-intellectualism glorifying the man of faith, the warrior, the businessman, or the master of practical know-how. Connected to this stress on cognition and thought came the focus on education discussed by Munro. Finally, in the ethos of interdependence, thought was "ideological" in Daniel Bell's sense. That is, it was based on the belief that norms can be deduced from objective givens, a standpoint in turn interwoven with a philosophical insistence on reification.[22]

A third characteristic of this ethos was "totalism." This can be seen in the goal of embracing a single doctrine covering all essential truths, of achieving oneness with the divine, of eliminating selfishness totally through unceasing efforts, and of being one with society. Because godlike autonomy was thus combined with a need to merge the self into the cosmos and the moral group, this autonomy can be distinguished from the concept of the ontologically ultimate, idiosyncratically creative individual basic to representative Western thinkers like J. S. Mill. As just mentioned, ego remained dependent on alter for moral guidance, even though the incompleteness of this guidance put the burden of freshly rethinking the truth on ego. Hence the paradoxical relation between autonomy and dependence.

This paradox was basic to our fourth characteristic, social inter-dependence, which was based on acts of both self-assertion and reciprocation. These acts involved the desire of the individual to subsume her or his own needs under those of a group both morally legitimated and concretely supportive in terms of this circle of morally reciprocating acts. To be sure, this circle of reciprocity involved more than horizontal patterns of mutual aid. Someone had to have the authority to make binding decisions about the specific content of reciprocation. But this grant of authority, whether in the family or in the polity, was subsumed under the concept of reciproca-tion (*kan-en pao-te*). Moreover, whether those in authority had "bestowed favors," thus generating the obligation to reciprocate, was open to doubt, and this doubt could be expressed by acting on the scholar's right to protest and by referring to the overarching moral authority of the classics. In late Ch'ing times, for instance, an official adduced the fact of allegedly low official salaries to suggest that the dynasty was not properly "bestowing favors" on the officials. Any individual, not just the one who had formal authority, could become a "model" defining the proper content of reciprocation. This pervasive concept of authority as a triangular structure, discussed in chapter 4, provided the individual with an "inner" psychological base which could through the "self-strengthening" of self-cultiva-tion be fortified against the onslaught of those "fears and anxieties" partly flowing from the activities of the "outer" political hierarchy. Although this "inner" life was vulnerable and thus inclined to feelings of dependence on "outer" authority figures, it was also potentially invincible and immune to the "fear" these figures could strike in weaker souls. Rather than submitting to them, the seri-ously Confucian individual sought to replace them with an "internal ruler" and thus autonomously to decide his moral obligations.

The individual, after all, merely emulated the sage, but he sought oneness with heaven. There simply was no other way to think about it. We then have to ask why Confucians thought about it that way. Whether we interpret "heaven" as an entity outside the self actually existing in some transcendent fashion or just as a symbol for a certain state of feeling within the self, the Neo-Confucian focus on heaven is a basic psychological fact that cannot be ignored. Oriented both toward "heaven" and toward persons distinguished purely in terms of their closeness to "heaven," the individual had recourse to a sense of morality and identity differentiated from the various particular cues of his social environment.

This moral-psychological fact could legitimate the rejection of one authority figure for another. For all of its stress on loyalty and hierarchy, Chinese society has been characterized by a remarkably fluid pattern of betrayal and intrigue. Individuals frequently oscillated between cooperation with the centralized state bureaucracy and support for smaller, often more ascriptive groupings, such as lineages, clubs, cliques, or secret societies, inhibiting political centralization. Indeed it was traditionally regarded as normal for individuals to oscillate back and forth between good and evil solidarities. "Good people" could turn into "bandits" and then turn back into "good people" depending on economic circumstances, while in many cases trusted officials erred, were sentenced as criminals, "renewed themselves" through expiation, and then were reinstated at the top of the bureaucracy. This perception of moral instability and the emphasis on moral "transformation" were just two sides of the same coin. Certainly the tissue of tightening the bonds of cooperation (*t'uan-chieh*), so central for all Chinese modernizers right and left, is connected to this oscillatory tendency.

All in all, the individual's capacity for thus autonomously deciding his allegiances could be combined with an acute sense of dependence on the support of his solidarity group because psychologically that outside moral power on which the individual perceived himself as depending was not rigidly ascribed to particular social roles. Rather, it was internalized to some extent. Thus in a free-floating way it could be shifted between different roles and could be projected onto a transcendent entity like heaven.

i. THE FEAR OF FAILURE

The fifth and final characteristic of this ethos was the sense of living along a perilous divide separating moral success from moral failure and, indeed, typically slipping down into the latter. This stemmed from the perception of elusive immanence; of the flow of evil within the self and throughout history; of the need constantly to struggle against this flow; and of the tendency of people to oscillate between commitment to this struggle and betrayal of it.

To the extent that the self successfully participated in a moral circle of reciprocation, it tapped godlike powers; experienced Mencian "joy" and a sense of Panglossian optimism dissolving the ultimacy of suffering and tragedy; participated in a community free of the distortions of self-interest; realized a sense of ontological oneness with the cosmos corresponding to its feelings of social interdependence; and behaved in accord with some "correct" "ideology" elucidating the conditions of both ontological oneness and social interdependence.

To a large extent, Chinese philosophy past and present has consisted of attempts to explain how to attain this state of moral success rather than self-consciously to describe the Confucian state of mind as poised between moral success and failure. Just because of this angle of vision, Chinese philosophy has tended to describe the human experience in terms making its insights often inaccessible to social scientists. Many of the latter, in turn, having undertaken to dismiss Confucian metaphysics as epiphenomenal froth on the ocean of behavioral phenomena, have not noticed operative feelings expressed only indirectly or in passing by Confucian scholars. Thus they have inaccurately identified the basic orientations of the educated elite with those virtues and moral imperatives prominently emphasized by this elite instead of with that state of mind as a whole in terms of which this elite sought to realize these virtues. Constantly perceiving themselves as on the brink of failure, the elite cannot be described as simply believing in a certain kind of ethical and political order. To recognize their basically troubled air is not to condemn them for their frailties but to do justice to the complexity and profundity of their worldview.

Thus poised on the brink of failure, the self was constantly anxious about disrupting its circle of moral reciprocity. This anxiety was expressed in that sense of predicament so basic to Neo-Confucian metaphysics. It was expressed in the probationary ethic, in terms of which officials often perceived at least other officials and probably themselves too as moral failures receiving justly inflicted punishments. The fear of disrupting the flow of reciprocity, of appearing as a "mean-minded person" pursuing selfish ends, was also basic to the fact that individuals did typically lapse into this pursuit only in ways calculated to minimize the risk of such disruption, relying on Machiavellian, indirect tactics or ambiguous cues to bring about selfishly desired patterns of behavior without tearing asunder the fabric of reciprocity. Therefore this Machiavellian tendency, now receiving increasing attention from political scientists, was perhaps due as much to the peculiar logic of Confucian ethics as to any more general Chinese genius for practicing the universal art of politics with unique finesse.

Yet while thus acting with cunning, caution, and fear to avoid moral failure, the individual often perceived himself and others as experiencing moral failure, as perpetuating that moral wilderness which typically filled the world. Hence, the traditional political culture also involved a set of attitudes articulated constantly as a response to this given situation. These consisted of a sense of tension between moral ideals and the status quo and a profound sense of doubt about how to conduct the moral struggle along its two basic fronts: elucidation of the conditions of cosmic oneness, and definition of complex economic and political institutions effectively providing a material basis for the flow of reciprocity on a society-wide basis. Fostered by the spectacle of historical disasters and by exegetical problems due to lapses in communication, this sense of doubt legitimated the flexibility needed to try out different kinds of policies. Thus searching for moral success, traditional scholars constantly put forward competing, controversial claims regarding linkage as well as the policies and structure of the bureaucracy. The history of these claims has been partly studied by intellectual historians, but the overarching set of perceptions in terms of which these claims were debated should be elucidated if we are to understand the shared orientations and political culture of the imperial elite.

One thus seems to be dealing with a general personality type seeking to subsume itself under a larger moral whole while oscillating between the euphoria of moral success, the anxiety of moral failure, and a troubled, doubt-ridden spirit of striving to achieve moral success. Neo-Confucian education not only could alter the cognitive skills with which one pursued this moral goal, it could also enlarge and redefine that moral whole to which one was oriented as well as one's own role in relation to it. Whether radically and zealously to aim for this enlargement or moderately to restrict one's ambitions to more local circumstances and familial problems was a choice presented by Confucian education to the male adult. Hence the centrality of the question of whether or not to try to become a sage. Perhaps the most basic aspect of the ethos of interdependence was the perception of the self as simultaneously capable of either polluting or exalting that expanding whole to which it belonged, thus simultaneously autonomous and subordinate to its reference group.

j. INTERDEPENDENCE IN MODERN TIMES

It seems clear that much of this ethos has persisted in the twentieth century, notably the continuing trend away from Western individualism; the totalistic emphasis on eliminating selfishness and achieving social oneness; the ontological faith in the oneness of spirit and matter, which has given Marxist materialism an intellectual context and support missing in the West; and the tendency toward "ideological" thought, common to the Communists, the Kuomintang, scientistic liberals like Yin Hai-huang, and tradition-oriented thinkers like T'ang Chün-i. True, Mao's sage-like position suggests that the traditional triangular paradigm of authority has been replaced by a more unitary system locating both sovereign political authority and the claims of ultimate moral insight in one person. However, we still see in the People's Republic of China an emphasis on respect for an overarching body of authoritative writings. Even in the famous "Little Red Book," circulated during the Cultural Revolution of the late sixties as a sacred compendium of Mao's wisdom, Mao is defined as "the greatest Marxist-Leninist of our age," a leader whose moral authority flows from truths established by dead sages, and Western ones at that. In this definition can certainly be seen the continuing need to separate the source of the society's ultimate, overarching truths from the pronouncements of the current ruler. Moreover, with Mao's stress on cultivating a creative tension between the bureaucracy and mass criticism, the split between sovereign political authority and the claims of moral insight reappears. Certainly it is in terms of this split rather than by establishing legally autonomous foci of political power that Mao has sought to set up a system of checks and balances limiting abuses of power.

k. THE TRADITIONAL IMPULSE TO TRANSFORM TRADITION

Moreover in the transformative impulse to reject Confucian fundamentalism and institutional Confucianism, the ethos of interdependence merged with foreign ideals. As a new outlook spreads, there is always a blurred interaction between new ideas and indigenous influences inclining an audience toward them.[23] The complex intellectual pedigrees of transformative movements in late Ch'ing times cannot be reduced to a contrast between imported, transformative orientations and indigenous, stagnative ones. At the very least, we can distinguish between: (a) the vital prerequisite of a widely shared, psychologically deep-seated belief in the meaningfulness of a total societal transformation overturning historically inherited forms and realizing a widely appreciated vision of morality; (b) the specific political and technological content of that transformation; and (c) the situational conditions leading people to adopt a particular vision of transformation. I would suggest that Western influences in late Ch'ing times have had more to do with the latter two factors than the first. Revealing a universally valid, cosmically grounded spirit of morality buried beneath the "accumulated" moral debris of history (*chi-pi*) and using it as a lever with which to transform one's current society is a Confucian cliché which seems to have informed the major paradigms of revolutionary action adopted by Chinese in our century. Once freed from the "inner" and "outer" predicament posed by Neo-Confucianism and from the traditionally deplored miasma of imperial despotism, the human will could not but find history malleable. Therefore it is not clear that the emergence of revolutionary thought in China was contingent on the importation of any Promethean or Faustian will.

5. Optimism (k)

After all, it is not original to suggest that the influence of basic, indigenous, universalistic ideas, whether the Lu-Wang concept of "mind," the Taoist view of the "natural," or the Buddhist emphasis on "compassion," can be found in the key radical attacks made on the established Confucian order at the turn of the century, such as K'ang Yu-wei's notion of "eliminating the nine spheres of distinction," T'an Ssu-t'ung's idea of "burst out of the net [of traditional social bonds]," and Chang T'ai-yen's (1868–1936) radically critical perspective on Confucian values.[24]

We should keep in mind that T'an's famous "burst out of the net" is virtually identical in wording and somewhat similar in meaning to Lu Chiu-yüan's "burst out of the net." The idea of *p'o* (breaking through and destroying) morally wrong ways of thinking and unjustified constraints was a theme common to Lu, T'an, and K'ang, though the latter two modernizers added a quite new definition of these constraints, impetuously identifying them with many or all of the traditional institutional forms. Lu Chiu-yüan was more exclusively concerned with the moral consciousness of the individual, but he was inspired by a similar vision of an almost Promethean, spiritually liberating moment of destruction: "Rush ahead with utter determination, burst out of the net, burn off the thorns, wash away the pools of stagnant filth!"[25] In both cases, a diffuse notion of something external to an inner moral being, oppressingly binding it down and so hindering its proper expression, is used to depict an object which should be destroyed.

It is important to note, however, that whatever the differences in emphasis between the various Neo-Confucian thinkers, the basic conceptualization of a cosmic morality transcending the given, corrupted sociopolitical order was integral to the overarching intellectual grammar of Neo-Confucians rather than merely peculiar to certain compartmentalized, unusually radical trends, such as the T'ai-chou school. This is an important point because an attitude can be regarded as a key cultural orientation with large-scale behavioral effects only if there actually is evidence that it existed in the form of a psychologically deep-seated way of thinking and feeling characteristic of an important social class with the power to influence political and economic developments. In this case, the evidence lies in the fact that the Neo-Confucian sense of predicament was expressed in the form of perceptions, not claims, clichés common to virtually the whole body of Neo-Confucian writing, not theories peculiar to an unusually original and controversial writer. If an influential intellectual like K'ang Yu-wei had not been able to appeal to an audience indigenously and diffusely sensitized to the existence of a cosmic morality transcending the given political order, his task of understanding the need to break out of the traditional mold and of conveying that understanding to the educated classes would have been far more difficult than it actually was, if not totally impossible. It is hardly an accident that when many Chinese intellectuals in the twentieth century viewed themselves as autonomous, creative thinking beings responding to the challenges of political crisis and cultural transition by consciously holding the cultural traditions of both East and West at a critical distance and evaluating them in terms of an open philosophic inquiry aimed at universal truth, they sought support for the radically pure autonomy of their position in the ideas of Lu-Wang Confucianism.[26] And it should not be overlooked that some of them came directly from this stance to the acceptance of Communism.

If, then, the radical rejection of the Chinese tradition did have some roots in this tradition, conversely traditional ideas in modern China did not readily serve as the basis for cogent conservative arguments against revolutionary change. This is another paradox that is only now beginning to attract scholarly attention. It proved almost impossible to build up conservative sentiment in the Burkean manner by emphasizing the value of the historical tradition distinct from its possible function as a vehicle of cosmic truths. Thus probably more than in the modernizing West, conservative arguments made in a purely pragmatic way were vulnerable to the charge of moral betrayal (*hsiang-yüan*). Not to mention the fact that because of the basic orientations regarding the individual and the community noted above, the concept of private property, always a rallying point for conservatives East and West, could not become a foundation stone of any Chinese political philosophy, as it did with Locke and Rousseau. Other axioms too, familiar to us as a part of this Western philosophy of property, freedom, individualism, and angst, could not be reconciled with these basic Chinese orientations, notably the idea that "it is entirely possible to construct an ideal political society out of bad human materials."[27]

1. THE NEW OPTIMISM AND TECHNOLOGY

Certainly the revolutionary Marxist emphasis on "victory over nature" has a technological dimension imported from the West, but the main business of the ancient sages had been to think up and carry out economic projects like river dredging in order to "control the ten thousand things" and to "put in order heaven and earth."

It is here, however, that a striking discontinuity with the past has occurred. What the West quite definitely did bring was not the concept of social and economic transformation per se but the belief that with modern technology, new techniques of political participation (whether liberal or Communist), and new forms of knowledge, the "outer" realm of economic and political problems, regarded as largely intractable since the euphoria of Wang An-shih's "new policies," could in fact be reformed. This belief was congruent with the optimism of Chou Confucians like Mencius but directly contradicted the sense of predicament basic to Neo-Confucianism. Thus it necessarily carried with it a sense of escape from predicament, an immense sigh of relief. In considering changes in the Chinese worldview during the last century, therefore, we should take into account not only new conceptualizations, some metaphysical, some anti-metaphysical, of the problems of life and of the methods available to solve them but also a new level of optimism about the efficacy of available methods, a new view of the extent to which methods matched problems. Putting the matter within the context of our ethos of interdependence, we can say that for many Chinese in the twentieth century, the belief that a society according with the morality of interdependence could in practice be realized grew much stronger than it had been for many centuries. The material as well as the political and ideological means were at hand. An era of moral success rather than moral failure was about to begin, and the resulting enthusiasms were channeled into one political "movement" after another, partially dissolving old suspicions, creating new solidarities, and even recalling ancient Chou dreams by unifying the moral empathies of the polity, the village, and the family.

Most crucial here is the fact that the Western promise of material progress was welcomed not by people with just the normal human desire for rising living standards but by people for whom this very question of "the people's livelihood" was philosophically of the utmost importance.[28] Any morally appealing ideology that could resolve this question was bound to impress Chinese intellectuals, especially given that prominent strain in Confucian thinking according to which the very fact of moral action outweighs any considerations of theoretical truth or pure erudition.[29] For such intellectuals, the fact that material progress had actually taken place somewhere in the world and was about to take place in China was in effect like the indisputable materialization of a religious being whose reality had always been regarded as just outside the bounds of proof. Consequently, as transformative action in the "outer" realm appeared ever more feasible to modern Chinese, the search for transformative power within the mind was relaxed. The "inner" predicament of moral purification and metaphysical linkage became less acute and central, and a kind of Panglossian optimism spread over much Chinese thought.

This tremendous change in the Chinese worldview was not primarily the result of a breakthrough on the part of any outstanding thinker. Weber said that "prophecy" can alter value systems, but the spiritual direction of a society can be as easily changed by new ideas so obviously true that only the platitudes of the uninspired can do them justice. For instance, the influential comprador and journalist Cheng Kuan-ying (1842–1923) was an intelligent person but certainly not a learned and profound thinker. Writing during the last Ch'ing years, he explained that by adopting Western technology, the Chinese could finally achieve that mastery of both ultimate principle and the outer world for which the ancient sages had called.[30] To make his point, he used the distinction between *tao* (true way) and *ch'i* (concrete thing) found in the *Classic of Changes*. His view of world history, echoed again and again by conservatives down to T'ang Chün-i, was that the Chinese had excelled in understanding the *tao*, Westerners, in mastering "concrete things." Both sides had suffered from this imbalance, but now both could learn from each other to achieve a perfect form of learning and civilization "joining together material things and ultimate principle."

Particularly significant for us is that Cheng, as was common in late Ch'ing times, argued that Western technology should be adopted not only because it was a superior way to achieve national power but also because, according to the meaning of the *Classic of Changes*, "the spiritual cannot be exhaustively known unless one masters practical matters." Certainly this was a cunning way of manipulating the classics in order to legitimate Westernization. Just as crucial, however, Cheng was plausibly pointing out that the "outer" transformation promised by Western technology was a basic Confucian goal. Moreover, in charging that Confucian scholars since Han times had neglected this goal by "lapsing into emptiness" and "engaging in lofty discussions of principle and the heaven-conferred nature," Cheng was hardly making an original and controversial point. On the contrary, his view merely echoed widely accepted criticisms of Neo-Confucianism made since at least the seventeenth century. While both the renascent Legalist tradition and the beginnings of nationalism turned late Ch'ing reformers toward the goal of "wealth and power," it was an obvious truth to Cheng's audience that material progress would satisfy a living Confucian desire which neither Neo-Confucianism nor any other Ch'ing trend had satisfied.

After all, compassion for the suffering of others was a point endlessly reiterated in the Confucian quest to overcome "selfishness." One need merely recall Wang Yang-ming's feelings of unbearable agony as he witnessed the misery of his countrymen: "Indeed there are cases when people see their fathers, sons, or brothers falling into a deep abyss and getting drowned. They cry, crawl, go naked and barefooted, stumble and fall. They hang onto dangerous cliffs and go down to save them. . . . Now to stand beside those drowning and make no attempt to save them but to bow, talk, and laugh is possible only for strangers who have no natural feelings of kinship, but even they will be considered to have no sense of pity and to be no longer human beings."[31]

Similarly, on the eve of the reform of 1898, K'ang Yu-wei described the predicament of Neo-Confucianism. All the discussions of the classics, he said, came down to "nothing but linen clothes in the summer, furs in the winter, saving the people from suffering according to their needs at the time." Chu Hsi, however, "while he knew something about examining one's character and correcting one's faults, had little to offer in the way of relieving the people's suffering."[32]

Both K'ang Yu-wei and Cheng Kuan-ying broke with the past in perceiving a previously absent "outer" force which made escape from this predicament possible. Banal to us as part of so many simplistic Chinese theories arguing that Westernization must be balanced by the spirituality of the East, this perception is usually dismissed as the more enlightened side of a Sinocentric response to the humiliations of Western imperialism. Its very banality, however, testified to the force of its truth. Into the "outer" world, previously barren of all hope for transformation, had suddenly come a new dynamic force, *kung-i-chih ching* (technology in its most refined form). Neither was this force "almost imperceptible in its subtlety." As a "fully manifest" vehicle of transformation, it was unprecedented in the Chinese experience.

Since at least the time of Liu Tsung-chou in the seventeenth century, Chinese intellectuals had been familiar with the view that the *tao* could be found only in *ch'i* (concrete things). What was new was the idea that a much higher level of material success could be attained in the handling of "concrete things." This revelation, moreover, made sense because it meshed with a widespread traditional image, that of the Chinese people as living "impoverished" in a land overflowing with natural resources waiting to be tapped. Paradoxical for a "backward" economy, this cultural myth reinforced the enthusiasm of the early modernizers. The superabundance of China's natural resources, for instance, was presupposed by K'ang Yu-wei, Cheng Kuan-ying, and the famous reformer and journalist Wang T'ao (1828–1897). "China's iron-producing places are innumerable. . . . China's coal mines are everywhere," Wang exclaimed.[33] Cheng Kuan-ying's rhetoric was flowery when he claimed that if the Chinese utilized "technology in its most refined form," they would eventually realize a world unified through the "benevolence" of the "true king." This hope, however, was built on a new reality perceived as unavailable before the coming of the West.

5. Optimism (l)

Small wonder then that K'ang and his influential disciple Liang Ch'i-ch'ao came to share a vision of the external, physical cosmos as dynamically vibrant with a creative energy waiting to be tapped through the external mechanisms of organization and science. In the late 1880s, K'ang Yu-wei echoed the Neo-Confucian Chang Tsai in viewing man's moral existence as part of one cosmic process stemming from a "primal ether of materialization." K'ang, however, viewed this ether as a dynamic aspect of external things, identifying it with electricity.[34] This faith in the "outer" cosmos as permeated with transformative power was complemented by the rapidly spreading view of history as an upward evolutionary process.[35] While this partly Spencerian outlook merged with the indigenous historical philosophy of the renascent New Text school, represented by K'ang, it could hardly have taken root without the advent of Western technology.[36]

Taking advantage of a changed cosmological environment, K'ang no longer had to continue the Neo-Confucian search for that transformative power present only in the transcendent, "almost imperceptible," and "totally still" source of movement within the mind (see chapter 3, section k). As epitomized later in Fung Yu-lan's philosophy (see section q below), the transformative power of the sage thus was relocated within the external natural and historical processes, and the redefinition of Chinese society as "backward" was correlated to the belief, found almost universally in the thought of twentieth-century China, that history moves in stages according to an evolutionary, teleological process. Such is the origin of modern Chinese "materialism."

I believe that Hao Chang's profound analysis of how the pivotal late Ch'ing thinker Liang Ch'i-ch'ao turned from the ideal of sagehood to that of the "new citizen" can be related to these questions. In chapter 9 of his book, Chang shows how Liang, by 1905, believed in the ideal of a "new citizen" who, motivated by a "collectivistic sense" of "group consciousness," participated in the affairs of his nation and displayed a spirit of "martial prowess." According to Liang, the "new citizen" backed up his "civic virtues" with a "private morality" consisting of virtually the whole Neo-Confucian repertoire of *kung-fu* (efficacious moral efforts). Thus from Liang's standpoint, the "new citizen" had to be "constantly on guard against even the faintest emergence of selfishness in the innermost recesses of his mind," and the "effort toward self-examination, self-reproach, and self-mastery could not be overemphasized." As Chang points out, however, Liang's concept of *kung-fu* was explicitly and entirely divorced from the metaphysical and cosmological context integral to it in the Neo-Confucian literature, including even the most basic concepts like *li* (principle) and *ch'i* (ether of materialization).

The moral efforts of the individual within his own mind, in other words, were disconnected from any transformative forces in the cosmos. Participation in the "outer," physical life of the nation, not *kung-fu*, had become the only way to help realize the opportunities for transformation presented by the given natural and historical structure of the world. When *kung-fu* was thus no longer the vehicle of cosmic transformation, the ideal of sagehood necessarily lost a central part of its meaning. The connection between the decline of this ideal and the rising faith in outer transformative processes again confirms the point that Neo-Confucians regarded their quest for sagehood as a way to struggle for transformative power.

m. THE NEW OPTIMISM AND RADICAL POLITICAL REORGANIZATION

Besides this perception of a new technology that could "save the people from their suffering," the new faith in "outer" transformation was based on the perception of new possibilities in the field of political organization. This is an obvious aspect of modern Chinese thought going back to the enthusiasm of the late Ch'ing reformers for European, American, and Japanese forms of government. Immense optimism in the manipulability of the political environment was a central aspect of K'ang Yu-wei's *Ta-t'ung-shu* (The Book of Universal Commonwealth), which he began to write in the late 1880s. Most striking, an optimistic faith in the almost magical results of devising the right constitution animated the early republican politicians, as Nathan has shown.

Yet fascinated as they were with the Western devices of political participation, these modernizers were not just turning to a view of political structure without roots in their own tradition. We can leave aside the various claims made by K'ang, Liang and others that

5. Optimism (m)

ancient Chinese thinkers from Mencius to Kuan Chung had antici-
pated the political principles developed in the modern West. What
is clear is that in opting for one or another of the Western models of
government, Chinese reformers were turning to a vision of political
action which in fact did most specifically accord with the Confucian
idea of radical political action (see chapter 3, section v). Had this
concept not been familiar to them as a vision of the most excellent kind of government, their enthusiasm for the new forms of
government could hardly have arisen so naturally. This momentous
break with the moderate realism of Ming-Ch'ing times was already
basic to K'ang Yu-wei's concept of reform, which inspired the Kuang-
hsü emperor in 1898. It was also epitomized by Liang Ch'i-ch'ao's
"statism."[37]

n. THE NEW OPTIMISM AND IDEOLOGICAL
PROGRESS

This radical vision of society as shaped by impulses flowing out of
the center of the political arena, moreover, was psychologically
associated with a belief in the imminence of a new level of knowledge
finally bringing all happening into a coherently linked whole. The
more the political center could master the laws of the cosmos, the
more effectively it could call on the energetic support of the whole
population. This belief in the imminence of great intellectual progress also can be traced back to early modernizers like Cheng Kuan-
ying and K'ang Yu-wei. It was basic to Chinese scientism, as
D. W. Y. Kwok has analyzed it, including, obviously, Maoism. It
is found in the Panglossian spirit of T'ang Chün-i (see chapter 2). It
also pervades Ho Lin's account of Chinese philosophical trends,
written in 1945. Moreover, it was buttressed by the victory over
Japan, and then, of course, by Mao's victories and successes. However, it was perhaps expressed most strikingly in the prophecies of
Shen Yu-ting made at the Nanking meeting of the Chinese Philosophical Association in early 1937:

> Whatever the various considerations involved, philosophy in China is
> about to have an unprecedented revival, and the Chinese people will
> on the basis of philosophy find a fundamental form of thought able to
> promote the revival of their nation. This is an inevitable phenomenon,
> because history has the rhythm of its wave-like motion. To say that

the culture of China's second period [which lasted from the Wei-Chin period through the Ch'ing] has already come to a close is equivalent to saying that the culture of China's third period is just about to come into being. Moreover we know that the culture of this third period is bound to return anew to the spirit of the first period, that socially practical, robust, positively creative spirit. . . . This is so because every time a new culture comes into being, it takes the form of a reaction against the old culture, it constitutes a revolution. At the same time, it is a return to the cultural spirit of the first period, a return to antiquity. Only with revolution can there be a true return to antiquity, and only with a return to antiquity can there be a true revolution.

The active cause of this third period of culture will be Confucian philosophy in its true self-awareness. The dynamic culture of the third period will in all aspects stand in contrast to the quiescent culture of the second period, and without any deliberately devised plan will match the dynamic culture of the first period. This new culture will come out of a new philosophy. This third period of culture will be rich with organizational capabilities. Whether in the case of social organization or the organization of thought, this culture will take as its basic condition a powerfully dynamic spirit of logic. Therefore Chinese philosophy henceforth will be systematic, no longer having its old lack of coherence. It will make manifest the quality of systematic thought latent in the philosophy of the first cultural period. This system is the great system of idealistic philosophy with its [Confucian] emphasis on exhaustively understanding true principle and exhaustively realizing one's heaven-conferred nature. Positive government, a positive morality of freedom, only in the culture of the third period will they become possible.[38]

Not the promise of science specifically but the more general feeling that a "new" understanding of "spirit" was imminent—this is what animated these philosophers a few months before the Japanese invaded Shanghai. Shen's passionate statement vividly exemplifies the importance in modern times of the completely traditional belief that "thought" is the basis of morality and political power.

o. IDEOLOGY, SINOCENTRISM, AND NATIONALISM

Of course, the new "thought" was at least partly based on the revelations of Western science. From the Levensonian standpoint, we might even claim that any insistence on including any Chinese ideas at all was just an attempt to assuage the sense of wounded cultural pride: the Sinocentric Chinese were bound to search for an ideology giving a boost to their nationalistic collective ego. Westernizers like Yin Hai-kuang have also denounced Sinocentrism.

Yet nationalism and the hatred of imperialism are common throughout the Third World without necessarily leading to enthusiastically collectivistic movements able to dissolve many of the traditional barriers of peasant particularism. This enthusiasm in China, therefore, should be understood in terms of the distinctive ideas which it involved.

I believe it has been hard for us to appreciate the sources of Chinese optimism particularly because they include a perception of science different from that with which we are most familiar in the West. We in the West, it is perhaps fair to say, have been preoccupied with the threat posed by science to the realization of ultimate hopes, the "philosophical struggle between science and religion," as Fung Yu-lan regarded it in the 1920s. In China, however, this very threat was posed not by science but by the traditional metaphysical and political situation and was in fact largely removed by the advent of science. While our perception of the increasing lack of fit between our problems and the methods available to solve them has perhaps brought about a deepening sense of predicament and angst in the West, the Chinese to a large extent have experienced in the last century a rising sense of impending solution. It is partly for this reason, I believe, that China today, in contrast to so much of the rest of the world, Communist and capitalist, is a strongly "ideological" society, to use Daniel Bell's term. The combination of the Messianic impact of science as a tool for solving the horrendous problems of the "outer" world and the traditional definition of morality as a code of cognitively known, objective truths has been overwhelming for nearly all Chinese intellectuals, right and left. How could scientific methods capable of solving the problem of "the people's livelihood" fail to be aglow with a moral code? It is this ideological current which flows behind the strident optimism typical of the pronouncements of the Chinese Communist Party. "Pessimistic views are groundless. The future of mankind is infinitely bright." Such was the response of the People's Republic of China to the problems of the "population bomb" being discussed at the United Nations conference on population held in Bucharest in 1974. This optimism, moreover, is grounded not only in ideology but also in the almost unique way that China has pulled itself out of the material misery in which the rest of the Third World is mostly still mired.

p. THE NEW OPTIMISM AND THE QUESTION OF CULTURAL DESPAIR

This new optimism is obvious when one looks at modern Chinese thought against the background of the Neo-Confucian sense of predicament. Yet it has been essentially ignored by modern Chinese scholars, who have complained of the political humiliations and intellectual disarray brought about by the Western impact, and by Western scholars, who have suggested that modern Chinese intellectuals have been passing through an "identity crisis" or a period of "cultural despair." Not self-doubt and the relaxation of worldly commitment, but a powerful belief that one's moral ideals are fully valid has been a common response of Chinese intellectuals to our turbulent century. No one has been more torn by the tragedies and spiritual upheavals of modern Chinese history than Yin Hai-kuang, but a few weeks before his death from cancer in 1969 he wrote: "I affirm the positive values of rationality, freedom, democracy, and love, and moreover I am confident that these are the eternal values needed if mankind is to survive."[39]

Admittedly, the Chinese have perceived this last century as one of constant upheavals and agonizing crises, but they have also viewed these upheavals as part of an upward, evolutionary process, a positive, creative ferment leading to a better order of things and involving not only *luan* (chaotic upheaval) but also various powerful *yün-tung* (movements) oriented to good ends. This point is illustrated by the mixed connotations of those words used almost interchangeably to denote these upheavals, words like *tung-luan* (upheaval and enormous activity), *tung-tang* (enormous activity and upheaval), *tung-yao* (earthshaking upheaval and activity), *tung-pien* (enormous activity and social transformation), and *pien* (social transformation). For many Chinese, it is only the many *tung-yao* resulting from the Western impact that have enabled China to shake off its "stagnancy" through *pien-ko* (social transformations and reforms).[40]

5. Optimism (p)

This sense of living in a historical period of creative ferment was connected to the fundamental paradigm of political action in modern China, "struggle" (*tou-cheng, fen-tou, fen-chan, chan-tou*). This paradigm was the opposite of any spirit of intellectual despair or moral uncertainty. We are familiar with it as an aspect of Communist thought, but it was basic also to the thought of an anti-Communist liberal like Yin Hai-kuang. From his collected political writings, which cover the years 1945–1960, and his book on Chinese culture, published in 1966, as well as the sayings of his last years, he emerges as one determined to "struggle" for ideals in which he had an almost unwavering faith. The terminology of "struggle" appears frequently in his writings, although Yin once objected to the Marxist connotations of *tou-cheng* (struggle).[41] In 1966, he called for persons able to "struggle forward in order to create a new age."[42] "Life," he said, "is a process of uninterruptedly struggling forward, and it should be so even more for an intellectual."[43] Just before his death, he described himself as one who "wages a totally uncompromising struggle against irrationalism, obscurantism, narrowmindedness, and dogmatism."[44] Like the Marxists, Yin viewed the forces "against" which he had to struggle as "hateful," not as some morally neutral cultural or psychological pattern. As he put it at one point, "Bolshevism . . . is . . . a poisonous snake . . . swallowing up freedom and human rights."[45] Facing such enemies, one had to be willing to die for the truth, "caring for nothing but the distinction between right and wrong."[46] Such courage, in turn, depended on a sense of immense inner pride. Yin spoke of "walking along with one's head held high . . . . unashamed before either heaven above or men below." This explicitly Mencian stance of pride and autonomy was basic to his thought. Only one willing to die for his principles, unmoved by any material considerations, is "truly a person who can stand on the earth with heaven unobstructed above him." Such a person can "undertake great responsibilities, shape heaven and earth, and struggle forward to create a new age."[47]

Moreover, we should not forget that to the extent that they perceived themselves as confronting an enormous historical crisis, the Chinese were not simply thrust into a totally novel, unprecedented situation of shock. Whatever the unprecedented aspects of the situation created by the Western impact, and we have just noted that these were positive as well as negative, the Chinese have traditionally regarded humiliating and convulsive disasters as a normal part of their history and indeed as serving to define the moral-political missions to be undertaken by succeeding generations. Certainly the feelings of humiliation and shock expressed by Liang Ch'i-ch'ao around 1897 with regard to the Manchus' conquest of China in 1644 were as emotionally intense as any he expressed regarding the victories of Western and Japanese imperialism.[48] And his feelings were hardly different from those of scholars in the seventeenth century who, witnessing the Ming collapse, felt they were living in a time when "heaven is falling down and the earth is collapsing," when "the blood vessels of the state have been severed, the temples of the dynasty have been overturned, the dikes have collapsed with dead fish strewn about rotting, and nothing can be done to retrieve the situation."[49] In this context we should take into account Hsü Fu-kuan's view of the Confucian standpoint as primordially a response to the disasters and suffering of the world (*yu-huan i-shih*).[50] Reacting to the crises of the late nineteenth century and of the twentieth, the Chinese were able to draw on the moral resources of a culture which for centuries had to a large extent defined moral action precisely as a process of coping with almost unbearable disasters. Consequently, one may suggest that whatever the intellectual disarray with which the Chinese entered the twentieth century, they were readying themselves in a traditionally familiar way to wipe away their most recent humiliations, and their determination to do so was increasingly shaped by a new wave of almost Messianic optimism.

In this light, the fact that some modernizing intellectuals, like Liang Ch'i-ch'ao, still remained preoccupied with Neo-Confucian writings on the travails of moral effort does not necessarily mean that they remained entrapped within the Neo-Confucian sense of predicament. As already indicated, Liang's continuing involvement in the Neo-Confucian tradition, leading him in 1905 to publish a new edition of Huang Tsung-hsi's study of Ming thought, was interwoven with a variety of new perspectives.[51] Nor should Chang T'ai-yen's pessimism about the possibility of any real progress resulting from the application of modern technology be regarded as a central intellectual current in the twentieth century, although many people shared his feelings. It can better be regarded as a sign that the newly spreading optimism had already gained enough ground to provoke an intellectual reaction. Nor was much of an impact made by Wang Ching-an's gloomy conclusion, so close to dominant Humean trends in the West, that knowledge synthesizing the realms of value and fact was impossible, that "ideology," in other words, was impossible. A student of Schopenhauer, Nietzsche, and Kant, Wang held that "The theories which can be loved cannot be regarded as true, and the theories which can be regarded as true cannot be loved."[52]

One obviously does not want to claim that modern China's intellectual history has been simply dominated by the rise of optimistic, transformative philosophical systems. As in the past, the intellectual scene remained highly heterogeneous. Many millions of people, taking a traditionally familistic, a romantic, or even a simply anomic attitude toward life, remained skeptical if not ignorant of the doings of the system-builders. Consequently it is not only the variety of transformative philosophical systems but also their complex relations to more accommodative worldviews with which any complete account of this period would have to deal. Nevertheless it is clear that the development of these philosophical systems attracted much attention and was integral to the growing determination to restructure Chinese society.

q. THE NEW OPTIMISM AND THE AGENDA OF MODERN CHINESE PHILOSOPHY

The agenda of modern Chinese philosophers can best be understood against the backdrop of this rising optimistic faith in an "outer," historical process of transformation leading to the ideals of interdependence and based on the advent of a new technology, new political forms, and new forms of knowledge. On the one hand, these thinkers worried about how to harness these "outer" forces in political and organizational terms, partly expressing conflicting class interests and political convictions as they argued over which pattern of action was the leading vehicle of historical progress. How could one best obtain a handle on the outer world? In this discussion, they considered different groups, such as "cultures" in the East and the West, classes, political parties, governments, international alliances, and other cosmopolitan structures, such as the Comintern; institutional structures, such as democracy or capitalism; patterns of activity, such as the upheavals of war, political movements, economic developments, and "history" as a whole; the nature of Man as an inevitable force for progress; and the moral enlightenment resulting from scientific knowledge.

In the thought of Yin Hai-kuang, for instance, the vehicles of progress were scattered in China and the rest of the world, and the task of the thinker was to identify them and somehow fit them together. In this respect, Yin was typical of all leading Chinese thinkers in the twentieth century, right and left. For him, world history was shaped by the twin drives of Man: a noble desire to realize greatness by pursuing values like science and freedom, and a selfish desire for immediate material gain, aggravated by a tendency to be confused by the "empty talk" of false ideologies. This selfish desire, Yin wrote in 1966, had led to various patterns of tyranny, such as Communism and the Confucian empires. Upheavals, like that caused by World War I, similarly released tides of immoral and ideologically confused behavior throughout the world. Amidst these historical vicissitudes, Yin was often doubtful that any Chinese political party, government, or social class could serve as a vehicle of progress, and he had little faith in capitalism or any form of economic development per se.[53]

Nevertheless, he repeatedly saw powerfully progressive forces at work in the "outer" world of current history. In 1945, he saw Man's desire for freedom effectively expressed in the leadership of the Kuomintang. Despite all difficulties, it was leading China along the "correct road," the "great road" of "modernization" and "liberation" from external oppression.[54] By 1949, Yin found hope no longer in the Kuomintang but in "the tendency of China's historical development" and in "the universal desire of the people for rationality, freedom, and food." Chinese Communism would fail because it clashed with these desires.[55] Then in the 1950s and 1960s, Yin thought more in terms of international alliances. In 1966, he saw Taiwan as just one part of the "Free World," which was led in Asia by Japan and India. China's situation was just one part of the world struggle between freedom and Communism, a typically Cold War view which nevertheless epitomized the modern Chinese image of history as a dynamically transformative, cosmopolitan process.[56]

Within China itself, however, the political situation was dark. In 1960, Yin put his hope in a social class, the "intellectuals," and argued for the establishment of an opposition party on Taiwan.[57] After this effort was crushed by the Kuomintang, Yin increasingly saw himself as a latter-day Wang Fu-chih, a spiritual exile cultivating *ko-li chih-hui* (the wisdom to refind one's strength by withdrawing from the world for a time).[58] In the meantime, however, Mao had found that China's masses and mass organizations constituted an effective vehicle of progress.

Apart from thus sorting out the forces of the "outer" world, China's modern thinkers dealt with the question of defining the "ideology" needed as the foundation of social and political morality. Whether they approached this problem in a scientistic or in an anti-scientistic, humanistic way, they shared the same rationalistic determination to deduce morality from a definite idea of the nature of existence, just as Neo-Confucians had. The variety of modern answers to this problem ranged from the scientistic emphasis on some form of material existence, to Fung Yu-lan's theory of a "true" realm of forms known through "logic," to the exegesis of T'ang Chün-i, who looked for the ultimate unit of existence in the inner life and defined it as "the point at which empathies are interchanged." Then, depending on one's ontological position and political convictions, an analysis of Chinese history and culture could be developed.

What especially distinguished all these efforts from Neo-Confucian philosophy was the fact that the need to clarify epistemological and ontological problems was no longer intertwined with the need to show how a transformative power could be activated. Nothing could be more static or even dead than Fung Yu-lan's vision of a purely "formal" realm of logical forms serving as moral ideals. Fung did not need any dynamically transformative metaphysics. He could simply point out that if one turned from the purely formal realm of "the true" to that of "the actual," one empirically discovered that, in the case of societies, the technology of production determined productive methods, which in turn determined a particular form of morality (except for certain "unchanging" virtues and the "spirit" peculiar to a culture). Therefore, as China was now beginning to industrialize, it was passing through "an age of transition" leaving behind the family-centered system of economic and social organization.[59]

Similarly, T'ang Chün-i could define the spiritual basis of society purely in terms of a personal moral condition without worrying, as Neo-Confucians had had to, about how this process of self-realization could be translated into an outwardly effective transformation of society. As we have seen (chapter 3, sections k and o), T'ang regarded "the points at which empathies are interchanged" as the "concrete happenings" primordially constituting experience, and so he turned from the Neo-Confucian preoccupation with the oscillation between rest and movement to a view of movement as the ultimate given. This change, however, did not primarily signify a shift from quiescence to dynamism, since, on the whole, dynamic activity was crucial to both positions.

It is rather the connection of the state of rest to the process of tapping a transformative cosmic force, conceptualized in organismic terms, which we should keep in mind here. Neo-Confucians were searching less for quiescence than for a transnatural hookup between ethical striving and the physical movements of the cosmos, or at least for the pathos of control over such a hookup. Therefore they clung to the terminology allowing them to visualize and symbolize this hookup. T'ang, however, living in a world where the possibility of this hookup has been denied by science, and where the need for this hookup has been obviated by historical developments, could redefine the spiritual struggle as purely a matter of moral purification. On this point, he was really in accord with Liang Ch'i-ch'ao (see chapter 5, section 1).

To be sure, as an idealist, T'ang proposed to reestablish the organic unity of all existence by deriving both my moral life and outer processes from one *t'ien-hsin* (heavenly mind) (see chapter 2, section c). This idealism, however, remained a feeble philosophical construct. The harshly independent realities of the outer world, with its Mao Tse-tungs and Richard Nixons prancing about, could hardly be reduced to manifestations of a single "heavenly mind." Consequently, despite his idealism, T'ang presented a philosophy in which the individual merely realized the high "value" latent in her personal experience, while history, on its own, so to speak, marched ahead in a partly tragic but invariably dynamic way.

Therefore this modern reliance on the dynamism of the "outer" world has not only generated a sense of escape from predicament but also brought with it a new problem, perhaps even a dilemma. Just because this process of transformation was external to the self, it lacked any necessary connection to the personal quest for truth and morality. This quest could not lead directly to a hope of control over the fate of one's society, and it could not be easily identified with any form of personal participation in any "outer" societal process. Whether in the thought of Fung Yu-lan (before 1949), T'ang Chün-i, or Yin Hai-kuang, the worldwide forces reshaping China appeared as impersonal historical tendencies, and the Chinese *yün-tung* (popular movements) which partly constituted these forces typically seemed different from if not hostile to the personal quest for truth and morality. While all these thinkers called on Chinese to devote themselves heroically to the "struggle" for a better world, they could not show any "inner" connection between the philosophical and moral foundation of this struggle and the political organizations through which societal change was occurring. While I could be one with "heaven," as T'ang urged, or in accord with *chen-li* (truth), as Yin urged, neither "heaven" nor "truth" was one with any of the vehicles of outer transformation. The heaven with which the individual could find oneness was a metaphysically castrated heaven without the capacity to issue any "mandate" to any political structure.

The new vision of a transformative outer cosmos, therefore, raised the linkage problem in a new form. In terms of the ethos of interdependence, social oneness flowed from a commitment to a single form of thought which simultaneously explicated the dynamics of the cosmos and the group. Part of the importance of Maoism lies in the fact that it offered an answer to this problem, using dialectical cosmological laws to show how selfless participation in mass movements constituted the very essence of the personal quest for truth and morality. In Mao's thought, the *kung-fu* (efficacious moral efforts) of the individual were once more organically connected to the processes of transformation. Nevertheless, for many Chinese intellectuals, Mao's synthesis failed to bridge the gap between the inner search for truth and outer transformative processes, since it appeared to them as based more on political pronouncements than on that authentically critical spirit of doubt and discussion so basic to the Chinese intellectual tradition. The full significance of Mao's thought, I believe, will become clearer when we stop regarding it as the terminal climax of Chinese intellectual history and view it as part of a varied, ongoing effort to resolve China's current ideological dilemma.

This dilemma seems to stem from a contradiction in China between the standards of truth which a successful ideology must meet and the urgent need for an ideology justifying the spirit of self-sacrifice on which the successful mobilization of the Chinese nation depends. An intellectually tenable ideology elucidating the oneness of cosmological, moral, and political processes is most difficult to devise, but so long as the ethos of interdependence defines the conditions of moral commitment in China, the public-spirited mobilization of the nation will partly depend on the successful propagation of just such an ideology. It follows, then, that Chinese thinkers will have to continue trying to formulate such an ideology unless they begin to question the very premises of interdependence and look for an alternative pattern of moral commitment and selfhood differentiating ethical from cosmological questions. This kind of philosophic or religious "breakthrough," however, does not seem to be on the horizon.[60]

r. CONCLUSION: MAO'S ACHIEVEMENT AND THE ETHOS OF INTERDEPENDENCE

To sum up, Westernization and modernization helped realize powerful, long-frustrated hopes in China, especially the hope of establishing a morally interdependent society founded on a proper cosmology, "radically" centralized, and able to master its "outer" problems. There is no need to deny that Mao let out and constructively channeled the previously suppressed anger of the "dependent" personality and the exploited masses, as certain behavioral scientists and Marxists respectively tell us. Such anger, however, arises when morally defined hopes are frustrated. How the angry person will act, therefore, depends not only on the fact that he is angry but also on the kind of hope he wants to satisfy. To the extent that Mao has aroused fervent support, his radical transformation has not only allowed the expression of anger but also has satisfied an intense desire for a certain kind of morally integrated society. It is the explosive mixture of this long-frustrated desire and the new possibilities of thought and action brought by the West which has fueled China's transformation.

It was Mao's contribution to build on the work of the earlier modernizers in designing the conditions of this mixture. The earlier reformers had enthusiastically discussed the new instrumentalities of wealth and power without being able to explain them as part of a single cosmic, societal, and "inner" process of moral transformation. The moral hollowness of their proposals, their failure to tap the resources of the Chinese spirit, and their understandable obsession with Westernization have been cogently criticized for decades from a variety of perspectives, especially that of conservative thinkers like Fung Yu-lan, Ho Lin, and T'ang Chün-i, but also that of Yin Hai-kuang. A proponent of "self-strengthening" like Hsüeh Fu-ch'eng (1838–1894) could call for efforts to imitate "the Westerners' way of figuring out how to obtain wealth and power," and, like Ch'ing officials generally, he repeated the slogan of *shang-hsia i-hsin* (superiors and inferiors with one mind devoting themselves to the public good).[61] He had no way, however, of evoking such a spirit of unity on a large scale and channeling it into these instrumental activities.

It was, therefore, easy to stress the importance of numerous kinds of technical and even social or cultural improvements, but these early thinkers could only stumble toward the new ideological synthesis their nation required. Hao Chang has pointed out that some of them were concerned with perennial existential problems as well as modernization. Yet we can also see them as struggling to explain how a focus on the external instrumentalities of life could be a way of realizing one's "inner" moral nature within the context of an "interdependent" society and cosmos. Mao's organizational success cannot be separated from the fact that, building on the heritage of May Fourth scientism, he was able to develop an ideology at least partly solving this problem, especially through his equation of practical, selfless work devoted to "the people" and the inner dignity of the individual.

The Sinification of Marxism thus can be seen in the way it came to express and implement the traditional ethos of inter-dependence, not only in explicit doctrinal or strategic shifts, such as Mao's emphasis on the peasants as a revolutionary force. Though alien to the Western world, the ethos he has evoked is not demon-strably pathological, and it certainly cannot be judged by the psychology of upper-class Americans who profess admiration for it. Perhaps the lesson that Mao has taught the world is that to mobilize a vast peasant population, a government has to build on an indigenous heritage of moral ideals which happens to lend itself to the exigencies of complex organization. Just because he has succeeded by depending on this heritage, he has failed to devise a universally valid path of development which can be readily followed by societies with basically different cultural traditions.

If then the Chinese are enthusiastically embracing moderni-zation as a meaningful way of realizing an ethos rooted in their history,[62] their problems are not necessarily those of a people aimlessly drifting away from their traditional moorings without either a clear sense of identity or sufficient capital to industrialize. As Mark Elvin has pointed out, the Chinese perhaps were and still are caught in an economic "high-level equilibrium trap."[63] Getting out of it, however, is only one aspect of their central problem. Their struggle seems to revolve more around the variety of obstacles— psychological, intellectual, and political as well as economic— impeding the continuing integration of their society in terms of the ethics of interdependence.

I have tried to suggest a connection between the realization of the new solidarities in the People's Republic of China, tending to merge the moral empathies of the polity, the city, the village, and the family, and the pattern of mass enthusiasm based on the optimistic feeling that China is entering an era of moral and material progress. It follows that if this optimism declines, if the power structure and the economy are once again perceived as slipping down into the pit of moral failure, these new solidarities and the newly designed collectivities which depend on them will be weakened, and a less politicized, more "capitalistic," and more particularistic kind of social order may once more appear.

Whether this connection between Messianic enthusiasm and the socialist pattern of solidarity is important remains to be seen. One may also ask to what extent this enthusiasm and the belief in Maoist ideology with which it is intertwined depend on the charisma of Mao's personality and on the widespread respect for his authority. Because enthusiasm and charisma are both likely to fade or end one way or another, the socialist order in the PRC can easily be seen as endangered.

On the other hand, the institutionalization of this order has probably acquired a momentum of its own, and as the highest hopes of Communism are dashed and as compromises with recalcitrant realities become increasingly unavoidable, Maoist enthusiasm may give way to a more sober and traditional definition of the current order as a partial moral failure. Possibly within the context of this perception, the tradition-rooted idea of a politically creative tension between sovereign political authority and the claims of moral insight can be further adapted so as to satisfy the interests of various social classes, intellectuals as well as peasants, and a more eclectic, pessimistic, and moderate body of ideology can be developed to legitimate these new channels of authority. That such an ideology would partly hark back to the Neo-Confucian tradition of "moderate realism" and inward spiritual struggle and anxiety is certainly a possibility. At any rate, the dichotomy in Chinese political thought between belief in and skepticism about a totalistic, morally transformed, and polity-dominated social order goes back many centuries, and the attempt to define, both institutionally and ideologically, some viable middle ground between these two alternatives is bound to remain important in the future.

We are thus brought back to the importance of Max Weber's cross-cultural analysis of the Confucian ethos. His perspective was partly different from ours. He was asking why in the seventeenth and eighteenth centuries the indigenous development of the West led to capitalism and the indigenous development of China did not. He concluded that China's failure was due largely to the effects of the Confucian ethos, and his conclusion still carries weight today, even though his early analysis of this ethos was erroneous. We however live in a world where the development of the major societies is based on a mixture of indigenous factors and cosmopolitan influences. We consequently are led to ask: why in this kind of world are some societies more effective than others in coping with their problems and rising to the challenges of modernization? While Weber had to explain China's failure, we have to explain its success, but paradoxically our answer, like Weber's, emphasizes the role of the indigenous ethos. How can this distinctive factor be ignored as we compare the modern development of China with that of other Third World nations which, similarly exposed to cosmopolitan, Western influences, have struggled less effectively with the problems of economic backwardness and political integration? This ethos, we have argued, is connected not only to the fact of China's success but also to the particular character of this success and to the problems of political integration and philosophical synthesis which the Chinese people continue to confront.

Consequently, the study of Chinese modernization does not just revolve around the issues of technology, economics, and political conflict, and unraveling the complexities of the Confucian "spirit" is not just a task for devotees of Spenglerian *Geisteswissenschaft*, philosophizing opponents of May Fourth scientism, and intellectual historians. Rather it is essential for understanding those unique cultural and social orientations which, probably more than any other factor, have shaped the course of Chinese history. That, I believe, is an historiographical lesson which we can learn from the Chinese humanists cited here as well as the sociological tradition of Max Weber.

Notes

1. *The New York Times*, Nov. 24, 1975, p. 35.

2. For a discussion of the concept of political culture, see Gabriel A. Almond and G. Bingham Powell, Jr., *Comparative Politics—A Developmental Approach* (Boston: Little, Brown and Co., 1966), ch. 3.

3. Given the sexist bias integral to traditional Chinese culture, many of the apparently universal traditional concepts about human life implicitly refer only to males, or perhaps better, to a mode of existence shared by males and females but attaining its fullest realization only in the case of males. That a woman could become a sage was inconceivable to the typical Confucian, I believe, and we do not need to translate *chün-tzu* as "true gentleman or lady." It is hard to say just how rare was the view ascribed to Huang Tsung-hsi (1610–1695) that women too should serve as officials, but it was unusual. See Kao Chun, *Huang Li-chou cheng-chih ssu-hsiang yen-chiu* (A Study of Huang Tsung-hsi's Political Thought; Yang-ming-shan: *Chung-kuo wen-hua hsüeh-yüan*, 1967), p. 64. One is reminded of Plato's view that talented women are as fit as talented men to play the highest roles in the ideal republic. Like Huang's, Plato's was a highly theoretical notion which did little to shape widespread norms of behavior. It is merely curious that, for instance, in the Ming period there were female palace "officials" up through the fifth grade and that at least one woman obtained the degree of "Bachelor"; see T'ao Hsi-sheng and Shen Jen-yüan, *Ming Ch'ing cheng-chih chih-tu* (The Governmental Institutions of the Ming and Ch'ing Dynasties; Taipei: The Commercial Press of Taiwan, 1967), p. 201. Whether sexism in imperial China inhibited the development of universalistic and modernizing orientations more than did sexism in the West is a complex issue which has not yet been studied. At any rate, when modern scholars refer to Confucian notions of the self or of human beings, they can usually assume a sexist bias and use masculine pronouns in their translations, although here and there they can roughly infer a reference to females as well. These considerations underlie the usages in this study, but I confess that often I use "his" where "her or his" would be more accurate, because the latter set of words is awkwardly long and because "her" alone in this context would sound strange to most readers.

4. Max Weber, *The Religion of China*, H. H. Gerth, trans. (Glencoe: The Free Press, 1951), pp. 227, 235. Wrestling in his typically disorganized, redundant, but repeatedly brilliant fashion with the Gargantuan task of contrasting Puritan and Confucian orientations, Weber not only saw Confucian society as emphasizing magic, ceremony, tradition, kin ties, and "personalist associations" but also astutely sought to account for the emotional quality of Chinese interpersonal relations, the large

amount of distrust in Chinese society, and the paradoxical Chinese preoccupation with wealth. "How can all this be explained?" he asked (pp. 231–32, 237). His answer, however, largely consisted of what we can now easily recognize as a caricature of Confucian thought. Emphasizing the valid point that there "were no prophets raising ethical 'demands' in the name of a supra-mundane God" (p. 142), he inaccurately concluded that Confucians were purely "this-worldly" and "bereft of metaphysical interest" (pp. 144, 154); regarded the actual world as "the best of all possible worlds" and as free of "radical evil" (pp. 227–28); and so were virtually innocent of any "tension" between their moral ideals and actuality (pp. 235, 227). "Tension toward the 'world' had never arisen because, as far as known, there had never been an ethical prophecy of a supramundane God who raised ethical demands" (pp. 229–30). Without this tension, Weber went on, the individual lacked any "inward" moral struggle comparable to the Puritan's striving for "systematic control of one's own nature which was regarded as wicked and sinful" (p. 244), any "autonomous ethic" (p. 142), any "internal measure of value," or any "autonomous counterweight in confronting this world" (p. 235). The emotional side of this lack of self-assertion was the "cool temper" of the Chinese, in terms of which "every inordinate passion, especially wrath, *ch'i*, produced evil charms" (p. 233). Thus the Confucian "desired neither to be saved from evil nor from a fall of man, which he knew not. He desired to be saved from nothing except perhaps the undignified barbarism of social rudeness" (pp. 156–57). "Propriety" was his overriding concern: "Controlled ease and correct composure, grace and dignity in the sense of a ceremonially ordered court-salon characterize this man" (pp. 156, 244, 162–63, 228). His ultimate goal, far from any ideal of sagehood, was "only long life, health, and wealth in this world and beyond death the retention of his good name." With this lack of any striving for moral autonomy, "pious conformism with the fixed order of secular powers reigned supreme" (p. 228). Far from asserting his own sense of moral responsibility for the empire, the Confucian felt that "everything depended upon the behavior of the officials" (p. 153). Study, divorced from any search for moral self-fulfillment, "consisted of the mere assimilation of existing ideas" (p. 163). Without the sense of moral autonomy and "tension," "there was no leverage for influencing conduct through inner forces freed of tradition and convention" (p. 236). Even if one grants that this last proposition has some validity, and I do not, the premises in terms of which Weber explained it, presented above, are grossly inaccurate, as made clear in chapter 3. One can easily see how Weber's analysis led to the emphasis, still prevalent today, on the "stagnative" and "authoritarian" character of Confucian orientations. On the similarity between Weber's and Fingarette's conclusions, see chapter 5, note 18. De Bary, in his profound work on Neo-Confucianism, has expressed doubts about Weber's thesis similar to mine, a fact which strengthens my argument. See Wm. Theodore de Bary et al., *The Unfolding of Neo-Confucianism* (New York: Columbia University Press, 1975, hereafter referred to as *Unfolding*). De Bary sees in Neo-Confucianism an emphasis on the individual and his autonomy (*ibid.*, pp. 161, 10, 27); a sense of "rational transformation" and "moral dynamism," which perhaps played a positive role at least in the modernization of Meiji Japan (*ibid.*, pp. 148, 7–9, 21–22, 25); compatibility with "the development of scientific inquiry" (*ibid.*, pp. 204, 167); and "values" possibly still important in China today (*ibid.*, p. 205). For the difference between de Bary's perspective and my argument, see chapter 3, section a.

5. S. N. Eisenstadt, ed., *The Protestant Ethic and Modernization* (New York: Basic Books, Inc., 1968), pp. 25–27.

6. Lucian W. Pye, *The Spirit of Chinese Politics* (Cambridge, Mass.: The M. I. T. Press, 1968), p. 30.

7. The Chinese views are described in chapter 1. Solomon is the leading American exponent. See Richard H. Solomon, *Mao's Revolution and the Chinese Political Culture* (Berkeley: University of California Press, 1971). See reviews of this work by F. W. Mote and T. A. Metzger in *The Journal of Asian Studies*, 32:1 (November 1972), pp. 101–20. In my review, I tried to sum up Solomon's position as follows (page numbers refer to Solomon's book): "Closely connected to Lucian W. Pye's views in his *The Spirit of Chinese Politics* (Cambridge, Mass.: The M. I. T. Press, 1968), Solomon's thesis revolves around the concept of a 'dependency social orientation' (p. xiv). This dependency orientation was shaped by attitudes connected to pressures of great economic scarcity; by Confucian ideology; and by patterns of socialization, particularly the strictness with which children were treated at home beginning around the age of six, and the authoritarian nature of education in the schools. Children learned that their own opinions, emotions, and aggressive impulses had to be severely curbed, and that they should consistently defer to the views of those having authority over them. This lack of legitimated channels for the expression of emotional and aggressive impulses generated several interconnected attitudes: an abhorrence of aggressive behavior, which was perceived as causing *luan* (chaos, disorder); a lack of 'self-esteem' and of confidence in one's own aggressive impulses and autonomous judgments, complemented by a feeling of dependence on superiors for moral guidance; a placing of collective interests over individual ones; a projection of the lack of self-esteem onto one's peers, with a resulting sense of distrust permeating many social relations and undermining friendships; and a set of attitudes towards authority. As just indicated, this set included feelings of 'deference' (p. 4) and, even more, a feeling of 'impotence' before power (p. 113). It also consisted of a sense of anxiety and frustration caused by the harshness with which authority was imposed against the direction of one's own impulses; anger, which evolved from this anxiety when a person felt that those in authority had failed to provide the benefits for which one depended on them (pp. 75–78); a desire to avoid contact with those in authority so as to avoid frustrations; and a desire to climb up the ladder of authority so as to enjoy the feeling of having others submit to ego (p. 79). What this set of attitudes excluded was the notion of legitimated protest against those in authority (p. 210), or at least protests of a direct sort, since appeals to third parties for intercession were common (p. 79, pp. 128–29)." Solomon's views are echoed in Lloyd E. Eastman, *The Abortive Revolution* (Cambridge, Mass.: Harvard University Press, 1974), chapter 7.

8. See his "'New Confucianism' and the Intellectual Crisis of Contemporary China." This will appear in a forthcoming volume on modern Chinese conservatism edited by Charlotte Furth.

9. Ho Lin, *Tang-tai Chung-kuo che-hsüeh* (Contemporary Chinese Philosophy: Nanking: *Sheng-li ch'u-pan kung-ssu*, 1947).

10. *Ibid.*, p. 68.   11. *Ibid.*, pp. ii, 67.   12. *Ibid.*, p. 2.

13. *Ibid.*, pp. 26–27.   14. *Ibid.*, pp. 11–12.   15. *Ibid.*, pp. 77, 55.

16. Joseph R. Levenson, *Confucian China and its Modern Fate—The Problem of Intellectual Continuity* (Berkeley: University of California Press, 1958), p. xvi.

17. See especially Fung Yu-lan's *Hsin li-hsüeh* (A New Philosophy Based on the School of Chu Hsi; Hong Kong: *Chung-kuo che-hsüeh yen-chiu-hui*, 1961) (the preface to the first edition was written in 1938 in Kunming); his *Hsin shih lun* (A New Discussion of the Issues of the Practical World; Kowloon: *Shih-tai shu-chü*, the year of

publication is not given but this book was written immediately after the completion of *Hsin li-hsüeh*, and the preface to the first edition was finished in 1939); and his *Hsin yüan-tao* (A New Analysis of Philosophy in China; Hong Kong: *Chung-kuo che-hsüeh yen-chiu-hui*, 1961) (the preface to the first edition was written in 1944). The latter book has been translated by E. R. Hughes as *The Spirit of Chinese Philosophy* (Boston: Beacon Press, 1967). For the basic influence of Russell's neo-realism and of Spinoza on Fung in the early 1920s, see Fung Yu-lan, *Jen-sheng che-hsüeh* (The Philosophy of Life; Kowloon: *Shih-hsüeh shu-tien*, date of publication not given). For a discussion of Fung and his other publications, see Wing-tsit Chan, *Religious Trends in Modern China* (New York: Columbia University Press, 1953), pp. 43–53, and the same scholar's *A Source Book in Chinese Philosophy* (Princeton: Princeton University Press, 1963), pp. 751–55. For some of Fung's views after converting to Marxism, see his articles in *Pei-ching ta-hsüeh hsüeh-pao—jen-wen k'o-hsüeh—che-hsüeh-p'ien*, vol. 1 (1955–1956). For a critique of Fung's interpretation of Chu Hsi, see chapter 3, note 210, and for further remarks about Fung's philosophy, see chapter 5, section q.

18. For Yin's turn to traditional values and his biography, see Ch'en Ku-ying, comp., *Ch'un-ts'an t'u-ssu—Yin Hai-kuang tsui-hou-te hua-yü* ("The Silk-worms Continue to Spit Out Silk until the Hour of their Death"—Yin Hai-kuang's Last Words; Taipei: *Shih-chieh wen-wu kung-ying-she*, 1969). For his scientistic use of contemporary social science categories to criticize Confucian culture and its continuing influence in modern China, see his *Chung-kuo wen-hua-te chan-wang* (An Appraisal of Chinese Culture and its Prospects; 2 vols.; Taipei: *Wen-hsing shu-tien*, 1966). Culture Book House in Hong Kong has put out two other editions of this book, in 1969 and 1971. For the development of his liberal political views from 1945 to 1960, see Yin Hai-kuang, *Yin Hai-kuang hsüan-chi—ti-i-chüan—she-hui cheng-chih yen-lun* (The Collected Writings of Yin Hai-kuang, Vol. 1, Social and Political Writings; Kowloon: *Yu-lien ch'u-pan-she yu-hsien kung-ssu*, 1971). Recently published is *Yin Hai-kuang shu-hsin-chi* (The Collected Letters of Yin Hai-kuang; ed. by Lu Ts'ang; Hong Kong: *Wen-i shu-wu*, 1975). Writings on Yin include *Yin Hai-kuang hsien-sheng chi-nien-chi pien-wei-hui*, comp., *Yin Hai-kuang hsien-sheng chi-nien-chi* (Essays in Memory of Yin Hai-kuang; Kowloon: *Yu-lien shu-pao fa-hsing kung-ssu*, 1971), and T. A. Metzger, "Yin Hai-kuang: The Meaning of Liberal Protest in Contemporary China," unpublished. For some discussion of Yin's thought, see chapter 5, sections p and q.

19. See D. W. Y. Kwok, *Scientism in Chinese Thought, 1900–1950* (New Haven: Yale University Press, 1965).

20. Li I-yüan and Yang Kuo-shu, eds., *Chung-kuo-jen-te hsing-ko: k'o-chi tsung-ho-hsing-te t'ao-lun* (Symposium on the Character of the Chinese—An Interdisciplinary Approach; Nankang, Taipei, monograph series B. no. 4 of the Institute of Ethnology, Academia Sinica, 1972), pp. 381–83. One focus of this seminar was childhood socialization, and its viewpoints in this regard are described in chapter 1. The seminar was also interested in single-factor genetic theories of Chinese culture, asking, without very satisfactory results I believe, whether the main cultural traits of traditional China should be causally ascribed to familism and the ethical teachings the latter involved; a diffuse tradition of respect for authority found in and out of the family; the character of agricultural or peasant life and the associated phenomena of economic backwardness; a "past time orientation"; or the patterns of childhood socialization. A third theme, worked out with far more fruitful results, was that of

changes in values and social structure accompanying modernization. Particularly stimulating to me were Wu Ts'ung-hsien's sociological analysis of such changes in the Taiwan peasant sector and Yang Kuo-shu's use of attitudinal surveys to compare the values of two large groups of college students, one examined in 1948, the other, around 1964–65. The seminar also had a fourth focus, defining the inherited "national character" of the Chinese. It is true that none of its conclusions in this regard are particularly new, and that vast reaches of evidence from studies in China's technological, economic, and social history were ignored as the seminar put forward various broad generalizations in a largely impressionistic way. Nevertheless, this exceptionally qualified group of behavioral scientists arrived at a rough consensus which must be given great weight by any scholar asking cross-cultural questions about the traditional civilization, such as questions about the failure to develop capitalism. They tended to agree on two points, which in turn refer to apparently intertwined syndromes. First, they were much concerned with a special pattern of authority, which some of them analyzed applying Western notions of dependency and of the authoritarian personality. This issue is discussed in my book, especially in chapter 4, but their second area of consensus should perhaps be outlined here. One could sum up this view as holding that the Chinese had a relatively passive way of dealing with objects in their environment, whether inherited norms, social objects, or natural objects. Thus the seminar at various times referred without reservations to the following alleged traits, which can all be regarded as subtraits of this passivity: a strong respect for the authority of inherited ways, sometimes viewed as a "past time orientation" (p. 29); the "stagnating" of basic social, economic, and political institutions (p. 57); lack of an emphasis on social activism, e.g. on adventuresomeness, on courage, on heroic military action, on political extremism (pp. 245–46); conversely, a stress on the avoidance of violence, on peace, on avoiding social activism except in times of extreme crisis (pp. 138–39, 149); a lack of individual initiative in solving problems (p. 245); a lack, notably among the peasants, of a differentiated, rationalistically instrumental orientation designed maximally to exploit material, economic opportunities (p. 361); lack of emphasis on analytical, systematic, scientific thinking (p. 418); a stress on accommodation with rather than conquest of the external, particularly the natural environment (p. 245); and a need to harmonize with the supernatural as well as the natural forces in the environment (p. 188). One could add a tendency to avoid directness in the articulation of political interests. Supporting an authoritarian tendency, this passivity also distinguished the Chinese form of authoritarianism from other kinds. Finally, the implicit ideological currents in the seminar are also interesting. Almost entirely absent was any Levensonian desire to demonstrate the validity of Chinese values relative to Western ones or to play down the contributions of Western social scientists working on China. The dominant spirit was what I would call a May Fourth sociology viewing the traditional traits as still very much present and as deficient compared to those of societies like the U.S.A., although this "inferiority complex" was criticized in the seminar (p. 421). At the same time, an "unideological" approach to modernization, stressing technological and behavioral patterns and thus contrasting with the common emphasis, left, right, and liberal, on moral transformation, is found in much of the writing. Wu Ts'ung-hsien's article is a good example. Long and excellent bibliographies are included.

21. Ho Lin, p. 19.   22. *Ibid.*, p. 2.

23. Levenson, pp. xv–xvi. Professor Yin's view is in an unpublished research memorandum which he gave me in the winter of 1967–68.

24. Ho Lin, pp. 1–66. Among Ho's many illuminating comments I would note his elucidation of the closeness of Fung Yu-lan's metaphysical position to that of Chin Yüeh-lin (pp. 31–36), whom the young, entirely scientistic Yin Hai-kuang looked up to as a mentor in the late 1930s, and his comments on the philosophical considerations underlying the historical works of Fung and T'ang Yung-t'ung (pp. 23–25, 80). On Fung, see note 17 above, chapter 5, section q, and chapter 3, note 210.

25. See Henry Stuart Hughes, *Consciousness and Society; The Reorientation of European Social Thought, 1890–1930* (New York: Knopf, 1961), and Talcott Parsons, *The Structure of Social Action* (New York: The Free Press of Glencoe, 1961).

26. Hao Chang, *Liang Ch'i-ch'ao and Intellectual Transition in China, 1890–1907* (Cambridge, Mass.: Harvard University Press, 1971), p. 112.

27. For instance, the Chinese behavioral scientists who recently participated in the Academia Sinica's symposium on the "national character" of the Chinese both examined and accepted this assumption. See eg. Li I-yüan and Yang Kuo-shu, pp. 47–49.

28. F. G. Bailey, "Chaos, Order, and Competition: A Perspective for Political Anthropology," unpublished. See also p. 251, note 2, below.

29. *Pei-ching ta-hsüeh hsüeh-pao—jen-wen k'o-hsüeh—che-hsüeh-p'ien*, vol. 1 (1955–56), p. 125. The mischievous but insightful remark about Marx is made by Stanislav Andreski in S. N. Eisenstadt, ed., *The Protestant Ethic and Modernization*, p. 56.

30. I use the term "ideology" mostly in this special sense found in Daniel Bell, *The End of Ideology* (The Free Press of Glencoe, Illinois, 1960), p. 16. Bell here refers to ideologies as "intellectual systems that could claim *truth* for their views of the world," and as putting "the claims of faith" above the "claims of doubt." Admittedly, because any body of political attitudes is a mixture of both kinds of claims and is likely to contain key moral propositions phrased as statements of fact, Bell's distinction between "ideology" and "anti-ideological" standpoints seems problematic. Nevertheless his view is suggestive in distinguishing between outlooks focused either more or less on explicitly demonstrating their verifiability as a comprehensive body of ontological, moral, and political theory. In the light of his use of the term "ideology," Chinese political thought in traditional times was as ideological as Maoism. According to Schurmann's use of the term, however, Chinese political orientations became largely ideological only with the rise of the PRC, since he essentially defines "ideology" as a way of thinking peculiar to modern, large-scale organizations. In other words, Schurmann uses the term to explicate the rise of new orientations in China, while I seize on another meaning of the term to refer to an aspect of Chinese political thought which has apparently remained constant since traditional times. See Franz Schurmann, *Ideology and Organization in Communist China* (Berkeley: University of California Press, 1968), pp. 3, 7, 8, 18, 49. Aside from this question of definition, I would agree with Schurmann to the extent of recognizing that however one analyzes the continuities and discontinuities in the development of Chinese political orientations, some of the changes that have occurred must be connected to the character of the organizations set up in the PRC. However, Schurmann's view that new orientations associated with these organizations have "replaced" the traditional "ethos" except for some "lingering vestiges of Confucian humanism" (pp. 7–8) is not based on any attempt carefully to discuss the materials connected to this ethos. Moreover, the questions raised by his theoretical framework are not just terminological. One can agree with his view that ideas consciously formulated and consciously concerned with goals and action play an especially large role in "organi-

zations" as opposed to other kinds of groups (p. 18), since this is a matter of definition regarding which there is a wide consensus among social scientists. However I find it difficult to accept Schurmann's view that all the main organizational orientations in the PRC can be identified with such a set of consciously formulated ideas (p. 8). On the contrary, any organization operates *also* in terms of the cultural orientations shared by its members. This can be seen from Robert H. Silin's acute analysis of large-scale business organization on Taiwan, as yet unpublished, or, more generally, from the vast body of social theory collected by Talcott Parsons and others and published in two volumes as *Theories of Society* (New York: The Free Press of Glencoe, Inc., 1961). Finally, Schurmann's attempt to conceptualize the difference between China's traditional orientations and the ideology of the PRC is not useful, because the distinguishing characteristic he ascribes to the latter ("express values and goals of sociopolitical action and achievement") can just as well be ascribed to the former, and vice versa (see p. 8).

    31. Don C. Price, *Russia and the Roots of the Chinese Revolution, 1896–1911* Cambridge, Mass.: Harvard University Press, 1974), pp. 2–5. Price's brilliant study emphasizes the continuity between central Confucian values and those of the early reformers and radicals. Especially important is his analysis of "the revolutionary vocation," developed in chapter 7. This analysis partly converges with T'ang Chün-i's concept of Confucian selfhood and autonomy, described in chapter 2, below.

CHAPTER ONE — DEPENDENCY AND THE
HUMANISTIC THEORY
OF CHINESE FAMILISM

    1. Li I-yüan and Yang Kuo-shu, pp. 227–56. For a brief discussion of this book, see Introduction, note 20. For an outline of Solomon's position, see Introduction, note 7.

    2. This point, admittedly, is made explicitly only in a similar analysis by Hsü Ching; see Li I-yüan and Yang Kuo-shu, p. 206.

    3. *Ibid.*, pp. 234, 246.   4. *Ibid.*, pp. 206, 221–23.

    5. *Ibid.*, p. 251–52. The emphasis in the theory of dependency on the severity with which children were treated as a factor producing a specifically Chinese personality pattern is not too convincing, because the harshly severe treatment of children has not been peculiar to Chinese culture. Obviously the humanistic theory of familism, with its emphasis on the ideological and emotional atmosphere of Chinese family life, is not so vulnerable to this kind of criticism. For a review of some of the more recent literature on the rather gruesome history of child rearing in the West, see Lawrence Stone, "The Massacre of Innocents," in *The New York Review of Books*, Nov. 14, 1974, pp. 25–31.

    6. Li I-yüan and Yang Kuo-shu, pp. 128–29, 131, 133, 135–37.

    7. *Ibid.*, p. 221

    8. These terms and quotations are found in the Morohashi dictionary. See chapter 4 for self-assertion in the Ch'ing bureaucracy.

    9. Li I-yüan and Yang Kuo-shu, pp. 163–74.   10. *Ibid.*, p. 231

    11. *Ibid.*, p. 167. This concept was adduced by the historian Wei Cheng-t'ung in the course of the seminar's discussion of Yang's paper. The centrality of this concept is clear also from T'ang Chün-i's analysis, discussed in chapter 2, and from Professor

1. Dependency

Lien-sheng Yang's famous and seminal article "The Concept of 'Pao' as a Basis for Social Relations in China," in John K. Fairbank, ed., *Chinese Thought and Institutions* (Chicago: The University of Chicago Press, 1957), pp. 291–309.

12. This passage is found under the thirty-seventh hexagram of the *Book of Changes*. See 2:215 in *The I Ching—The Richard Wilhelm Translation Rendered into English by Cary F. Baynes* (2 vols.: New York: Pantheon Books, 1952).

13. Li I-yüan and Yang Kuo-shu, p. 9.   14. *Ibid.*, p. 215.

15. *Ibid.*, pp. 159–60, 170.   16. *Ibid.*, p. 81.   17. *Ibid.*, pp. 150, 152.

18. Yin Hai-kuang, *Chung-kuo wen-hua-te chan-wang*, 2:617–18.

19. Li I-yüan and Yang Kuo-shu, p. 151.

20. *Ibid.*, p. 146.   21. *Ibid.*, pp. 169, 144–46.   22. *Ibid.*, pp. 138, 146, 157.

CHAPTER TWO — T'ANG CHÜN-I'S CONCEPT OF
CONFUCIAN SELF-FULFILLMENT

1. T'ang Chün-i, *Chung-kuo wen-hua-chih ching-shen chia-chih* (The Value of the Spirit of Chinese Culture; Taipei: *Cheng-chung shu-chü*, 1972). Hereafter referred to as "T'ang." This book was completed in 1951, and in its introduction T'ang gives a brief intellectual autobiography (pp. i–vi). Although preparation of the final manuscript took only eight months and was carried out under hectic conditions in Hong Kong, where T'ang had to write it largely out of his memory with few books to refer to, this book is the direct product of a decade of intense study and writing, beginning with the time, around 1940, when T'ang shifted his philosophical position much closer to that of Hsiung Shih-li and began his long intellectual association with Mou Tsung-san. T'ang's publications on the "spirit" of Chinese culture go back to about 1934, but before 1940, he could not accept the idealistic position of Hsiung and Ou-yang Ching-wu and had not yet been won over by German idealism. Thus the relation of the transcendent to human consciousness was not yet clear to him. At one point he held that any concept of ultimate being transcending the empirical was no more than "an abstraction which one clings to the way deluded people cling to the material world" (this is perhaps too literal a translation of the term *chih-cho*, discussed in note 17 below). After turning into the idealist path around 1940, when he was passing through a time of great personal hardship and intense thought about the problems of morality and mortality, T'ang entered a decade of study during which he never again felt any need to change his ultimate philosophical position, and during which he used this position to reexamine "one by one" all the major issues of culture, science, and political theory, finding in each case what he felt was "the correct interpretation" and feeling that the validity of his standpoint was being increasingly corroborated by many of the important publications appearing at that time, such as those by Hsiung, Mou, Ch'ien Mu, Liang Shu-ming, and Fang Tung-mei. As the major product of this decade in his life, *Chung-kuo wen-hua-chih ching-shen chia-chih* is an historical document in its own right and is distinguished by a special degree of philosophic brilliance and fresh enthusiasm. In his introduction to it, T'ang was forced to apologize for the heavy demands made on the reader by difficult parts of the book which, "touching on recondite aspects of philosophical questions," could not be written in a "popularized" way. His own view of the importance of this work is also expressed in his foreword to his *Jen-wen ching-shen-chih ch'ung-chien* (The Reconstruction of the Humanistic Spirit; 2 vols; Hong Kong: *Hsin-ya yen-chiu-so*, 1955), where (p. ii) he states that this more recent book is not so complete and "rig-

orous" in its "presentation of basic concepts" as are the last three sections of *Chung-kuo wen-hua-chih ching-shen chia-chih*. In *Che-hsüeh kai-lun* (An Introduction to Philosophy; 2 vols.; Taipei: *T'ai-wan hsüeh-sheng shu-chü*, 1974), 1:129–31, 1:136–37, T'ang reaffirms the basic standpoint in *Chung-kuo wen-hua-chih ching-shen chia-chih*. He argues here that different geographical, economic, and living conditions in China, India, and the West led in early times to different primordial ways of thought, and that Indian and Chinese thought involved a more direct and authentic grasp of moral experience than did Western thought, which was too "external," "rational," and dependent on "universal categories." T'ang's other works include *Chung-kuo che-hsüeh yüan-lun* (Studies on the Foundations of Chinese Philosophy; 2 vols.; Kowloon: *Hsin-ya shu-yüan yen-chiu-so*, 1968 and 1974). In English, his articles can be found in Charles A. Moore, ed., *The Chinese Mind* (Honolulu: East-West Center Press and University of Hawaii Press, 1967), in Wm. Theodore de Bary, ed., *Self and Society in Ming Thought* (New York: Columbia University Press, 1970), and in *The Unfolding of Neo-Confucianism*. See also p. 277, note 60, below.

2. T'ang pp. 348–49.

3. T'ang p. 179. T'ang admits that this kind of differentiation "also manifests a kind of spiritual attitude which has value," but his account of it ("when they are interested in seeking truth, they go to a library, school, or association devoted to intellectual pursuits") is laced with sarcasm.

4. *Ibid.*, p. 115. In thus summing up the nature of Greek thought, T'ang had not yet taken into account works like Werner Jaeger, *Paideia: The Ideals of Greek Culture*, 3 vols. (New York: Oxford University Press, 1943–1945), the first German edition of which came out in 1933. Seeking to define "the Greek ideal of culture," Jaeger refers to an "organic point of view" which has more in common with Chinese culture as viewed by T'ang than with Greek culture as viewed by T'ang. See *ibid.*, 1: xvii–xxiv.

5. T'ang, pp. 89–101.   6. *Ibid.*, p. 91.   7. *Ibid.*, pp. 93, 106.

8. *Ibid.*, pp. 90, 188.   9. *Ibid.*, pp. 91, 93.   10. *Ibid.*, p. 93.

11. *Ibid.*, pp. 91, 97. For the Neo-Confucian idea of free will, see chapter 3, section o.

12. *Ibid.*, pp. 91–92.   13. *Ibid.*, pp. 58, 61, 115, 93–94, p. 141.

14. *Ibid.*, p. 183.   15. *Ibid.*, p. 92.

16. *Ibid.*, p. 119. On the imagery of water in the conceptualization of reality by Neo-Confucians see chapter 3, section j, etc.

17. *Ibid.*, pp. 114, 155. This idea of *chih-cho* (holding) connotes the Buddhist notion of clinging in a deluded way to the material world, an idea with some resemblance to the Confucian notion of *p'ien-hsia ku-chih* (onesidedly narrow, stuck in an obstinately unmoving position), since both concepts associate immorality with an image of unnatural fixity. Perhaps the *locus classicus* of this image, involving the idea of wrongly trying to "hold" something which cannot be fixed in one spot, is the twenty-ninth chapter of the *Tao-te-ching*. For an example of this idea of "holding" or "clinging" in the thought of Chinese Buddhists, see Chi-tsang's (549–623) use of *chih* (hold) in Fung Yu-lan, *Chung-kuo ssu-hsiang-shih* (A History of Chinese Philosophy; 2 vols.; anonymous Taiwan edition), 2:672. This is translated in Fung Yu-lan, *A History of Chinese Philosophy*, trans. by Derk Bodde, 2 vols. (Princeton: Princeton University Press, 1953), 2:252. For the idea of "holding" in Neo-Confucianism, see chapter 3, section u. Concerned with avoiding the philosophical and moral fault of *chih-cho* (artificially clinging to and trying to keep static the inherently moving),

2. T'ang Chün-i

T'ang Chün-i in his *Chung-kuo wen-hua-chih ching-shen chia-chih* does not bring up the philosophical question of reification. So long as ultimate being (e.g. "heaven") is conceptualized as something inherently moving, one can without any difficulty maintain that it exists objectively as a transcendent thing: the danger of *chih-cho* had been avoided, and the danger of reification is not recognized. Possibly preoccupation with the former danger blunted awareness of the latter. Yet T'ang, at least by the late 1950s, was worrying about whether "universals" were real except as ideas within the mind. See *Che-hsüeh kai-lun*, 1:66–67.

18. T'ang, pp. 49–50, 179.

19. *Ibid.*, pp. 94, 96–101. It is only through this idea of "emptiness" that the crucial Neo-Confucian emphasis on "total stillness" etc. enters T'ang's analysis. See chapter 3, section k.

20. *Ibid.*, pp. 212, 287, 203.   21. *Ibid.*, p. 113.

22. Yin Yai-kuang, *Yin Hai-kuang hsüan-chi*, p. 501. Huang Tsung-hsi and Ch'üan Tsu-wang, comps., *Sung Yüan hsüeh-an* (Notes on the Confucian Scholars of the Sung and Yüan Dynasties; 3 vols.; Taipei: *Shih-chieh shu-chü*, 1961), 2:944.

23. T'ang, pp. 63, 95.   24. *Ibid.*, pp. 106–7.

25. *Ibid.*, pp. 331–33, 65, 106–7.

26. *Ibid.*, pp. 128, 145, 156.   27. *Ibid.*, p. 138.

28. *Ibid.*, pp. 66, 108. I suspect I have concocted the phrase *chiao-kan-chih chi* out of T'ang's almost identical *chiao-kan* and *kan-t'ung-chih-chi* but still believe T'ang himself uses it. *Chiao-kan* was a Neo-Confucian term: Chu Hsi, for instance, referred to "the interchange of empathies" between yin and yang. See Ch'ien Mu, *Chu-tzu hsin-hsüeh-an* (A New Scholarly Record on Chu Hsi; 5 vols.; Taipei: *San-min shu-tien*, 1971), 1:270. Hereafter referred to as "Ch'ien Mu." See Wei-ming Tu's excellent review article dealing with this book, "Reconstituting the Confucian Tradition," *Journal of Asian Studies*, 33, no. 3 (May 1974).

29. Arthur O. Lovejoy, *The Great Chain of Being* (New York: Harper Torchbooks, 1960), pp. 10–14.

30. T'ang, p. 137.   31. *Ibid.*, p. 108, p. 153.

32. *Ibid.*, pp. 95, 153, 102, 332–33, 158. Strictly speaking, a good number of these characteristics I ascribe to *chiao-kan-chih chi* are explicitly ascribed by T'ang to the processes of the "mind." My way of putting it, which is entirely justified in terms of T'ang's view of the relation between mind and experience, as the reader will see, is more convenient relative to the structure of my exposition. T'ang's exegesis is based, in the best style of a truly empirical phenomenology brilliantly alluding to traditional Chinese concepts, on the observation of given aspects of experience which anyone can observe for himself, whatever may be the problems of interpretation. This can be realized only if we leave the path of synopsis to quote T'ang directly. Let us look at a part of his discussion which deals largely with what I have called the second and third steps of his exegesis. His discussion is aimed at distinguishing between the quality of unreflective immediacy found in each moment of living experience (our first step) and the static, conceptual world of intellectually apprehended universals, to which the mind somehow relates these living moments (our second step). His thrust throughout is that the moment of experience itself, best summed up as *chiao-kan-chih chi*, inherently combines both these dimensions, so that conceptual universals are not something in the mind which the mind then brings to experience. Experience itself, with its given meshing of subjective mind and outer appearances, is what both dimensions, immediacy and conceptual universals, simultaneously inhere in. But for the sake of facilitating our understanding, T'ang looks at the

matter in terms of characteristics of the mind, and he thus cites three characteristics of the mind which, he holds, traditional Chinese philosophers have always focused on: *chih* (the capacity to know), which refers here purely to the mind's cognitive grasp of static concepts distinct from the immediate flow of experience; *hsü-ling ming-chüeh* (intelligent awareness in its pure, naturally given form, empty of any consciously specific concepts or sensations), the existence of which is demonstrated by the implicit consideration that there must be some aspect of the mind open to new impressions, some "empty" space, so to speak, into which new impressions can enter; and *shen* (the spiritual impulse), which refers to the capacity of the mind not only passively to open itself to new experience but actively to "extend" itself into the unreflective immediacy of the present and the future, that is, to act (in my account of T'ang's exegesis, the idea of *shen* is implicit in that of *chiao-kan-chih-chi*). (On *shen*, see chapter 3, section d.) At the same time, whatever are the various dimension of each moment of experience, T'ang, in a way reminiscent simultaneously of Kant and Wang Yang-ming, infers that these dimensions constitute the objective cosmos itself. Here is some of his discussion:

Thus all the knowledge in one's memory is no more than a storing of the past. When one makes judgements in meeting an experience in the present, then on the one hand one depends on reviving this memorial knowledge of the past which has coagulated in the mind, and on the other hand one depends on directly receiving that which appears in the immediate present. These two processes are fused to bring into being a judgement on the present turn of things, to determine one's attitude toward the present turn of things. This is what is called the mind's *shen* (spiritual impulse). The "Great Commentary" of the *Classic of Changes* says: "The spiritual impulse is for apprehending that which is about to be; the capacity to know is for storing memories of the past." This storing of memories is done by preserving in obscured form within the mind that which the mind received in a vivid form, it is the yin aspect of the mind. The capacity of the spiritual impulse to apprehend that which is about to be stems from the mind's extending itself to that which appears in the immediate present while in the same act reviving that which it received in the past, causing that which has been preserved as obscure to become vivid again. This is the mind's yang aspect. It is in terms of this yang aspect, whereby the mind extends to that which appears in the immediate present, that the mind becomes part of the world it encounters. Yet what appears in the immediate present, [interwoven as it is with] this very process of the mind's extending and moving, also at the same time is that which the mind receives and so can enter the yin aspect of the mind, forming memorial knowledge . . . . what is referred to in Western psychology as paying attention to, anticipating, or responding in a judgmental way to the ever-new flow of sense impressions, or as the activity of the will and the imagination, all this in the terminology of Chinese psychology falls under the idea of the mind's *shen* (spiritual impulse). . . . The capacity to know concerns what has already been realized. the spiritual impulse concerns what is about to be. In all cases, that which has been realized is always in the process of being fused with that which is about to be. Were there not that which is about to be, all would enter the dark and the cosmos would be no more. That the cosmos endures hangs entirely on the fact that what is about to be is able forever to transcend the limits of that which has already been realized. . . . Therefore the spiritual impulse which grasps that which is about to be sets the direction for the process of knowing, and the latter, in terms of which memories of the past are stored, cannot control the direction of the spiritual impulse. (Tang, pp. 100–102)

One cannot help but mischievously wonder how T'ang would react to the impertinent suggestion that in the Confucian balance between *chih* and *shen*, *shen* failed to exert enough "control," being almost overpowered by *chih*, a situation summed up by the idea of *shu erh pu-tso* (to transmit truths rather than create something new).

33. T'ang, p. 66.   34. *Ibid.*, pp. 101, 108.   35. *Ibid.*, p. 332.

36. *Ibid.*, p. 333. In his *Chih-te chih-chüeh yü Chung-kuo che-hsüeh* (The Intuition of Noumenal Reality and Chinese Philosophy; Taipei: *T'ai-wan shang-wu yin-shu-kuan*, 1970), Mou Tsung-san makes the same argument in a more rigorous way. Mou points out that the "intuition of noumenal reality," which Kant denied was possible, is precisely that *te-hsing-chih chih* (knowledge of one's ultimate moral nature) which Neo-Confucians have emphasized since Chang Tsai. If Kant is right, says Mou, "all of Chinese philosophy is impossible" (*ibid.*, intro., p. 2). Having described the Neo-Confucian concept of this noumenal reality as a boundless oneness of all things somehow known through one's moral awareness (*ibid.*, pp. 184–88), Mou asks how we can know that this concept has an objectively real referent and is not just a subjective idea (*ibid.*, p. 190). In his answer, I believe, he fails to weigh all the possibilities in a sufficiently critical way. Let us agree with Mou that the concept of this boundless oneness can be more generally formulated as that in our moral experience which gives us the feeling that we are acting in accord with a universal moral imperative. Kant also referred to this aspect of experience, calling it "free will," and Mou equates Kant's "free will" with the "original mind" of Confucians (*ibid.*, p. 190). Whether or not Mou's equation does justice to the different cultural nuances involved, we do seem to experience this dimension of universality when we have a moral experience, such as the "feeling of unease" caused by the suffering of someone else (*ibid.*, p. 193). Mou then goes on to argue that when Kant held that this dimension could not be known as a noumenon or "thing-in-itself," he overlooked its concreteness: "Since [free will] appears in our concrete experience as a form of conscious activity, why can't it reflect on itself and become self-aware, that is, why can't it, on the basis of its inherent awareness, reflect on itself, directly intuit its own nature as a purely intelligible entity [not a sense impression], and cause itself to appear exactly as it inherently is? The basis for the possibility of the intuition of noumenal reality lies in this 'living awareness'" (*ibid.*, p. 194). (I have had to translate this passage just a bit freely in order to make its meaning plain in English.) Mou, in other words, argues that this felt dimension of universality is totally knowable in its essence since it is an inner part of the morally active mind, not an outer phenomenon. His argument, therefore, depends on the epistemological "transparency" of this dimension of universality, i.e. its actually being in its essence what it appears to be.

The problem appears to be as follows. We know there are moral experiences, e.g. "a sense of unease" caused by the suffering of someone else. Moreover, as Mou notes, we seem necessarily to "speak" of these experiences by referring to this dimension of universality, mentioning, say, "God," "natural law," the "original mind," or "the ultimate nature of benevolence" (*ibid.*, p. 193). Moreover, as an integral part of this experience, this verbal reference denotes something felt in us. But what is this something? If it is epistemologically transparent, as Mou holds, then it could be the kind of universally present cosmic force which people have so often tried to describe in words. On the other hand, it could be just a psychic process which involves a sensation of epistemological transparency, and which is experienced as inherently possessing unique and universal value—a "pathos," to use Lovejoy's term. Certainly we cannot be rigidly opposed to all reductionism in the interpretation of human experience, and things are not always what they seem to be. Whether based on a pathos or on a noumenal reality, this dimension of universality, I feel, is equally "high" and noble, a sufficient basis for a life full of "value." Kant has been accused of cosmic impiety, and Mou's insistence on involving the whole cosmos in my moral sentiments strikes me as similarly gratuitous. If man is really *wan-wu-chih ling* (the spiritual being among the ten thousand things), why can't he be responsible for his own moral sentiments? Mou's sense of dependence on the cosmos, like T'ang's, reflects, I would suggest, the influence of the ethos of interdependence (see chapter 5). In more specifically philosophical terms, Mou's concept of moral consciousness as a universal noumenal reality can be seen as an attempt to defend the basic Neo-Confucian idea of *hsü-ling ming-chüeh* (intelligent awareness in its pure, naturally given, cosmically indivisible form, empty of any consciously specific sensations or concepts) against Kantian objections (on this Neo-Confucian concept, see chapter 3, section d). The latter concept, however, connotes the crucial idea of *ching* (state of rest), while Mou, like T'ang, describes a consciousness which is primordially active (see chapter 3, section k).

37. T'ang, p. 156.   38. *Ibid.*, pp. 93–94.   39. *Ibid.*, p. 148.

40. *Ibid.*, p. 168.   41. *Ibid.*, pp. 119–20.

42. *Ibid.*, pp. 139–40, 157. In holding that a person can find in himself a primordially given feeling which can and should serve as the basis of his moral life, T'ang takes a position similar to that of Western psychologists who optimistically emphasize that some of the constitutionally most basic "needs" of human beings are for empathetic interaction with others. For instance, Carl Rogers, in a section with the Mencian title "Basic Trustworthiness of Human Nature," holds that ". . . the basic nature of the human being, when functioning freely, is constructive and trustworthy . . . . one of his own deepest needs is for affiliation and communication with others . . . . his need to be liked by others and his tendency to give affection will be as strong as his impulses to strike out or to seize for himself." However, the specific content of these ultimately basic, morally positive feelings is not the same for Rogers and T'ang. Where Rogers sees a "need to be liked by others," T'ang sees a sense of gratitude, a sense of obligation owed to someone or something, a sense that life is not a right but a gift putting one eternally in debt. This divergence of viewpoints as to the most basic content of empathetic feeling suggests that such a feeling is bound to be culturally peculiar rather than cosmically universal. T'ang's position, however, in both this book and his later *Che-hsüeh kai-lun*, is that the Chinese syndrome of cultural and environmental conditioning tended more than the Western to stimulate a sense for the universally real and true (*shih-tsai-kan*). For T'ang, if the constitutionally most basic need of a particular person is a "need to be liked by others," that person's grasp of his own reality has already been damaged and blocked by a mistaken tendency to cling statically to self-centered impulses (*chih-cho*) (see footnote 17 above). By comparing T'ang's views to those of Rogers, we can see how two different philosophic and cultural traditions have led to two specifically different concepts of mental health. See Carl R. Rogers, *On Becoming a Person* (Boston: Houghton Mifflin Company, 1961), p. 194.

43. T'ang, p. 109. In their *Chung-yung* form (chapter 25), *ch'eng-chi* and *ch'eng-wu* appear in different sentences as distinct concepts, but making a single phrase out of them was common. See e.g. Jung Chao-tsu, *Ming-tai ssu-hsiang-shih* (A History of Thought in the Ming Dynasty; Taipei: *T'ai-wan k'ai-ming shu-tien*, 1969), p. 27.

44. *Ibid.*, pp. 153–54.   45. *Ibid.*, pp. 30, 140, 157.

46. T'ang's point about the presence of the supreme ultimate in the existence of each thing is taken from Neo-Confucianism, presumably from Chu Hsi's writings. Chu Hsi's view, in turn, reflects the influence of Hua-yen and T'ien-t'ai Buddhism. For Chu Hsi's view, see Ch'ien Mu, 1:275.

47. T'ang, pp. 22–23, 26–27, 38.

48. *Ibid.*, p. 159. On Weber's thesis, see Introduction, note 4. These points are developed further in the following chapters.

49. *Ibid.*, pp. 203, 189, 49, 322.

50. *Ibid.*, p. 307. The common translation of *hsiang-yüan* as "goody-goody" does not do justice to its connotation of evil. A goody-goody is an affected person who refuses to commit minor sins, like drinking. A *hsiang-yüan* is a hypocrite who refuses to carry out moral acts that require one courageously to resist currently powerful, immoral trends. Thus Confucius and Mencius called him "the enemy of virtue." A goody-goody is often really virtuous.

51. *Ibid.*, pp. 295–99.   52. *Ibid.*, p. 298. Ch'ien Mu, 2:28.

53. T'ang, p. 299. *Hao-chieh* was used informally by Ch'ing officials to denote an outstanding official. Thus it did not just refer to heroic rebels.

54. On this *li* as a major bureaucratic virtue, see Thomas A. Metzger, *The Internal Organization of Ch'ing Bureaucracy* (Cambridge, Mass.: Harvard University Press, 1973), p. 48.

55. On "fears and anxieties," see chapter 3, section e. For Lu Chiu-yüan's statement, see Fung Yu-lan, *Hsin yüan-tao*, p. 180.

56. T'ang, p. 322.   57. Lovejoy, *Great Chain*, pp. 288–314.

58. T'ang, pp. 283, 43, 305.   59. Li I-yüan and Yang Kuo-shu, p. 206.

60. T'ang, pp. 283–84.

61. *Ibid.*, p. 288. On creativity, see chapter 3, section o.

62. Philippa Foot, "Sincerely Yours," *The New York Review of Books*, March 8, 1973, pp. 23–24.

63. Weber, *The Religion of China*, p. 235. See note 42 above for the difference between the Confucian view of mental health and some American views.

64. T'ang, pp. 283, 286.   65. Li I-yüan and Yang Kuo-shu, pp. 190–91.

66. Solomon, pp. 70–71. T'ang, pp. 306–307. *K'uang* and *chüan* also had the pejorative meaning of failing to hit the golden mean by being too impetuous or too cautious. For a deeper discussion of *k'uang*, see Julia Ching's book on Wang Yang-ming, *To Acquire Wisdom* (New York: Columbia University Press, 1976), pp. 25–27.

67. A number of valuable articles dealing with the concept of the individual in Chinese thought can be found in Charles A. Moore, ed., *The Chinese Mind* (Honolulu: East-West Center Press, University of Hawaii Press, 1967).

CHAPTER THREE — THE NEO-CONFUCIAN SENSE

OF PREDICAMENT

1. This sense of predicament, however, has some connection to that *yu-huan i-shih* (sense of anxious concern over the troubles of the world) which Hsü Fu-kuan and others have viewed as a basic aspect of Chinese thought emerging at the beginning of the Chou period. I am much indebted to Professor Hao Chang for pointing this out. See Hsü Fu-kuan, *Chung-kuo jen-hsing-lun shih—hsien-Ch'in-p'ien* (A History of Chinese Views of Human Nature—Section on the Pre-Ch'in Period;

3. Sense of Predicament

Taipei: The Commercial Press of Taiwan, 1969), pp. 20–21. My discussion differs from Hsü's in dealing specifically with the Neo-Confucian *Problematik* and in the view of anxiety it takes. While this early Chou sense of concern involved both worry caused by suffering in the world and, at least implicitly, anxiety caused by the possibility that one may fail to realize one's goal, the latter kind of anxiety is central to my discussion.

    2. Mou, *Chih-te chih-chüeh yü Chung-kuo che-hsüeh*, p. 188. For "definition of the situation," an elegant formulation on which I greatly rely in this study, believing that it directs our attention to culture as shaping the perceived setting of our experience, not only our ideals, see William I. Thomas, "The Four Wishes and the Definition of the Situation," in Parsons *et al.*, eds., *Theories of Society*, 2 vols., (New York: Free Press, 1961), 2:741–44. Kenneth Burke's profound concept of a "grammar of motives" has been borrowed to form the term "grammar of action" and other such terms found in my discussion. See Kenneth Burke, *A Grammar of Motives and A Rhetoric of Motives* (Cleveland: The World Publishing Company, Meridian Books, 1962). I suppose that my methodology in this chapter reflects a spreading tendency among intellectual historians to emphasize shared patterns of discourse and rhetoric and "conceptual vocabularies" rather than intellectual biography. This tendency can be seen in the recent work of scholars like Michel Foucault, H.D. Harootunian, and Tetsuo Najita. An outstanding example of this trend is J. G. A. Pocock's *The Machiavellian Moment* (Princeton: Princeton University Press, 1975), which shuns intellectual biography in order to elucidate "sub-philosophical" "ideas and conceptual vocabularies" and so "reconstruct a scheme of ideas within which the sixteenth-century mind sought to articulate the equivalence of a philosophy of history" (pp. 3–4). Apparently Pocock's search for underlying "paradigms" of political action constituting patterns of "political culture" shared by different thinkers reflects his extensive backround in political science (pp. 506, 523). The approving account of his methodology in Felix Gilbert's review (*The Times Literary Supplement*, March 19, 1976) confirms my impression that peasants are not the only people whose shared cultural orientations should be studied, and that the shared orientations of intellectuals cannot be understood without word-for-word analysis of their habitual utterances. This point applies with particular force to non-Western cultures the ordinary values of which are most difficult for outsiders to grasp. (I am most grateful to Ramon H. Myers for bringing to my attention these writings by Pocock and Gilbert.) While a variety of intellectual historians are thus almost inevitably coming to apply the anthropological concept of culture to the study of historical ways of thought, my own perspective goes back to the training I received from Robert N. Bellah while a graduate student at Harvard. His profound sociological approach to the problems of East Asian civilization has basically influenced all my work as a historian. What might then be called the cultural approach to intellectual history represents a sixth way of studying shared cultural orientations. For the other five, see pp. 11–14 above.

    3. Cited by David S. Luft in his Ph.D. dissertation, "Robert Musil: An Intellectual Biography, 1880–1924" (Harvard University, Department of History, 1972), p. 262.

    4. *Unfolding*, p. 12. Huang Tsung-hsi, *Ming-ju hsüeh-an* (Notes on the Confucian Scholars of the Ming Dynasty; Taipei: *Shih-chieh shu-chü*, 1961), p. 1 of "Principles of Compilation."

    5. Chu Ch'ien-chih, *Li Chih—shih-liu shih-chi Chung-kuo fan feng-chien ssu-hsiang-te hsien-ch'ü-che* (Li Chih—A Forerunner in Sixteenth-Century China of the Movement Against Feudal Thought; Wuhan: *Hu-pei jen-min ch'u-pan-she*, 1957), p. 68.

3. Sense of Predicament

6. Mou Tsung-san, *Hsin-t'i yü hsing-t'i* (The Moral Consciousness and Moral Nature of Man; 2 vols; Taipei: *Cheng-chung shu-chü*, 1970), p. 49. An invaluable aid for the study of Neo-Confucianism is Wing-tsit Chan, *A Source Book in Chinese Philosophy*. Also basic is the same scholar's *An Outline and an Annotated Bibliography of Chinese Philosophy* (Yale University, New Haven, Connecticut: Far Eastern Publications, Sinological Series No. 4, 1969). A handy introduction to Neo-Confucianism is in Yu-lan Fung, *A Short History of Chinese Philosophy* (New York: The Macmillan Company, 1960). For a deeper understanding of Neo-Confucianism, I recommend especially T'ang Chün-i's *Chung-kuo che-hsüeh yüan-lun*, an authoritative work of scholarship illuminating the historical development and meaning of Confucian ideas, as well as the two volumes edited by de Bary, *Unfolding* and *Self and Society in Ming Thought*.

7. See James T. C. Liu, *Ou-yang Hsiu—An Eleventh-Century Neo-Confucianist* (Stanford: Stanford University Press, 1967), and, on Ssu-ma Kuang's thought, Hou Wai-lu *et al.*, *Chung-kuo ssu-hsiang t'ung-shih* (A Comprehensive History of Chinese Thought; 5 vols.; Peking: *Jen-min ch'u-pan-she*, 1957–1960), 4a:511–21.

8. See Hsiao Kung-ch'üan, *Chung-kuo cheng-chih ssu-hsiang-shih* (A History of Chinese Political Thought; 6 vols.; Taipei: *Chung-hua ta-tien pien-yin-hui*, 1966), 4:449–81; T'ao Hsi-sheng, *Chung-kuo cheng-chih ssu-hsiang shih* (A History of Chinese Political Thought; 4 vols.; Taipei: *T'ai-wan lien-ho shu-chü*, 1964), 4:138–55; and Hao Chang, "On the *Ching-shih* Ideal in Neo-Confucianism," *Ch'ing-shih wen-t'i*, vol. 3, no. 1 (November 1974).

9. On Li Chih (Li Cho-wu), see Chu Ch'ien-chih and de Bary's excellent article in *Self and Society in Ming Thought*.

10. For Buddhism, see Kenneth K. S. Ch'en, *Buddhism in China* (Princeton: Princeton University Press, 1964), pp. 389–470, and *Unfolding*, pp. 39–140. For Taoism, see *Self and Society in Ming Thought*, pp. 291–330.

11. On Fang I-chih, see Willard J. Peterson's article in *Unfolding*; on P'u Sung-ling, see Chun-shu Chang and Hsüeh-lun Chang, "The World of P'u Sung-ling's *Liao-chai chih-i*: Literature and the Intelligentsia during the Ming-Ch'ing Dynastic Transition," in *The Journal of the Institute of Chinese Studies of The Chinese University of Hong Kong*, vol. 6, no. 2 (December 1973):401–23.

12. Wang Yang-ming, *Wang Wen-ch'eng kung ch'üan-shu* (Complete Works of Wang Yang-ming, *Ssu-pu ts'ung-k'an* edition), p. 101, translated in Wing-tsit Chan, comp., *Instructions for Practical Living and Other Neo-Confucian Writings by Wang Yang-ming* (New York: Columbia University Press, 1963), p. 122. Hereafter Wang and Chan. I have, naturally, greatly relied on Professor Chan's masterful translation, sometimes just copying it. However in many of the translations below I have inserted my own wording.

13. Li I-yüan and Yang Kuo-shu, pp. 137, 158.

14. *Ibid.*, pp. 342–43, 361.

15. For instance, while moral effort for the masses meant mainly practicing "industriousness and frugality" in order to achieve "wealth" and "status," the goal of Confucian "self-cultivation" was a transvaluation of these material goals demanding that the self focus directly on purely spiritual values. The scope of these goals was different too. The Neo-Confucian consciously aimed for that immense spiritual leverage needed to transform the total society, eliminating all misery and moral failure everywhere, while ordinary persons normally pursued benefits limited just to their own families and accepted the continuation of moral failure and economic misery in their social environment. Thus the Neo-Confucian often perceived his

world as totally malleable, while the masses perceived the problems of their world as largely intractable, at least relative to their own efforts. But this also meant that the Neo-Confucian goal was really unattainable, while ordinary persons could often fulfill their main obligations by getting married, having children, and carrying out tasks well within their practical powers. In this light, therefore, there was no ultimate, existentially inescapable predicament for the masses, only predicaments arising out of circumstances which could often be avoided.

The arenas of Neo-Confucian and popular moral action differed not only in terms of malleability. The morality of the common people was realized basically in terms of a territorially small micro-arena made up mainly of relatives, neighbors, and local supernatural beings. It was also an arena experienced largely in a sensory rather than an abstract way. On the other hand, the macro-arena of the elite was territorially large, was visualized in a more abstract way, and tended to center on *wu-hsin* (the mind of the self), the people, heaven and earth, and those *chih-tu* (governmental institutions) which comprised a unique cockpit of power in terms of which all could be controlled. It was the very physical vastness and abstractness of this macro-arena which necessitated an emphasis on extremely generalized, universalistic moral norms, especially *ching, jen*, and *ch'eng*, under which Neo-Confucianism subsumed the other virtues. Certainly a more particularistic mix of norms dominated the micro-arena.

16. *Ibid.*, p. 49.   17. *Unfolding*, p. 24. See *ibid.*, p. 156 for the same point.

18. *Ibid.*, p. 161.

19. *Ibid.*, p. 24. Wei-ming Tu similarly emphasizes that in Neo-Confucianism, "experiential knowledge was always considered superior to speculative theory." See *ibid.*, p. 523.

20. T'ang, *Che-hsüeh kai-lun*, 1:7–12, 1:40–45.

21. Ch'ien Mu, 2:131. All references to "Ch'ien Mu" are to *Chu-tzu hsin-hsüeh-an*.

22. Ch'ien Mu, *Chung-kuo chin-san-pai-nien-te hsüeh-shu-shih* (A History of Chinese Thought During the Last Three Centuries; 2 vols.; Taipei: *T'ai-wan shang-wu yin-shu-kuan*, 1966), 1:77.

23. Wang, p. 74, Chan, p. 52.   24. Wang, p. 67, Chan, p. 33.

25. Wang, p. 75, Chan, p. 53. For Wang's reliance on cognitive propositions, see section u below. For a sensitive summary of the Neo-Confucian attitude toward the importance of verbalization as well as the indispensable role of non-verbalized understanding, see T'ang, *Chung-kuo che-hsüeh yüan-lun*, 1:219–22.

26. T'ang, *Che-hsüeh kai-lun*, pp. 128–31, 136–37. Mou Tsung-san has the same view. See Mou, *Chih-te chih-chüeh yü Chung-kuo che-hsüeh*, p. 346. On Mou's philosophic position, see chapter 2, note 36.

27. *Unfolding*, pp. 157–58. On Mou Tsung-san's thought, see chapter 2, note 36.

28. Ch'ien Mu, 2:198, 2:374, 2:383, 2:365, 1:126.

29. T'ang, *yüan-hsing-p'ien*, p. 609.

30. *Self and Society in Ming Thought*, p. 155.   31. Ch'ien Mu, 1:185, 1:142.

32. T'ang, *yüan-hsing-p'ien*, p. 545.   33. Ch'ien Mu, 1:124.

34. *Ibid.*, 2:4. See Hu Shih's excellent discussion of Chu Hsi's emphasis on the need to "doubt" in *The Chinese Mind*, pp. 115–19.

35. Jung Chao-tsu, *Ming-tai ssu-hsiang-shih* (A History of Thought in the Ming Dynasty; Taipei: *T'ai-wan k'ai-ming shu-tien*, 1969), p. 101.

36. Wang, p. 66, Chan, p. 29.   37. Wang, p. 57, Chan, p. 9.

38. Ch'ien Mu, 2:248.   39. *Ibid.*, 1:362.   40. *Ibid.*, 2:440.

3. Sense of Predicament

41. *Ibid.*, 2:188. For an explanation of this process, see section o.
42. T'ang, *yüan-hsing-p'ien*, p. 611.   43. Wang, p. 57, Chan, p. 8.
44. *Unfolding*, p. 518. Chu Hsi might have regarded such ritualism as a "dead method."
45. T'ang, *yüan-hsing-p'ien*, p. 611.
46. Ch'ien Mu, 2:428.   47. T'ang, *yüan-lun*, 1:5–26.
48. For a typical example containing many of these clichés, see the passages from Chan Jo-shui's (1466–1560) writings cited in Jung Chao-tsu, p. 62.

The reader is referred to David S. Nivison's article on the assumptions about knowing, believing, being, and acting which underlay the traditional discussion of the relation between cognitive clarity and morality. This issue illustrates the importance of probing beyond philosophical propositions into the widely shared assumptions in terms of which such propositions were addressed to meaningful problems. For many Chinese, that cognitive grasp of the ultimate order of things needed to be moral included an understanding of the relation of understanding itself to the state of moral action. Because it was widely assumed that the grasp of this relation simultaneously was needed as a moral guideline, inherently brought about right action, and yet paradoxically was accessible only to one who already had the moral purity to see things in the right light, the question of this relation remained central and elusive. That is, given this assumption, it was clear that a right understanding of this relation would transform one's moral existence, that the unsatisfactory condition of one's life demonstrated one's lack of this understanding, and that one had to try to fathom the nature of this relation. Only by taking this persisting cultural attitude into account can one understand why Sun Yat-sen's famous formula "knowledge is difficult, action is easy," which Westerners have generally regarded as a pathetically simpleminded attempt to philosophize, was looked on as a tremendous intellectual breakthrough by even an acute student of modern philosophy like Ho Lin. See Ho Lin, pp. 84–86. For Nivison's article, see Arthur F. Wright, ed., *Studies in Chinese Thought* (The American Anthropological Association, vol. 55, no. 5, part 2, memoir no. 75, December 1953), pp. 112–45.

49. Wang, p. 92, Chan, p. 100. Yü Ying-shih, *"Ts'ung Sung Ming ju-hsüeh-te fa-chan lun Ch'ing-tai ssu-hsiang-shih—shang-p'ien—Sung Ming ju-hsüeh-chung chih-shih-chu-i-te ch'uan-t'ung* (A Discussion of Ch'ing Intellectual History from the Standpoint of the Development of Sung-Ming Neo-Confucianism—Part One— The Tradition of Intellectualism in Sung-Ming Neo-Confucianism," *Chung-kuo hsüeh-jen*, 2 (September 1970), pp. 23–25. One can argue that Lu Chiu-yüan also wanted cognitive clarity. He emphasized realization of the mind as "principle," referred to what the sages had "said" to "make principles clear," and held that "One should make efforts to know about human nature, tendencies in human affairs, and the principles of things." See T'ang, *yüan-hsing-p'ien*, p. 413. Most important, like nearly all Confucians, he attributed the rise of immorality to both selfish desires and false "ideas." See *ibid.*, p. 419.

50. Ch'ien Mu, 1:142.   51. *Ibid.*, 1:135, 1:399.
52. *Ibid.*, 1:382, 2:412.   53. *Ibid.*, 2:52, 2:54.   54. *Ibid.*, 2:42.
55. *Ibid.*, 2:39, 2:61.   56. *Ibid.*, 1:122, 2:46.
57. I do not recall Chu Hsi's using *ching-chieh*, but he could have. See *ibid.*, 2:28 for his use of the similar *shih-chien*, and *ibid.*, 1:42 for *shih-chieh*. *Shih-chieh*, like *ching-chieh*, did not necessarily refer to the "realm" of experienced events; it could also, as in the latter example, refer to the "realm" of abstract *li* (principles).

For Ming examples, see Jung Chao-tsu, pp. 117, 121. This significant tendency mentally to encapsulate the world of experience within a "realm" distinct from one's inner spiritual space seems to have been borrowed from Buddhism. See Chi-tsang's (549–623) reference to the "*ching* (realm) of the ten thousand things" in Fung Yu-lan, *Chung-kuo ssu-hsiang-shih*, 2:672. This is translated in Fung Yu-lan, *A History of Chinese Philosophy*, 2:252. Possibly conceptualization of a "realm" was associated with the idea of that to which one wrongfully "clings." See chapter 2, note 17.

58. Ch'ien Mu, 2:207–8.

59. *Ibid.*, 2:149. Wang, p. 87, Chan, p. 86. For a Han example, see Fung, *ssu-hsiang-shih*, 2:547, translated in Bodde, 2:90.

60. Ch'ien Mu, 2:412.

61. Wang Hsien-ch'ien, ed., *Hsün-tzu chi-chieh* (Hsün-tzu with Collected Commentaries; Taipei: *I-wen yin-shu-kuan*, 1967), p. 556. Translated in Burton Watson, *Hsün-tzu—Basic Writings* (New York: Columbia University Press, 1969), p. 129.

62. Ch'ien Mu, 1:131.   63. *Ibid.*, 1:134.

64. For T'ang Chün-i's valuable explanation of *hsü*, *ming*, *ling*, and *shen*, see Moore, *The Chinese Mind*, pp. 271–73. The terms *hsü-ling*, *hsü-ling ming-chüeh*, *chih-chüeh*, *hsü-ling chih-chüeh* all interchangeably meant "intelligent awareness in its pure, naturally given, cosmically indivisible form, empty of any consciously specific concepts or sensations."

65. Hou Wai-lu, 4b:625.   66. *Ibid.*, 4b:626–27, 637. Ch'ien Mu, 2:99.

67. Ch'ien Mu, 1:97.   68. *Ibid.*, 1:94, 2:201.

69. Jung Chao-tsu, p. 25.   70. *Ibid.*, pp. 21–22.

71. On Chu Hsi's and Wang Yang-ming's use of the idea of *chu-tsai*, see below in this section and Ch'ien Mu, 1:369–70. On the idea of an "internal ruler" in Chou thought, see Donald J. Munro, *The Concept of Man in Early China* (Stanford: Stanford University Press, 1969), pp. 59–64, 89. On the Neo-Taoist idea of "overcoming things," see Fung, *ssu-hsiang-shih*, 2:607, translated in Bodde, 2:189. The reference in *Chuang-tzu* is in *Chu-tzu chi-ch'eng* (A Complete Collection of the Works of the Ancient Scholars; 8 vols.; Peking: *Chung-hua shu-chü*, 1959), 3:51.

72. Ch'ien Mu, 2:13, 1:70. The idea of "encompassing" heaven and earth comes from the *Classic of Changes*. See *Shih-san-ching chu-shu* (The Thirteen Classics with Commentaries and Subcommentaries; 8 vols.; Taipei: *I-wen yin-shu-kuan*, 1965), 1:147.

73. Jung Chao-tsu, p. 38.   74. *Hsün-tzu*, p. 33, Watson, p. 23.

75. Ch'ien Mu, 2:246.   76. *Ibid.*, 1:97, 1:136.

77. Wang, p. 65, Chan, p. 27.   78. Wang, p. 80, Chan, pp. 66–67.

79. T'ang, *yüan-hsing-p'ien*, pp. 532–33.   80. Ch'ien Mu, 2:25.

81. *Ibid.*, 2:82, 2:47.   82. *Ibid.*, 1:159.   83. *Ibid.*, 2:16, 2:201.

84. *Ibid.*, 1:136.   85. *Ibid.*, 1:88.   86. *Ibid.*, 1:238.

87. *Ibid.*, 2:53, 1:103, 1:126, 1:39.   88. *Ibid.*, 1:143, 1:260.

89. *Ibid.*, 1:88.   90. *Ibid.*, 2:99.

91. For the key passages in *Mencius*, *Lun-yü*, *Chuang-tzu*, and *Lao-tzu*, see T'ang, *Che-hsüeh kai-lun*, 1:21–22. See also *Hsün-tzu*, pp. 31–32, Watson, p. 22.

92. De Bary makes a similar point. See *Unfolding*, p. 163.

93. Ch'ien Mu, 2:47, 1:293.

94. Mou Tsung-san, *Hsin-t'i yü hsing-t'i*, 1:17–18. Mou suggests here that Sung Neo-Confucians differed from the great Chou Confucians in making explicit the oneness of key ethical and metaphysical elements, such as *jen* and heaven, where

the Chou thinkers had merely spoken of a close connection. My point about the distinctiveness of the Neo-Confucian concern with linkage accords with this formulation by a great authority, but I differ from him in arguing that making this question of linkage explicit marked a major divergence from Chou thought, an awareness that the wholeness of existence taken for granted by Chou Confucians was in fact problematic, something that could be lost if not thought through and demonstrated.

95. Ch'ien Mu, 1:38.   96. T'ang, *che-hsüeh yüan-lun*, 1:1–26.

97. Ch'en, *Buddhism in China*, p. 66.

98. Ch'ien Mu, 2:44, 1:112.   99. *Unfolding*, p. 161.

100. Fung, *ssu-hsiang-shih*, 2:809, trans. in Bodde, 2:419.

101. See note 57 above. On subsumption, see section d.

102. Ch'en, *Buddhism in China*, pp. 70–71, 6, and Chan, *A Source Book in Chinese Philosophy*, pp. 370–74. See note 222 below.

103. Ch'ien Mu, *Chung-kuo chin-san-pai-nien-te hsüeh-shu-shih*, 1:1–5. Whether Wang An-shih actually failed or was only perceived as a failure by most Neo-Confucians is an important question. Recent work suggests that the Sung bureaucracy was unusually efficient in the control it could exert on village affairs and commerce, that Wang's reforms were to a significant extent part of a broad and continuous pattern of reform, that Wang was admirably cautious and practical in implementing his reforms, and that the latter were strikingly successful, especially in solving the state's financial crisis, reducing some of the economic burdens carried by the lower classes, and improving the efficiency and strength of the military. Great light on the Sung bureaucracy has been shed by Peter J. Golas, "The Sung Financial Administration" (unpublished) and Brian E. McKnight, *Village and Bureaucracy in Southern Sung China* (Chicago: The University of Chicago Press, 1971). An illuminating discussion of Wang's reforms supporting the above points is in Ch'i Hsia, *Wang An-shih pien-fa* (The Reforms of Wang An-shih; Shanghai: *Shang-hai jen-min ch'u-pan-she*, 1959). Views current just some ten years ago to the effect that Wang's reforms "achieved no conspicuous successes" are therefore being abandoned in favor of a more complex and favorable evaluation, as can be seen from J. K. Fairbank, E. O. Reischauer, and A. M. Craig, *East Asia: Tradition and Transformation* (Boston: Houghton Mifflin, 1973), pp. 128–29. Historians used to ask "Why did Wang fail?" They are now asking "Did he fail?" James T. C. Liu's important study, *Reform in Sung China* (Cambridge, Mass.: Harvard University Press, 1959), does not deal with the question of the extent of Wang's success, following the traditional view that Wang's reforms basically failed, but it does on p. 10 indicate that much of the criticism directed at Wang has been less concerned with any failure of his reforms during Shen-tsung's reign than with the somewhat irrational charge that the notorious postreform, which occurred after Wang's death, was somehow his fault.

104. Ch'ien Mu, 1:377. *Hsün-tzu*, p. 228, Watson, p. 44.

105. Ch'ien Mu, 2:39, 1:99. Of course, the sages themselves had grasped the *ta-t'ou-nao-ch'u*, but it was not made clear in their "words." For this basic theme of a lapse in communication, see chapter 5, section e.

106. *Ibid.*, 1:75.   107. *Ibid.*, 1:70.   108. *Ibid.*, 1:54–55.

109. *Ibid.*, 1:481, 1:494.   110. *Ibid.*, 1:371.

111. *Ibid.*, 1:69. The phrase on "assisting" heaven and earth is from chapter 22 of the *Doctrine of the Mean*. See also section r below for Chu Hsi's striking statement on the concrete "efficacy" of the sage's power to rectify the whole world.

112. Wang, p. 77, Chan, p. 60. Wang, p. 80, Chan, p. 68.

113. Wang, p. 154, Chan, p. 249. Wang, p. 60, Chan, p. 14.

114. Wang, p. 77, Chan, p. 60.

115. Wang, p. 148, Chan, p. 234. See note 313, below.

116. *Unfolding*, p. 203.

117. Wang, p. 75, Chan, p. 56. For the eight steps, see Chan, *Source Book*, pp. 86–87. After working out this interpretation of Wang's tendency to turn sagehood into a matter of personal ethics and to play down the sage's power to transform the cosmos and the polity, I was pleased to realize that my point is probably sound but certainly unoriginal. It is similar to Fung Yu-lan's. See *Hsin yüan-tao*, pp. 202–4, Hughes trans., *The Spirit of Chinese Philosophy*, pp. 215–18. For Wang's passionate commitment to the goal of saving the whole world from material suffering, see especially Wang, p. 121, Chan, pp. 168–69.

118. Ch'eng Hao is cited in *Hsin-yüan-tao*, p. 167.

119. Wang, p. 99–100, Chan, pp. 119–21.

120. Although Chu Hsi said that "Heaven and earth belong to the realm of ordinarily experienced forms" (Ch'ien Mu, 1:244), heaven was certainly a metaphysical entity, and Chu Hsi spoke of the "mind" of "heaven and earth," which consisted of the effective intention to "bring things into being." See *ibid.*, 1:55. Thus "heaven and earth" somewhat transcended the experiential. Fung Yu-lan exaggerated a bit when he said that traditional Chinese philosophers "never looked at space and time as differentiated from things and affairs" (see *Hsin li-hsüeh*, p. 76). Obviously, *yü-chou* means "space and time," and Chu Hsi spoke of *tso-ch'u ku-chin t'ien-ti-chien wu-hsien shih lai* (bring about a limitless number of events in that realm of past and present, heaven and earth). See Ch'ien Mu, 1:286. Nevertheless, the idea of "heaven and earth" was far more basic than that of space and time. On *t'ien-ming*, see section p.

121. Wang, p. 106, Chan, p. 132. Another example of Wang's monism is in Wang, p. 129, Chan, p. 189. For the *I-ching*'s distinction, see *Shih-san-ching*, 1:158.

122. T'ang Chün-i has pointed out that Confucian thinkers never experienced doubt about "the objective reality of the natural world" (T'ang, pp. 136–37). Yet it is true that the general Neo-Confucian preoccupation with the transnatural power of the self was complemented by a feeling that the relationship between outer cosmos and inner consciousness was a mysterious one easily allowing for speculations going beyond common sense. This relationship was connected to the prevalent concept of an indivisible cosmic consciousness (see section d). Yet within this framework, there were different points of emphasis. With his view of man as "the filial son of heaven and earth," Chang Tsai pictured the cosmos as an entity largely outside the self, but Lu Chiu-yüan pictured an indivisible cosmic mind with his statement that "All that is in space and time is my mind, my mind is all that is in space and time." See T'ang, *Che-hsüeh kai-lun*, 1:113–14. Both Chu Hsi and Wang Yang-ming inclined toward the idea of the cosmos as a monad, that is, an indivisible whole found in each of its parts. Thus Chu Hsi said that "in the case of each thing, there is the supreme ultimate," a concept probably influenced by T'ien-t'ai and Hua-yen Buddhism. See Fung, *ssu-hsiang-shih*, 2:902–3, Bodde, 2:541, and Hou Wai-lu, 4b:601. Wang largely followed Lu's emphasis on the indivisible mind, which he also described as a set of things pervaded by a single ether of materialization. The passages in Wang, p. 143, Chan, pp. 221–22, are most useful to pinpoint the difference between Wang's position and subjective idealism. Wang suggested that something like a flower on a tree is "not external to your mind," but rather than viewing the flower

as a function of my private mind, he in effect held that my private mind and the flower were part of one indivisible substance, "a single ether of materialization." Since all things were part of this ether, they could "mutually pervade each other" (*hsiang-t'ung*). This idea of "mutually" reflects Wang's feeling that other things are as real as the private mind. His ontological starting point, as indicated in the above passages, was not my mind but the "one body" formed by "heaven, earth, the ten thousand things, and man." I believe Wang's tendency toward what we may term subjective idealism is best understood as stemming from his effort to solve the problem of linkage. He found himself unable to pursue his solution without claiming that outer "things" were no more than aspects of inner moral "intentions" (*i*). See sections r and u. More generally, his sort of idealism was only a short step away from the above assumptions about the existence of an indivisible cosmic consciousness (*hsü-ling ming-chüeh*) and the monad-like character of the cosmos.

123. Ch'ien Mu, 1:276.　　124. *Ibid.*, 1:270, 2:133, 1:424.

125. Wang, p. 72, Chan, p. 48.

126. T. A. Metzger, *The Internal Organization of Ch'ing Bureaucracy* (Cambridge, Mass.: Harvard University Press, 1973), p. 34.

127. Connected to the idea of the dyads was another ontological assumption, that of the single but mulifaceted entity. The image of a tree, with its roots, branches, and leaves, or of the human body with its various organs, was sometimes used to articulate this assumption. Wang's monism presupposed the idea that such an entity was possible. See e.g. Wang, p. 129, Chan, p. 189. As in this case, the word *ch'u* (point at which, qua) was often used to express the idea of one aspect among a number of aspects.

128. Hou Wai-lu, 4b:625.　　129. Ch'ien Mu, 2:1.

130. Wang Yang-ming tended to use "mind" and "ether of materialization" interchangeably. See note 122 above. While Huang Tsung-hsi said "Filling all of heaven and earth is only the heaven-conferred nature as an aspect of the ether of materialization and matter," he also said "All that fills heaven and earth is mind" (Ch'ien Mu, *san-pai-nien*, pp. 24, 27). Liu Tsung-chou's position was entirely similar (*ibid.*, 1:45). Wang Fu-chih (1619–1692), often called a "materialist," said: "There is no mind apart from things, there are no things apart from mind" (*ibid.*, 1:102). Neo-Confucians observed the differences between "mind" and "matter" and between the "inner" and the "outer," but they essentially relegated all these to the realm of the experiential and rather emphasized the distinction between the metaphysical and the experiential, trying to overcome the gap between these two. The difference between mind and matter was important to them only insofar as they had to consider the best way to conceptualize the experiential realm so as to facilitate its linkage with the metaphysical.

131. Fung, *ssu-hsiang-shih*, 2:828, 2:826; Bodde, 2:449, 2:446. *Shih-san-ching*, 1:154, 1:171.

132. Ch'ien Mu, 2:123.　　133. T'ang, *yüan-hsing-p'ien*, p. 558.

134. Ch'ien Mu, 2:82.　　135. *Ibid.*, 2:28.　　136. *Ibid.*, 2:133.

137. *Ibid.*, 1:45.　　138. *Ibid.*, 2:44.

139. T'ang, *yüan-hsing-p'ien*, pp. 474–75.　　140. Ch'ien Mu, 2:14.

141. T'ang, *yüan-hsing-p'ien*, p. 475. Another passage which is helpful for understanding what Neo-Confucians assumed about the nature of the mind is the following from Chu Hsi cited in Ch'ien Mu, 2:117. "The mind is consciousness as realized in the case of human beings. It is that which finds mastery through its inner equilibrium while responding to outer events." This formulation would perhaps

strike Wang Yang-ming as drawing the distinction between inner equilibrium and outer response in a heavy-handed way, but basically this was a totally unoriginal and uncontroversial way of pointing out that the mind was a phasic kind of thing which responded to outer stimuli; that it also had an inner state; and that the character of its responses depended on the quality of its inner state. It was this perception of the structure of the mind which made Neo-Confucians concerned above all with the perfection of this inner state as the way to perfect one's outer responses.

142. *Ibid.*, pp. 557–68. Ch'ien Mu, 2:123, 2:134.

143. Hou Wai-lu, 4b:625. For a brief critique of Fung's interpretation of Chu Hsi, see note 210 below.

144. T'ang, *yüan-hsing-p'ien*, pp. 558–59, 637. I have slightly reshuffled the sequence of these passages quoted from T'ang but without any alteration in meaning.

145. T'ang, introduction, p. 2.

146. One might argue that they are subsumed under what I have described as step three of T'ang's exegesis, that is, under the idea of the mind's spirit-like (*shen*) ability to "extend" itself into the world in an openly receptive way "empty" of the biases stemming from its memorial knowledge. T'ang's neglect of the phases in the context of his work as a philosopher is also evident in *Che-hsüeh kai-lun*, where they are barely mentioned. In *ibid.*, 1:140–44, he gives a sketch of Neo-Confucian thought about the cultivation of the mind without mentioning the phases (understandable for such a thumbnail outline). In *ibid.*, chapter 19, which treats the development of Confucian metaphysics, including thought about the moral development of the mind, the phases are again not mentioned, as T'ang emphasizes the *I-ching's* idea of cosmic creativity and the elimination of the selfish impulses adulterating the force of this creativity within us. Only in *ibid.*, 1089–90 are the phases briefly mentioned in connection with the idea that the correction of actual feelings which are improper presupposes an underlying, inner potentiality for the perfect expression of feelings.

147. Wang, p. 71, Chan, p. 43. The tendency to overemphasize *ching* (rest) at the expense of "movement" was prominent and was resisted by Wang and Chu Hsi. See Ch'ien Mu, 2:277.

148. To be sure, we should not exaggerate the contrast between T'ang's view of movement and the Neo-Confucian view of oscillation between rest and movement. After all, both views refer to an ultimate ground of existence transcending movement in the spatio-temporal sense (see sections l and m). Nevertheless, the Neo-Confucian insistence on the reality of a totally still point of existence entirely free of the experience of empathy is basically different from T'ang's view that this "concrete" experience of empathy is the ultimate reality from which the structure of the cosmos must be inferred. Again, one has to consider that persistent tendency among some Neo-Confucians, such as Chang Nan-hsüan, Wang Yang-ming, and Liu Tsung-chou, to insist that this totally still point of existence was completely immanent in concrete experience. Such a view does indeed appear to converge with T'ang's. This is a profound problem that cannot be easily clarified. I would emphasize that Wang's metaphysical bias, as described in sections m and u, was not shared by T'ang. See also chapter 5, sections l and q.

149. Chang, *Liang Ch'i-ch'ao*, pp. 54–55, 67–69, 87–91.

150. Ch'ien Mu, 2:152.   151. *Ibid.*, 2:141. Chan, *Source Book*, p. 601.

152. Ch'ien Mu, 2:133.   153. *Ibid.*, 2:135.

154. *Ibid.*, 2:123–24, 2:131–34, 2:142–43.   155. *Ibid.*, 2:123, 2:142.

156. *Ibid.*, 2:145.   157. *Ibid.*, 2:137, 2:128–29.   158. *Ibid.*, 1:123.

159. *Ibid.*, 2:129.   160. *Ibid.*, 2:130–31.   161. *Ibid.*, 2:132–33.

3. Sense of Predicament

162. *Ibid.*, 2:156. T'ang, *yüan-hsing-p'ien*, p. 563.

163. Ch'ien Mu, 2:131.

164. *Ibid.*, 2:141. In translating this passage, I have thrown in a couple of nuances which are a bit clearer in the parallel passage cited in *ibid.*, p. 147. I have also been helped by Prof. Chan's translation in *Source Book*, pp. 601–2.

165. Ch'ien Mu, 2:137–38.   166. *Ibid.*, 2:131.   167. *Ibid.*, 2:147.

168. *Ibid.*, 2:150.

169. *Ibid.*, 2:142. See T'ang, *yüan-hsing-p'ien*, pp. 543–44, 557–74 for a similar account of Chu Hsi's spiritual development with regard to the problem of the phases.

170. *Ibid.*, 2:144.   171. *Ibid.*, 2:148.   172. *Ibid.*, 2:131.

173. T'ang, *yüan-hsing-p'ien*, pp. 416–17.

174. *Ibid.*, p. 544.   175. *Ibid.*, p. 637.

176. Chan, *Instructions for Practical Living*, p. xi.

177. Wang, p. 149, Chan, p. 236.   178. Wang, p. 60, Chan, pp. 16–17.

179. Wang, p. 85, Chan, p. 82.   180. Wang, p. 76, Chan, p. 56.

181. Wang, p. 56, Chan, p. 7.   182. Wang, p. 63, Chan, p. 23.

183. Wang, p. 56, Chan, p. 7.   184. Wang, p. 72, Chan, p. 47.

185. Wang, p. 150, Chan, pp. 239–40.   186. Wang, p. 78, Chan, p. 62.

187. Wang, p. 147, Chan, pp. 231–32.   188. Wang, p. 67, Chan, p. 34.

189. Wang, p. 71, Chan, p. 43.   190. Wang, p. 79, Chan, p. 65.

191. Wang, p. 85, Chan, p. 82.

192. Wang, pp. 66, 69, 72, 73, 74, 81, 83, 106, 108, 151. Chan, pp. 30, 39, 47, 49, 52, 72, 76–77, 134, 139, 244.

193. Wang, p. 73, Chan, pp. 50–51. For these views, see section l.

194. Wang had still more arguments to demonstrate the interpenetration of movement and rest. One point, made a bit unclearly, was that since principle meant an absence of both movement and selfish desire, to act without selfish desire was a case of "movement while yet at rest." The other argument was that "If one is in the middle of daily affairs and so is aware of outer objects and empathetically pervades them with one's response, this is certainly a case of movement, but this movement does not add anything to the phase of utter stillness." In other words, since rest and movement coexisted without changing each other's character, the presence of the one did not imply the negation of the other. Consequently the idea of "moving, yet lacking motion" made sense.

195. T'ang, *yüan-hsing-p'ien*, p. 434. T'ang adds that Wang subsumed the idea of "cautious and fearful" under that of "spontaneous moral knowledge."

196. This whole exchange is in Wang, pp. 107–8, Chan, pp. 135–37. For the sake of clarity, I have reordered the sequence of questions and points raised. I disagree with a part of Professor Chan's translation. Where at the bottom of p. 136 he has "Activity and tranquillity appertain to the time when the mind comes into contact with things, whereas in the original substance of the mind there is no distinction between activity and tranquillity," I read the text to say: "The moment just when the phases of movement and rest meet is the ultimate substance of the mind. It definitely is outside any distinction between movement and rest."

197. Wang, p. 67, Chan, p. 34.   198. Wang, p. 75, Chan, p. 55.

199. Wang, p. 72, Chan, p. 47.

200. Huang Tsung-hsi, *Ming-ju hsüeh-an*, p. 75. For Wang's three stages, see Chan, pp. xxix–xxx.

201. Ch'ien Mu, 1:488.   202. Hou Wai-lu, 4b:634.

203. Wang, p. 60, Chan, p. 17.

204. Wang, pp. 66, 71–72, 74, 77, Chan, pp. 30, 46, 52, 60.
205. T'ang, *yüan-hsing-p'ien*, pp. 420–21.
206. T'ao Hsi-sheng, *cheng-chih ssu-hsiang*, 4:128–29.
207. T'ang, *Che-hsüeh kai-lun*, 1:134.
208. Ch'ien Mu, *san-pai-nien*, 1:23–24.
209. Ch'ien Mu, 1:238, 1:45, 1:406.
210. I believe that many readers have been misled by Fung Yu-lan's influential interpretation of Chu Hsi, which fails to show how Chu Hsi's dualism is combined with a strong sense of immanence. Presumably any theory of dualism must acknowledge some junction between the metaphysical and the experiential realms, but the extent and character of this junction is a major variable in ontological theory with significant cultural implications. It was precisely the special prominence and expansiveness of this conjunction in Confucian thought, even Chu Hsi's, that made possible the idea of virtue as dissolving any disjunction between the metaphysical and the experiential realms, and this idea, whether from T'ang Chün-i's standpoint or that in my book, was basic to the Confucian concept of self and community. Yet in Fung's discussion, only Chu Hsi's dualistic concept of this disjunction is made clear. It is notably on this point that Ch'ien Mu's interpretation is superior.

It is of course true that Chu Hsi stressed the distinction between the metaphysical and the experiential (*hsing-erh-shang* and *hsing-erh-hsia*), equating *li* (principle) with the former and *ch'i* (ether of materialization) with the latter. This is fundamentally the distinction between "that which concretely appears" and "the general principle in terms of which this concrete thing is what it is" (Fung, *Chung-kuo ssu-hsiang-shih*, 2:896, slightly mistranslated in Bodde's generally excellent work, Fung, *A History of Chinese Philosophy*, 2:534). As Fung puts it, "It is reasonable to say that *li* transcends time and space and is changeless, while *ch'i* is in time and space and exists amidst the processes of change" (Fung, *ssu-hsiang*, 2:906, Fung, *History*, 2:545). In Fung's *Hsin-li-hsüeh*, pp. 24–26, this distinction is formulated as that between "the true" and "the real."

Fung, however, omits any reference to the ambiguous remarks in Chu Hsi's writings expressing Chu Hsi's reluctance to draw too absolute a boundary between these two realms. For instance, describing the relation between "mind" and "the heaven-conferred nature," Chu Hsi could not just reiterate his basic points, which were that "mind" was an aspect of *ch'i* and "nature" was *li*. Rather he said that this relation was "something like being one and yet two, two and yet one" (Ch'ien Mu, 2:36). Thus simplistically regarding Chu Hsi's *li-ch'i* distinction as an absolute one, Fung compares it without qualification to the Greek distinction between "form" and "matter" (Fung, *ssu-hsiang*, 2:903, 2:908, 2:915, Fung, *History*, 2:542, 2:547, 2:556). Still more, Fung pictures Chu Hsi as ascribing the source of evil entirely to the material realm of *ch'i* (Fung, *ssu-hsiang*, 2:912–913, Fung, *History*, 2:552–553), while he describes Chu Hsi's *li* (or *t'ai-chi*) as the realm of "the good" (Fung, *ssu-hsiang*, 2:899, Fung, *History*, 2:537). Yet for Chu Hsi the "good" quality of "principle" was found in the "feelings" of the concrete "mind" at least when "not yet issued," and, conversely, the "selfish material desire of man is hidden in heavenly principle" (Ch'ien Mu, 1:406). Therefore Fung's description of Chu Hsi's philosophy as simply aligning the good–evil distinction with the *li–ch'i* distinction is a serious mistake.

Fung's interpretation suffers most, I believe, from the fact that he concentrates almost entirely on Chu Hsi's account of external cosmic forces, failing to elucidate Chu Hsi's complex view of the "mind" as a unique entity which, although an aspect of *ch'i*, could through moral effort become *li*, thus dissolving the disjunction between the metaphysical and the experiential. In fact, Fung barely if at all mentions the ideas of sagehood and "oneness with heaven" in his chapter on Chu Hsi. Similarly omitted are Chu Hsi's ideas that *ch'eng* (sincerity) was both "principle" and a possible condition of the "mind"; that from a certain standpoint "*jen* is mind" (while also being principle); and that, similarly, "man is heaven" (Ch'ien Mu, 2:407–408, 2:24, 1:366). I would sum up Chu Hsi's position by saying that while "the mind" apart from moral effort was an aspect of *ch'i* only tinged with the almost imperceptible presence of *li*, the result of perfect moral effort was to imbue the mind totally with *li*: "In the case of one who is *jen*, the mind is *li*" (Ch'ien Mu, 1:362). Chu Hsi's position, therefore, only partly differed from Lu Chiu-yüan's.

Erasing that logical distinction between "the real" and "the true" so basic to Fung's *Hsin-li-hsüeh*, this dimension of Chu Hsi's thought is thus ignored in Fung's classic study of the history of Chinese philosophy, but Fung was well aware of it. As he pointed out in *Hsin-yüan-tao*, pp. 199–203 (translated in *The Spirit of Chinese Philosophy*, pp. 212–17), it was just such a failure to distinguish rigorously between "the real" and "the true" which was characteristic of all Confucian thinkers (with the partial exception of Wang Yang-ming), and which led to the false Confucian concept of the sage as one who could through knowledge of general principles become "one with the ten thousand things" and so exert a decisive influence on the actual flow of events. Fung thus was well aware that Confucian metaphysics emphasized that man had a transnatural power to transform the cosmos, and he rejected this emphasis as philosophically untenable. See section o.

211. Wang, p. 99, Chan, p. 119. T'ang, *yüan-hsing-p'ien*, pp. 420–21. For Wang's emphasis on the power of evil, see section r.

212. Ch'ien Mu, 1:412. For "bad [portion of] ether of materialization," see *ibid.*, 1:491.

213. *Ibid.*, 1:399.   214. *Ibid.*, 1:88, 1:367.   215. Hou Wai-lu, 4b:634.

216. Ch'ien Mu, 1:84. The use of water as a simile to describe the mind's vulnerability, contrasting with Mencius' use of water as a simile for the force of goodness, goes back at least to *Hsün-tzu*. See *Hsün-tzu*, pp. 560–61, Watson, p. 131. See also Ch'ien Mu, 1:97 for *po-t'ao* (stormy waves).

217. Ch'ien Mu, 1:90.   218. *Ibid.*, 1:440.   219. *Ibid.*, 1:487.

220. Fung, *ssu-hsiang-shih*, 2:916, Bodde, 2:557–58. Chan, *Source Book*, p. 52. See note 216 above.

221. Ch'ien Mu, 1:487. Hou Wai-lu, 4b:631. On the Sung criticism of Mencius, see Hsia Chün-yü's article in his *Sung-hsüeh kai-yao* (Essentials of Sung Thought; Shanghai: Commercial Press, 1937), pp. 56–76. This Confucian shift away from Mencian optimism can also be related to the rise of a more pessimistic political outlook which I have labeled "moderate realism" (see section v below).

222. While the Neo-Confucian emphasis on the mind's moral fragility clearly had roots in Chou thought, it also reflected the influence of Buddhist thought, which typically stressed that what appears as a self is merely a "momentary collection" of the "five aggregates," and as such is dominated by egotistic cravings and false notions about what is real. Such cravings were regarded as "the root of all evil," as Professor Ch'en notes, especially since they led to retribution, according to the belief in karma. Thus Buddhist writers such as Hsi Ch'ao (336–77) viewed the mind as the constant source of dark feelings leading to evil. See Ch'en, *Buddhism in China*, pp. 70–71, 6–8. Another example of this Buddhist emphasis on consciousness as dominated by evil and illusion is the "Consciousness-only School" of Hsüan-tsang (596–664), which held that of the eight levels of consciousness, seven served

to generate evil and delusion. See Chan, *A Source Book*, pp. 370–74. Certainly, besides this sense of moral fragility, Buddhists emphasized that the mind, or at least some minds, had the positive power to overcome evil and illusion. For instance, Tao-sheng (d.434) followed and elaborated on the "fundamental Mahāyāna [tenet] that all sentient beings possess the Buddha-nature in them, and that all are capable of attaining Buddhahood." See Ch'en, p. 115. The influential Ch'an school also emphasized that "everyone possesses the Buddha-nature," and the Hua-yen and T'ien-t'ai schools came to similar conclusions with their theories about the total interpenetration of the realms of ultimate being and phenomenal existence. See Chan, pp. 396, 407, 428. One has to ask, though, whether this Buddhist sense of the mind's positive capability can be equated with the Neo-Confucian emphasis on the mind's transnatural power. Can, for instance, the "untainted seeds" found on the purest level of consciousness (*ālaya*), according to Hsüan-tsang, be compared with the "incipiences" of moral feeling perceived by Neo-Confucians? I would tentatively say not. These "incipiences" were part of an ever-beneficent cosmic force, while the realm of *ālaya* was conceived of as a sort of incessant, impersonal flux. Moreover, Neo-Confucians drew on their cosmic force to shape the concrete world outside, while the *ālaya* consciousness was more a realm to which one escaped, leaving the concrete world behind. Just as Buddhism rejected the Confucian idea of an organic interpenetration of the realms of ultimate being and experience (see section f), so it was perceived by Neo-Confucians as failing to recognize the transnatural power of the mind, as discussed below in this section.

223. 2:34–35.   224. Wang, p. 73, Chan, p. 49.

225. By an "evaluating mind," Munro means a capacity to "distinguish between the naturally noble and base positions and the naturally proper and improper actions of things." See Munro, pp. 11–12. By "cognitive capacity" I mean the capacity to pursue the goal of cognitive clarity, which, as discussed in section d, involved more than distinguishing right from wrong. See note 269 below.

226. Ch'ien Mu, 1:90, 1:372, 1:44–45, 1:37, 1:131.

227. Ch'ien Mu, 1:124. Chu Hsi's use here of the image of "the thousand forks in the road, the ten thousand roads" to describe the field of moral choice is interesting in the light of Fingarette's observation that the *Lun-yü*'s failure to use the "image of the crossroads, an obvious elaboration of *Tao* imagery to us," illustrates the "absence of a developed language of choice and responsibility" in *Lun-yü*. See Herbert Fingarette, *Confucius—the Secular as Sacred* (New York: Harper Torchbooks, 1972), pp. 18–20. For my critique of Fingarette's thesis, see chapter 5, note 18. The Chinese word used in modern times to translate the Western word "freedom" is *tzu-yu*, which could be used traditionally to mean acting as one pleased, as in the phrase *ts'ao-tsung tzu-yu* (manipulate affairs as they please). In an edict of about 1763, the emperor blamed high regional officials who let their private secretaries act this way. See *Ch'in-ting Ta-Ch'ing hui-tien shih-li* (Imperially Endorsed Precedents and Regulations Supplementary to the Collected Statutes of the Great Ch'ing Dynasty), 8:6360. This book is a reprint of the 1899 edition and is found in *Ch'in-ting Ta-Ch'ing hui-tien t'u shih-li* (The Imperially Endorsed Collected Statutes of the Great Ch'ing Dynasty, with the Annotated Maps and Other Visual Aids, and the Supplementary Precedents and Regulations; 24 vols.; Taipei: *Ch'i-wen ch'u-pan-she*, 1963).

228. Ch'ien Mu, 2:28. This reference to *tsui* is a quote from *Mencius*, chap. 11; see Chan, *Source Book*, p. 54.

229. Wang, p. 64, Chan, p. 25. Wang, p. 81, Chan, p. 70.

3. Sense of Predicament

230. Ch'ien Mu, 2:374.   231. Wang, p. 75, Chan, p. 54.
232. Wang, p. 153, Chan, p. 248.   233. Wang, p. 65, Chan, p. 29.
234. Metzger, *Internal Organization*, pp. 48–50.
235. The "seven feelings" are mentioned in the *Li-yün* chapter. See Jung Chao-tsu, p. 96, for Wang Yang-ming's argument that all seven, including material desire and fear, are "spontaneous moral knowledge in action" and "outside any distinction between good and bad," unless misused.
236. Ch'ien Mu, 2:371, 2:366, 1:495.   237. *Ibid.*, 2:376.
238. Jung Chao-tsu, p. 98.   239. Ch'ien Mu, 2:187–88.
240. *Ibid.*, 1:124.   241. *Ibid.*, 1:69.   242. *Ibid.*, 2:365–66, 1:371.
243. Chan, *Source Book*, pp. 107–108 (my translation differs slightly from Professor Chan's). A naturalistic interpretation of Hsün-tzu's concept of the cognitive mind can be found in Munro, *The Concept of Man in Early China*, p. 80, and in T'ang Chün-i, "*Hsün-tzu yen 'hsin' yü 'tao' chih kuan-hsi pien-i* (An Essay on the Relation of 'Mind' and 'Tao' in Hsün-tzu's Thought)," in *The Journal of the Institute of Chinese Studies of the Chinese University of Hong Kong*, 4, no. 1 (September 1971):8. T'ang emphasizes that for Hsün-tzu, the mind was "a mind bringing about a humanistic order of things"; Munro interprets Hsün-tzu's view of the mind in terms of Hsün-tzu's concept of "man's unique behavioral constancy, that of forming or participating in social organizations." Both interpretations exclude the possibility that for Hsün-tzu the mind had a diffuse transnatural power interacting with the cosmos as a whole, but I would argue that it had. The following are only some of the preliminary points to be considered. As is widely recognized, the cosmos for Hsün-tzu was not just a naturalistic, phenomenal entity impinged on by people only in terms of instrumental knowledge and action. It was a normative order constituted by the complementary functions of heaven, earth, and the true gentleman. It also served as a normative standard, for instance by showing the naturalness of social hierarchy. Moreover, "heaven and earth produced" the ordering agent of the cosmos, i.e. the true gentleman. Most basic, Hsün-tzu repeatedly made two complementary points: although lacking any tendency to reward and punish human beings, heaven and earth were inherently and diffusely amenable to the moral action of the true gentleman, and the latter had the power to control the former. For instance: "It is through the rules of moral propriety that heaven and earth are joined, the sun and moon shine, the four seasons proceed in order.... The true gentleman puts in order heaven and earth ... [and] participates in the processes of heaven and earth." The "great man" whose mind had attained "the state of great clarity and brightness" had a total understanding explicitly encompassing all time and space. Moreover, his "brightness matches the sun and moon; his greatness matches the eight directions." The immensity of this mental power was frequently expressed by the use of "great," as in "great principle," which was one term for the object of the understanding of the "great man." See *Hsün-tzu*, pp. 431, 33–34, 499, 228, 212, 491, 555–56, and Watson, pp. 79, 23, 94, 44–45, 36, 91, 128–29.

This concept of a potential cosmos-ordering brightness in the mind has to be considered together with Hsün-tzu's concept of the mind's potential total objectivity. The key passage is in *Hsün-tzu*, pp. 553–56, Watson, pp. 127–29. The point here is that Hsün-tzu did not just in a practical way urge people to be fair (*kung*) so as to avoid resentment, a view found in Legalism. Rather, as T'ang Chün-i makes clear, he emphasized that fairness involved a mental state described with terms like "empty," "one," "state of absolute rest," and "almost imperceptible in its subtlety" (*wei*).

"One" was involved because in finding an overarching standard by which two conflicting claims could be weighed, a person's mind necessarily moved from two to one. Yet this "one" was not just an ordinary number and perhaps, like "one" in the *Tao-te ching*, connoted the "root" or the "source" of things. Perceiving this "one," the mind was in contact with something "absolutely at rest," was "empty" of any bias, was apprehending something "elusively subtle," and so was "fearful" in its constant efforts to avoid the "danger" of falling into the obscurity of misunderstanding. The idea of "absolutely at rest" (*ching*) as a form of mental perfection is reminiscent of the *Classic of Changes*' *chi-jan pu-tung* (total stillness without movement), which was regarded by Neo-Confucians as a state coinciding with the unadulterated presence of heaven. Moreover, Hsün-tzu in this context spoke of a quality transcending the spatio-temporal distinction between movement and a rest, a quality crucial to Neo-Confucians, as we have seen (see sections l and m): "The mind is always in movement, but it still involves that which one calls absolute rest." So important to Chu Hsi, the image of water perturbed by wind was used in *Hsün-tzu* to show how the mind stood in constant danger of being deluded. In this stress on being "fearful," *Hsün-tzu* shares the epistemology of the *Tao-te-ching* and *The Doctrine of the Mean*. It is in this context that Hsün-tzu mentions another idea basic to Neo-Confucianism, that of *chi* (incipient, almost imperceptible phase in the movement of something): "Therefore, a true classic says: 'How dangerous is the situation of the human mind! Almost imperceptible in its subtlety is the mind of the *tao!*' These incipient motions apprehended by a mind in danger trying to grasp what is almost imperceptible in its subtlety! Only the true gentleman with a totally illuminated understanding can know them." See *Hsün-tzu*, p. 560, Watson, p. 131 (my translation differs from Watson's). Moreover, with its "fearful" focus on the "one," the mind was like the *tao* (true way), which, "constant and unchanging in its essence, encompasses all change." Even more, while the *tao* "encompasses all change," "the mind is that which brings to completion and controls the *tao*." See *Hsün-tzu*, pp. 550, 591, and Watson, pp. 126, 147. These ideas about the "changes" of "heaven and earth" as "encompassed" by a *tao* which the mind in turn controls through its absolute objectivity, brightness, and "fearful" concentration form a single intuition or gestalt basic to the outlook of *Hsün-tzu* and so cannot be dismissed as rhetoric, hyperbole, or metaphor. It is especially in its grandiose vision of the ultimate object of knowledge, of the ability of the mind to carry on the knowing process to this final point, and of the total, diffuse power over the cosmos which humans can thus attain that *Hsün-tzu* goes well beyond the lexicon of naturalism and humanism. Even apart from the fact that Hsün-tzu presupposed that knowledge of noumena was possible, his humanism was that of a godlike superman, not that of an ordinary person as this term is understood in the West. Himself accepting without hesitation Hsün-tzu's stress on absolute objectivity as a reasonable interpretation of ordinary mental life (see chapter 2), T'ang Chün-i may have been less predisposed than some Western readers to find in *Hsün-tzu* a transnatural concept of the mind. Yet my emphasis on this transnatural aspect is partly supported by T'ang's own view, expressed in *Che-hsüeh kai-lun*, 1:138, that Hsün-tzu, holding that the virtue of the sage "encompassed heaven and earth," shared with Confucius and Mencius the idea that man should "attain the virtue of heaven," an idea which, T'ang says, "involved a religious and metaphysical feeling and realm." For a further critique of Munro's position, see note 269 below.

244. T'ang, *Che-hsüeh kai-lun*, 1:113.

3. Sense of Predicament

245. Ch'ien Mu, 3:495. T'ang, *yüan-hsing-p'ien*, p. 534. See note 222 above.
246. Fung Yu-lan, *Hsin yüan-tao*, pp. 202–4, translated in *The Spirit of Chinese Philosophy*, pp. 215–18. Fung's point here that Ch'an Buddhism largely avoided ascribing such a transnatural power to the sage reinforces our point above (see note 222). Fung's analytical framework in *Hsin yüan-tao* is more fully developed in his *Hsin li-hsüeh*.
247. Wang, p. 108, Chan, pp. 137–38.
248. Wang, pp. 121–22, Chan, pp. 168–71.
249. For an excellent discussion of quiet sitting, see de Bary's remarks in *Unfolding*, pp. 171–72.
250. Jung Chao-tsu, p. 287.   251. Ch'ien Mu, 1:84. See note 216 above.
252. *Ibid.*, 2:237. Wang Yang-ming also used the image of a mirror. See section e.
253. *Ibid.*, 2:5.
254. Wang, p. 59, Chan, pp. 12–14. Lu Chiu-yüan referred to *ch'i-ping*. See T'ang, *yüan-hsing-p'ien*, p. 413.
255. Ch'ien Mu, 1:496.   256. *Ibid.*, 1:480–81.
257. *Ibid.*, 1:491, 1:480, 1:498, 1:487.
258. *Ibid.*, 1:491, 1:482–83.   259. *Ibid.*, 1:480–81, 1:495.
260. *Ibid.*, 1:489–90.   261. *Ibid.*, 1:495.   262. *Ibid.*, 1:481.
263. *Ibid.*, 1:491.   264. *Ibid.*, 1:493, 1:488.   265. *Ibid.*, 1:377, 1:497.
266. *Ibid.*, 1:494, 1:497, 1:486, 1:481.
267. *Ibid.*, 1:481. See note 15 above.   268. T'ang, *yüan-lun*, 1:504.
269. Ch'ien Mu, *Chung-kuo chin-san-pai-nien-te hsüeh-shu-shih*, 1:40. Chu Hsi's concept of *ch'i-ping*, what Munro would call a theory of natural or biological inequality, raises questions regarding Munro's position, which is that Confucians emphasized "natural equality," holding that "people's natural differences had little effect on their future performance as members of society." See Munro, p. 12. Munro notes but does not sufficiently emphasize that the theory of natural inequality was alive in Neo-Confucianism (p. 177). To be sure, Chu Hsi's idea of *ch'i-ping* may have involved a significant transition from more optimistic Chou views, as noted elsewhere (see section o). The extent of this shift, however, depends on the degree of pessimism already present in Chou and Han thought. For instance, Wang Ch'ung (first century A.D.) believed in natural inequality. He used the concepts of *ch'i* (vital force) and *ping* (endowed with) to refer to outstanding persons who are "endowed with a great deal of heaven's vital force." Like Chu Hsi, moreover, Wang combined this theory of natural inequality with a belief in the validity of moral effort. See Fung, *ssu-hsiang-shih*, 2:589, Bodde, 2:152. Tung Chung-shu also assumed that every individual "received" a portion of the "vital force" in the cosmos, and he held that this *ch'i* included "evil," which was manifested "in" a person's "mind" as a sense of "greed." He said that "the *ch'i* of both greed and benevolence are in a person," though he does not seem to have said that different individuals received differently mixed portions of *ch'i*. See Chan, *Source Book*, p. 274, and chapter 35 of *Ch'un-ch'iu fan-lu* (*Ssu-pu ts'ung-k'an*). *Mencius* seems to allude to an awareness that because individuals have different natural endowments, the identical impulse of morality develops differently in different persons, just as identical seeds of wheat grow differently depending on the nature of the soil in which they are planted, as well as on the watering and the care they receive (see Chan, *Source Book*, p. 55). This awareness would mesh with Mencius' elitism. At the very least, Munro's statement that there "was no belief in a Fate that inhibited self-cultivation" (p. 90) cannot be applied to Confucian thought generally.

3. Sense of Predicament

Munro's interpretation of Chou views about "Fate" and evil are similar in that, if we follow them, the contrast between Chou Confucianism and Neo-Confucianism would probably be greater than some leading Chinese authorities would allow. While Neo-Confucians definitely saw evil desires and intentions arising in the mind, Munro (p. 90) holds that "environmental conditions, for the ancient Chinese, were the primary 'source of evil.' Thus the path to privilege was still open to all, because evil could not be traced to the inherent nature of any man." I would, however, make two points in arguing that Chou Confucians too regarded evil as based on human traits as well as environmental conditions. First, for both Mencius and Hsün-tzu, thought was needed to become moral, and people tended to think incorrectly, partly on account of the direct and the more subtle effects of egotism, partly because of a lack of perspicacity. The existence of the latter factor was perhaps not explicitly singled out but was implied, for instance, by Mencius' view that "heterodox doctrines delude the people." The way to eliminate this delusion, for Mencius, was not to change environmental conditions but "to argue." Second, Chou Confucians emphasized selfish desires as a central cause of evil. To overcome these, one had to "look within oneself"; one could not just try to change one's environment. Thus Confucius said one should "overcome self-centeredness," Hsün-tzu (*Hsün-tzu*, p. 325) condemned "the mind which lusts after profit," and Tung Chung-shu, as we have just seen, referred to the "*ch'i* of greed" as "in a person." Even if Hsün-tzu himself never called human nature "evil," a possibility Munro mentions (p. 77), he at least regarded unrestrained material desires as a force bringing about evil. This point is basic to his emphasis on ritual. As discussed in note 243, moreover, Hsün-tzu viewed the mind as in constant danger of lapsing into immorality and misunderstanding. Certainly Confucians made euphoric statements about how improving the economic conditions of the masses would eliminate evil, but their view of evil went beyond such statements. Policies improving these conditions had to be administered by an elite whose own minds had reached a state of impartiality eliminating all the subtly distorting influences of egotism. If Munro would hold that this process of enlightenment was seen as resulting from proper education, which was an environmental factor, I would answer that for Hsün-tzu and Mencius, educational success depended not only on being exposed to good teachers but also on being willing and able to make the internal effort to grasp their teachings. No teacher could spare an individual from the difficulties and uncertainties of "looking within oneself."

A final point concerns Munro's effort to demonstrate a convergence between Hsün-tzu and Mencius by discounting not only Hsün-tzu's view that human nature is evil but also Mencius' emphasis on man's heaven-derived flow of spontaneous moral feeling, which Munro ascribes to Mencius' "logical confusion of the ideal man with the actual man" (p. 72). Whether or not Mencius was confused in holding that human nature was naturally good, his view had an enormous impact on Confucian attitudes. As we have seen, T'ang Chün-i cogently argues that just this Mencian stress on the good cosmic flow of empathetic feeling distinguishes the Chinese "spirit" from the Western one. On the other hand, Munro's discussion of how Mencius and Hsün-tzu ascribed some of the same features to the mind, such as the capabilities of evaluation and command, constitutes one of the most valuable parts of his important book.

270. Hou Wai-lu, 4b:905–908.   271. T'ang, *yüan-hsing-p'ien*, pp. 538–52.

272. Ch'ien Mu, 3:368–69. Fung, *ssu-hsiang-shih*, 2:938, Bodde, 2:586.

273. T'ang, *yüan-hsing-p'ien*, pp. 531–33. Fung, *ssu-hsiang-shih*, 2:938, Bodde, 2:585.

3. Sense of Predicament

274. Yü Ying-shih, pp. 22–23.   275. Ch'ien Mu, 3:399.

276. Fung, *ssu-hsiang-shih*, 2:877–79, Bodde, 2:509–12.

277. Wang, p. 106, Chan, p. 132.   278. Ch'ien Mu, 1:94.

279. Wang, p. 60, Chan, pp. 16–17.

280. T'ang, *yüan-hsing-p'ien*, pp. 538–39.   281. Hou Wai-lu, 4b:884.

282. *Ibid.*, 4b:637.   283. T'ang, *yüan-hsing-p'ien*, p. 417.

284. See note 211 above.

285. Wang's view of history as dominated by the "selfish" spirit of the "hegemon" (*pa*) was virtually identical with Chu Hsi's. Wang's view is in Wang, pp. 100–101, Chan, pp. 121–22. Chu Hsi's view of history after the Three Dynasties as dominated by selfish desires was expressed in his debate with Ch'en Liang (1143–1194). See Hou Wai-lu, 4b:724.

286. Wang, p. 56, Chan, p. 7.

287. While Chu traced the existence of evil to various cosmic circumstances and extensively discussed "what heaven has decreed," these topics are virtually unmentioned in *Ch'uan-hsi-lu*. Similarly, Chu's idea of concrete events as a turbulent stream rushing aginst the mind (*kun-kun chiang-ch'ü*) and threatening to "overcome" (*sheng*) it was avoided by Wang. Phrases suggesting the fragility of the mind, like "fears and anxieties," were used by Wang but more rarely than by Chu. Referring to incipient issuance, Chu often used *chi* (incipient, almost imperceptible phase in the movement of something), a concept immediately connoting the difficulties of moral effort, but this word is almost never used in *Ch'uan-hsi-lu* (for a rare exception, see Wang, p. 157, Chan, p. 257). Wang preferred to regard emerging feelings as *i* (intentions) or *nien* (thoughts). Wang also talked less about *li* (effort) than did Chu (see section o). Nor did Wang talk of the difficulties of "getting a hold" on the elusive process of moral cultivation, a favorite theme of Chu Hsi's (see section f). Although admitting it was often "covered over" by selfish desire, Wang often referred to the "mind's ultimate substance" as "always shining," perhaps thus implying that it was easy to perceive. For Wang's reference to moral effort as "easy," see Wang, p. 78, Chan, p. 62.

288. Ch'ien Mu, 2:117. See also *ibid.*, 2:99, 1:93, 1:57.

289. See note 59 above.   290. T'ang, *yüan-hsing-p'ien*, p. 544.

291. *Ibid.*, pp. 433–34.   292. Ch'ien Mu, 1:75.

293. *Ibid.*, 2:36, 2:34, 1:286, 1:99.   294. *Ibid.*, 1:277, 1:241, 1:433.

295. *Ibid.*, 1:287.   296. *Ibid.*, 1:44–45.

297. *Ibid.*, 1:275, 2:32, 1:360, 1:366.   298. *Ibid.*, 1:360, 1:107.

299. *Ibid.*, 1:276.

300. *Ibid.*, 2:3. See note 64 above for the concept of an indivisible consciousness.

301. *Ibid.*, 1:276.   302. *Ibid.*, 1:433.   303. *Ibid.*, 2:19.

304. *Ibid.*, 1:362. See note 210 above.   305. *Ibid.*, 2:3, 1:139, 2:13–14.

306. *Ibid.*, 1:52–53. On Chu Hsi's use of Chang Tsai's concept, see section 1.

307. *Ibid.*, 2:27, 1:54, 2:37.   308. *Ibid.*, 1:276, 1:432–34, 1:293.

309. For instance, some assertions of linkage evoked a "metaphysical pathos" which guaranteed plausibility or just seemed self-evident. For instance, man's link to heaven could be demonstrated by playing on the concepts of *sheng* (to give birth to) and *tung* (to move). Since "movement" was found both in the heavenly process of unceasingly "giving birth" to things and in man's sense of "compassion," man in terms of the latter was linked to the former (*ibid.*, 1:360). The same pathos allowed one to link man and heaven by saying: "*Jen* is that conscious spirit in terms of which heaven and earth give birth to things" (*ibid.*, 1:349). (At the same time, of course, it

was a human virtue.) It was equally self-evident to say that "if one speaks of the supreme ultimate, then with this come yin and yang" (*ibid.*, 1:36); "since heaven has produced this man, heaven also is in this man" (*ibid.*, 1:366); or "the finest essence of the supreme ultimate, it is reasonable to say, is always present in the [ten thousand things]" (*ibid.*, 1:276). Of course Han metaphysics had demonstrated how the various existents "respectively matched" each other, an approach Chu Hsi was comfortable with (*ibid.*, 2:47, 1:293). Other assumptions also facilitated conceptualization of oneness, notably a tendency to regard the knowing process almost as a way of physically incorporating the object known: "Someone asked: 'How do you explain the way the mind's intelligence is able to grasp the finest essence of all principles and control the ten thousand things?' Chu Hsi said: 'Say a principle is fixed here. The mind then applies this principle. But to do this the mind must know it. In knowing it, the mind is related to it just as a hungry or thirsty person is related to drinking or eating" (*ibid.*, 2:13). Similarly, the notion of empathetically entering the being of that which one studies was connoted by common verbs denoting "understand" like *t'i-hui, t'i-jen*, or *t'i-yen*.

310. *Ibid.*, 2:197.   311. Ch'ien Mu, *san-pai-nien*, 1:25.

312. T'ang, *yüan-hsing-p'ien*, p. 412. Similarly, Ch'ien Mu traces Huang Tsung-hsi's way of collapsing *pen-t'i* into *kung-fu* ("the mind is without any ultimate substance; ultimate substance is what efficacious moral efforts come to") back to Liu Tsung-chou and Wang Yang-ming. See Ch'ien Mu, *san-pai-nien*, 1:45.

313. Said Wang: "Only after one has experienced pain can one know pain. The same is true of cold or hunger. How can knowledge and action be separated?" See Wang, p. 58, Chan, p. 10. Wang similarly argued that the actual practice of governmental administration was the same as "the investigation of things." See Wang, pp. 132–33, Chan, pp. 197–98. However, Wang also said that Confucius, who had never taken charge of a government, understood all governmental principles. See section g above.

314. Wang, p. 64, Chan, pp. 24–25. This passage also describes Hsü Ai's conversion experience. See also Wang, p. 83, Chan, p. 75; Wang, p. 60, Chan, pp. 15–16; Wang, p. 82, Chan, p. 73.

315. Wang, p. 59, Chan, p. 14.   316. Wang, p. 129, Chan, p. 189.

317. Wang, p. 141, Chan, p. 218.   318. Wang, p. 151, Chan, p. 243.

319. Wang, p. 106, Chan, p. 134.   320. Wang, p. 60, Chan, p. 15.

321. Wang, p. 67, Chan, p. 32.   322. Wang, p. 149, Chan, p. 235.

323. Wang, pp. 105–6, Chan, p. 132.   324. Wang, p. 108, Chan, pp. 137–38.

325. This question is clarified in T'ang Chün-i's article in *Unfolding*. Besides the "four-sentence teaching" referred to above, the idea that the distinction between good and evil was based on something transcending this distinction can be found in Wang, p. 134, Chan, p. 202. In Wang, p. 157, Chan, pp. 256–57, Wang makes very clear that the distinction between good and evil was entirely in the realm of specific, consciously formed concepts (*nien*) and so was distinct from the pure, naturally given, indivisible consciousness of the cosmos (see section d), which was identical with "the mind's ultimate substance." Wang's idea, therefore, was quite logical. If moral responses (*ying*) were to be based on a total lack of selfish impulses and thus a sense of oneness with the cosmos, they would have to be based on an awareness transcending the distinction between good and bad.

326. Wang, p. 72, Chan, p. 46. See chapter 2, note 17.

327. Wang, p. 56, Chan, pp. 6–7. Wang, p. 65, Chan, p. 28.

328. Jung Chao-tsu, p. 38.

329. They are described more fully in my *Internal Organization*, pp. 74–79.
330. See note 103 above.
331. Metzger, *Internal Organization*, p. 75. On ambivalence, see *ibid.*, pp. 66–74.
332. Ch'ien Mu, *san-pai-nien*, 1:15.   333. *Ibid.*, 1:79–81.
334. Ch'ien Mu, 1:198–99. Metzger, *Internal Organization*, p. 69.
335. Ch'ien Mu, 3:388–89.   336. *Ibid.*, 2:243.   337. *Ibid.*, 1:21.
338. *Ibid.*, 1:124.   339. *Ibid.*, 1:368, 1:89.   340. *Ibid.*, 1:377.
341. *Ibid.*, 1:381–82.
342. *Ibid.*, 2:365. I am not saying that *ti-wei* here fully has the flavor of the modern term, which often connotes the longing for social prestige, but it perhaps has a bit of this flavor.
343. *Ibid.*, 1:348.   344. *Ibid.*, 1:362, 2:413.
345. *Unfolding*, pp. 543–77.   346. *Ibid.*, pp. 194–96.
347. Ch'ien Mu, *san-pai-nien*, 1:19–20.
348. See Lu Pao-ch'ien, "*Lun Ch'ing-tai ching-hsüeh* (On the Study of the Classics During the Ch'ing Period," *Li-shih hsüeh-pao*, no. 3 (February 1975), pp. 1–22. Lu holds that Ch'ing textual studies arose mainly out of the *ching-shih* trend of the seventeenth century combined with the increasing emphasis on textual research as a way for the Ch'eng-Chu and Lu-Wang schools to try to refute each other. He thus agrees with Ying-shih Yü in emphasizing the desire to establish metaphysical truth as a major motive for engaging in textual studies, but Lu tends to see this desire as a polemical tendency, while Yü sees it more as part of the inner logic of Confucian thought.
349. Yü Ying-shih, pp. 19, 32.
350. This point emerges most clearly from Chung-ying Cheng's analysis of Wang Fu-chih's concept of *ch'i* in *Unfolding*, pp. 473–85.
351. Ch'ien Mu, 1:23–24.   352. T'ang, *yüan-hsing-p'ien*, p. 484.
353. This is also, by and large, the conclusion that John Watt draws from his extensive study of Ch'ing local government; see John R. Watt, *The District Magistrate in Late Imperial China* (New York: Columbia University Press, 1972), p. 97. Watt here shows how the Confucian emphasis on *jen* was at odds with the realities of local administration, a situation bringing about a "conflict of roles: between the role learned in study and the role required in practice." In my view (*Internal Organization*, pp. 89–91, p. 66), this conflict was not so clearcut, because the values developed through learning included an ambivalent appreciation of Legalist methods. Nevertheless, whether or not cushioned by feelings of ambivalence, the bureaucrats' perception of social reality stood in sharp contrast to the ideal of social oneness basic both to their education and the official rhetoric of the bureaucracy (*shang-hsia i-hsin*, etc.).
354. Parsons *et al.*, eds., *Theories of Society*, 1:664–70.

CHAPTER FOUR — NEO-CONFUCIANISM AND THE
POLITICAL CULTURE OF LATE IMPERIAL CHINA

1. Seymour Martin Lipset, *Political Man* (Garden City, N.Y.: Anchor Books, 1963), p. xx.
2. Solomon, pp. xiv–xv.   3. Metzger, *Internal Organization*, chapter 4.
4. *Ibid.*, pp. 255–60.
5. These edicts are taken from the 1899 edition of *Ta-Ch'ing hui-tien shih-li*

(Precedents and Regulations Supplementary to the Collected Statutes of the Great Ch'ing Dynasty), and are found in *Ch'in-ting Ta-Ch'ing hui-tien t'u shih-li*, 22:17051–17075. The following observations are taken from a paper I gave at the March 1975 meeting of the Association of Asian Studies, "Ch'ing Political Culture and the Imperial Rhetoric of Moral Condemnation."

6. *Shih-li*, 22:17066.   7. *Ibid.*, 22:17068.   8. *Ibid.*, 22:17058.

9. Metzger, *Internal Organization*, pp. 261–67.

10. Ch'ien Mu, *san-pai-nien*, 1:41–42. The view that *yü* (material desires) are integral to one's *hsing* (heaven-conferred nature) had a long history. Apart from certain Taichow thinkers, we may note that even Wang Yang-ming leaned in this direction when he discussed the *Li-chi's* "seven feelings," which included *yü*. See chapter 3, note 235.

11. T'ang, *yüan-hsing-p'ien*, p. 501.

12. For Fan's statement that "A scholar should be the first to become concerned with the world's troubles and the last to rejoice in its happiness," see James T. C. Liu's article, p. 111, in John K. Fairbank, ed., *Chinese Thought and Institutions* (Chicago: The University of Chicago Press, 1957).

13. Ch'ien Mu, 2:336, 2:453.   14. Jung Chao-tsu, pp. 21–22.

15. Solomon, pp. 103–4.   16. See chapter 3, sections c and h.

17. Metzger, *Internal Organization*, pp. 250–54.

18. *Ibid.*, pp. 89–90.   19. Solomon, p. 83.

20. Chu Ch'uan-yü, *Sung-tai hsin-wen-shih* (A History of the Flow of News in the Sung Dynasty; Taipei: *Chung-kuo hsüeh-shu chu-tso chiang-chu wei-yüan-hui*, 1967), pp. 274–78.

21. Shen Ming-chang, *Ming-tai cheng-chih-shih* (A Political History of the Ming Dynasty; Taipei: Shen Ming-chang, 1967), pp. 32–33.

22. See p. 153 in Charles O. Hucker's article in Fairbank, ed., *Chinese Thought and Institutions*.

23. Arthur W. Hummel, ed., *Eminent Chinese of the Ch'ing Period*, 2 vols. (Washington: United States Government Printing Office, 1943), 1:306–7. *Shih-li*, 22:17067. *Ch'ing-shih lieh-chuan* (Biographies of Persons Prominent in the History of the Ch'ing Dynasty; 10 vols.; Taipei: *Chung-hua shu-chü*, 1962), 75:3b–4b.

24. Fu Tsung-mao, *Ch'ing-tai chün-chi-ch'u tsu-chih chi chih-chang chih yen-chiu* (A Study of the Functions and Organization of the Grand Council of the Ch'ing Dynasty; Taipei: Cultural Foundation of the Chia-hsin Cement Company, 1967), pp. 214–15.

25. *Ch'ing-shih lieh-chuan*, 61:19b–21.

26. Metzger, *Internal Organization*, pp. 158–60, 267–68, 241–45.

27. *Ibid.*, pp. 328, 267. On Chu Hsi's statement, see Ch'ien Mu, 1:377.

28. *Shih-li*, 8:6361. The view that there are many arrogant fools who pretend that they are superior persons or sages is illustrated by the complementary feelings of disgust expressed by Li Chih and Wang Shih-chen (1525–90). See *Self and Society in Ming Thought*, pp. 178, 204–5. Li Chih himself was an example of this "arrogant" personality type (*ibid.*, p. 193).

29. Metzger, *Internal Organization*, pp. 337, 156–58.

30. Watt, *The District Magistrate in Late Imperial China*, pp. 176–77.

31. *Shih-li*, 7:6060–6061, 8:6359–6363. See also Metzger, *Internal Organization*, pp. 150–55. Important statistical work on the average length of tenure in various offices has recently been published in Taiwan by Li Kuo-ch'i and Wei Hsiu-mei. Professor Kwang-Ching Liu and I plan a review article on their findings.

32. Metzger, *Internal Organization*, pp. 158–60.

33. *Ibid.*, pp. 161–62, pp. 176–77. The need to make the emperor's position awesome was emphasized beginning at least with Ssu-ma Ch'ien's monograph on ritual.

34. See de Bary's article on *Ming-i tai-fang lu* in Fairbank, ed., *Chinese Thought and Institutions.*

35. Metzger, *Internal Organization*, pp. 66–71.

CHAPTER FIVE — THE ETHOS OF INTERDEPENDENCE IN AN AGE OF
RISING OPTIMISM AND WESTERNIZATION

1. Immanuel C. Y. Hsü, *The Rise of Modern China* (New York: Oxford University Press, 1970), pp. 562–63.

2. This point emerged out of a conversation with Professor Charlotte Furth.

3. Lucien Bianco, *Origins of the Chinese Revolution, 1915–1949* (Stanford: Stanford University Press, 1971), p. 1.

4. See, for instance, Shih-chiang Lu, "Research Note: Confucian Tradition and Innovation," in *Ch'ing-shih wen-t'i*, vol. 3, no. 4 (December 1975):100–104. His particular point here, that the Confucian tradition "may have provided certain important ideological elements forming the foundation of and motivation for innovation," meshes specifically with my argument in section k.

5. Parsons *et al.*, eds., *Theories of Society*, 2:1378.

6. Li I-yüan and Yang Kuo-shu, p. 49.   7. Munro, p. 162.

8. See Introduction, note 18, for bibliographical information about Yin.

9. Solomon, p. 512.

10. See Price, *Russia and the Roots of the Chinese Revolution*, and Frederic Wakeman Jr., *History and Will: Philosophical Perspectives of Mao Tse-tung's Thought* (Berkeley: University of California Press, 1973).

11. Studying philosophy at Columbia University around 1920, Fung Yu-lan feared that the truths of science and materialism destroyed man's spiritual hopes, turning him from a "high" being into a "low" creature without an immortal soul, freedom, or a history of human achievements with long-lasting "value." Fung was fully familiar with the Western "debate between science and metaphysics," which turned on this fear. See his *Jen-sheng che-hsüeh*, pp. 224–26. Moreover, this controversy was echoed in China when, in 1923, a lengthy debate took place between believers in science and those upholding the validity of a more metaphysical approach to the problem of moral values; see Kwok, pp. 135–60. Yet it seems clear, especially from Kwok's book, that the fear that a philosophy of materialism destroyed the basis for a life of "value" remained largely academic in China, and I would link this fact to the traditional concept of matter, which, in Confucian thought, was a teleologically rich substance. See also chapter 3, section x, and notes 130 and 350.

12. This is from K'ang's essay on the *Li-yün* chapter of *Li-chi* and is cited on p. 112 of *Chung-kuo che-hsüeh-shih tzu-liao hsüan-chi—chin-tai-chih pu (1840–1919)* (Selected Materials on the History of Chinese Philosophy—Section on the Modern Period [1840–1919]; comp. by *Chung-kuo k'o-hsüeh-yüan, Che-hsüeh yen-chiu-so, Chung-kua che-hsüeh-shih-tsu*; Peking: *Chung-hua shu-chü*, 1959).

13. Weber, *The Religion of China*, pp. 229–30.

14. T'ang, *ching-shen chia-chih*, pp. 328, 335.

15. See Robert N. Bellah, *Beyond Belief* (New York: Harper and Row, Publishers, 1970), p. 12. Bellah approvingly cites Geertz's definition: "A religion is a system of

symbols which acts to establish powerful, pervasive, and long-lasting moods and motivations in men by formulating conceptions of a general order of existence and clothing these conceptions with such an aura of factuality that the moods and motivations seem uniquely realistic." Bellah's own definition—"the most general mechanism for integrating meaning and motivation in action systems"—leaves aside Geertz's "aura of factuality" and so covers more abstract philosophies like Neo-Confucianism still better. It is striking that the three beliefs and two psychological characteristics listed by William James as fundamental to the religious life, which he had explored in his carefully inductive way using mainly Christian materials, were indeed central to Neo-Confucianism with only one possible exception. This is his idea of "inner communion" with that higher, spiritual force in the cosmos, a concept not entirely congruent with the "spiritual nurture" of the Neo-Confucians. Yet this is no more than a quibble: for James, such "communion" did not have to be with an anthropomorphic god, and the flow of "spiritual energy" which "communion" led to was integral to "spiritual nurture" as well. See William James, *The Varieties of Religious Experience* (New York, Mentor Books, 1958), p. 367. Re-reading James after completing my study, I find that methodologically my work to a large extent simply follows James's premises, a result unconsciously arrived at. Particularly congenial to me is his naturalistic but highly empathetic approach to religion as a "state of mind," his emphasis on "inarticulate feelings of reality," and a number of his categories, notably those of the "divine" and the "godlike." See *ibid.*, pp. 40, 73, 42–47. James also strikingly refers to a peculiarly religious serenity that perfectly exemplifies what Neo-Confucians called "knowing what heaven has decreed." See *ibid.*, p. 53.

16. See, for instance, Arthur P. Wolf, ed., *Religion and Ritual in Chinese Society* (Stanford: Stanford University Press, 1974), and especially Maurice Freedman's attempt to "consider Chinese religion as a whole" while ignoring the writings of Chinese humanists who have partly sought to do precisely this.

17. I am indebted to my colleague David K. Jordan for a conversation tending to support this observation, though he should be spared responsibility for it.

18. See Herbert Fingarette, *Confucius—The Secular as Sacred*. Fingarette himself leans toward a current philosophical movement which seeks a middle path between subjectivism and behaviorism or formalism (p. 54). With this middle path, one hypostatizes neither the individual nor society (p. 76). Rather, in a manner reminiscent of Whitehead, George H. Mead, and T'ang Chün-i, one emphasizes the relational and social character of human experience. The philosophy of Confucius, Fingarette holds, already pointed to this path in that, for Confucius, "The ceremonial act is the primary, irreducible event" of the good human life (p. 14). As illustrated by ordinary social acts like shaking hands (p. 9), the ceremonial act involves not only the "stance, the literal stand and spatial attitude of the actor" (p. 55), but also the "directional, aim character of" the act (p. 54), though not in its "subjective" intent. It is a physically shared, lived social experience with a "conventional" form rooted in "tradition" (p. 63), and it inherently has a quality of "solemnity and lightness of heart," "holy beauty," and even "magic," in terms of which "human dignity" is realized (pp. 76, 3, 64). Conversely, according to Fingarette, Confucius rejected a subjectivist approach to human existence; did not "systematically" locate man's "spiritual dimension 'inside' the individual" (p. 46); and did not believe that man is "holy by virtue of his absolute possession, within himself and independently of other men, of a 'piece' of the divine, the immortal soul" (p. 78). Consequently, for Confucius, the emphasis is not on "self-realization" (p. 72); man "is not an ultimately autonomous

273

being who has an inner and decisive power, intrinsic to him, a power to select among real alternatives and thereby to shape a life for himself" (p. 34); the ideas of "moral responsibility, guilt, deserved (retributive) punishment, and repentance" are not central (p. 24); and, in effect, Weber's tension is missing, in that there is little "personal power as over against society or the physical environment" (p. 35). I believe that this interpretation involves some textual oversights, and that Confucius' outlook could not have been that different from that of Neo-Confucianism, which, as I have tried to show, was characterized by these very views allegedly absent from the philosophy of Confucius, or at least strongly tended toward them. Certainly if one is willing to regard *tao-hsin* (the mind of the *tao*) as "the immortal soul," one has to say that Neo-Confucians believed that man is "holy by virtue of his absolute possession, within himself and independently of other men, of a 'piece' of the divine, the immortal soul." The fact that Fingarette's view of Confucius does have significant textual support reminds us that we need to look further into the relation of Confucius' ideas to Neo-Confucianism. It is interesting, moreover, that Fingarette's emphasis on ceremony is similar to Max Weber's view of Confucianism (see Introduction, note 4, and chapter 3, note 227), although Weber hardly matched Fingarette's enthusiasm for the "dignity" of the ceremonial act. One can suppose that had distinctively Neo-Confucian views not arisen in imperial China, Weber's view of a stagnatively ceremonial culture might have been largely justified.

19. Bellah, *Beyond Belief*, p. 57.   20. See Introduction, note 20.

21. This valuable point about the emphasis on thought as the basis of morality is taken from Robert H. Silin's Ph.D. dissertation "Management in Large-scale Taiwanese Industrial Enterprises" (Harvard University 1971). See chapter 3, note 48.

22. See Introduction, note 30, for this concept of "ideology."

23. This formulation was developed by Don C. Price in a talk given at the San Diego meeting of Asian Studies on the Pacific Coast, June 14, 1974.

24. Ho Lin, pp. 3–5, 7.

25. Cited in Fung, *Hsin-yüan-yao*, p. 180, trans. in Hughes, pp. 193–94.

26. Ho Lin, p. 19.

27. A. O. Lovejoy, *Reflections on Human Nature* (Baltimore: The Johns Hopkins Press, 1961), pp. 38–39. Lovejoy here discusses the importance of this idea in eighteenth-century thought regarding checks and balances in government.

28. A collection of references to the importance of the people's economic well-being in famous documents from Chou through Ch'ing times can be found in Chou Chin-sheng, *Chung-kuo ching-chi ssu-hsiang-shih* (A History of Chinese Economic Thought; 4 vols.; Taipei: Chou Chin-sheng, 1965) 3:921–37. The elaborate emphasis on sheer material prosperity in K'ang Yu-wei's *Ta-t'ung-shu* can also be noted in this context. Max Weber astutely noted: "In no other civilized country has material welfare ever been so exalted as the supreme good" (*The Religion of China*, p. 237).

29. Probably a locus classicus of this viewpoint is Tzu-hsia's statement in book one of the *Lun-yü* about his regarding as learned a person of upright conduct even though this person has "not studied." This strain can also be found among Tung-lin scholars like Kao P'an-lung and Ku Hsien-ch'eng. The latter, reacting against the excessive intellectualizing of some Neo-Confucians, said: "Ever since antiquity, what the sages have taught is merely to do good and eliminate evil. Doing good is realizing what one originally has, eliminating the bad is eliminating what one originally lacked. Whether you are referring to the ultimate substance of things or the problem of moral cultivation, this is the issue. What both of these matters come

to is simply the same thing." See Ch'ien Mu, *Chung-kuo chin-san-pai-nien-te hsüeh-shu-shih*, 1:9, 1:11. Given this prominent though not dominant *philosophical* emphasis on the primacy of practical morality over philosophy, scholars whose philosophical training involved study of the Confucian tradition could find reasons to embrace a political movement solving the morally crucial problem of the people's livelihood even if they disagreed with this movement's theoretical positions regarding history, epistemology, and so on. This question is related to the issue of "anti-intellectualism" raised by Ying-shih Yü.

30. This essay of Cheng's, "The True Way and the World of Concrete Things," is found in *Chung-kuo che-hsüeh-shih tzu-liao hsüan-chi*, pp. 104–6. For Cheng's biography and ideas, see Yen-p'ing Hao, *The Comprador in Nineteenth Century China* (Cambridge, Mass.: Harvard University Press, 1970), 196–206.

31. Wang, p. 121, Chan, pp. 168–69, *Self and Society in Ming Thought*, pp. 159–60.

32. This is from the preface to his famous study *Confucius as a Reformer*, cited in *Chung-kuo che-hsüeh-shih tzu-liao hsüan-chi*, pp. 122–23.

33. Cited in *Chung-kuo chin-tai ssu-hsiang-shih ts'an-k'ao tzu-liao chien-pien* (Selected Reference Materials on China's Modern Intellectual History; comp. by Shih Chün *et al.*; 2 vols.; Peking: *San-lien shu-tien*, 1957), 1:160–61.

34. *Chung-kuo che-hsüeh-shih tzu-liao hsüan-chi*, p. 191. This passage is from K'ang's famous *Ta-t'ung-shu*. See L. G. Thompson, trans., *Ta T'ung shu: The One-World Philosophy of K'ang Yu-wei* (London: Allen and Unwin, 1958). On K'ang's and Liang's cosmology, see chapter 3, section k, and Chang, *Liang Ch'i-ch'ao*, pp. 54–55, 67–69, 87–91. I would argue that already with his earliest extant writings, around 1886, K'ang's thought completely exemplified the shift analyzed here, that is, the shift from a "church"-like accomodation with the status quo to a "sect"-like zeal for the total moral transformation of the world, from the Neo-Confucian preoccupation with the *kung-fu* of the "inner" life to a focus on "outer" processes, from the Neo-Confucian sense of predicament to an optimistic faith in the imminence of great intellectual, technological, economic, and political progress, and from "moderate realism" to "radicalism." K'ang's shift from the generally more oblique Ch'ing orientation toward sagehood to a personally direct quest for sagehood was also part of this shift to a transformative outlook. Therefore, while K'ang is usually seen as struggling unsuccessfully to save the Confucian heritage by advancing implausible arguments about its compatibility with modernization, he can also be viewed as successfully initiating modern China's crucial tradition of transformative thought, incorporating into his philosophic system some of the most basic points common to all the subsequent systems, including Mao's. In other words, the shift from K'ang's Confucianism to anti-Confucian scientism was not necessarily more of a watershed than was K'ang's own shift from the accomodative worldview dominant in the Ch'ing period. Again, the question of context deserves more attention than the usual biographical approach has allowed for. How one gauges the importance of a particular thinker depends on some understanding of the trends which preceded him. Thus Howard was unable to analyze K'ang's earliest writings, holding, for instance, that when K'ang extolled "the almost magical powers of the emperor," he was merely expressing "traditionally Confucian" views. Indeed if one is unaware that the Confucian tradition included alternative views regarding the polity and regarding the role of the self in relation to the polity, how can one recognize a shift from one of these alternatives to another? See Richard C. Howard, "K'ang Yu-wei (1858–1927): His Intellectual Background and Early Thought," in Arthur F. Wright

and Denis Twitchett, eds., *Confucian Personalities* (Stanford: Stanford University Press, 1962), p. 308. These points regarding K'ang, which I will try to develop in a forthcoming article, are supported by the evidence in Professor Hsiao's masterful study of K'ang, although his perspective differs from the one put forward here. See Kung-chuan Hsiao, *A Modern China and a New World* (Seattle: University of Washington Press, 1975).

35. See especially Benjamin I. Schwartz, *In Search of Wealth and Power—Yen Fu and the West* (Cambridge, Mass.: The Belknap Press of Harvard University Press, 1964).

36. On the New Text school, which argued for the authenticity of New Text versions of the classics and the revival of which began in the late eighteenth century, see Chang, *Liang Ch'i-ch'ao*, pp. 21–26.

37. See the many references to statism in Chang, *Liang Ch'i-ch'ao*, and note Liang's enthusiasm for the *Kuan-tzu's* totalitarian vision of national mobilization expressed in his *Kuan-tzu chuan* (A Biography of Kuan-tzu; Taipei: *T'ai-wan Chung-hua shu-chü*, 1963). So far as I am aware, the only modern political trend possibly rejecting the traditional model of "radical" centralization as described in chapter 3, section v, was the federalist movement of the 1920s, which Grieder regards as "a feeble and a losing cause." See Jerome B. Grieder, *Hu Shih and the Chinese Renaissance* (Cambridge, Mass.: Harvard University Press, 1970), p. 195. On the early republican "constitutionalist faith," see Andrew J. Nathan, *Peking Politics, 1918–1923* (Berkeley: University of California Press, 1976), chapter 1.

38. Ho Lin, pp. 46–47.   39. *Yin Hai-kuang hsüan-chi*, p. ii.

40. These remarks are taken from my "On Political Culture."

41. *Yin Hai-kuang hsüan-chi*, pp. 130–39.

42. Yin, *Chung-kuo wen-hua-te chan-wang*, 2:618.

43. Ch'en Ku-ying, *Ch'un-ts'an t'u-ssu*, p. 32.

44. *Yin Hai-kuang hsüan-chi*, p. ii.

45. *Chung-kuo wen-hua-te chan-wang*, 2:383.   46. *Ibid.*, 2:644.

47. *Ibid.*, 2:618, 2:533. *Yin Hai-kuang hsien-sheng chi-nien-chi*, p. 53.

48. Sun Hui-wen, *Liang Ch'i-ch'ao-te min-ch'üan yü chün-hsien ssu-hsiang* (The Thought of Liang Ch'i-ch'ao on Popular Rights and Constitutional Monarchy; Taipei: *Kuo-li T'ai-wan ta-hsüeh wen-hsüeh-yüan*, 1966), p. 15.

49. Ch'ien Mu, *san-pai-nien*, 1:15, 1:18.   50. See chapter 3, note 1.

51. Chang, *Liang Ch'i-ch'ao*, pp. 272–74.   52. Ho Lin, pp. 6, 29.

53. *Yin Hai-kuang hsüan-chi*, pp. 600–601. In this article for *Tzu-yu Chung-kuo* (Free China), written in 1960 on the question of starting an opposition political party, Yin, as might be expected, was not ready to give credit to the Kuomintang for Taiwan's economic progress, which, he wrongly maintained, would cease as soon as U.S. aid ceased. Political antagonisms aside, Yin's basic emphasis on the moral foundations of political power, combined with his strongly critical view of KMT rule, precluded any pragmatic appreciation of Taiwan's economic progress as laying down some of the foundations for social and moral progress in general. Moreover, the institution of capitalism did not arouse any sense of commitment in Yin, although he praised it in 1950 as a desirable alternative to totalitarian control of the economy. See *ibid.*, p. 115.

54. *Ibid.*, p. 4.   55. *Ibid.*, p. 56.

56. Yin, *Chung-kuo wen-hua-te chan-wang*, 2:673.

57. *Yin Hai-kuang hsüan-chi*, p. 602.

58. Ch'en Ku-ying, p. 37, *Yin Hai-kuang hsien-sheng chi-nien-chi*, p. 51.

59. Fung, *Hsin shih-lun*, pp. 58, 63, 198–99.

60. This idea of a "breakthrough" has been used by Bellah. In his classic article "Religious Evolution," Bellah deals with the kind of fundamental restructuring of beliefs which would be involved were Chinese thinkers to replace the ethos of interdependence with another definition of selfhood and moral commitment. For this article, see *Beyond Belief*, pp. 20–50. For a better understanding of the new problem of linkage faced in modern Chinese philosophy, see T'ang Chün-i's *Chung-kuo jen-wen ching-shen-chih fa-chan* (The Development of China's Humanistic Spirit; Taipei: *T'ai-wan hsüeh-sheng shu-chü*, 1974). On p. 316, for instance, T'ang argues that while the "outer" search for scientific knowledge and better political organization is rich with promise, this promise cannot be really realized unless this "externalized," "objectified" world is integrated with the "inner" search for value, "making the inner and the outer one." This book first came out in 1957, but in 1974 T'ang felt it still represented his basic outlook (*ibid.*, p. i).

61. *Chung-kuo chin-tai ssu-hsiang-shih ts'an-k'ao tzu-liao chien-pien*, 1:163.

62. De Bary makes a similar suggestion in *Unfolding*, p. 205.

63. Mark Elvin, *The Pattern of the Chinese Past* (Stanford: Stanford University Press, 1973), pp. 298–316. Elvin's thesis has won considerable acceptance among economists. See e.g. Robert F. Dernberger's article in Dwight H. Perkins, ed., *China's Modern Economy in Historical Perspective* (Stanford: Stanford University Press, 1975).

Bibliography

Not all Western sources cited in notes are listed here.

Bellah, Robert N. *Beyond Belief*. New York: Harper and Row, 1970.

Chan, Wing-tsit. *Religious Trends in Modern China*. New York: Columbia University Press, 1953.

———, comp. *A Source Book in Chinese Philosophy*. Princeton: Princeton University Press, 1963.

———, comp. *Instructions for Practical Living and other Neo-Confucian Writings by Wang Yang-ming*. New York: Columbia University Press, 1963.

Chang, Hao. *Liang Ch'i-ch'ao and Intellectual Transition in China, 1890–1907*. Cambridge, Mass: Harvard University Press, 1971.

Ch'en Ku-ying 陳鼓應 comp. *Ch'un-ts'an t'u-ssu—Yin Hai-kuang tsui-hou-te hua-yü* 春蠶吐絲—殷海光最後的話語 ("The Silk-worms Continue to Spit out Silk until the Hour of their Death"—Yin Hai-kuang's Last Words). Taipei: Shih-chieh wen-wu kung-ying-she, 1969.

Ch'i Hsia 漆俠. *Wang An-shih pien-fa* 王安石變法 (The Reforms of Wang An-shih). Shanghai: Shang-hai jen-min ch'u-pan-she, 1956.

Ch'ien Mu 錢穆. *Chung-kuo chin-san-pai-nien hsüeh-shu-shih* 中國近三百年學術史 (A History of Chinese Thought During the Last Three Centuries). 2 vols. Taipei: T'ai-wan shang-wu yin-shu-kuan, 1966.

——— *Chu-tzu hsin-hsüeh-an* 朱子新學案 (A New Scholarly Record on Chu Hsi). 5 vols. Taipei: San-min shu-tien, 1971.

Ch'in-ting Ta-Ch'ing hui-tien t'u shih-li 欽定大清會典圖事例 (The Imperially Endorsed Collected Statutes of the Great Ch'ing Dynasty, with the Annotated Maps and Other Visual Aids, and the Supplementary Precedents and Regulations). 24 vols. Taipei: Ch'i-wen ch'u-pan-she, 1963.

Ch'ing-shih lieh-chuan 清史列傳 (Biographies of Persons Prominent in the History of the Ch'ing Dynasty). Comp. and pub. by Chung-hua shu-chü. 10 vols. Taipei: 1964.

Chou Chin-sheng 周金聲. *Chung-kuo ching-chi ssu-hsiang-shih* 中國經濟思想史 (A History of Chinese Economic Thought). 4 vols. Taipei: Chou Chin-sheng, 1965.

Chu Ch'ien-chih 朱謙之. *Li Chih—shih-liu shih-chi Chung-kuo fan feng-chien ssu-hsiang-te hsien-ch'ü-che* 李贄—十六世紀中國反封建思想的先

Bibliography

驅者 (Li Chih—A Forerunner in Sixteenth-Century China of the Movement Against Feudal Thought). Wuhan: Hu-pei jen-min ch'u-pan-she, 1957.

Chu Ch'uan-yü 朱傳譽. *Sung-tai hsin-wen-shih* 宋代新聞史 (A History of the Flow of News in the Sung Dynasty). Taipei: Chung-kuo hsüeh-shu chu-tso chiang-chu wei-yüan-hui, 1967.

Chu-tzu chi-ch'eng 諸子集成 (A Complete Collection of the Works of the Ancient Scholars). Comp. by Chung-hua shu-chü on the basis of an earlier edition published by Shih-chieh shu-chü. 8 vols. Peking: Chung-hua shu-chü, 1959.

Chung-kuo che-hsüeh-shih tzu-liao hsüan-chi—chin-tai-chih pu (1840–1919) 中國哲學史資料選輯—近代之部 (Selected Materials on the History of Chinese Philosophy—Section on the Modern Period [1840–1919]). Comp. by Chung-kuo k'o-hsüeh-yüan, Che-hsüeh yen-chiu-so, Chung-kuo che-hsüeh-shih-tsu. Peking: Chung-hua shu-chü, 1959.

Chung-kuo chin-tai ssu-hsiang-shih ts'an-k'ao tzu-liao chien-pien 中國近代思想史參考資料簡編 (Selected Reference Materials on China's Modern Intellectual History). Comp. by Shih Chün 石峻 *et al.* 2 vols. Peking: San-lien shu-tien, 1957.

de Bary, Wm. Theodore *et al. Self and Society in Ming Thought.* New York: Columbia University Press, 1970.

―――― *The Unfolding of Neo-Confucianism.* New York: Columbia University Press, 1975.

Eisenstadt, S. N., ed. *The Protestant Ethic and Modernization.* New York: Basic Books, 1968.

Fingarette, Herbert. *Confucius—The Secular as Sacred.* New York: Harper Torchbooks, 1972.

Fu Tsung-mao 傅宗懋. *Ch'ing-tai chün-chi-ch'u tsu-chih chi chih-chang-chih yen-chiu* 清代軍機處組織及職掌之研究 (A Study of the Functions and Organization of the Grand Council of the Ch'ing Dynasty). Taipei: Cultural Foundation of the Chia-hsin Cement Company, 1967.

Fung Yu-lan 馮友蘭. *Jen-sheng che-hsüeh* 人生哲學 (The Philosophy of Life). Kowloon: Shih-hsüeh shu-tien, n. d.

―――― *Hsin li-hsüeh* 新理學 (A New Philosophy Based on the School of Chu Hsi). Hong Kong: Chung-kuo che-hsüeh yen-chiu-hui, 1961.

―――― *Chung-kuo ssu-hsiang-shih* 中國思想史 (A History of Chinese Philosophy). 2 vols. Anonymous Taiwan edition.

―――― *Hsin-yüan-tao* 新原道 (A New Inquiry into the Development of Philosophy in China). Hong Kong: Chung-kuo che-hsüeh yen-chiu-hui, 1961.

―――― *Hsin shih-lun* 新事論 (A New Discussion of the Issues of the Practical World). Kowloon: Shih-tai shu-chü, n. d.

Ho Lin 賀麟 *Tang-tai Chung-kuo che-hsüeh* 當代中國哲學 (Contemporary Chinese Philosophy). Nanking: Sheng-li ch'u-pan-she, 1947.

Hou Wai-lu 侯外廬 *et al. Chung-kuo ssu-hsiang t'ung-shih* 中國思想通史 (A Comprehenisve History of Chinese Thought). 5 vols., physically in the form of 6 books. Peking: Jen-min ch'u-pan-she, 1957–1960.

280

Hsia Chün-yü 夏君虞. *Sung-hsüeh kai-yao* 宋學概要 (Essentials of Sung Thought). Shanghai: Commercial Press, 1937.

Hsiao Kung-ch'üan 蕭公權. *Chung-kuo cheng-chih ssu-hsiang-shih* 中國政治思想史 (A History of Chinese Political Thought). 6 vols. Taipei: Chung-hua ta-tien pien-yin-hui, 1966.

Hsü Fu-kuan 徐復觀. *Chung-kuo jen-hsing-lun shih—hsien-Ch'in-p'ien* 中國人性論史—先秦篇 (A History of Chinese Views on Human Nature—Section on the Pre-Ch'in Period). Taipei: The Commercial Press of Taiwan, 1969.

Hsün-tzu. See Wang Hsien-ch'ien.

Huang Tsung-hsi 黃宗羲. *Ming-ju hsüeh-an* 明儒學案 (Notes on the Confucian Scholars of the Ming Dynasty). Taipei: Shih-chieh shu-chü, 1961.

—— and Ch'üan Tsu-wang 全祖望. *Sung Yüan hsüeh-an* 宋元學案 (Notes on the Confucian Scholars of the Sung and Yüan Dynasties). 3 vols. Taipei: Shih-chieh shu-chü, 1961.

Jung Chao-tsu 容肇祖. *Ming-tai ssu-hsiang-shih* 明代思想史 (A History of Thought in the Ming Dynasty). Taipei: T'ai-wan k'ai-ming shu-tien, 1969.

Kao Chun 高準. *Huang Li-chou cheng-chih ssu-hsiang yen-chiu* 黃梨洲政治思想研究 (A Study of Huang Tsung-hsi's Political Thought). Yang-ming-shan: Chung-kuo wen-hua hsüeh-yüan, 1967.

Kwok, D. W. Y. *Scientism in Chinese Thought, 1900–1950.* New Haven: Yale University Press, 1965.

Levenson, Joseph R. *Confucian China and its Modern Fate—The Problem of Intellectual Continuity.* Berkeley: University of California Press, 1958.

Li I-yüan 李亦園 and Yang Kuo-shu 楊國樞 eds. *Chung-kuo-jen-te hsing-ko: k'o-chi tsung-ho-hsing-te t'ao-lun* 中國人的性格—科際綜合性的討論 (Symposium on the Character of the Chinese: An Interdisciplinary Approach). Nankang, Taipei: monograph series B, no. 4 of the Institute of Ethnology, Academia Sinica, 1972.

Liang Ch'i-ch'ao 梁啓超. *Kuan-tzu-chuan* 管子傳 (A Biography of Kuan-tzu). Taipei: T'ai-wan Chung-hua shu-chü, 1963.

Lovejoy, Arthur O. *The Great Chain of Being.* New York: Harper Torch Books, 1960.

Lu Pao-ch'ien 陸寶千. *"Lun Ch'ing-tai ching-hsüeh* 論清代經學 (On the Study of the Classics During the Ch'ing Dynasty)." In *Bulletin of Historical Research* (*Li-shih hsüeh-pao*), put out by the Graduate Institute of History and the Department of History, National Taiwan Normal University, no. 3 (February 1975):1–22.

Metzger, Thomas A. "On Chinese Political Culture," *The Journal of Asian Studies*, 32, no. 1 (November 1972):101–5.

—— *The Internal Organization of Ch'ing Bureaucracy.* Cambridge, Mass.: Harvard University Press, 1973.

Mote, F. W. "China's Past in the Study of China Today—Some Comments on the Recent Work of Richard Solomon," *The Journal of Asian Studies*, 32, no. 1 (November 1972):107–20.

Bibliography

Mou Tsung-san 牟宗三. *Hsin-t'i yü hsing-t'i* 心體與性體 (The Moral Consciousness and Moral Nature of Man). 2 vols. Taipei: Cheng-chung shu-chü, 1970.

———— *Chih-te chih-chüeh yü Chung-kuo che-hsüeh* 智的直覺與中國哲學 (The Intuition of Noumenal Reality and Chinese Philosophy). Taipei: T'ai-wan shang-wu yin-shu-kuan, 1970.

Munro, Donald J. *The Concept of Man in Early China*. Stanford: Stanford University Press, 1969.

Pei-ching ta-hsüeh hsüeh-pao—jen-wen k'o-hsüeh—che-hsüeh-p'ien 北京大學學報—人文科學—哲學篇 (The Journal of Peking University, Humanistic Sciences, Philosophy Section).

Pye, Lucian W. *The Spirit of Chinese Politics*. Cambridge, Mass.: The M. I. T. Press, 1968.

Schurmann, Franz. *Ideology and Organization in Communist China*. Berkeley: University of California Press, 1968.

Shen Ming-chang 沈明璋. *Ming-tai cheng-chih-shih* 明代政治史 (A Political History of the Ming Dynasty). Taipei: Shen Ming-chang, 1967.

Shih-san-ching chu-shu 十三經注疏 (The Thirteen Classics with Commentaries and Subcommentaries). 8 vols. Taipei: I-wen yin-shu-kuan, 1965.

Solomon, Richard H. *Mao's Revolution and the Chinese Political Culture*. Berkeley: University of California Press, 1971.

Sun Hui-wen 孫會文. *Liang Ch'i-ch'ao-te min-ch'üan yü chün-hsien ssu-hsiang* 梁啓超的民權與君憲思想 (The Thought of Liang Ch'i-ch'ao on Popular Rights and Constitutional Monarchy). Taipei: Kuo-li T'ai-wan ta-hsüeh wen-hsüeh-yüan, 1966.

T'ang Chün-i 唐君毅. *Jen-wen ching-shen-chih ch'ung-chien* 人文精神之重建 (The Reconstruction of the Humanistic Spirit). 2 vols. Hong Kong: Hsin-ya yen-chiu-so, 1955.

———— *Che-hsüeh kai-lun* 哲學概論 (An Introduction to Philosophy). 2 vols. Taipei: T'ai-wan hsüeh-sheng shu-chü, 1974.

———— *Chung-kuo che-hsüeh yüan-lun* 中國哲學原論 (Studies on the Foundations of Chinese Philosophy). 6 vols. Kowloon: Hsin-ya shu-yüan yen-chiu-so, 1974, 1968, 1976, 1973, 1974, 1975.

———— *Chung-kuo wen-hua-chih ching-shen chia-chih* 中國文化之精神價值 (The Value of the Spirit of Chinese Culture). Taipei: Cheng-chung shu-chü, 1972.

———— "*Hsün-tzu yen 'hsin' yü 'tao' chih kuan-hsi pien-i* 荀子言「心」與「道」之關係辨義 (An Essay on the Relation of 'Mind' and 'Tao' in Hsün-tzu's Thought)." In *The Journal of The Institute of Chinese Studies of The Chinese University of Hong Kong*, 4, no. 1 (September 1971):1–21.

T'ao Hsi-sheng 陶希聖. *Chung-kuo cheng-chih ssu-hsiang-shih* 中國政治思想史 (A History of Chinese Political Thought). 4 vols. Taipei: T'ai-wan lien-ho shu-chü, 1964.

———— and Shen Jen-yüan 沈任遠. *Ming Ch'ing cheng-chih chih-tu* 明清政治制度 (The Governmental Institutions of the Ming and Ch'ing Dynasties). Taipei: The Commercial Press of Taiwan, 1967.

Wang Hsien-ch'ien 王先謙, ed. *Hsün-tzu chi-chieh* 荀子集解 (Hsün-tzu with Collected Commentaries). Taipei: I-wen yin-shu-kuan, 1967.

Wang Yang-ming 王陽明. *Wang Wen-ch'eng kung ch'üan-shu* 王文成公全書 (Complete Works of Wang Yang-ming). Ssu-pu ts'ung-k'an edition.

Watson, Burton, trans. *Hsün Tzu—Basic Writings*. New York: Columbia University Press, 1969.

Watt, John R. *The District Magistrate in Late Imperial China*. New York: Columbia University Press, 1972.

Weber, Max. *The Religion of China*, trans. by Hans H. Gerth. Glencoe: The Free Press, 1951.

Yin Hai-kuang 殷海光. *Chung-kuo wen-hua-te chan-wang* 中國文化的展望 (An Appraisal of Chinese Culture and its Prospects). 2 vols. Taipei: Wen-hsing shu-tien, 1966.

—— *Yin Hai-kuang hsüan-chi—ti-i-chüan—she-hui cheng-chih yen-lun* 殷海光選集—第 1 卷—社會政治言論 (The Collected Writings of Yin Hai-kuang—Volume 1—Social and Political Writings). Kowloon: Yu-lien ch'u-pan-she yu-hsien kung-ssu, 1971.

—— *Yin Hai-kuang shu-hsin-chi* 殷海光書信集 (The Collected Letters of Yin Hai-kuang). Lu Ts'ang 盧蒼 ed. Hong Kong: Wen-i shu-wu, 1975.

Yin Hai-kuang hsien-sheng chi-nien-chi 殷海光先生紀念集 (Essays in Memory of Yin Hai-kuang). Comp. by Yin Hai-kuang hsien-sheng chi-nien-chi pien-wei-hui 殷海光先生紀念集編委會. Kowloon: Yu-lien shu-pao fa-hsing kung-ssu, 1971.

Yü Ying-shih 余英時. *"Ts'ung Sung Ming ju-hsüeh-te fa-chan lun Ch'ing-tai ssu-hsiang-shih—shang-p'ien—Sung Ming ju-hsüeh-chung chih-shih-chu-i-te ch'uan-t'ung* 從宋明儒學的發展論清代思想史—上篇—宋明儒學中智識主義的傳統(A Discussion of Ch'ing Intellectual History from the Standpoint of the Development of Sung-Ming Neo-Confucianism—Part 1—The Tradition of Intellectualism in Sung-Ming Neo-Confucianism)." In *Chung-kuo hsüeh-jen*, 2 (September 1970):19–41.

Glossary and
Terminological Index

When a word has more than one meaning, usually just that one meaning relevant to the contents of this book is given. Also omitted are names and titles given in the bibliography, reign titles, the names of emperors, some exceptionally famous names, and place names. When a translation in this glossary differs from one in the main part of the text, it is the former which is of more general applicability. A Romanized syllable lacking any tonal marking is an unstressed syllable to be pronounced without any of the four tones.

mìng 命 (what heaven has decreed) 127–34

míng 明 (bright; clear) 67, 255 n64

mìng-chīh-chèng 命之正 same as chèng-mìng, 130

Míng-í tài-fǎng-lù 明夷待訪錄, 272 n34

míng-pièn 明辨 (see distinctions clearly) 64, 66, 140

mò 末 (derivative, secondary aspect) 84

nèi 內 (inner) 84

nièn 念 (consciously formed idea) 32, 268 n287, 269 n325

Ōu-yáng Chìng-wú 歐陽竟無 8, 244 n1

Ōu-yáng Hsiū 歐陽修 52

pà 霸 (hegemon) 190, 268 n285

pāo 包 (enfold) 65

pèi 備 (set forth) 126

p'èi 配 (match) 72

p'èi-t'iēn 配天 (match heaven) 38

p'éi-yǎng kuó-chīa-chīh yüán-ch'ì 培養國家之元氣 (nourish the original vital force of the state) 199

pěn 本 (root; basis) 84

pěn-ján-chīh miào 本然之妙 (finest essence of the ultimate nature of something) 84

pěn-t'ǐ 本體 (ultimate substance) 70, 114, 142, 146, 147

pì 蔽 (cover over and hide) 124, 138

pì 弊 (corrupt practice) 60, 199

p'ì-lòu 僻陋 (unsophisticated and vulgar) 67

piǎo 表 (outwardly manifest) 101

pièn 變 (transform) 83, 223

pièn 辨 (distinguish between) 66

pièn-huà ch'ì-chíh 變化氣質 (morally transform one's material substance) 111

pièn-kó 變革 (fundamental changes and reforms) 223

pièn-pì chìn-lǐ 鞭辟近裏 (cut to the core) 149

pièn-shìh 便是 a copula, 143

p'iēn-hsiá kù-chìh 偏狹固滯 (one-sidedly narrow, stuck in an obstinately unmoving position) 67, 245 n17

p'iēn-nèi 偏內 (one-sidedly emphasize inner things) 67

p'iēn-wài 偏外 (one-sidedly emphasize outer things) 67

pìng 病 (harmful shortcoming) 60

pǐng 稟 (receive as one's constitutional endowment from heaven) 129

pìng-t'ùng 病痛 (harmful shortcoming) 60, 126

pó-hsüéh 博學 (broad learning) 64

pō-t'aó 波濤 (stormy waves) 114, 262 n216

p'ò 破 (destroy) 123, 124, 212

pù-chī-chīh ts'ái 不羈之才 (talented person unfettered by convention) 44

pú-lì 不力 (to fail to put out effort) 116

pú-tùng-hsīn 不動心 (imperturbable mind) 69

P'ú Sūng-líng 蒲松齡 53

shàng-hsìa ì-hsīn 上下一心 (superiors and inferiors devoting themselves with one mind to the public good) 232

Shào Yūng 邵雍 121, 144

shén 神 (spirit) 67, 121, 247 n32, 255 n64

shén-míng-chīh chǔ 神明之主 (that which controls through the spiritual force of its brightness) 66

shèn-ssū 慎思 (thinking with utmost care) 64

shěn-wèn 審問 (examining and inquiring) 64

General Index

This General Index supplements the detailed Table of Contents and the Glossary and Terminological Index. Generally, the latter includes references to Chinese historical figures, while this General Index covers modern scholars, Chinese and Western. There are exceptions, however. Modern Chinese scholars who do not appear as authors in the Bibliography are listed in the Glossary and Terminological Index, and the following Chinese historical figures are listed in this General Index: Chu Hsi, Hsün-tzu, Liang Ch'i-ch'ao, Mao Tse-tung, Mencius, Sun Yat-sen, and Wang Yang-ming. The references below to modern scholars pertain only to their interpretative positions, not to their work on purely factual or textual questions.

student of Chinese culture, 11;
and his Mencian moral ideals, 26,
195–96, 224; and Manichaeanism,
109; and "ideology," 210; and
Sinocentrism, 222; and
"struggle," 223–24; and his
concept of the "outer" world,
227–28, 230; and his writings,
240 *n*18

Yü Ying-shih, 64, 136, 162; *see also*
Anti-intellectualism

Studies of the East Asian Institute

The Ladder of Success in Imperial China, by Ping-ti Ho. New York: Columbia University Press, 1962.

The Chinese Inflation, 1937–1949, by Shun-hsin Chou. New York: Columbia University Press, 1963.

Reformer in Modern China: Chang Chien, 1853–1926, by Samuel Chu. New York: Columbia University Press, 1965.

Research in Japanese Sources: A Guide, by Herschel Webb with the assistance of Marleigh Ryan. New York: Columbia University Press, 1965.

Society and Education in Japan, by Herbert Passin. New York: Bureau of Publications, Teachers College, Columbia University, 1965.

Agricultural Production and Economic Development in Japan, 1873–1922, by James I. Nakamura. Princeton: Princeton University Press, 1966.

Japan's First Modern Novel: Ukigumo of Futabatei Shimei, by Marleigh Ryan. New York: Columbia University Press, 1967.

The Korean Communist Movement; 1918–1948, by Dae-Sook Suh. Princeton: Princeton University Press, 1967.

The First Vietnam Crisis, by Melvin Gurtov. New York: Columbia University Press, 1967.

Cadres, Bureaucracy, and Political Power in Communist China, by A. Doak Barnett. New York: Columbia University Press, 1967.

The Japanese Imperial Institution in the Tokugawa Period, by Herschel Webb. New York: Columbia University Press, 1968.

Higher Education and Business Recruitment in Japan, by Koya Azumi. New York: Teachers College Press, Columbia University, 1969.

The Communists and Chinese Peasant Rebellions: A Study in the Rewriting of Chinese History, by James P. Harrison, Jr. New York: Atheneum, 1969.

How the Conservatives Rule Japan, by Nathaniel B. Thayer. Princeton: Princeton University Press, 1969.

Aspects of Chinese Education, edited by C. T. Hu. New York: Teachers College Press, Columbia University, 1970.

Documents of Korean Communism, 1918–1948, by Dae-Sook Suh. Princeton: Princeton University Press, 1970.

Japanese Education: A Bibliography of Materials in the English Language, by Herbert Passin. New York: Teachers College Press, Columbia University, 1970.

Economic Development and the Labor Market in Japan, in Koji Taira. New York: Columbia University Press, 1970.

The Japanese Oligarchy and the Russo-Japanese War, by Shumpei Okamoto. New York: Columbia University Press, 1970.

Imperial Restoration in Medieval Japan, by H. Paul Varley. New York: Columbia University Press, 1971.

Japan's Postwar Defense Policy, 1947–1968, by Martin E. Weinstein. New York: Columbia University Press, 1971.

Election Campaigning Japanese Style, by Gerald L. Curtis. New York: Columbia University Press, 1971.

China and Russia: The "Great Game," by O. Edmund Clubb. New York: Columbia University Press, 1971.

Money and Monetary Policy in Communist China, by Katharine Huang Hsiao. New York: Columbia University Press, 1971.

The District Magistrate in Late Imperial China, by John R. Watt. New York: Columbia University Press, 1972.

Law and Policy in China's Foreign Relations: A Study of Attitudes and Practice, by James C. Hsiung. New York: Columbia University Press, 1972.

Pearl Harbor as History: Japanese-American Relations, 1931–1941, edited by Dorothy Borg and Shumpei Okamoto, with the assistance of Dale K. A. Finlayson. New York: Columbia University Press, 1973.

Japanese Culture: A Short History, by H. Paul Varley. New York: Praeger, 1973.

Doctors in Politics: The Political Life of the Japan Medical Association, by William E. Steslicke. New York: Praeger, 1973.

The Japan Teachers Union: A Radical Interest Group in Japanese Politics, by Donald Ray Thurston. Princeton: Princeton University Press, 1973.

Japan's Foreign Policy, 1868–1941: A Research Guide, edited by James William Morley. New York: Columbia University Press, 1974.

Palace and Politics in Prewar Japan, by David Anson Titus. New York: Columbia University Press, 1974.

The Idea of China: Essays in Geographic Myth and Theory, by Andrew March. Devon, England: David and Charles, 1974.

Origins of the Cultural Revolution, by Roderick MacFarquhar. New York: Columbia University Press, 1974.

Shiba Kōkan: Artist, Innovator, and Pioneer in the Westernization of Japan, by Calvin L. French. Tokyo: Weatherhill, 1974.

Insei: Abdicated Sovereigns in the Politics of Late Heian Japan, by G. Cameron Hurst. New York: Columbia University Press, 1975.

Embassy at War, by Harold Joyce Noble. Edited with an introduction by Frank Baldwin, Jr. Seattle: University of Washington Press, 1975.

Rebels and Bureaucrats: China's December 9ers, by John Israel and Donald W. Klein. Berkeley, University of California Press, 1975.

Deterrent Diplomacy, edited by James William Morley. New York: Columbia University Press, 1976.

House United, House Divided: The Chinese Family in Taiwan, by Myron L. Cohen. New York: Columbia University Press, 1976.

Cadres, Commanders and Commissars: The Training of the Chinese Communist Leadership, 1920-1945, by Jane L. Price. Boulder, Colorado: Westview Press, 1977.

Contemporary Japanese Budget Politics, by John Creighton Campbell. Berkeley: University of California Press, 1976.

The Medieval Chinese Oligarchy, by David Johnson. Boulder, Colorado: Westview Press, 1976.

Escape from Predicament: Neo-Confucianism and China's Evolving Political Culture, by Thomas A. Metzger. New York: Columbia University Press, 1976.